BEYOND FOUNDATIONS

Developing as a Master Academic Advisor

Edited by
Thomas J. Grites
Marsha A. Miller
Julie Givans Voller

JB JOSSEY-BASS™
A Wiley Brand

NACADA
The Global Community for Academic Advising

Library of Congress Cataloging-in-Publication Data

Names: Grites, Thomas J. (Thomas Joseph), 1944- editor. | Miller, Marsha A.,
  1950- editor. | Givans Voller, Julie, 1969- editor.
Title: Beyond foundations : developing as a master academic advisor / [edited
  by] Thomas J. Grites, Marsha A. Miller and Julie G. Voler.
Description: San Francisco, CA : Jossey-Bass & Pfeiffer ; Hoboken, NJ : John
  Wiley & Sons, 2016. | Includes index.
Identifiers: LCCN 2016020540 (print) | LCCN 2016025635 (ebook) |
  ISBN 9781118922897 (cloth) | ISBN 9781118923085 (pdf) |
  ISBN 9781118923078 (epub)
Subjects: LCSH: Counseling in higher education.
Classification: LCC LB2343 .G66 2016 (print) | LCC LB2343 (ebook) | DDC
  378.1/97—dc23
LC record available at https://lccn.loc.gov/2016020540

Cover design: Wiley

Printed in the United States of America
FIRST EDITION
HB Printing   10 9 8 7 6 5 4 3 2 1

This book is dedicated to all who practice academic advising at the master level and to those who aspire to achieve this level. May you use its contents to advance your advising practice, further student success, and contribute to the academic advising field.

CONTENTS

ACKNOWLEDGMENTS

The idea for a book explicitly for those who advise at the master level grew from discussions with Erin Null, then a staff member at Jossey-Bass. NACADA: The Global Community for Academic Advising began its long and productive relationship with Jossey-Bass with the development and publication of the first edition (2000) of *Academic Advising: A Comprehensive Handbook*. Much has changed in the field of academic advising since 2000; as a result of discussing those changes with Erin, a three-book series took shape to address the broadening scope of advising practice.

With the publication of this book, NACADA and Jossey-Bass complete the academic advisors core resources library:

- *The New Advisor Guidebook: Mastering the Art of Academic Advising* (Advising 101—the informational component),
- *Academic Advising Approaches: Strategies That Teach Students to Make the Most of College* (Advising 201—the relational component), and
- *Beyond Foundations: Developing as a Master Advisor* (Advising 301—the conceptual component).

Beyond Foundations is the first of its kind: a book dedicated to those who have not only mastered the basics of the field but who wish to contribute to the professional development of academic advisors on their campuses and in academe.

We owe a debt of gratitude to a number of individuals who contributed to the production of this text. First, we thank the master advisors who reviewed the book's outline and initial chapter drafts; their insights into what master advisors need in a book (and in the field) were invaluable.

Contributors

Brian Buckwald, Hunter College, City University of New York

Subhasish Dasgupta, George Washington University

Joanna Davis, University of Missouri–Kansas City

Sonia Esquivel, United States Air Force Academy

Susan Fread, Lehigh County Community College

Gayle Juneau-Butler, University of Nevada, Las Vegas

Amber Kargol, Iowa State University

Shanai Lechtenberg, Linfield College

Holly Martin, University of Notre Dame

Craig M. McGill, Florida International University

Chrissy Renfro, Laramie County Community College

Maggie L. Shedian, Elon University

Fanie Zis, Alexander College

We also thank the authors for sharing their expertise. Authors are the unsung heroes of any edited book. Not only do they expend extensive time and effort crafting drafts based upon the editors' outline and their areas of expertise but they also respond to reviewer suggestions and make multiple revisions so that the content of the book is built from cover to cover. The authors met the challenge of writing to meet a variety of expectations in extraordinary fashion; they are some of the best and brightest practitioners in the advising field. Each has our undying gratitude.

We also thank the production staff who made the book possible, starting with Nancy Vesta, NACADA's copy editor extraordinaire. Nancy brought her keen eye and over 20 years of experience editing advising literature to this book. Our words cannot begin to express our thanks to Nancy. We also thank the NACADA Executive Office staff, including Executive Director Charlie Nutt, graduate research assistants Taylor Mather and Rebecca Rowlison, and Marketing Manager Bev Martin, for their support throughout two years of book production. We thank the Jossey-Bass team who picked up where Erin Null left off: Pete Gaughan, Alison Knowles, Aneesa Davenport, and Connor O'Brien (to name just a few). We value your expertise and your belief in us as editors, NACADA as an organization, and all who advise students.

Finally we thank you, the master advisor, reading this book. We trust that you will find validation for your advising practice as you acquire new ideas and strategies so you can boost student success, impact your campus, and contribute to the advising field.

THOMAS J. GRITES
MARSHA A. MILLER
JULIE GIVANS VOLLER
EDITORS

THE EDITORS

Thomas J. Grites has been directly involved in the academic advising process in higher education for over 40 years. He was instrumental in forming the National Academic Advising Association and served as its second President. He has served as a consultant, program evaluator, and faculty development workshop leader on more than 100 campuses.

His publications have linked the importance of academic advising to many diverse areas within higher education. His publication, *Academic Advising: Getting Us Through the Eighties*, was used for academic advising program reviews for many years. He was coauthor of *Developmental Academic Advising*, the standard text for advisor training programs for many years. He has authored more than 70 journal articles, books, book chapters, program evaluations, and consultant reports. He has delivered over 120 conference presentations. He was coeditor of the second edition of *Academic Advising: A Comprehensive Handbook*.

Grites has taught courses in general teaching methods, freshman seminar, a basic skills course in critical thinking, a graduate course on developmental academic advising at Teachers College, Columbia University, and most frequently a transfer student seminar at Stockton University. He has also served on his local board of education for over 30 years.

He is a native of Danville, Illinois. He earned his bachelor's and master's degrees from Illinois State University and a PhD from the University of Maryland. Both institutions have awarded him distinguished alumni awards; he was inducted into the College of Education Hall of Fame at Illinois State during its 150th anniversary and homecoming celebrations on October 13, 2007. Tom resides in Absecon, New Jersey.

Marsha A. Miller, a NACADA member since 1988, began her academic career as a history major at the University of Missouri, where she served as a peer advisor in the College of Education. She has graduate degrees from the University of Iowa and Emporia State University; she advised and taught at Cloud County Community College for 14 years. At Cloud, she served as chair of the faculty committee that restructured the advising program and was director of that program when it received the NACADA Advising Award and the Noel-Levitz citation for Excellence in Student Retention.

Miller has been a member of the NACADA Executive Office staff since 2002 and serves as NACADA's Assistant Director for Resources and Services. She regularly presents at conferences and publishes articles. She was coeditor (with Jayne K. Drake and Peggy Jordan) of the 2013 NACADA/Jossey-Bass book *Academic Advising Approaches: Strategies That Teach Students to Make the Most of College* and coauthored a chapter and glossary of terms included in the most recent NACADA/Jossey-Bass book, *The New Advisor Guidebook: Mastering the Art of Academic Advising* (2015). She was a coeditor of the first edition of *Comprehensive Advisor Training and Development: Practices That Deliver* (2009). She is managing editor for NACADA-produced books and established the NACADA Clearinghouse of Academic Advising Resources on the web.

In addition, Miller served as a faculty member of the NACADA Summer Institute for 9 years. She is the NACADA Director on the board of the Council for the Advancement of Standards in Higher Education and answers member questions regarding advising-related concerns.

Julie Givans Voller is a research and planning strategist for the Maricopa County Community College District in Arizona. Her work supports the Maricopa Priorities initiative—a multiyear, district-wide effort to increase collaboration and promote student success and mobility in the District's 10 colleges and 2 skills centers. Previously, she served as the Director of Academic Advising, Transfer, and Assessment Services at Phoenix College (PC). At PC, the flagship college of the Maricopa District, she initiated and implemented local and district-wide innovations to improve students' experience and learning through academic advising and student affairs.

Prior to joining the Maricopa District, Givans Voller was Director of Academic Advising for the College of Liberal Arts and Sciences at Arizona State University. As an administrator, her work focused on managing change, integrating technology into academic advising, and designing and delivering programs for advisor training and professional development.

Givans Voller's credentials include regional and national conference presentations, serving as a founding Cochair of the NACADA Pre-Law Interest Group, and membership on the Publications Advisory Board. She was a member of the executive board of the Western Association of Pre-Law Advisors. She contributed to two NACADA webinars related to advisor professional development. She has authored articles on citizenship learning through advising, professional development, and advisor reward and recognition, and was lead editor for *Comprehensive Advisor Training and Development: Practices That Deliver* (2009).

She earned her doctorate in Educational Leadership and Innovation from Arizona State University in 2013.

THE AUTHORS

Karen L. Archambault, EdD, a long-time advocate for student success, currently serves as Executive Director of Enrollment Management at Rowan College at Burlington County, New Jersey, where she oversees recruitment, financial aid, and the registrar's office as well as several retention programs for high-risk students. In prior work experiences, she worked in areas of recruitment, advising programs, and retention as well as new student programs and faculty support. While her experience spans a wide range of functional areas, Archambault's research interests are in transfer student preparation and retention and in cross-campus efforts that support student success. She received her bachelor's degree from Salisbury University and her master's degrees from Old Dominion University and Trinity Washington University. She completed her doctorate in Educational Leadership at Rowan University.

Jennifer L. Bloom, EdD, joined the Department of Educational Leadership and Research Methodology at Florida Atlantic University in August 2015 as an associate professor and Coordinator of the Higher Education Leadership Master's Degree Program. She previously served as a clinical professor and the Director of the Master's Degree Program in the Higher Education & Student Affairs Program housed in the Department of Educational Leadership and Policies at the University of South Carolina from 2007 to 2015. Prior to this position, she served as the Associate Dean for Student Affairs and the Medical Scholars Program at the University of Illinois College of Medicine at Urbana-Champaign. She earned her doctorate in Higher Education Administration from the University of Illinois at Urbana-Champaign in 1995. Bloom is a cofounder of the appreciative advising and appreciative education movements.

Susan M. Campbell earned her BS in Speech and Theatre from Ball State University, her MS in Adult Education from the University of Southern Maine, and her EdD in Higher Education Administration from the University of Massachusetts at Amherst. Campbell currently serves as senior advisor to the Dean for the Lowell Institute School at Northeastern University. She served as President of NACADA, has held other leadership positions within the association, and received the NACADA Virginia N. Gordon Award in 2005. She participated in the 2005 AASCU graduation rate outcomes study and on a task force for the AASCU/NASULGC Voluntary System of Accountability Project. Her publications include contributions to the *NACADA Guide to Assessment in Academic Advising* (2005); the 2005 NACADA monograph, *Peer Advising: Intentional Connections to Support Student Learning*; both editions of *The Distance Learner's Guide* (1999, 2004), published by Prentice Hall; and the second edition of the *Academic Advising Handbook* (2008) published by Jossey-Bass. She also coauthored a chapter in the 2013 NACADA/Jossey-Bass book, *Academic Advising Approaches: Strategies That Teach Students to Make the Most of College.*

Hilleary Himes is the Director of Advising and the Division of Undergraduate Studies Program Coordinator in the College of Earth and Mineral Sciences at the Pennsylvania State University. She earned her BA in Anthropology from Penn State, her MA, also in Anthropology, from the University of Montana, and is currently earning her doctorate in Educational Theory and Policy. Himes is an active member of the NACADA Theory, Philosophy, and History of Advising Commission, serving on the Steering Committee from 2012 to 2014, and is serving as a mentor in NACADA's Emerging Leaders Program. Her research interests include developing philosophy and theory for academic advising, understanding the influence of socio-economic status on students' educational experiences, and the history of higher education and academic advising.

Chrissy L. Davis Jones is the Associate Dean of Student Development at Spokane Falls Community College (SFCC) in Spokane, Washington. Her responsibilities at SFCC include direct oversight of academic advising and counseling, new student orientation, placement and proctor testing services, and peer services as well as an academic early alert system. She is also actively involved with various local, state, and national organizations. She is a long-standing member of NACADA and has served on the NACADA Professional Development Committee, Awards Committee Program, the Faculty Advising Commission, and the Advisory Board as well as in a faculty position for the Administrators' Institute. She earned her bachelor's of Social Work at the University of Wyoming, a master's of Social Work from the University of Denver, and a doctorate of Education in Higher Education from the University of North Texas.

Peggy Jordan is a professor of Psychology at Oklahoma City Community College. She also served as the Director of the Center for Learning and Teaching and as a student development counselor. For the first 20 years of her professional career, Jordan worked in various state agencies and in private practice. After years of teaching clients coping skills and strategies to enhance motivation and feelings of worth, Jordan returned to the college campus with a strong belief that teaching and advising students offer them the greatest opportunities for empowerment. Jordan coauthored a chapter in the second edition of the *Academic Advising Handbook* (2008) and was coeditor for the NACADA monograph *Advising Special Student Populations* (2007). She has written for other NACADA monographs and for the *NACADA Journal*. Jordan served as a faculty member for the NACADA Faculty Seminar and Summer Institute and has presented numerous workshops for NACADA regional and national conferences.

Marc Lowenstein earned degrees in Philosophy from Colgate University and the University of Rochester. He taught philosophy at several institutions before shifting to a career in administration at Richard Stockton College (now Stockton University) in New Jersey. His positions there included Dean of Professional Studies and Associate Provost. He retired in 2012. Lowenstein has published a number of articles and spoken at numerous local, regional, and national conferences. His areas of interest include the ethics, the theory and philosophy, and the future of advising. In 2014, NACADA presented him with the Virginia Gordon Award for Excellence in Academic Advising.

Jeffrey McClellan is an associate professor of Management and academic advisor at Frostburg State University. He is also the Codirector of the College of Business Leadership Development Center. He earned a PhD in Leadership Studies from Gonzaga University. McClellan is a former advising administrator and an experienced consultant, trainer, and speaker. He has conducted more than 70 presentations at professional and academic conferences; facilitated or performed more than 100 professional presentations, speeches, training sessions, and consultations for numerous businesses, nonprofit organizations, and universities; and published more than 50 book reviews, articles, and chapters on leadership, administration, and advising. Most of McClellan's current work focuses on academic advising administration and on leadership, especially servant leadership and leadership in Latin America. He lives in Cumberland, Maryland, with his wife and six children.

Brett McFarlane currently serves as the Director of Academic Advising at the University of California (UC) Davis where he oversees campuswide advising initiatives, assessment of advising, advising training and professional development, advising technology advancements, and collaborative programming between academic and student affairs. Prior to taking his position at UC Davis, McFarlane served as the Director of Undergraduate Programs for the College of Engineering at Oregon State University and Director of Student Services for the School of Business at Portland State University. He holds a BS in Accounting from the University of Oregon, an MS in Postsecondary Adult and Continuing Education, and an EdD in Higher Education Leadership, both from Portland State University. His research interests focus on advising administration, student persistence, and advising assessment.

Craig M. McGill is a senior academic advisor at Florida International University. He holds master's degrees in Music Theory from the University of Nebraska–Lincoln and Academic Advising from Kansas State University; he is currently pursuing his doctorate in Adult Education and Human Resource Development with cognates in Gender Studies and Higher Education. An active member of NACADA, he recently finished a three-year term as the Florida liaison, the Emerging Leaders Program, and currently is a member of the Diversity Committee, the Sustainable Leadership Committee, the Steering Committee for the Commission for LGBTQA Advising and Advocacy, the Publications Advisory Board, and the *NACADA Journal* Editorial Board. He has published papers on a variety of subjects in academic advising, adult education, and musical theatre studies.

Susan McWilliams is the Assistant Provost for Undergraduate Programs and Core curriculum at the University of Southern Maine (USM). In this capacity, McWilliams oversees curriculum development and assessment. She also directs the USM Office of Community Engagement and Career Development. In this capacity, she oversees staff who assist students, faculty members, and community partners with service, volunteer, and internship opportunities. McWilliams received her BA in German and Sociology from Wesleyan University in Connecticut and her PhD in Sociology from the University of Washington.

Charlie L. Nutt was appointed the Executive Director of the National Academic Advising Association in October 2007. Prior to this, he served as the Associate Director of the Association for 5 years. In addition, he was also Vice President for Student Development Services at Coastal Georgia Community College for 9 years and assistant professor of English/Director of Advisement and Orientation for 6 years. He received his AA from Brunswick College, BSEd from the University of Georgia, and MEd and EdD in Higher Educational Leadership from Georgia Southern University. Nutt has had vast experience in education. In addition to his 15 years as a teacher and administrator at Coastal Georgia Community College, where he originated the College Advisement Center and Orientation Program, which was awarded a Certificate of Merit by NACADA in 1995, he has taught English in grades 9 through 12, served as a department chair and assistant principal in a high school, and served as director of development and admission at a private K–12 institution. Presently, he teaches graduate courses in the College of Education in the Department of Counseling and Educational Psychology at Kansas State University. He has also been instrumental in the development of the NACADA/K-State Graduate Certificate in Academic Advising and several other NACADA professional development initiatives.

Rich Robbins is Associate Dean of Arts and Sciences at Bucknell University. He has developed advising programs at two institutions and headed advising programs at four institutions. He currently teaches in the Kansas State University master's program in academic advising. He has made over 150 professional presentations (including 40 on assessment) as well as dozens of campus consultations specifically on assessment of advising, and he is author or coauthor of four separate chapters on assessment of advising in various texts. His service to NACADA includes Chair of the Research Committee, member of the Council, Board of Directors, and several committees and task forces, as faculty and Chair of the Summer Institute and Assessment Institute, and as faculty for the Administrators' Institute. He is a member of the NACADA Consultants and Speakers Service and coeditor of the *NACADA Journal*. In 2011, Robbins received the Service to NACADA Award and also received the 2013 NACADA Virginia N. Gordon Award for Excellence in Advising.

Matthew M. Rust serves as the Director of Campus Career and Advising Services at Indiana University–Purdue University Indianapolis. In this role, he coordinates professional development, technology incorporation, and outcomes assessment within academic advising and career development. His professional background includes academic advising, career exploration, outcomes assessment, and first-year seminar teaching. Rust earned a BA in Political Science and Philosophy/Religion from Butler University, an MS in Student Affairs in Higher Education from Miami University, and a JD cum laude from North Carolina Central University School of Law. Admitted to the North Carolina State Bar in 2011 (currently inactive), Rust regularly presents on legal issues in advising as well as liberal education and assessment. Rust currently serves on the Editorial Board of the *NACADA Journal*.

Janet Schulenberg earned her undergraduate degree in Biology and Anthropology from SUNY Geneseo and her MS and PhD in Anthropology from the Pennsylvania

State University. She serves as Associate Director for Technology and Curriculum in the Division of Undergraduate Studies at Penn State. Prior to returning to Penn State, she was an assistant professor of Anthropology at SUNY Potsdam. Schulenberg is past Chair of the NACADA Research Committee and the Theory, History, and Philosophy of Advising Commission. She coauthored "The Historical Foundations and Scholarly Future of Academic Advising" in the 2010 NACADA monograph, *Scholarly Inquiry in Academic Advising*, and "Advising Is Advising: Toward Defining the Practice and Scholarship of Academic Advising" in *NACADA Journal*, Volume 28, Number 1.

Leigh S. Shaffer received the BA and MA degrees in Psychology from Wichita State University in 1969 and 1971, and he received the PhD in Social Psychology from the Pennsylvania State University in 1974. He is professor emeritus of Sociology, Department of Anthropology and Sociology, West Chester University. He is now retired and living in Columbia, Missouri. He has served as coeditor of the *NACADA Journal* since 2009. He has authored or coauthored several articles on academic and career advising from a human capital approach.

During the past 25 years, **George E. Steele** has presented at the NACADA Annual Conference on topics related to working with undecided students, advising theory, and use of technology in advising. He has also written more than two dozen publications addressing these topics. He has been recognized for his work by NACADA in various ways, including the Service to NACADA Award and the Virginia N. Gordon Award. In addition, he has served in a variety of NACADA leadership roles. In his professional career, Steele has served as the Executive Director of the Ohio Learning Network, an organization that assisted Ohio higher educational institutions to assess, adopt, and deploy technology for online learning and student services. Prior to this position, he directed the advising program at the Ohio State University for undecided and major-changing undergraduates. Currently, Steele is a consultant working with institutions on topics related to his interests and teaching online for The Ohio State University.

Carolyn Thomas is the Dean and Vice Provost for Undergraduate Education at the University of California (UC) Davis and a professor of American Studies. As a faculty member, she served as an undergraduate and graduate student advisor for programs in American Studies and Cultural Studies. In her administrative role, she collaborates with deans, associate deans, and advising directors to enhance advising resources and partners with the Director of Academic Advising to improve advising practices throughout the UC Davis community. She is also the former recipient of the Chancellor's Award for Distinguished Undergraduate Mentoring at UC Davis.

Beverly A. Wallace has extensive experience as a faculty advisor for graduate and undergraduate majors and undeclared students. She received a PhD and MEd in Educational Psychology from the University of Alabama and an MA in English Education (Secondary) from Southeastern Oklahoma State University. She has contributed numerous publications and presentations in the areas of student learning and motivation.

Stephen O. Wallace serves as Coordinator of Developmental Education and Advising Development at Shippensburg University of Pennsylvania. He has extensive experience in advising and student support services. He received a PhD in Educational Administration from the University of Alabama and MEd in Adult and Higher Education from the University of Oklahoma. He has published in various NACADA publications and the *NADE Digest* and presented at the 2008 NACADA Annual Conference.

INTRODUCTION

Thomas J. Grites, Marsha A. Miller, and Julie Givans Voller

The best way to predict your future is to create it.

—Abraham Lincoln (1809–1865)

This book provides a path for the future of academic advising and those who practice it at a mastery level by

o delving deeply into the foundations and development of academic advising as a significant component of higher education;

o reflecting on master advisors' consistent and primary goal of fostering student success; and

o examining the contexts in which master advisors practice the craft in the 21st century.

This book completes a series of joint NACADA: The Global Community for Academic Advising and Jossey-Bass publications, the advisor core library, that build upon Habley's (1987) work in which he delineated the components of academic advising as *informational* (advisor knowledge), *relational* (advisor communication skills and approaches), and *conceptual* (advisor understanding of ideas and theories) to advise students effectively. Thus the three books provide a functional curriculum for the practice, research, and scholarly inquiry that comprise academic advising. The audience for this book includes experienced advising practitioners, active researchers, engaged scholars, and the upper level administrators of these individuals. For the purpose of this book, we call this group *master advisors*.

The first book in the core library series, *The New Advisor Guidebook: Mastering the Art of Academic Advising* (Folsom, Yoder, & Joslin, 2015), explains the broad spectrum of roles, responsibilities, and the requisite skills and knowledge necessary to successfully practice as an academic advisor. The *Guidebook* also establishes the base of a pyramid structure (illustrated in chapter 3 of this book) that reflects the organizational and informational aspects of the advising process. It can be considered (in course numbering parlance) as Advising 101.

The second book of the core library, *Academic Advising Approaches: Strategies That Teach Students to Make the Most of College* (Drake, Jordan, & Miller, 2013), provides a wide range of strategies that connect academic advising approaches to the practices that have emerged since the 1970s. The *Approaches* book builds upon the central part of the pyramid by reflecting the relational strategies that advisors use in their craft. It is considered Advising 201.

This final volume in the series, *Beyond Foundations: Developing as a Master Advisor*, synthesizes advisor knowledge and beliefs about the rapidly changing world of higher education in an effort to identify, confront, and resolve the current and the impending challenges facing the field of academic advising in the near future. *Beyond Foundations* provides the opportunity for master advisors to create their own future. It completes the apex of the pyramid by imposing the conceptual framework that the field of academic advising needs to establish. It is considered Advising 301.

As academic advising professionals (both those whose primary role within an institution is to advise students and those who advise as part of their faculty responsibilities) look to the future, a number of unresolved, perhaps even confusing, fundamental aspects related to the advising process need to be (re)examined. The nature of the academic advising process is characterized by diversity in terms of practitioners (e.g., faculty and staff advisors), appropriate credentials for academic advisors, organizational delivery systems, types of institutions, and student clienteles, so conclusive resolutions may not—and perhaps should not—result from an examination of the individual or collective aspects of advising. Marsha A. Miller (chapter 3), Susan M. Campbell and Susan McWilliams (chapter 4), and Karen L. Archambault (chapter 6) describe these distinct elements and offer suggestions for accommodating the dilemmas they pose for the practitioner. These quandaries have created obstacles to the construction of a universally accepted definition of academic advising. Nevertheless, the concerns related to the academic advising process need to be reviewed.

Understanding the Foundation and Development of Advising

As the importance of the role of academic advising gained recognition as a visible force in higher education, a number of scholars examined the nature underlying it. Burns Crookston (1972/1994/2009) and Terry O'Banion (1972/1994/2009) raised the level of consciousness about academic advising in articles now considered classics in the advising literature. Although the importance of these concepts went unrecognized at the time, they established a cornerstone for the acknowledgment of academic advising as a significant factor in facilitating the success of college students.

As the debate over a definition grew, a number of terms appeared to describe the process, most notably *theory* and *philosophy* (described by Hilleary Himes and Janet Schulenberg in chapter 1). Subsequently, terms such as *concept, approaches,* and *purpose* appeared in the advising literature. Many of these terms are used interchangeably to describe the nature of academic advising. In the future, academic advising professionals (practitioners, researchers, and scholars) will be challenged to distinguish among these terms when using them to describe their work. For our purposes in this book, we suggest that the following differences be examined:

- o *Theory.* While the debate about whether a unified theory of academic advising can or should exist continues (Lowenstein, 2014), the meaning of *theory* needs to be elucidated because it currently is not used universally, varying according to traditional academic disciplines. For example, theory in the arts and humanities fields is based on beliefs and analyses of numerous phenomena used to anticipate responses, but those in the natural and social science fields seek to prove or disprove whether interactions result in specific outcomes (Lowenstein, 2014). Simply referring to a *theory* of academic advising, without fully defining the term or context does little to advance the understanding or field of advising (Himes & Schulenberg, 2013).

o *Philosophy*. Although frequently used as a companion to *theory*, *philosophy* can connote different meanings, depending on the context in which it is used. An institutional philosophy (e.g., religious) may not fully comport with one's personal philosophy about specific issues. In many situations, however, one's beliefs, intentions, values, assumptions, and reflections likely enter the conversation as evidence of a personal philosophy. Furthermore, one's (personal) philosophy could, in fact, conflict with a theoretical perspective. The use of *philosophy* in the absence of understood parameters could create confusing, or even conflicting, conversations.

o *Concept*. NACADA adopted the term *concept* in 2006 when agreement on a specific definition of academic advising could not be reached (NACADA: The Global Community for Academic Advising [NACADA], 2006). This broader term suggested a fundamental idea, description, or understanding that enhanced certain specific explanations. Those drawn to this term must recognize and acknowledge whether it is used in reference to the NACADA Concept of Academic Advising (NACADA, 2006) or in a more generalized way.

o *Approaches*. The editors of the second book of the series intentionally chose this term for the title (Drake et al., 2013, p. xi) and specified that the approaches described therein are derived from various theories and employ certain strategies for implementing each approach. In chapter 2, Peggy Jordan has presented enhanced applications of several major theories.

Understanding the Goal of Advising: Student Success

The ultimate goal of every academic advisor seems clear: Help each student achieve his or her own success. Upon deeper inspection, the goal seems elusive: What does *success* mean? Who decides when success is achieved? Does a student's success reflect the behaviors or characteristics of advisors, advising programs, or institutions? To clarify the roles and importance of advising in higher education, questions on the meaning of success require answers in the not-so-distant future. In chapter 5, Stephen A. Wallace and Beverly O. Wallace explore success and offer suggestions for resolving the confusion that has emerged in the discussion of it.

The higher education agenda in the United States offers a clear answer to all the questions on success: graduation rates. More recently, the goal has evolved to include part-time and transfer students who graduate from college but not necessarily from the institution of initial enrollment. However, these performance measures do not recognize students who do not claim graduation as their sole criterion for success or those with goals that do not include a degree or certificate. No one knows the number of students who fall into these categories. Furthermore, no systematic means of ascertaining the goals for nondegree students has been established, which certainly precludes any ability to determine whether they had achieved their educational goals before they left college.

Perhaps more alarming than the latest definition bestowed on higher education, *student success* is rarely defined in the literature or in the programs designed to result in this outcome. Graduation is presumed to be *the* criterion for student success, and it is rapidly becoming a surrogate for institutional success or failure. If graduation is the proxy for success, then the role of academic advising is defined: Get students graduated! However, this characterization of the advising role and related edicts often comes from those unaffiliated with higher education institutions. Furthermore, advisors may be held accountable for ensuring that students graduate. Academic advising advocates have been quick to take some credit for improved retention rates, but are they ready to accept some responsibility for unmet graduation criteria?

Each academic advisor must appreciate the meaning attached to *student success* by campus, unit, and advisor. In his description of the human capital approach to career advising in chapter 9, Leigh S. Shaffer extends the call for clarity and development to students. Rather than succumb to the default criterion (graduation), advisors must determine, accept, and monitor alternative measures to demonstrate the success of the unit or the institution. Some may set the bar for success through measures of student satisfaction with the institution and the academic advising provided; completion of the student goals specified upon matriculation, with documentation of reasons for noncompletion as indicated by the students; established student learning outcomes; or postattendance behaviors such as transferring, attending graduate school, or entering the workplace. For example, a student who plans to transfer to another program or institution meets the criterion (i.e., demonstrates success) when she or he changes programs or colleges, not when an external party says the student has succeeded. In chapter 17, Thomas J. Grites encourages master advisors to monitor various sources and conditions that could create challenges in the future, and in chapters 14 and 15, Rich Robbins provides assessment strategies critical to documenting the establishment and achievement of specific advising goals.

Understanding the Master Advisor Concept

In selecting the title for this book, we created our own challenge: Determine the characteristics of a master academic advisor. We looked at various descriptors for this term—one qualified to teach, one with consummate skill, one whose work serves as a model, one having authority, and so forth—and we determined that all the descriptors probably apply to academic advisors who aspire to earn such a distinction.

Although we were confronted with the diverse nature of the field of academic advising, we call for further exploration of the criteria for master advisor recognition. Such a distinction will affect the future of academic advising as a profession, field, and discipline that can be studied. In chapter 7, Marc Lowenstein and Jennifer L. Bloom provide a strong foundation for understanding professionalism.

Because of the rapid changes in higher education over the last few years, academic advisors must lead, adapt, and produce results. Identifying and developing influential leaders cannot be left to chance, and master advisors must exert their leadership qualities. Brett McFarlane and Carolyn Thomas (chapter 11) describe a number of efforts that master advisors use to advocate for change on their campuses, including building coalitions, providing intentional professional development efforts, and garnering the support of upper level administrators.

The provision of a set of criteria by which individuals seek and receive acknowledgment for status as master advisors is addressed by Chrissy L. Davis Jones (chapter 10), who explains that those assuming a leadership role must also demonstrate

- up-to-date knowledge of the overall higher education landscape,
- understanding of the literature and research in academic advising,
- appropriate application of institutional policies and knowledge about their effects on the academic advising process,
- ability to articulate the rationale behind and proposals for enhancing the academic advising program, and
- engagement with professional development activities that have improved the ability to lead.

In chapter 12, Jeffrey McClellan explains current and desirable rewards and career ladders that motivate and retain master advisors. In chapter 13, Julie Givans Voller describes numerous professional development approaches for advisors that support their aspirations to become master advisors.

Folsom et al. (2015) provided a comprehensive description of the specific knowledge, skills, and behaviors that meet the criteria for their foundational mastery of advisor development. In this volume, Matthew M. Rust (chapter 8) addresses critical legal issues confronted by master advisors, and George E. Steele (chapter 16) shares a model for master advisors to harness technology that supports academic advising as a teaching.

Since the inception of NACADA in 1979, scholars and practitioners alike have struggled with the term *professional advisor*. Many who advise students as their primary function and those who have become academic advising administrators understand the term. However, many have criticized it because it seems to exclude the many excellent faculty advisors and may even suggest that faculty members who advise do not subscribe to the same high standards of practice as those specifically hired to advise students.

As the editors of *Beyond Foundations,* we have taken the position that the preferred term for the group of academic advisors who spend the majority of their time in direct academic advising or advising-related activities (managing, assessing, training, advocating, etc.) should be *primary-role* advisors. This term clearly delineates this group from the faculty members who advise but whose primary role is teaching. We are further emboldened to use this term because the NACADA Awards Program began using the term *primary role* in 2001 (along with *secondary role*) and subsequently recognized excellent faculty advisors in a separate category, as first seen with the Outstanding Advising Award winners in 2002.

We also confronted the long-standing debate on the distinction (or not) of academic advising as a profession. We assert that those engaged in academic advising are members of a profession. Authors, researchers, presenters, and practitioners in academic advising frequently use this term rather freely, regardless of the debate surrounding it. Lawyers, landscapers, and lyricists are members of their professions, and we contend that advisors should think no less of themselves. Therefore, we asked our authors to use this term to reinforce our affirmation. Craig M. McGill and Charlie L. Nutt, in the final chapter (18) of this book, address the current and future state of this debate.

Finally, in discussions and in the literature, advisors use the term *field of academic advising,* and we encourage the continued use of it. Academic advising as a *field* refers to the continued expansion of research and literature that advances advisors' work and influence. We contrast *field of academic advising* with the term *academic advising discipline.* Academic disciplines incorporate the research and literature within a field into the subjects taught and studied within graduate programs, and those in a discipline espouse "theories and concepts that can organize the accumulated specialist knowledge effectively" (Krishnan, 2009, p. 9). To meet this articulated standard, the field needs to establish at least one theory of academic advising. The difficult task of establishing an organized academic advising theory was delineated by Lowenstein (2014) and is acknowledged in McGill and Nutt's chapter.

With this book, we provide the rationale and direction for moving practitioners beyond the fundamental roles of academic advisors to become campus advocates, leaders, researchers, and scholars within the field; in so doing, advisors can become a research-based discipline worthy of doctorate programs. Through well-conceived statements and explanations about advising practice, strategies, and concepts, the profession will gain recognition for advisor contributions to higher education and student success—however it is defined.

References

Crookston, B. B. (2009). 1994 (1972): A developmental view of academic advising as teaching. *NACADA Journal, 29*(1), 78–82. (Reprinted from *Journal of College Student Personnel, 13,* 1972, pp. 12–17; *NACADA Journal, 14*[2], 1994, pp. 5–9)

Drake, J. K., Jordan, P., & Miller, M. A. (Eds.). (2013). *Academic advising approaches: Strategies that teach students to make the most of college.* San Francisco, CA: Jossey-Bass.

Folsom, P., Yoder, F., & Joslin. J. E. (Eds.). (2015). *The new advisor guidebook: Mastering the art of academic advising.* San Francisco, CA: Jossey Bass.

Habley, W. R. (1987). *Academic advising conference: Outline and notes.* The ACT National Center for the Advancement of Educational Practices (pp. 33–34). Iowa City, IA: ACT. Retrieved from www.nacada.ksu.edu/Portals/0/Clearinghouse/advisingissues/documents/AcademicAdvisingConferenceOutlineandNotes.pdf

Himes, H., & Schulenberg, J. (2013). *Theoretical reflections: Theory and philosophy should always inform practice.* Retrieved from http://www.nacada.ksu.edu/Resources/Academic-Advising-Today/View-Articles/Theoretical-Reflections-Theory-and-Philosophy-Should-Always-Inform-Practice.aspx#sthash.5EiItAXH.dpuf

Krishnan, A. (2009). *What are academic disciplines? Some observations on the disciplinarity vs. interdisciplinary debate.* United Kingdom: University of Southampton and ESRC National Centre for Research Methods. Retrieved from eprints.ncrm.ac.uk/783/1/what_are_academic_disciplines.pdf

Lowenstein, M. (2014, August 12). Toward a theory of advising. *The Mentor: An Academic Advising Journal.* Retrieved from https://dus.psu.edu/mentor/2014/08/toward-a-theory-of-advising/

NACADA: The Global Community for Academic Advising. (2006). *The NACADA concept of academic advising.* Retrieved from http://www.nacada.ksu.edu/Resources/Clearinghouse/View-Articles/Concept-of-Academic-Advising.aspx

O'Banion, T. (2009). 1994 (1972): An academic advising model. *NACADA Journal, 29*(1), 83–89. (Reprinted from *Junior College Journal, 42,* 1972, pp. 62, 63, 66–69; *NACADA Journal, 14*[2], 1994, pp. 10–16)

THE EVOLUTION OF ACADEMIC ADVISING AS A PRACTICE AND AS A PROFESSION

Hilleary Himes and Janet Schulenberg

Study the past if you would define the future.

—Confucius (551–479 BC)

Those who wish to effect change in the role and status of academic advising within higher education need an understanding of the structural obstacles to and opportunities for innovation. We provide an overview of the history of the academic advising field with particular focus on areas with lasting ramifications for status and practice. In tracing the history of academic advising from a structuration perspective, we found three important influential trends: expansion of the purposes for attending higher education, the emergence of academic disciplines and their influence in knowledge generation, and changes in theoretical perspectives and perceived roles of academic advising.

Reader Learning Outcomes

From studying this chapter, advisors will use knowledge gained on the history of advising to

- identify several influences on the development of academic advising in the United States,
- select participation opportunities that may influence future change, and
- explain implicit and explicit structures of the institutional system and their relationship to the local and global history of academic advising.

Over the past two centuries, academic advising has emerged as an increasingly important component of higher education. Attention to the purposes, guiding principles, and outcomes of advising has increased, and as the field matures, practitioners increasingly view advising as a profession. In line with this movement, master academic advisors must gain an understanding of the ways the history of advising affects their daily interactions with students and the role of practice within higher education. Further, those who wish to effect change need to know the structures and roles that create obstacles to and opportunities for innovation. This chapter provides an overview of the history of the academic advising field with particular focus on areas with lasting ramifications on status and practice.

Scholars have divided the history of academic advising into four eras:

1. Prior to 1870, academic advising was a largely unrecognized activity.

2. Between 1870 and 1970, the role of academic advising was recognized, but remained largely unexamined by both practitioners and other stakeholders.

3. Between 1970 and 2003, academic advising gained greater recognition and examination by practitioners (Frost, 2000; Kuhn, 2008).

4. From 2003 to present, academic advising practitioners attempt to intentionally clarify and convey the role of advising, including that of advising as a profession (Cate & Miller, 2015).

A current focus of advising scholarship is on illuminating the distinctive role of advising in higher education and elevating it in the eyes of others, such as higher education administrators, students, and the general public (Schulenberg & Lindhorst, 2008; Shaffer, Zalewski, & Leveille, 2010). The historical development of the field sheds light on the reasons that those in higher education, including those who advise students, do not consistently value the practice or the expertise of advisors. It also points toward opportunities for change.

Structuration theory informs this discussion. It places social structures (defined roles, institutions, rules, etc.) in a dual role (Giddens, 1984). Social structures shape human practices by defining the goals that can and cannot be accomplished by an actor in a particular social role. Despite the boundaries, actors create and reproduce social structures (Giddens, 1984) that both constrain and enable human action. Further, they effect changes to systems both unintentionally and intentionally:

> Human agents [are] "knowledgeable" and "enabled" [implying] that those agents are capable of putting their structurally formed capacities to work in creative or innovative ways. And, if enough people or even a few people who are powerful enough act in innovative ways, their action may have the consequence of transforming the very structures that gave them the capacity to act. (Sewell, 1992, p. 4)

The recent discussion of academic advising as a profession reflects social structures that both enable and constrain academic advisors. As a result, those in positions to innovate benefit from an understanding of the history of academic advising.

The history of academic advising within higher education as viewed from a structuration perspective reveals three influential trends:

o The social and professional roles higher education played for individuals expanded and grew complicated. Increased access to higher education, evolution of the social needs for an educated citizenry, and changes in credentialing for the professions are connected to both an increase in curricular complexity and the enrollment of an expanding and increasingly diverse student body.

o As academic disciplines emerged and the role of knowledge generation gained importance in the funding model for higher education institutions, faculty members became decidedly specialized in their disciplines (Raskin, 1979). At the same time, stakeholders recognized the need for specialization in helping students. Efforts to meet the need for specialized skills and knowledge led to the creation of a student personnel cadre (Cook, 2009), many with backgrounds in psychological theory and method.

o Particularly since 2000, practitioners and other stakeholders have paid increasing attention to the examination of academic advising philosophy, practice, and evaluation (Frost, 2000; Kuhn, 2008; Schulenberg & Lindhorst, 2010). Changes in the particular theoretical perspectives and perceived roles of academic advising as well as the differential implementation of academic advising among higher education institutions contributed to the current shape and status of academic advising.

These historical trends inform past and present views of academic advising, create the boundaries for current practices and structures, and suggest areas critical to future directions and professionalization of the field. We encourage readers to gain familiarity with the historical accounts of advising by Frost (2000), Grites (1979), Kuhn (2008), as well as Schulenberg and Lindhorst (2010), as this chapter omits details articulated by other authors.

The First Advising Era (1620 to 1870): Academic Advising Is Unrecognized

Frost (2000) and Kuhn (2008) characterized the First Advising Era (1620–1870) as a period when academic advising was undefined within American higher education. By the turn of the 19th century, higher education had transformed dramatically, creating the need for students to make academic decisions with the aid of an academic advisor. The previous 200 years of higher education perpetuated the structures and roles from which academic advising emerged.

Prior to the American Revolution, nine colleges existed in the colonies, and they enrolled few students, predominantly from wealthy classes (Rudolph, 1990). These earliest institutions unified church and state, creating institutions for elite education and socialization for those destined for political and social leadership, primarily as ministers. By 1750, college affiliation had become a mark of prestige, providing formal socialization of males likely to hold positions of power and providing families a network of social connections that reinforced the existing social hierarchy (Rudolph, 1990; Thelin, 2004; Vine, 1976). Few individuals attended college, and fewer graduated. Colleges played little or no role in credentialing for any professional field (Thelin, 2004); rather, colleges provided young teenage boys an education in manhood through strict intellectual and physical discipline as role modeled and enforced by teachers (Thelin, 2004; Vine, 1976). In particular, institutional leaders meant to prevent the effeminization of society, which they feared would be a consequence of allowing the children of the social and political elite to spend their adolescence with coddling mothers (Vine, 1976).

During this time, relationships between students and teachers were extremely formal and hierarchical. They mainly revolved around disciplinary issues (Thelin, 2004). Students lived and learned in austere environments. As the authoritarian figures, faculty members wielded power over students, who frequently challenged faculty authority with outbursts of riotous behavior. During this era, students and faculty members remained structurally separated, and the notion of a nurturing relationship between a faculty member and a student was antithetical to the role of higher education in socializing elite boys.

Following the American Revolution, the purposes of higher education institutions shifted from educating the clergy toward "educating citizens for a new republic" (Frost, 2000, p. 5). During this period, the enlightenment ideal of an educated citizenry prevailed: Persons put the welfare of the country ahead of individual interests. The colonial universities shed their historical ties to particular religious denominations and aligned control with the state (Thelin, 2004). A broader population of students was educated in subjects in keeping with enlightenment values: applied sciences (e.g., agriculture), professions (e.g., medicine, civics), and modern languages (particularly French). Immediately following the Revolution and into the 19th century, "The American college was conceived of as a social investment" (Thelin, 2004, p. 58). By the end of the 19th century, however, the civic purpose had diminished.

> As the public displaced the public servant in the conduct of civil affairs, the college was denied some of its sense of purpose. As Americans lost their sense of society and substituted for it a reckless individualism, there was less demand on the colleges to produce dedicated leaders. . . . In time colleges would be more concerned about the expectations of their students than about the expectations of society. (Thelin, 2004, pp. 59-60)

From 1783 to 1899, more than 450 colleges were founded and enrollments increased a hundredfold (Geiger, 2000). The western frontier was growing, in part because church denominations sought to offer religious-sponsored education to local residents and in part because of the need for educated individuals on the frontier (Rudolph, 1990; Thelin, 2004). Through this expansion of institutional mission and increase in number of institutions, a wider range of individuals gained access to college. In particular, the number of colleges for women and Blacks, as well as institutions specifically geared toward the emerging sciences of engineering and agriculture (e.g., land grant institutions), increased dramatically (Geiger, 2000). These changes in mission and college-attendance patterns laid the foundation for aspects of American higher education still relevant today. Much more research on the development of academic advising at these emerging institutions is needed; this summary is largely informed by developments at universities.

Of particular salience for this period, classical curricula were evolving and becoming increasingly focused on practical disciplines such as natural sciences and philosophy. Connected to this, more faculty members developed disciplinary specializations. As a result individual faculty members no longer taught all classes for a cohort; rather, each taught within disciplinary areas, and institutions often hired young scholars who had been educated abroad. By the 1830s, some institutions no longer required the student to learn Latin and Greek, and others allowed junior and senior students to select optional studies (Sack, 1963). Also at this time, some college presidents instituted changes such as formal matriculation and established new roles for faculty, including as an academic advisor. In an 1840 letter to his mother, Rutherford B. Hayes, a student at Kenyon College in Ohio, explained the role of advisor to his mother:

> A new rule has been established that each student shall choose from among the faculty some one who is to be his adviser and friend in all matters in which assistance is desired and is to be the medium of communication between the student and faculty. This I like very much. My patron is a tutor in the Grammar School who has graduated since I came here. Upon the whole, the President governs very well for those who intend to take every opportunity to evade the laws. But he is rather hard on those who are disposed to conduct themselves properly. (Hayes & Williams, 1922, p. 54)

The intention behind the creation of an advisor role and the subsequent effects on students, faculty members, and institutions remain unclear. Tutors, like the one chosen by Hayes, were recent graduates, who were likely of a similar age to enrolled students. As Hayes indicated, faculty members and presidents served as in loco parentis disciplinarians. Other letters sent home by Hayes described turbulent relationships between faculty members and students that often resulted in students' dismissal from college (Hayes & Williams, 1922). During this era, the few college enrollments were further diminished by dismissals (apparently a common form of discipline). In fact, these low enrollments cost the President of Kenyon College his job (Douglass, 1844).

Nineteenth-century students differed from their 18th-century counterparts. They were older, more indulged, operated with a sense of honor, and expected more luxury. Student clubs (eating clubs) had been formed in the colonial era. Later, honor societies were formed by and for students who did not want to rebel against the faculty or indulge in drink or sport. Collegiate sports and other student activities associated with higher education institutions had gained popularity by 1840 (Frost, 2000; Geiger, 2000).

The Second Era (1870 to 1970): Academic Advising
Remains Unexamined

The Second Advising Era has been defined as a period during which institutions created the particular role of a primary academic advisor, but the goals, methods, and
theories that guided practice were largely undefined and unexamined (Frost, 2000).
Several key elements affected the development of academic advising: knowledge
expanded as did the college curriculum, student–faculty relationships similar to those
of the post-Revolution remained, student enrollment and diversity increased, and
student support systems—informed by the emerging field of educational psychology—proliferated (Frost, 2000; Kuhn, 2008; Schulenberg & Lindhorst, 2010).

Curricular expansion in the late 19th and early 20th centuries exerted an impact
on the history of academic advising (Schulenberg & Lindhorst, 2010). Curricular
expansion related to academic advising was embodied in the 1880s at The Johns
Hopkins University, which created topical areas of focus—the beginning of undergraduate majors—and the creation of a formal role of academic advisors to guide
and approve student choices for study (White & Khakpour, 2006). Around the same
time, Harvard University instituted a curriculum based on a system of electives and
shortly thereafter coupled that expansion of student choice by using academic advisors to guide students in these choices. Charles Norton (1890), a Harvard graduate,
described a provision that

> every student on his entrance to college is referred to a member of the Faculty, who
> will act as his adviser in regard to all matters in which he may stand in need of coun-
> sel, such, for instance, as a judicious scheme and choice of courses of study, and the
> best use of his time and opportunities in college in view of his proposed aims in after-
> life, or as to his social, economical, and moral interests. (p. 588)

Norton's description of advisors includes many responsibilities that remain within
the purview of academic advisors today.

The 18th-century faculty member as disciplinarian continued well into the 19th
century; the few exceptional accounts of beloved faculty members suggest that close
relationships between students and faculty were not the norm. The underlying goal
of advising appears to include guidance for students in making meaningful choices
for their education and to advocate for and mediate the student–faculty relationship
(Gilman, 1886):

> The adviser's relation to the student is like that of a lawyer to his client or of a physi-
> cian to one who seeks his counsel. The office is not that of an inspector, nor of a
> proctor, nor of a recipient of excuses, nor of a distant and unapproachable embodi-
> ment of the authority of the Faculty. It is the adviser's business to listen to difficulties
> which the student assigned to him may bring to his notice; to act as his representative
> if any collective action is necessary on the part of the board of instruction; to see that
> every part of his course of studies has received the proper attention. (p. 575)

The ideal role of advisor was to facilitate the development of maturity through student choice of educational focus (Schulenberg & Lindhorst, 2010). Yet in practice, advising was predominantly characterized by the approval of course and major selection, not the relationship and conversation meant to underlie such approval. For example, at Harvard,

> sympathetic mentors . . . were the more needed in the era when personal liberty and free election bewildered many students, left them drifting without rudders, the sport of every breeze. The Board of Freshman Advisers was set up in 1889, but they did little except address the entering class en masse, approve study cards, and invite the advisee to a pallid luncheon in the Colonial Club. (Morrison, 1936, p. 403)

Although academic advising appears to have been founded as a means for bringing students and faculty members closer together, the evidence suggests that no such relationship became the norm in 20th-century American higher education.

The 20th-century expansion of higher education included increasing numbers and diversity of students to institutions of all types (Schulenberg & Lindhorst, 2010). Educational emphasis shifted toward intellectual growth of students and away from their social, moral, and religious development (American Council on Education Studies [ACE], 1949). In addition, the emerging field of educational psychology contributed to the progressive education movement, which emphasized the whole person and individual differences (Schetlin, 1969).

During the first half of the 20th century, the push to study education through a scientific lens contributed to a growing emphasis on practice based on assessment and statistical method (Schetlin, 1969). Schools used IQ tests to determine students' abilities and potential, which allowed placement in course work that best fit their ability level. Founded in a growing literature base on student needs, institutions provided support in the form of orientation, psychological counseling, tutoring, and other services: "With the growth of our understanding and appreciation of the significance of individual differences, some institutions have endeavored to develop the science of advising to keep pace with our more accurate knowledge of human nature" (Hopkins, 1926, p. 25).

Most of these emerging student personnel areas were informed by the growing scholarship in educational psychology as applied to practice by specialists. *The Student Personnel Point of View* (ACE, 1949), created by educators "who were deeply concerned about the welfare and needs of their students" (Schetlin, 1969, p. 63), championed the focus on the whole student and a range of psychosocial needs, including mental, physical, social, spiritual, intellectual, and vocational aspects of individual development (ACE, 1949).

Because few envisioned academic advising as a specialist field, a body of literature about advising was not developed, nor were theories intentionally and consistently applied to practice (Raskin, 1979). As with the original advising roles for faculty in the 19th century, advising in the 20th century was seen as "an extra job added on to the teaching workload" (Raskin, 1979, p. 101). However, Hopkins's 1926 summary of the state of student services at 14 institutions suggests that, like other fields, academic advising needed specialists.

Hopkins (1926) thought the addition of academic advising responsibilities to faculty duties impossible because of other demands placed on them for teaching and research. Hopkins recognized that advisors must understand more than institutional structure and program requirements. A multi-institution study revealed that in the mid-1920s advisors were expected to master complex interpersonal skills that allowed them to interpret student information, gather additional information about students' interests, and identify areas in which the student may need support to engage in a full and honest conversation (Hopkins, 1926).

In this era, the terms *guidance* and *counseling* referred interchangeably to psychological counseling, vocational guidance, and academic advising; practice in all of these areas was informed by clinical methods developed in psychology (Williamson, 1937). The intermingling of the advancing field of psychology, emerging career counseling practice, and guidance in educational decision making was based on the assumptions that students' abilities were fixed, that academic decisions and vocational decisions were linearly linked, and that the primary aim of education was to increase employability (MacIntosh, 1948). These assumptions, which according to structuration theory may or may not be recognized by those acting on them, have shaped the evolution of academic advising and resulted in expanding the original focus of advising on academic decision making to include a broader perspective on guidance, particularly in career decision making.

Some scholars of the mid-20th century recognized that students make academic decisions within a larger personal and social context than had been regularly considered:

> It does not seem reasonable to allow a student to pick and choose his studies from the curriculum without asking any questions as to what the courses are, what relationship they have to other courses, and where they may eventually lead. (MacIntosh, 1948, p. 135)

This perspective on the role of advisor conforms with the charge to advisors as originally outlined at Harvard and Johns Hopkins. However, after World War II, educators increasingly recognized complex influences and factors that affect a student's educational planning and the need to incorporate social sciences research into academic advising. For example, several publications from the 1950s called for greater attention by faculty members and counselors to student processes in making sense of academic decisions (Hardee, 1955; Havemann & West, 1952). In some cases, this role was shifted from faculty members to specialists in academic advising.

The first dedicated academic advisors and advising units were created during the 1950s (Gordon, 2004). The first primary-role advisors—representatives of the institution whose main responsibility was advising students—often came from counseling and psychology backgrounds and applied theoretical perspectives and methods from these backgrounds to practice (Schulenberg & Lindhorst, 2008). Principles of educational psychology as documented in *The Student Personnel Point of View* (ACE, 1949) informed practice of the first primary-role advisors by creating sets of purposes, assumptions, theories, and methods for working with students and evaluating that work; the guidance differed from that offered by faculty advisors, who were steeped in their respective disciplines (Raskin, 1979). The move toward a psychological basis for advising enabled primary-role advisors to create new structures (e.g., more units devoted to advising) and also constrained their actions by differentiating their advising from that offered by faculty members.

Despite the growing specialization of advisors in the mid-20th century, inconsistency in practice and purpose remained. During the 1950s, Robertson (1958) completed a survey of advising by visiting 20 institutions of higher education to learn more about patterns of operation and common challenges. He observed diversity in program structure and philosophy across institutions and similar diversity across departments within large institutions. Robertson affirmed the perceived importance of helping students navigate academic problems by facilitating student recognition of issues and understanding of their educational directions. In practice, however, advising was predominately clerical in nature. Although more institutions were implementing programs designed to support students, many of the participants in Robertson's study viewed students' desire for guidance as suspect or weak. In response, Robertson expressed concern about the future of advising, calling for the development of a clear philosophy to guide practice. Of particular note, he called for evaluation of advising, in part to prevent unfair criticism of the practice and to mitigate defensiveness and power struggles among students and faculty members.

By the 1960s, institutions had been transformed by both the accelerated research activity promoted by the National Science Foundation and the increased enrollments facilitated by the financial support provided through the GI Bill for veterans (Frost, 2000). The different historical trajectories came together in the structures and cultures that still affect academic advising practice today: faculty allegiance to the discipline, sometimes before the institution; advising as clerical bookkeeping and tracking of degree requirements; and perceptions that students who need help are weak and those who desire to provide them help are coddling or enabling.

The Third Era (1970 to 2003): Academic Advising Is Examined

The Third Advising Era is characterized by an emergence of a more distinct role for academic advising in higher education and increased attention to the purposes, theories, and methods applied to practice. During this era, a wider range of the American population, particularly women and students of color, accessed higher education. Between the 1960s and 1980s, enrollment in higher education increased nearly 400%, as institutions enlarged their enrollment capacity (National Institute of Education, 1984; Snyder, 1993). Consistent with earlier eras of expansion, the greater amount and variety of student needs prompted the continued growth of support structures for students. However, despite the upturn in nationwide enrollments, many institutions also experienced increased attrition, inspiring stakeholders to recognize academic advising as critical for helping students succeed (Frost, 1991).

As understanding of student needs expanded, those in student counseling acknowledged the distinct issues, theories, and methods of practice associated with career counseling, psychological counseling, and academic advising. At some institutions, more individuals were employed in primary-role academic advising positions (Frost, 2000), many of whom had academic backgrounds in human services (Gordon, 2004; Schulenberg & Lindhorst, 2008). At these institutions, the expectations for the faculty role in advising remained unexamined; however, primary-role advising appears to have largely supplemented faculty advising, especially in advising undeclared students (Habley, 1988).

The Student Personnel Point of View (ACE, 1949) directly informed the developmental advising movement of the 1970s and 1980s. Building on the emphasis of counseling during the 1950s, efforts to integrate the faculty, teaching, and the growing field of educational counseling increased (Crookston, 1972/1994/2009; Hardee, 1959, 1970), while at the same time, the number of primary-role advisors also rose (Gordon, 2004; Schulenberg & Lindhorst, 2008). The differing perspectives used to inform advising practice contributed to a growing gap between the faculty and advising staffs. These trends facilitated the developmental versus prescriptive rhetoric of the 1970s through 1990s, which posited faculty advising in opposition to advising done by primary-role advisors. The term *professional advisor*, now routinely interchanged with *primary-role advisor*, lingers as a manifestation of the third era rhetoric.

The increased number of academic advisors whose practice was informed by perspectives and skill sets that differed markedly from their faculty peers created a divide between the advising done by faculty and primary-role advisors (Moore, 1976). In 1972, Burns Crookston and Terry O'Banion each connected advising practice to theories of student development and described advising as teaching (Crookston, 1972/1994/2009; O'Banion, 1972/1994/2009). Both of their writings attempted to reconcile student personnel perspectives with teaching and move all advisors toward a common ideal of practice. Through his treatise on developmental advising, Crookston provided clarity on the roles, purposes, and values of academic advising. Notably, the Crookston and O'Banion articles normalized the kind of help students seek through academic advising and each described the teaching roles of advisors addressing normal developmental issues.

As scholarship and attention to advising grew, attempts to clearly articulate the goals and purposes of practice within the academy continued. "[Coordinators of advising] realized that advising can be a single-direction activity to select courses and plan schedules or a process for individualized teaching" (Moore, 1976, p. 374). Efforts to refocus on teaching-oriented goals as the primary function of advising gained momentum.

The rise of dedicated advisors and the increased attention paid to the role of advising in student success led to the formation of the National Academic Advising Association (NACADA) in 1979. NACADA (now known as NACADA: The Global

Community for Academic Advising) facilitated the conversation about academic advising (Cate & Miller, 2015) by developing leadership within the cadre of academic advisors and garnering commitment to scholarship-based practice through publication venues, conferences, and commissions. The formalized network for sharing practices and theory added to practitioner awareness of student development theory and directed attention to sharing perceived best practices.

As the literature in student personnel concepts and academic advising expanded, the need to identify and support academic advising as a distinct field through scholarship was acknowledged with the first edition of the NACADA Journal printed in 1981. Yet, despite the growing network of advisors, a 1984 report by the National Institute of Education found that academic advising was one of the weakest components of the undergraduate academic experience. Consistent with calls for educational reform in K-12 schools in A Nation at Risk (The National Commission on Excellence in Education, 1983), stakeholders used the 1984 National Institute of Education report to examine the quality of education provided to college students. The 1984 report made the critical point that "many faculty members do not participate in advisement, and those who do often treat this responsibility perfunctorily" (p. 31). As in previous decades, advising remained a low status role and often functioned as an informational conduit rather than an important part of student learning and development.

In addition to the predominantly informational practice of advising, few programs implemented assessment that identified and measured desired learning outcomes or created comprehensive statements of the goals and purposes within the institution (Carstensen & Silberhorn, 1979). Further, the prevailing developmental approaches connected with neither practice nor the assessments used at the time to measure success (Carstensen & Silberhorn, 1979; Laff, 1994). Few studies related techniques of advising to educational outcomes. For example, the majority of advising assessments reviewed in 1982 consisted of surveys about student satisfaction with advising (McLaughlin & Starr, 1982). Another report based on survey responses from 820 colleges and universities indicated that the majority of institutions primarily relied on faculty members to provide academic advising. The majority of these institutions did not conduct formal assessment of the advising program, and 68% of those that reportedly conducted evaluations based them solely on advisee satisfaction (Carstensen & Silberhorn, 1979). From these and other studies conducted after 1965, McLaughlin and Starr (1982) found that students expressed overwhelming dissatisfaction with their academic advising, yet they wanted more contact with advisors.

From the 1970s through the 1990s, academic advising was delivered with many different models across and within institutions. National surveys of academic advising conducted by the ACT from 1979 to 1997 (Habley, 1988; Habley & Morales, 1998) indicated national trends toward organizational models in which faculty members and primary-role advisors shared responsibility for advising. The studies seemed to suggest a growing recognition that academic advising must be provided systematically. However, these reports also showed that practices supporting faculty advising were consistently unsystematic and undervalued; in addition, academic advising centers remained critically underfunded (Habley, 1988). For example, in 1997, only 23% of U.S. campuses required training for faculty advisors, and 31% provided recognition, reward, or compensation for faculty advising (Habley & Morales, 1998). The variation in advising models employed within and across institutions illustrates the diversity in theoretical bases for advising practice and the range of views about the goals of academic advising.

During the 1980s and 1990s, NACADA and the *NACADA Journal* as sources of research on academic advising grew in influence, and through opportunities to discuss important issues and build a literature base focused on advising, they encouraged contributions to address the evolving structure and role of advising practice. Of particular significance, NACADA fostered the assessment of academic advising and the application of technology to advising as described and advocated in *Transforming Academic Advising through the Use of Information Technology* (Kramer & Childs, 1996); these advances came at critical moments because state disinvestment and associated higher tuition costs for students generated calls for accountability.

The Fourth Era (2003 to Present): Role of Academic Advising Is Actively Examined

During the Fourth Era of Academic Advising, practitioners made a concerted effort to clarify the role of academic advising and to demonstrate the value of it to a wide range of stakeholders. During this time, U.S. higher education continued to accommodate increased enrollments (Aud et al., 2012); encourage internationalization of students (Institute of International Education, 2014); and focus directly on accountability, student retention, and completion (McPhail, 2011). At the time of this writing, U.S. institutions enroll a wider diversity of students than they had at other points in history, and these students (or their families) fund much more of the cost of college attendance than in any other era (Aud et al., 2012; Fischer & Stripling, 2014).

Since 2003, as evidenced by the expansion of disciplines and theories applied to advising, practitioners have come from more diverse educational backgrounds than ever before. Further, the advising community has grown through the establishment of a global network (i.e., NACADA). New ways of examining and explaining the role and work of academic advisors have augmented the primary theoretical paradigm of developmental advising. Stakeholders have attempted to further clarify and convey the important role of academic advising through three approaches: clarification of the distinct purposes of academic advising, careful examination of advising practice using diverse theoretical perspectives, and intentional contributions to scholarship in academic advising. Their efforts have enhanced the visibility of advising throughout the higher education community.

Several initiatives culminated in refocused attention on elucidating the purposes of advising: a NACADA-led project to intentionally define *academic advising* and *advisor competencies* (Cate & Miller, 2015); revised emphases on learning and teaching by the Council for the Advancement of Standards in Higher Education (Cook, 2009); and increased calls for clarification on the distinctive role of advising within higher education (Schulenberg & Lindhorst, 2008). In 2003, NACADA sought a definition of *academic advising*, and three years later the endeavor resulted in a concept statement that highlighted the integral role academic advising plays in the teaching and learning mission of higher education institutions; the NACADA Concept of Academic Advising laid out three components of practice: curriculum, pedagogy, and student learning outcomes (NACADA, 2006).

By incorporating new ways to examine academic advising, practitioner-scholars have continued to communicate the purposes of academic advising within higher education. Since 2003 they have expanded the advising literature base with theory from disciplines such as philosophy of science (Bridgen, 2014), education (Musser & Yoder, 2013), sociology (Himes, 2014), and a variety of humanities (Champlin-Scharff, 2010). Although the examination of advising has expanded in many ways, much of the recent literature has featured ideas derived from the perspectives of teaching and learning (Lowenstein, 1999), philosophy (Jackson, 2005), and Socratic self-examination (Kuhtmann, 2005) (chapter 2). Despite the positive growth created by applying theory from and making comparisons to other fields, some thought leaders in advising discourage the use of analogies to other disciplines to describe advising practice or purpose. They argue that scholarship strengthens and highlights the distinctive role advising plays within higher education (see, e.g., Schulenberg & Lindhorst, 2008). An advocate for developing a unique theory of advising, Marc Lowenstein (2013) has called for the reclamation of the original, ideal purpose of advising of helping students make meaning from curricular decisions.

As renewed discussions on the role and purposes of academic advising transpired, endeavors to refine advising practice, advisor qualifications, and assessment were also intensified. New resources to guide advising practice, such as *The New Advisor Guidebook: Mastering the Art of Academic Advising* (Folsom, Yoder, & Joslin, 2015) and *Academic Advising Approaches: Strategies That Teach Students to Make the Most of College* (Drake, Jordan, & Miller, 2013), further expounded on current research about students and education and made intentional connections of theory to practice. In addition, the NACADA Certification Task Force delineated five academic advisor competency areas across relational and informational areas (Cate & Miller, 2015). These competencies—conceptual knowledge of advising, knowledge of college student characteristics, skills and knowledge in career advising, communication and interpersonal skills, and institution-specific knowledge (NACADA, 2003)—reflect the core understandings required by academic advisors, who also must know the diversity in advising structures and models at various institutions.

Several authors have called for a focus on academic advising as a distinctive field worthy of scholarly attention (Lowenstein, 2013; Schulenberg & Lindhorst, 2008; Smith, 2013). In 2008, the coeditors of the *NACADA Journal* suggested that, rather than a dichotomy of research and practice, advising follows a continuum of activities for practitioner and researcher (Kuhn & Padak, 2008). In 2010, Aiken-Wisniewski,

Smith, and Troxel advanced Kuhn and Padak's idea further by calling for advisor-led research: "Academic advisors are uniquely positioned to both affect, and be affected by, important aspects of educational research" (p. 4). Their attempts to remove the division between educational researcher and academic advisor came at the same time that McGillin (2010) explained that advisors did not enjoy a consistent, scholarly voice within the academy.

To support advisors' abilities to undertake and support research, NACADA published *Scholarly Inquiry in Academic Advising* (Hagen, Kuhn, & Padak, 2010). The publication was designed to meet the needs of scholars in academic advising by addressing topics such as applying epistemology, generating scholarship from practice, and utilizing qualitative and quantitative methodologies.

The growth in research and the participation of primary-role advisors in scholarly inquiry has enabled meaningful action among advisors. The growing body of literature shows continued refinement to messages about the role, purpose, and practice of academic advising. However, the structural organization of advising within institutions, which is based on various purposes or advising responsibilities, dampens scholarship efforts; that is, many advisors receive little to no support for engaging in or contributing to scholarship (Aiken-Wisniewski et al., 2010; Schulenberg & Lindhorst, 2010). For example, advisors who see many students in short appointments—a result of resource decisions based on assumptions that advising is primarily informational—typically have limited time and resources to participate in scholarship. Until environments that allow advisors to deviate from historic social structures are created by advisors and administrators, many will struggle to find the means or encouragement to contribute to the literature base of advising. Advisors and administrators in environments that allow contributions to scholarship likely have insights about ways others might remove structural barriers to scholarly engagement.

Looking to the Future

Understanding the history of academic advising can help shed light on its future. Structuration theory provides a framework from which to understand the historical influences on academic advising and how social structures enable or limit actors to function. Throughout the history of academic advising, social structures within and beyond higher education (e.g., the changes in size and diversity of student enrollment and the formation of NACADA) have influenced advising. So have the perspectives, roles, and language used by practitioners, as seen in the influence of *The Student Personnel Point of View* (ACE, 1949) and the increased creation and use of scholarship. The history of academic advising shows the critical role practitioners continue to play in facilitating change:

> Lasting change is accomplished only when individuals within the institution, and particularly those more affected by the change, understand the need for change, develop ownership by virtue of participation in the planning for change, and become involved in the implementation of change. (Habley, 1988, p. 14)

Advising practitioners' awareness of the past structures and roles that have shaped contemporary academic advising remains critical for identifying strategies to change these social structures in the future. Moreover, practitioners' collaboration on and support of a comprehensive advising philosophy will inspire the continued examination and effectiveness of advising within higher education.

Both language and reward structures continue to perpetuate a division between primary-role and faculty advisors. Through all eras, both faculty members and staff have undertaken advising responsibilities without the necessary comprehensive theoretical base from which to inform their practice. Until publication of *Academic Advising Approaches: Strategies That Teach Students to Make the Most of College* (Drake et al., 2013), no central resource was available to help advisors apply theory to the practice of academic advising. However, the pace of scholarship has quickened, highlighting the importance of the professionalization of advising: "NACADA members should feel a sense of urgency in addressing the evident weak link between practice and the underlying knowledge base of academic advising" (Shaffer et al., 2010, p. 71).

Research specifically addressing questions in academic advising will contribute to the development of advising as a field—a distinctive branch of knowledge studied within higher education—and emphasize the importance of building a strong base of scholarship. As literature and research expand, advising gains momentum; however, scholar-practitioners must exercise care and intentionality so the path forward can be surveyed and purposefully constructed.

Through time, the views and philosophies of advising held by practitioners have influenced the direction and perception of advising within higher education and students' learning experiences. When differences between philosophies surface, as seen between faculty and primary-role advisors during the mid-20th century, ambiguity about the purposes of advising results. Moreover, institutions created advising programs out of existing structures that were informed by existing philosophies. Those local traditions and needs led to the creation of advising programs that vary in form, function, and practice.

The differences in purposes and models of advising have contributed to inconsistency and division in the roles of academic advisors across and within institutions; on many campuses, this ambiguity weakened the move toward professionalization. Inconsistency within academic advising has stubbornly exerted an influence for years. In 1948, MacIntosh quipped, "Before we can tackle the problem of advising and directing our students satisfactorily, we must develop a philosophy on which to base our actions" (p. 135). Sixty-eight years later, the content and the appropriateness of a comprehensive and consistent philosophy of advising remains hotly debated. In 2013, Lowenstein articulated the view that the future of advising depends on a purposeful focus on advisors helping students with academic decision making and advisors being recognized as educator peers with faculty members. Professionalization means that all who advise, regardless of their other institutional responsibilities, should embrace a common and clear purpose for advising interactions, share fundamental understandings developed through education, and share common standards of practice. With a strong understanding of the history of advising, an expansion of scholarship, and intentional actions by advising practitioners, we are optimistic that academic advising can achieve consistency.

As global change continues to alter the context of higher education, institutions can expect academic advising to play a key role in student success. The size and diversity of the student population will likely continue to extend demands for preparation in a fast-paced, globalized world. Educational trends affecting K-12 schools, such as the Common Core curriculum instituted in the United States, will affect the preparedness and goals of college students, and academic advisors will help them transition to higher education and craft a meaningful educational program.

As a coordinator in the global community, NACADA provides an important social structure that will enable individuals' abilities to contribute to and engage in advising consistent with professionalization. The application of structuration theory to examine history can be expanded as can studies based in new theoretical perspectives. Studies from a wide variety of institutions, including international institutions, will provide a better understanding of ways advisors can intentionally move forward so that the field evolves to better meet the educational mission of advising.

Aiming for Excellence

- o Reflect on a conversation with a student, faculty member, staff, or administrator at your institution. How have the historical trends influenced daily practice? Consider mission statements, vision statements, advising philosophies, advising models, and structures.

- o How has advising changed since you first experienced the field as a professional in higher education? Are these changes positive or challenging?

- o The history of academic advising presented in this chapter is based primarily on documents from large research universities; how does the history of your institution fit this narrative? To learn more about the development of academic advising at your institution, talk to administrators, faculty members, and staff and read institutional records.

- o How have academic advising structures and personnel positions evolved at your institution? How does the history compare to that of other institutions? Do you recognize any trends by institution type? Speculate on the reasons for the variation in institutional histories of advising.

- o What preconceived ideas about the nature of advising have you developed? Do your initial perceptions fit the history presented in this chapter? If they do not, how do they differ?

- o To learn more about and consider the forces acting on academic advising, attend a conference, seminar, or class that addresses current issues in education policy and theory. How can institutions and advisors intentionally direct advising and higher education?

o If a comprehensive statement of the role and purpose of advising were created, as MacIntosh (1948) advocated, what should be included and excluded from the statement?

References

American Council on Education Studies. (1949). *The student personnel point of view.* Washington, DC: Author.

Aiken-Wisniewski, S. A., Smith, J., & Troxel, W. G. (2010). Expanding research in academic advising: Methodological strategies to engage advisors in research. *NACADA Journal, 30*(1), 4–13.

Aud, S., Hussar W., Johnson, F., Kena, G., Roth, E., Manning, E., . . . Zhang, J. (2012). *The condition of education 2012* (Report No. 2012-045). Washington, DC: U.S. Department of Education, National Center for Education Statistics.

Bridgen, S. T. (2014). *Academic advising at a satellite campus of a large multi-campus university: A qualitative case study using systems theory constructs* (Unpublished doctoral dissertation). Available from ProQuest Dissertations and Theses. (AAT 3645902)

Carstensen, D. J., & Silberhorn, C. (1979). *A national survey of academic advising: Final report.* Iowa City, IA: American College Testing.

Cate, P., & Miller, M. A. (2015). Academic advising within the academy: History, mission, and role. In P. Folsom, F. Yoder, & J. E. Joslin (Eds.), *The new advisor guidebook: Mastering the art of academic advising* (pp. 39–52). San Francisco, CA: Jossey-Bass.

Champlin-Scharff, S. (2010). Advising with understanding: Considering hermeneutic theory in academic advising. *NACADA Journal, 30*(1), 59–65.

Cook, S. (2009). Important events in the development of academic advising in the United States. *NACADA Journal, 29*(2), 18–40.

Crookston, B. B. (2009). 1994 (1972): A developmental view of academic advising as teaching. *NACADA Journal, 29*(1), 78–82. (Reprinted from Journal of College Student Personnel, 13, 1972, pp. 12–17; *NACADA Journal, 14*[2], 1994, pp. 5–9)

Douglass, D. B. (1844). *Statement of facts and circumstances connected with the removal of the author from the presidency of Kenyon College.* Retrieved from https://archive.org/details/statementoffacts00doug

Drake, J. K., Jordan, P., & Miller, M. A. (Eds.). (2013). *Academic advising approaches: Strategies that teach students to make the most of college.* San Francisco, CA: Jossey-Bass.

Fischer, K., & Stripling, J. (2014, March 3). An era of neglect. *The Chronicle of Higher Education.* Retrieved from http://chronicle.com/article/An-Era-of-Neglect/145045/

Folsom, P., Yoder, F., & Joslin, J. E. (Eds.). (2015). *The new advisor guidebook: Mastering the art of academic advising.* San Francisco, CA: Jossey-Bass.

Frost, S. H. (1991). *Academic advising for student success: A system of shared responsibility.* Washington, DC: George Washington University, School of Education and Human Development.

Frost, S. H. (2000). Historical and philosophical foundations for academic advising. In
    V. N. Gordon & W. R. Habley (Eds.), *Academic advising: A comprehensive handbook*
    (1st ed.) (pp. 3–17). San Francisco, CA: Jossey-Bass.

Geiger, R. L. (2000). Introduction: New themes in the history of nineteenth-century colleges.
    In R. L. Geiger (Ed.), *The American college in the nineteenth century* (pp. 1–36).
    Nashville, TN: Vanderbilt University Press.

Giddens, A. (1984). *The constitution of society*. Berkeley: University of California Press.

Gilman, D. C. (1886). The group system of college studies in The Johns Hopkins University.
    The Andover Review, 5(30), 565–576.

Gordon, V. N. (2004). The evolution of academic advising: One institution's historical path.
    NACADA Journal, 24(1&2), 17–23.

Grites, T. J. (1979). *Academic advising: Getting us through the eighties*. Washington, DC:
    American Association for Higher Education.

Habley, W. R. (Ed.). (1988). *The status and future of academic advising: Problems and
    promise*. Iowa City, IA: ACT. Retrieved from http://eric.ed.gov/?id=ED346903

Habley, W. R., & Morales, R. H. (1998). Advising models: Goal achievement and program
    effectiveness. *NACADA Journal, 18*(1), 35–41.

Hagen, P. L., Kuhn, T. L., & Padak, G. M. (Eds.). (2010). *Scholarly inquiry in academic
    advising* (Monograph No. 20). Manhattan, KS: National Academic Advising
    Association.

Hardee, M. (1955). *Counseling and guidance in general education*. New York, NY:
    World Book.

Hardee, M. D. (1959). *The faculty in college counseling*. New York, NY: McGraw-Hill.

Hardee, M. D. (1970). *Faculty advising in colleges and universities*. Washington, DC:
    American College Personnel Association.

Havemann, E., & West, P. S. (1952). *They went to college: The college graduate in America
    today*. New York, NY: Harcourt, Brace and Company.

Hayes, R. B., & Williams, C. R. (1922). *Diary and letters of Rutherford Birchard Hayes,
    nineteenth President of the United States*. Columbus: Ohio State Archaeological and
    Historical Society.

Himes, H. A. (2014). Strengthening academic advising by developing a normative theory.
    NACADA Journal, 34(1), 5–15.

Hopkins, L. B. (1926). *Personnel procedures in education: Observations and conclusions
    resulting from visits to fourteen institutions of higher learning*. Washington, DC: The
    American Council on Education.

Institute of International Education. (2014). *Open doors data; International students:
    Academic level*. Retrieved from http://www.iie.org/en/Research-and-Publications/
    Open-Doors/Data/International-Students/Academic-Level/1954-2010

Jackson, R. (2005). Academic advising and philosophy. *NACADA Journal, 25*(2), 30–36.

Kramer, G. L., & Childs, M. W. (Eds.). (1996). *Transforming academic advising through the
    use of information technology* (Monograph No. 4). Manhattan, KS: National Academic
    Advising Association.

Kuhn, T. (2008). Historical foundations of academic advising. In V. N. Gordon, W. R. Habley, & T. J. Grites (Eds.), *Academic advising: A comprehensive handbook* (2nd ed.) (pp. 3–16). San Francisco, CA: Jossey-Bass.

Kuhn, T., & Padak, G. (2008). From the co-editors: What makes research important? *NACADA Journal, 28*(1), 1.

Kuhtmann, M. (2005). Socratic self-examination and its application to academic advising. *NACADA Journal, 25*(2), 37–48.

Laff, N. (1994). Reconsidering the developmental view of advising: Have we come a long way? *NACADA Journal, 14*(2), 46–49.

Lowenstein, M. (1999). An alternative to the developmental theory of advising. *The Mentor, 1*(4). Retrieved from http://dus.psu.edu/mentor/old/articles/991122ml.htm

Lowenstein, M. (2013). Envisioning the future. In J. K. Drake, P. Jordan, & M. A. Miller (Eds.), *Academic advising approaches: Strategies that teach students to make the most of college* (pp. 243–258). San Francisco, CA: Jossey-Bass.

MacIntosh, A. (1948). *Behind the academic curtain: A guide to getting the most out of college* (1st ed.). New York, NY: Harper.

McGillin, V. (2010). Foreword. In P. L. Hagen, T. L. Kuhn, & G. M. Padak (Eds.), *Scholarly inquiry in academic advising* (Monograph No. 20) (pp. 5–9). Manhattan, KS: National Academic Advising Association.

McLaughlin, B. M., & Starr, E. A. (1982). Academic advising literature since 1965: A *College Student Personnel Abstracts* review. *NACADA Journal, 2*(2), 14–23.

McPhail, C. J. (2011). *The completion agenda: A call to action.* Washington, DC: American Association of Community Colleges.

Moore, K. M. (1976). Faculty advising: Panacea or placebo? *Journal of College Student Personnel, 17,* 371–375.

Morrison, S. E. (1936). *Three centuries of Harvard.* Cambridge, MA: Harvard University Press.

Musser, T., & Yoder, F. (2013). The application of constructivism and systems theory to academic advising. In J. K. Drake, P. Jordan, & M. A. Miller (Eds.), *Academic advising approaches: Strategies that teach students to make the most of college* (pp. 179–196). San Francisco, CA: Jossey–Bass.

NACADA: The Global Community for Academic Advising (NACADA). (2003). *Academic advisor competencies.* Retrieved from http://www.nacada.ksu.edu/Resources/Clearinghouse/View-Articles/Academic-advisor-competencies.aspx

NACADA. (2006). *NACADA concept of academic advising.* Retrieved from http://www.nacada.ksu.edu/Resources/Clearinghouse/View-Articles/Concept-of-Academic-Advising-a598.aspx

The National Commission on Excellence in Education. (1983). *A nation at risk: The imperative for educational reform: A report to the nation and the secretary of education, United States Department of Education.* Washington, DC: Author.

National Institute of Education. (1984). *Involvement in learning: Realizing the potential of American higher education: Final report.* Washington, DC: Author.

Norton, C. E. (1890, June 1). Harvard University in 1890. *Harper's New Monthly Magazine, 81*, 581–592.

O'Banion, T. (2009). 1994 (1972): An academic advising model. *NACADA Journal, 29*(1), 83–89. (Reprinted from *Junior College Journal, 42*, 1972, pp. 62, 63, 66–69; *NACADA Journal, 14*[2], 1994, pp. 10–16)

Raskin, M. (1979). Critical issue: Faculty advising. *Peabody Journal of Education, 56*(2), 99–108.

Robertson, J. H. (1958). Academic advising in colleges and universities: Its present state and present problems. *The North Central Association Quarterly, 32*, 228–239.

Rudolph, F. (1990). *The American college & university: A history*. Athens: University of Georgia Press.

Sack, S. (1963). *History of higher education in Pennsylvania* (Vol. 2). Harrisburg: The Pennsylvania Historical and Museum Commission.

Schetlin, E. M. (1969). Myths of the student personnel point of view. *The Journal of Higher Education, 40*(1), 58–63.

Schulenberg, J., & Lindhorst, M. (2008). Advising is advising: Toward defining the practice and scholarship of academic advising. *NACADA Journal, 28*(1), 43–53.

Schulenberg, J., & Lindhorst, M. (2010). The historical foundations and scholarly future of academic advising. In P. Hagen, T. Kuhn, & G. Padak (Eds.), *Scholarly inquiry in academic advising* (Monograph No. 20) (pp. 17–28). Manhattan, KS: National Academic Advising Association.

Sewell, W. H. (1992). A theory of structure: Duality, agency, and transformation. *American Journal of Sociology, 98*(1), 1–29.

Shaffer, L., Zalewski, J. M., & Leveille, J. (2010). The professionalization of academic advising: Where are we in 2010? *NACADA Journal, 30*(1), 66–77.

Smith, J. S. (2013). From the President: Effectively articulating the purpose of advising. *Academic Advising Today, 36*(2). Retrieved from http://www.nacada.ksu.edu/Resources/Academic-Advising-Today/View-Articles/From-the-President-Effectively-Articulating-the-Purpose-of-Advising.aspx

Snyder, T. D. (1993). *120 years of American education: A statistical portrait*. Washington, DC: U.S. Department of Education, National Center for Educational Statistics.

Thelin, J. R. (2004). *A history of American higher education*. Baltimore, MD: The Johns Hopkins University Press.

Vine, P. (1976). The social function of eighteenth-century higher education. *History of Education Quarterly, 16*(4), 409–424. http://doi.org/10.2307/367723

White, M. R., & Khakpour, P. (2006, October 25). The advent of academic advising in America at The Johns Hopkins University. *The Mentor*. Retrieved from http://dus.psu.edu/mentor/old/articles/061025mw.htm

Williamson, E. G. (1937). *Student personnel work: An outline of clinical procedures* (1st ed.). New York, NY; London, England: McGraw-Hill.

2

THEORY AS THE FOUNDATION OF ADVISING

Peggy Jordan

He who loves practice without theory is like the sailor who boards ship without a rudder and compass and never knows where he may cast.

—Leonardo da Vinci (1452–1519)

Higher education must adapt to rapid changes in student populations and calls for increased safety measures and responses on campus and in communities. The result of international and global tensions as well as mental health issues students bring to the college campus, these changes challenge administrators and master advisors to keep pace. Advisor knowledge and use of theory benefit the individual student's progression toward goals and advance campus safety. By advising students as whole individuals, skilled advisors can more fully know the students they advise and with this understanding offer interventions that both promote student success and ensure appropriate referral to campus and community resources. Institutions can prevent problems by hiring highly skilled advisors who use appropriate theories, some of which are featured in the chapter, to address both typical and atypical situations.

Reader Learning Outcomes

From studying this chapter, advisors will use knowledge gained on the use of theory to summarize key points of

- Erikson's (1963) psychosocial theory of development,
- Chickering and Reisser's (1993) theory of identity formation,
- Marcia's (1980) ego identity theory,
- Schlossberg's transition theory (Schlossberg, Waters, & Goodman, 1995),
- Maslow's (1970) hierarchy of needs, and
- Holland's (1997) theory of career development.

Although it does not allow for a thorough exploration of all the theories that inform advising, this chapter offers descriptions of those most frequently encountered. In particular, case studies demonstrate use of the theories from psychosocial, humanistic, and career development, as used with advising approaches featured in *Academic Advising Approaches: Teaching Students to Make the Most of College* (Drake, Jordan, & Miller, 2013), to illustrate specific points. These theories are summarized for clarification or reminder.

Psychosocial Theories

Psychosocial theories are used to look at growth and change through stages of the life span. They explain developmental tasks and abilities, individual interactions in relationships, and life transitions, such as experienced when a young adult separates from parents to attend college and makes career choices. Psychosocial theories also describe the ways a person creates an identity that makes him or her unique (Evans, Forney, Guido, Patton, & Renn, 2010).

Erikson's Psychosocial Theory

Erik Erikson (1963) described eight stages or crises of development over the life span. An individual can reach a positive or negative resolution at each stage, depending on her or his interactions with the environment and personal internal processes. Healthy resolutions lead to positive outcomes of a crisis and integrate into the person's development. Negative resolutions, however, tend to cause discontinuities in development, which are carried over into subsequent stages. Although negative resolutions stemming from childhood crises can remain with a person into adulthood, the individual can mend developmental gaps through positive resolutions of later stages. For example, a person who never learned to trust authority figures can, through a steadfast and honest relationship cultivated by a teacher, mentor, advisor, or friend, learn to trust. Of the eight stages Erikson proposed, most advisors find stages five and six—identity versus role confusion and intimacy versus isolation—the most relevant in dealing with traditional college students. (Erikson, 1963)

Chickering and Reisser's Theory of Identity Formation

Arthur Chickering and Linda Reisser (1993) based their work on Erikson's (1963) comprehensive psychosocial theory. Chickering and Reisser's model demonstrates the ways college students change psychosocially through seven vectors: developing competence, managing emotions, moving through autonomy toward interdependence, developing mature interpersonal relationships, establishing identity, developing purpose, and developing integrity. Student growth along these vectors can transpire at different rates and may correspond to movement on other vectors. Typical students of traditional age explore the first three vectors in their initial college years and deal with the substance of the other vectors as juniors or seniors. However, individuals may work through the last three vectors throughout their entire life span.

Chickering and Reisser (1993) promoted frequent student–faculty contact and defined student development professionals as educators who collaborate with faculty members in the application of student development theory. Chickering and Reisser suggested educational environments that exert a potent influence on student development, and they thus proposed seven factors as key influences: institutional objectives, institutional size, student–faculty relationships, curriculum, teaching, friendships and student communities, and student development programs and services.

Marcia's Ego Identity Theory

James Marcia's (1980) theory is also based on Erikson's (1963) psychosocial theory. He focused on identity development in late adolescence and adulthood and presented four identity statuses or states: foreclosure, moratorium, identity achievement, and diffusion. Each state involves varying levels of crisis and commitment. Crisis is characterized as a period in which an individual explores new ideas or options through reading, participating in classes, or engaging in discussions with others. Commitment involves taking responsibility for one's own decisions rather than following parents' or others' recommendations.

Marcia (1980) described foreclosure as the most common status in which people accept without question the values, ideals, and goals of their parents or other authority figures. Individuals in foreclosure experience neither crisis nor commitment. Most people enter and leave a moratorium, characterized by crisis and no commitment, relatively quickly. The crisis occurs because individuals are actively questioning rules, values, and ideas they had previously accepted. If they continue to explore alternatives, they will likely reach identity achievement, the healthiest of Marcia's statuses. In identity achievement, individuals continue to experience a crisis because they continue to question and make independent decisions, which typically stimulate a feeling of anxiety and a sense of risk.

Identity-achieved individuals experience a high degree of commitment because they have made their own decisions after a thorough process of exploration. In the status of diffusion, individuals experience no crisis and no commitment because they make few independent decisions; rather they exhibit the greatest conformity as they rely on others to set their course. Those experiencing diffusion tend to be compliant and depend on external rather than internal authority (Evans et al., 2010).

Schlossberg's Transition Theory

Nancy Schlossberg focused on a transition theory based on life events involving change (Schlossberg et al., 1995). She believes that transitions reveal more important characteristics for understanding individual behavior than does chronological age.

Transition theorists look at a person's resources for coping with transitions and identifying sources of support. Schlossberg identified three types of transitions:

o anticipated—those an individual can predict, such as attending college;

o unanticipated—unpredictable events, such as divorce or early death of a
  spouse; and

o non-event—occurrences expected that did not materialize, such as experienced
  with failure to gain admission to medical school or not having children which
  had been planned.

With these types of transitions come three stages:

o moving in,

o moving out, and

o moving through.

In the first stage of transition, a person moves in or out. For example, students graduating from high school are moving out, but those starting college for the first time are
moving in. The moving through period begins once learners know the expectations
for them and the ways to navigate the system. Moving out can be experienced at the
end of one transition and before the beginning of the next.

Schlossberg devised a way to determine a person's ability to cope through these
phases. Her system is based on a ratio of assets and liabilities, referred to as the 4 Ss:
situation, self, support, and strategies. This assessment can help advisors understand
the reasons people react differently to the same transition and why one person may
react differently to a similar situation presented at different times in the person's life
(Schlossberg et al., 1995).

Maslow's Hierarchy: Humanist Theory

Humanistic theories approach the understanding of individuals through holistic
observation with an emphasis on the uniqueness of each person. Scholars developed
it in opposition to behaviorist and psychodynamic perspectives, which focus, respectively, on observable behavior while studying development and on emotions, the
unconscious, and the inner working of the mind (Santrock, 2015). As it was developed in reaction to these prior movements, humanism is sometimes called *the third
force* in psychology (Maslow, 1968).

Abraham Maslow (1970) created a hierarchy of needs that included physiological
needs, such as those for safety, socialization, and esteem, with self-actualization as
the pinnacle achievement. According to Maslow, lower order needs such as air, food,
and water must be met before a person can attempt to satisfy the next level of need.
Maslow's holistic approach, as it accounts for students' physical, social, and intellectual qualities when academic progress is considered (McLeod, 2007), makes his

theory particularly applicable to student learning. Maslow advocated practice in which students are shown respect and offered a supportive educational environment.

Holland's Career Development Theory

Career development theories, each with a different perspective on ways career choices and transitions are made over the life span, characterize the relevant literature for academic advisors. Many students ask questions about education choices and how they relate to career goals.

John Holland (1997) created a theory of career development using six personality types:

- Realistic—interested in working with objects and animals;
- Investigative—interested in working with ideas and science;
- Artistic—interested in creative and artistic activities;
- Social—prefer work with others that helps, guides, cures, or enlightens;
- Enterprising—prefer to lead or manage others to achieve goals; and
- Conventional—interested in working with data and in orderly and structured activities.

According to Evans et al. (2010, p. 33), Holland proposed a theory that "explored satisfaction, achievement, persistence, and degree of fit between persons and the environments in which they find themselves." An individual's personality can be assessed by looking at her or his top two or three scores on a Holland-based survey. The assessment takes into account both environmental and personal characteristics (Evans et al., 2010).

Reasons for Learning About Theories

Skilled academic advisors need to use theory to address students as whole individuals with idiosyncratic problems and needs. Theories can point to potential reasons for student behavior. With the insight these theories provide, advisors can interact with students to promote growth. Although advisors should meet with students to discuss degree plans and course requirements, institutions that hire only enough advisors to perform minimal informational functions miss the opportunities to positively influence retention and promote student success, decrease students' senses of isolation and confusion, and prevent issues that negatively affect the student, institution, or community. In this regard, advisors hired to cover only course scheduling are analogous to security staff who only hand out parking tickets. That is, just as policing parking spots does little to deter crime, advising limited to cursory registration functions does little to enhance student development.

Despite the slow pace at which higher education evolves, the world nonetheless is changing faster than ever before. Although empowered to search for nonspecialized courses and degree information online, students' increased use of technology does not translate to less need for academic advising; rather, they require trained and flexible advisors who can meet them in the best spaces to address their learning goals (chapter 18).

At the heart of student engagement on campus, academic advisors provide "perhaps the only opportunity for all students to develop a personal, consistent relationship with someone in the institution who cares about them" (Drake, 2011, p. 10). As the postsecondary world becomes more complex, those working on college campuses are stretched to accommodate students of greater diversity than previous cohorts. Advisors make the connections between students and the college and the various offices that influence students. Administrators at colleges and universities can take a reactive position to respond to changes as they occur, or they can be proactive and enlist master advisors to help initiate needed changes.

Although they should guide the practice of advisors, theories in advising differ from theories of advising (Lowenstein, 2014). Theories in advising are drawn from nonadvising fields, such as student development, social sciences, humanities, philosophy, and the sciences. Theories of advising distinguish advising from other activities and present it as a unique field of practice and thought. Although no theories have been accepted as specific to advising, either in whole or in part, Lowenstein (2014) has recently presented a promising possibility of integrative learning theory.

Navigating through the myriad theories that relate to advising proves a daunting task such that the most skilled advisors may ask, "Why learn about theory?" Three of the most important reasons explain the importance of theory in practice and scholarship:

o Theories organize and summarize a good deal of information with a few key ideas. This parsimony provides an uncomplicated way to examine a variety of situations.

o Theories generally offer more internally consistent information than common sense observations; without theory, advising practitioners risk offering contradictory recommendations or strategies to address student concerns.

o Most social science theories can be empirically tested through long-standing research methodologies; theories borrowed from the humanities provide unique lenses through which to view academic advising practice.

Advising should be an evidence-based practice in which theory is integrated with best practices, results of research, practitioner expertise, and the needs of students and institutions. *Scholarly Inquiry in Academic Advising* (Hagen, Kuhn, & Padak, 2010) offers excellent resources for those interested in learning to interpret or conduct quantitative and qualitative research in advising. The focus on evidence provided by tested research reduces the possibility that advisors will introduce biases, stereotypes, and misconceptions that can cloud the advising session. Scholarly research provides a standard of professionalism that protects students and institutions while elevating the field of advising. Practical information related to various approaches to advising students with diverse needs is available in *Academic Advising Approaches: Strategies That Teach Students to Make the Most of College* (Drake et al., 2013).

Case studies are particularly effective tools for understanding the usefulness of theory in practice. Four case studies—three brief and one detailed—provide examples of practice with theories, applications, and advising approaches.

Case Studies

Case studies provide an opportunity for advisors to learn the way others interact with students. They give context to the reading about theories and approaches to advising, and they offer more engagement than memorization of the theory components or advising approaches. One cannot apply rotely learned and recalled facts to alternatives presented in a set of circumstances never encountered; neither can one guess the practical recommendations or courses of action that may be necessary.

While no one correct answer usually applies to every advising issue, case studies help advisors take the perspective of another professional. Advisors should review each case and put themselves in the position of the advisor in the described situation. Specifically they should identify the problem, analyze the possible causes, and tentatively plan recommendations or actions. Then they can compare their ideas with those described as the case unfolds. They can also consider their own students who present similar circumstances. The following checklist offers guidance on approaching case studies:

1. Read the case carefully to capture salient details.
2. As if the advisor in the situation, make a note of additional information obtainable through questions or a records inquiry, document key points, and organize the information if the student presents it in a chaotic or nonsequential way.
3. Rank advising issues in order of importance, but remember that some concerns are interdependent such that addressing one problem may affect another aspect of the case.
4. List possible interventions and the desired effect of each.
5. Summarize solutions and provide a theoretical basis that supports the intervention or action.

Case studies illustrate the creativity and critical thinking skills used by master advisors. Of the triad of advising content—informational, conceptual, and relational—master advisors have gained proficiency with the informational part of their jobs and remain current on information as it changes. They also have a conceptual understanding of the interrelated parts of the academy, such as general education requirements and the overall value of a degree. However, acquiring mastery takes frequent training in the form of readings and discussions as well as attending workshops and conferences to grasp and stay abreast of relational advising skills that incorporate the application of theory. Administrators who appreciate the benefits to students of advisors trained to stay updated on the current state of education and advising provide the resources necessary for professional development.

Benefits to Students

Listing all the potential benefits of excellent advising compares with describing all relevant theories in advising: Both are impossible tasks. However, the noteworthy benefits, including increased student resilience, rates of retention and completion, and student connectedness as well as decreased numbers of students on probation or suspension, grab the attention of stakeholders throughout higher education. These positive student benefits from academic advising have been well documented (Higgins, 2003; Miller & Murray, 2005; Tinto, 1993; Williams, 2007).

Specifically, higher education administrators are required to examine college graduation statistics and determine ways their institutions can assist students in timely degree completion. In some states funding is tied to college or university graduation rates. Klepfer and Hull (2012) found that students who met with advisors persisted at higher rates at both 2-year and 4-year postsecondary institution than those who did not. In a study of first-generation college students, Swecker, Fifolt, and Searby (2013) found that every meeting with an advisor was associated with a 13% increase in the chance of a student being retained.

Skilled advisors, who are trained to inform their practice through theory, eliminate (or at least decrease) the anonymity of students on the largest campuses. Advisors not only listen to students and assist them with individual issues but they also serve as the voice for students whose needs have been unheard. Like the residents in a small town know (or know about) everyone in town, when hired in adequate proportion to the student population, advisors trained in the application of theory know students' needs, strengths, and problems.

Stigma concerning personal and mental health issues, as well as lack of training in broaching these concerns, has led to silence and inaction (Moll, 2014) that have negatively affected students, and in extreme cases, has compromised on-campus safety. In response, Moll suggested a voluntary standard for providing a psychologically safe work environment that includes mental health literacy training, which involves informing both knowledge and beliefs about mental health, offered in one or two sessions. Advisors' comfort in discussing mental health issues, coupled with increased knowledge about signs that may indicate a student's struggle, may increase their ability to appropriately refer students to the resources they may need. Colleges and universities with a climate of interpersonal knowing are safer places, and successful efforts rest on the expectation that advisors put forth great effort to relate to and know their students.

Decision makers in academe must understand that enforcing college safety requires more than adding security or police officers who can, at best, identify students breaking laws or institutional rules. One can argue that arming more on-campus police generates a false sense of security, but most recognize that real security comes from knowing who walks into classrooms, lives in student housing, and eats in the cafeterias. Advisors, who know and listen to students because they have the training, resources, and flexibility "to develop a personal, consistent relationship" may not only be the "only person who cares about" students (Drake, 2011, p. 10) but they may also be the first to recognize problems that need serious and immediate attention for the sake of the student, the campus, and the community.

When students enroll in college they bring their computers, cell phones, books, and other personal effects. They also bring their coping skills, preconceptions, emotions, vulnerabilities, and in short, the whole of themselves. Advisors can refer students to any number of on- and off-campus resources but cannot force a student to follow through with appointments or suggested courses of action. However, because of their level of personal commitment to students, advisors may have the greatest opportunity to participate in relationship with students, and as a result, may carry the influence necessary to inspire students to seek resources.

Case Study: Underdeveloped Academic and Communication Skills

Jerry, a first semester freshman, was 19 years old with unrealistic goals as revealed by a desire to be, despite lack of a math and science background, a nuclear physicist. "It is an important job." When pressed about the job duties of a nuclear physicist, Jerry produced correct information about a curricular pattern appropriate for eventual application to graduate programs and expressed excitement about gaining skills in math and science. The advisor, Chris, referred Jerry to the career center to gather more information about nuclear physics and possibly explore other areas of interest.

Jerry was impulsive, so seldom made an appointment, but returned often to Chris's office. As each setback was deemed a crisis needing immediate attention, Chris discovered that Jerry had poor coping skills. Chris made an effort to speak with Jerry at every impromptu visit but also explained that appointments were required for addressing serious issues.

Jerry talked incessantly to Chris, and the topics ran the gamut: Sometimes they revolved around problems with professors or an interesting science fiction episode of a television show. However, the thread running through all Jerry's meetings was the need to talk, never to listen, such that Chris could not interject a comment or suggestion. Although not pressured speech, Jerry's chatter revealed neither introspection nor thought-provoking ideas. So, Chris mostly listened, and when opportunity arrived, gave a few simple straightforward suggestions, none of which Jerry followed.

Although Chris sensed Jerry's increased agitation and could plainly see the failed math and science courses (and poor performance in the other classes), Chris could not have guessed the depth of Jerry's anger and frustration. Instead, Chris recommended many good remedies for Jerry's academic problems from on-campus tutors to withdrawing from a couple of classes in hopes that Jerry could pass some of the others. Jerry seemed determined and convinced that "I'll pass somehow."

Two weeks before the end of the semester, Jerry met with Chris, who was at first pleased by the happy tone to the meeting. "Jerry, it's great to see you in such a good mood. What's going on?" Jerry confided to following one of the professors and said, "I'll show her how it feels to have everything you care about taken from you." Alarmed, Chris remained calm and asked Jerry to explain. "I'll just break in through that cellar door and break a few things." After thanking Jerry for the candid response, Chris said, "I must tell the professor and security of your disclosure," and Jerry immediately recanted, "I was just talking. I wasn't really going to do it." Chris asked for an explanation on the comment "following the professor," which Jerry admitted had been true, and Chris adamantly explained that such behavior was beyond inappropriateness and strongly urged counseling. Although doubting that Jerry would act on the vandalism plans, Chris called security and the professor. Jerry finished the semester with a 0.80 grade point average and did not return the following semester.

Response to Case: Identity Formation Theory

Chris initially assessed Jerry as immature with unrealistic expectations and poor coping skills. While imposing as little stress as possible and using Chickering and Reisser's (1993) theory of identity formation, Chris looked at Jerry's position on the first three vectors: developing competence, managing emotions, and moving through autonomy toward interdependence.

Competence includes intellectual ability or the acquisition of subject matter knowledge and skills related to academic goals, which in Jerry's case meant nuclear physics. It includes critical-thinking skills and reasoning ability. Competence also includes physical well-being and ability to negotiate interpersonal relationships by working well with others and communicating effectively. Without academic progress and because of difficulty talking directly to professors, Jerry acted out in a negative way. This lack of interpersonal communication skills meant that Jerry's relationship with Chris was crucial to keeping unhealthy impulses under control.

Chris used a developmental advising approach by looking for normal growth patterns associated with traditional students and approached Jerry's complex educational, career, and personal issues in a holistic way. This approach translated to a focus on the deficits that affected Jerry's academic performance in college. Although Jerry did not return the subsequent semester, Chris had presented the opportunity to grow, which may have prevented Jerry from acting rashly and may resurface positively as Jerry tackles additional stressors and a possible return to academia in the future.

Addressing the needs and concerns of some students takes a considerable amount of time. When advisors are scheduled too tightly, they cannot intervene with students in a way that may avert serious outcomes for the student and others. Therefore, the expectation and mandate must come from the highest levels of administration that advisors be trained to know, listen to, and understand the potential impact of the narratives they hear. Although scheduling course work will remain a part of the advisor's job, advisors can do more for students, their unit, the institution, and higher education.

Master advisors advocate for students. They help a student use college channels to petition for improvements; they also help students get out of their own way to success. In serious situations, they may protect students from self-inflicted harm. At all times advisors behave in ways that enhance and encourage students and work toward decreasing or eliminating obstacles to students' progress toward their goals.

Skills Used in Advising

Master advisors are thoroughly grounded in the theories that lay the foundation for superior advising practices. Advisors come from many backgrounds and have become accustomed to a specific nomenclature and perspective about theory. As a result, advisors from the humanities may think very differently than advisors from business, science, or psychology. Regardless of diverse educational backgrounds and experience, many advising approaches share essential elements, which makes learning them manageable in a relatively short time. Most approaches are based on the following tasks or skills:

- establish a caring relationship with the student;
- exhibit clear communication and listening skills;
- possess knowledge of campus and community resources;
- engage students in inquiry and problem solving; and
- encourage and reinforce positive goals and behaviors.

The diversity of approaches that colors key elements of theory benefit students, who make meaning differently from each other just as advisors do. The many approaches to advising allow practitioners to switch effortlessly from one strategy to another to advise students.

Advisor or Counselor?

Although sometimes they may discuss the same issues with students, counselors and advisors serve different purposes for students and the institution. The similarities include approachability and excellent communication skills, such as nonverbal behaviors, facility with open and closed questioning, and multicultural awareness. In addition to building rapport like counselors, master advisors demonstrate knowledge about a broad spectrum of theories as they apply to college students. They also listen to students who broach sensitive, personal topics; no subject should be off limits for students to discuss with their advisor.

Despite their willingness to help, some advisors are reluctant to address certain personal issues with students for fear of crossing an ethical boundary into counseling; however, Kuhn, Gordon, and Webber (2006) identified five levels of involvement on an advisor–counselor continuum that often overlap: "informational, explanatory, developmental, mentoring, and counseling" (p. 25). They pointed out that "both advisors and counselors help students set goals so they can improve their personal functioning, identify barriers that may impact successful accomplishment of their goals, develop strategies to accomplish these goals, and assess whether or not the strategies are successful" (p. 26). The distinction is characterized by counselor assistance with personal problems that interfere with a student's life satisfaction, and master advisors help with issues that impede a student's success in college. Sometimes those issues are the same, and some students will consult both an academic advisor, for supportive services, and a mental health counselor, for therapeutic intervention, during the same period.

Case Study: Tragedy and Loss

Jess came to college with the intent to earn a bachelor's degree in nursing. Intelligent, motivated, hard working, and mature, Jess seemed to need only a little guidance to pave the path to completion. Therefore, Tristan was shocked to discover at a midsemester meeting that Jess was living in a car off campus and expressing doubts about completing the semester. Jess asked about the impact of withdrawal and tuition refunds. With Tristan's patient prodding, Jess shared a story that was both remarkable and troubling.

In the previous year, Jess's mother, who had been diagnosed with stage four breast cancer, arranged for Jess's father to reenter their lives shortly before she passed away. Without any recollection of life with him, Jess moved over 1,000 miles away to live with him, his wife, and their two children. Despite the sad circumstances, the reunion had been good: "I missed my mom, but I'm so grateful that my dad was in my life after all those years. I was just a baby when my parents divorced. It was great to have a family again."

Jess worked part-time and began taking the classes needed to apply to a nursing program; however, midway through the semester, Jess's father had a sudden, massive heart attack. He died before reaching the hospital. Shortly after the funeral, Jess's stepmother made clear that any joy over the reunion had not been shared: "You have your mother's car, so I'm giving you until the end of the week to move out." Without arguing, Jess packed up the car and tried to continue working part-time and keep up in school, tending to personal hygiene in the restrooms of gas stations and truck stops.

Moved by the profound tragedy of the story and silently wondering how long anyone could live on the edge like this and come out okay, Tristan commended Jess's resilience and then immediately enlisted others on campus who could offer help with the processes of applying for emergency assistance, shelter, and low-income housing. Tristan referred Jess for grief counseling and also explained that free legal services for students may help with claims for any inheritance money that may provide some long-term relief.

Response to Case: Maslow's Hierarchy and Schlossberg's Transition Theory

Tristan used common sense in referring Jess to on-campus services to meet basic needs for safety and shelter. However, in retrospect, Jess's place on Maslow's hierarchy became clear; discussion on course work and degree completion would come in time. Tristan also clearly recognized the applicability of Schlossberg's theory of development (Schlossberg et al., 1995): Jess demonstrated extreme adaptability, especially evident after the smooth initial transition from high school to college went unexpectedly awry. Jess's coping mechanisms and interpersonal skills were very advanced. Furthermore, based on academic preparedness, Jess's goals of becoming a nurse showed realistic and mature expectations.

Tristan's establishment of a good working relationship in a short time encouraged Jess to seek advising when the crises became insurmountable. Together, Tristan and Jess constructed a network of support resources necessary for Jess to stay in school and work part-time. Jess also took Tristan's advice to see a mental health counselor in the community, but Tristan was always available to give additional emotional support, which Jess accessed on occasion.

Although many students follow through on referrals to mental health professionals, some will not seek help; however, these same reticent students may see an academic advisor on campus, creating some conflict for advisors, who must resist assuming the role of counselor. Academic advisors can bear witness to a student's functioning and recognize a student's decline in mental health, and this role is appropriate for an advisor trained in theory. Academic advisors see the distress, hear the cries for help, and know that preventive measures are the best security measures for the student and for the campus.

Complex individuals do not experience problems in isolation. An academic problem may be related to a learning disability, family conflict, developmental issue, health problem, financial concern, or other situation. By knowing their advisees in their wholeness and their typical behavior, academic advisors are more likely to recognize when a student is in crisis than those with less access or interaction.

Case Study: Eating Disorder

A 22-year-old transfer student, Lenny had been a literature major and changed to archeology with a particular interest in Native American life and history. Lenny told Ari, the advisor for transfer students, that "I transferred because I thought it was time for me to grow up." Lenny had earned a 3.85 GPA, seemed a bit shy, and preferred to spend time alone; "I've never had a lot of friends." Ari suggested that Lenny consider joining the archeology club on campus and pointed to a few service opportunities of potential interest.

A couple of months later, when they crossed paths on campus, Ari was shocked by Lenny's appearance; something about Lenny looked not only different but also odd somehow, but Ari could not quite figure out the problem until they started talking. Then Lenny's obvious decreased weight explained the difference in appearance. Lack of eyebrows explained the oddness in it.

Ari was concerned that perhaps Lenny had been diagnosed with cancer or some other serious illness. "Why don't you come by later today so we can talk?" Lenny agreed, and during their appointment, Ari was straightforward: "I wanted to see you because I could tell you had lost a lot of weight, and your eyebrows are gone. I am concerned. Are you okay?"

Lenny explained a troubling self-imposed regime: "I am trying to lose weight, so I run a mile in the morning, a mile at noon, and a mile in the evening. I gave up all those sugary drinks—even those sports drinks have calories, you know—so I drink only water. I eat three saltine crackers a day. One day, I ate four, so I shaved my eyebrows as a reminder to never do that again." Ari also discovered that Lenny was missing classes and having difficulty focusing. Because Lenny's health was of greatest concern, Ari felt that parental intervention was necessary and encouraged Lenny to call home right then and there.

Lenny's parents wanted to speak to Ari, and after securing the proper written permissions from Lenny, Ari picked up the phone and learned about Lenny's history of eating disorders. Lenny's mother could be there the next day on the first flight, but she asked Ari to arrange a medical evaluation as soon as possible. Lenny was willing to go to the hospital emergency room and was immediately hospitalized and diagnosed with anorexia.

Analysis of Case: Prescriptive Advising

Ari answered all Lenny's questions as they selected classes for the semester. However, Ari did not explore Lenny's comments about leaving home and growing up; a few pointed questions would have revealed that Lenny had been in counseling before transferring to an out-of-state school. Ari may also have learned that Lenny had recently quit taking a prescribed anti-depressant medication. Such revelation would have spurred a referral to a community counseling center and supportive services on campus as well as more frequent follow-up advising appointments.

Advisors frequently and appropriately use a prescriptive approach to advising; however, a master advisor uses theory to determine when another approach may be more appropriate. In Lenny's case, proactive advising may have been the most appropriate. Ari missed the significant impact caused by this immature, shy, and solitary student moving far from family and support systems. Knowledge of any of the psychosocial theories, particularly Schlossberg's transition theory (Schlossberg et al., 1995), would have helped Ari uncover Lenny's struggle at college as caused by poor coping strategies and shortcomings in self-efficacy and resilience.

Use of Theory to Prevent Problems

Knowledge of theory does more than allow advisors to assist students as they journey through college. Some normative theories, for example, can be used to predict future behavior. Erikson's (1963) stages of psychosocial development point to developmental weak spots that may help advisors anticipate challenges students may encounter in the short term. That is, master advisors know students before a problem arises and can likely offer suggestions for preventing or promptly resolving it.

For instance, Schlossberg's theory helps advisors recognize transitions and the student's coping strategies and environmental supports (Schlossberg et al., 1995). If the advisee shows some difficulty in coping or a loss of support, the advisor points out college or community resources that the student may need to access in the near future. Not only might these resources provide help during challenges, foreknowledge of them may reduce stress for the advisee. As with potentially dangerous situations, master advisors provided with training and time can contribute to prevention of lesser or personal crises because they develop the strong, interpersonal relationships that promote student success, health and safety, and goal completion.

To function to their full potential as advocates and problem solvers, master advisors systematically read students' well-being. Adding a probing summary question toward the end of an advising session (e.g., "Are there any other concerns you would like to discuss?") can open up dialogue on students' unaddressed difficulties. If students point to safety concerns, advisors follow the protocol for campus reporting. Probing summary questions serve as more than information-gathering tools about the student's well-being or concerns; they clearly send a clear message of compassion.

Most students will voice few concerns, but those who may not intend to disclose abuse, eating disorders, stalking, or mental health issues may open up and feel relieved for the opportunity to talk with someone. Advisors can listen and appropriately refer students for the help they need. The student can then proceed to complete his or her higher education goals.

Some students may be receiving psychological treatment of some form, such as weekly outpatient counseling or short-term inpatient treatment. The master advisor listens to all the ways life issues may be interfering with a student's college success and suggests supportive services on campus that complement treatment received in the community. For example, a student with post-traumatic stress disorder may feel least anxious when seated by the door in a classroom, and an advisor can help the student arrange for an accommodation that involves a reserved seat. When advisors have questions about conflicting services, such as when a student is receiving counseling about an issue that also affects academic plans, advisors should seek permission to consult the mental health professional for an opinion and thus defer to the counselor's recommendation.

Case Study: Decision Making and Identity

by Craig M. McGill

Samantha is an 18-year-old forensic science major who entered college with a math deficiency. After her first semester of college, she had earned a 2.20 GPA. Samantha faces many prerequisite math classes before she can enroll in major courses.

During her first advising session, Samantha displayed an inflated ego and talked like a know-it-all. She was closed off, distant, and refused to take responsibility for any of her actions, always finding a way to blame others. For example, when asked about her grade of D+ in public speaking, Samantha complained about her instructor: "He was a jerk and didn't grade the projects like the syllabus said he would."

Samantha was meeting with Kendall, her advisor, to select a fall semester schedule. Kendall harbors uncertainty about both Samantha's commitment to and ability to complete a forensic science major: "Why don't you make an appointment with career services before our next appointment? We can use what you learn there in our next session."

A few weeks later, Kendall's concerns were validated when Samantha returned to drop her biology course. Like the speech professor, the biology instructor was "terrible" and was the reason she was failing. Samantha admitted to not understanding biology or chemistry, which are the core subjects for a forensic science major. Kendall asked, "Why do you want to major in forensic science if you dislike much of the required course work?" Samantha replied, "literally nothing else" interested her. "Have you considered criminal justice as a major? It is based on social sciences, which require fewer math classes and only core courses in chemistry and biology." She was not open to discussion, rejecting any potential alternatives, and Kendall realized that she selected forensic science just to say she had selected a major.

Tiring of the discussion on academics, Samantha shared that she was in love with her best friend, Joey, who was gay. She frequently accompanied Joey to gay bars and had stripped at one club for fun and a little extra money. She also admitted that she liked to bring Joey home with her to annoy her homophobic father, who she described as a "big shot lawyer" in her hometown. Samantha also claimed that her father physically abused his wife and had emotionally scarred her and her siblings.

Concerned, Kendall asked, "Have you ever considered therapy?" Samantha said her parents had insisted she be in therapy during high school, but it only "made things worse." Allegedly, the therapist accused Samantha of lying and broke the confidentiality agreement and shared the session's information with Samantha's parents.

After learning about her background, Kendall started to see the reasons for Samantha's immaturity, delayed development, and lack of commitment. When Kendall carefully posited a few ideas that might explain Samantha's faultfinding and lackadaisical attitude, Samantha did not disagree or become defensive, as she had done in their first sessions. Furthermore, she admitted that she could have done more to succeed in her public speaking course and that much of her superior demeanor served as a defense from childhood traumas.

Although forensic science was not a good fit for her, Samantha claimed no other interests. With the help of Kendall, she chose four courses for the fall term that could meet the general education requirements for most majors. She also agreed to make the appointment with career services and to get serious about exploring potentially interesting topics to study.

Less than a week later, Samantha showed up in Kendall's office. She had taken their latest conversation to heart and explained that because she enjoyed her gay friends, "Maybe I could do justice work for their rights or teach a course about gay and lesbian culture." As if compelled to say it, Samantha spontaneously shared that she sometimes likes to make out with girls but she definitely was not "that kind of person."

Kendall pointed out, "There is nothing wrong with being a lesbian, and students can feel safe in the confines of an advising appointment to share information about their sexual orientation if they choose." Samantha seemed to let down her guard and said, "Well, even if I was a lesbian, I could not let my family know. Even though I bring Joey home to upset my father, if he found out I was gay, he would stop paying for college. And he owes me at least that much for messing up my life." Careful not to encourage faultfinding, inflame the situation at home, or condemn her selfish manipulation of Joey, Kendall sympathetically nodded. The appointment ended with a discussion that, even though she would likely change her major, Samantha needed to pay serious attention to her remaining courses and perform as well as possible.

Response to Case: Career, Cognitive, Strengths-Based, and Student Development Theories

by Craig M. McGill

Samantha presents a complex array of issues to address. She has a low GPA, which may be related to her uncertain career goals and immature emotional development. Undecided on a major, she must be encouraged, even prodded, to undertake the effort to explore careers. Samantha demonstrates delays in her psychosocial development, particularly in identity development.

Career Development

Samantha needs to participate in exploratory studies to find a subject of interest. By recommending general education courses required for most majors, Kendall helps Samantha stay on track to graduation and receive some exposure to various topics. Kendall could consider asking Samantha to keep a journal about exciting topics and the activities, people, and events that make her happy. She should be reminded to think about hobbies, activities, and careers that have been of interest to her over the years; she should not rule out any topic at first. Of Marcia's (1980) four statuses of identity—diffusion, foreclosure, moratorium, and achievement—Samantha exhibits signs of moratorium: She is exploring, but with a few vague ideas in mind, has made no commitment.

Kendall could utilize Holland's (1997) theory of six vocational personalities and environments to find a work situation that matches Samantha's personality type. Holland based his research on the primary assumption that behavior results from an individual's interaction with the environment. Both environmental and personal characteristics are taken into account.

Kendall decided to use a strengths-based advising approach (Schreiner, 2013), which shifts the focus from problems to possibilities. Advisors using the strengths-based approach encourage advisees to discuss their successes, thus empowering them and making them feel understood by their advisor. Knowing that Samantha has faced some childhood challenges that may still be a source of discouragement for her, Kendall thinks that the focus on success may result in greater motivation, clearer direction, inspired confidence, and more engagement in the learning process for Samantha.

Student Development Theory

Kendall considers that Samantha may have received little support when she made mistakes in childhood and turns to Erikson's (1963) stage of autonomy versus shame and doubt as a possible explanation for her constant projected blame to others. This educated speculation further confirms to Kendall that the focus on strengths as a way to build up weaknesses is an ideal approach to help Samantha get control over her behaviors and decisions.

Although identity development continues throughout life, Samantha appears to be stuck in Erikson's identity versus role confusion of adolescence. She has adopted a negative identity based on defiance of her father, and she is struggling with her sexual identity. As a counselor might work with Samantha to resolve family and identity issues, Kendall's role as an academic advisor involves the acknowledgment of these issues in Samantha's decision making and academic performance. As his primary goal, Kendall seeks to help Samantha navigate her personal circumstances to be successful in college.

Summary

The case studies in this chapter shed light on how theoretical knowledge and advising approaches can aid students in reaching their educational goals and provide an invisible layer of security to the college and university campus. Higher education offers a climate rich in opportunities that promote advisors' continued learning and development. Just as crises often set the stage for growth in students, advisors should be introspective about their own change and growth.

Advisors often protest that learning and applying theory requires too much time and labor. However, a trial-and-error approach may be more time consuming and much less effective than practice informed by theory. No other practitioners exercise the freedom to guide their professional behavior dictated solely by common sense or individual wisdom.

Less than a month following the September 11, 2001, terrorist attacks in New York City, Washington, DC, and Pennsylvania, I flew from Boston to Ontario, Canada, to attend a NACADA conference. Most people on the flight were at least a little anxious about flying so soon after the attacks. Shortly after the flight was in the air, the pilot came on the intercom to give the customary airline welcome. Unlike I had experienced on other flights, he addressed the general anxiety about flying in the wake of the recent tragedies. He added, "In light of the September attacks on American soil, we have implemented additional security. It is you. Turn to your neighbors on your right and on your left. Introduce yourself. Find out who your fellow travelers are, where they are going, and the purpose of their trip. Get to know one another. If you have any concerns about one or more of your fellow travelers, let a flight attendant know. Thank you for your help in making this a safe flight."

Advisors must listen intently to hear students' real stories. They must see students clearly, without bias or preconceived ideas. Finally, they must be comfortable with their own skills to hear and see their students, and they must be trained well enough to know the approaches most appropriate for the well-being of their students and the campus at large. The post 9-11 reality means that, as the pilot said, each person bears responsibility for security, including the safety of students, colleagues, and members of the community. Of course, responsibility is born of compassion, not legal obligation. Advisors celebrate their students' victories, no matter how small. They also grieve for students who experience injustice, loss, and failure. The compassion of advisors makes them most responsible for students.

Colleges and universities cannot rely on expanding security and police forces to make campuses safe. In fact, advisors may be in the best position and could be the best trained to identify students in jeopardy or who represent a threat to themselves or others. However, to assume this important role fully, advisors must understand and apply multiple theories to their work with students.

Although not all institutions can train each advisor to the highest level, stakeholders should aspire to this goal. Of course, novice advisors will be hired and some will be striving to reach master status, but they should all inform their practice through theory. Knowledge of and skillful use of theories and approaches in advising allow the professional to organize the information students present and respond in a consistent, logical way. Theory-based practice offers the best way to help students reach their goals and enhance campus security in this changing world.

Aiming for Excellence

- Stay current with existing and new theories by reading comprehensive literature on theories, such as *Student Development in College: Theory, Research and Practice* (Evans et al., 2010). Periodically review the NACADA Clearinghouse to see articles on theories and approaches to advising.

- Send interesting research articles on theory to colleagues with an invitation to meet and discuss new ideas and trends. For example, schedule a casual meeting, such as a brown bag lunch, for colleagues to discuss ways theory informs advising practice on campus.

- Develop competence in different advising approaches by reading *Academic Advising Approaches: Strategies That Teach Students to Make the Most of College* (Drake et al., 2013).

- Connect with other professionals through NACADA by attending conferences and seminars. Become an active member of the NACADA Theory, Philosophy, and History of Advising Commission.

- Present a PowerPoint on an area of theory at a NACADA conference and send a related write-up to *Academic Advising Today: Voices of the Global*

Community. In addition, use the information gained to conduct extensive research, possibly in collaboration with others, and submit the results to the *NACADA Journal*. The following ideas may help you generate topics for publication and venues for research:

o Write a case study that features use of a specific theory and an advising approach.

o Identify at least 10 Clearinghouse articles concerning the use of theory in advising and write a summary of each using APA citations (American Psychological Association, 2009).

o Describe the differences in theory-based advising and personal counseling.

o Write an argument and rationale for the use of theory in advising.

o Ask for or reserve time in meetings so that advisors can present short case studies that demonstrate useful application of theory. Encourage advisors to share a difficult encounter to initiate discussion and to solicit suggestions from the group.

o Take the initiative to start a candid discussion with colleagues and administrators as well as those in the behavioral response (or similar) team, judicial affairs, general counsel, and public safety units across campus about the value of increasing campus safety by strengthening the relationship between students and advisors. Make the case that creation of an environment that inspires trust and comfort may encourage troubled students, or those in their social circle, to speak up and seek help.

o View the NACADA DVDs "Scenes for Learning and Reflection" (available from the NACADA online store). After viewing the DVDs respond to the following prompts:

   o Determine the particular theory or approach each advisor is using.

   o Would other theories or approaches be helpful in working with the student(s)?

   o Do you think changing the advisors' interaction with students (based on theory) would have led to different outcomes?

   o Do some theories or approaches work better with certain kinds of advisees, such as students on academic probation?

References

American Psychological Association. (2009). *Publication manual of the American Psychological Association* (6th ed.). Washington, DC: Author.

Chickering, A. W., & Reisser, L. (1993). *Education and identity*. San Francisco, CA: Jossey-Bass.

Drake, J. K. (2011). The role of academic advising in student retention and persistence. *About Campus, 16*(3), 8–12.

Drake, J. K., Jordan, P., & Miller, M. A. (Eds.). (2013). *Academic advising approaches: Strategies that teach students to make the most of college.* San Francisco, CA: Jossey-Bass.

Erikson, E. H. (1963). *Childhood and society* (2nd ed.). New York, NY: Norton.

Evans, N. J., Forney, D. S., Guido, F. M., Patton, L. D., & Renn, K. A. (2010). *Student development in college: Theory, research, and practice.* San Francisco, CA: Jossey-Bass.

Hagen, P. L., Kuhn, T. L., & Padak, G. M. (Eds.). (2010). *Scholarly inquiry in academic advising* (Monograph No. 20). Manhattan, KS. National Academic Advising Association.

Higgins, E. M. (2012). *Advising students on probation.* Retrieved from http://www.nacada.ksu.edu/Resources/Clearinghouse/View-Articles/Advising-students-on-probation.aspx

Holland, J. L. (1997). *Making vocational choices: A theory of vocational personalities and work environments* (3rd ed.). Odessa, FL: Psychological Assessment Research.

Klepfer, K., & Hull, J. (2012). *High school rigor and good advice: Setting up students to succeed.* Retrieved from http://www.centerforpubliceducation.org/Main-Menu/Staffingstudents/High-school-rigor-and-good-advice-Setting-up-students-to-succeed/High-school-rigor-and-good-advice-Setting-up-students-to-succeed-Full-Report.pdf

Kuhn, T., Gordon, V. N., & Webber, J. (2006). The advising and counseling continuum: Triggers for referral. *NACADA Journal, 26*(1), 24–31.

Lowenstein, M. (2014, August 12). Toward a theory of advising. *The Mentor: An Academic Advising Journal.* Retrieved from https://dus.psu.edu/mentor/2014/08/toward-a-theory-of-advising/

Marcia, J. E. (1980). Identity in adolescence. In J. Adelson (Ed.), *Handbook of adolescent psychology* (pp. 159–187). New York, NY: Wiley.

Maslow, A. H. (1968). *Toward a psychology of being* (2nd ed.). New York, NY: D. Van Nostrand.

Maslow, A. H. (1970). *Motivation and personality* (2nd ed.). New York, NY: Harper & Row.

McLeod, S. A. (2007). *Maslow's hierarchy of needs.* Retrieved from http://www.simplypsychology.org/maslow.html

Miller, M. A., & Murray, C. (2005). *Advising academically underprepared students.* Retrieved from http://www.nacada.ksu.edu/Resources/Clearinghouse/View-Articles/Academically-underprepared-students.aspx

Moll, S. E. (2014). The web of silence: A qualitative case study of early intervention and support for healthcare workers with mental ill-health. *BMC Public Health, 14*(1), 1–23. doi:10.1186/1471-2458-14-138

Santrock, J.W. (2015). *Life-span development* (15th ed.). New York, NY: McGraw-Hill.

Schlossberg, N. K., Waters, E. B., & Goodman, J. (1995). *Counseling adults in transition* (2nd ed.). New York, NY: Springer.

Schreiner, L. (2013). Strengths-based advising. In J. K. Drake, P. Jordan, & M. A. Miller (Eds.), *Academic advising approaches: Strategies that teach students to make the most of college* (pp. 105–120). San Francisco, CA: Jossey-Bass.

Swecker, J. K., Fifolt, M., & Searby, L. (2013). Academic advising and first-generation college students: A quantitative study on student retention. *NACADA Journal, 33*(1), 46–53.

Tinto, V. (1993). *Leaving college: Rethinking the causes and cures of student attrition.* Chicago, IL: University of Chicago Press.

Williams, S. (2007). *From theory to practice: The application of theories of development to academic advising philosophy and practice.* Retrieved from https://www.nacada.ksu .edu/Resources/Clearinghouse/View-Articles/Applying-Theory-to-Advising-Practice.aspx

3

BUILDING UPON THE COMPONENTS OF ACADEMIC ADVISING TO FACILITATE CHANGE

Marsha A. Miller

There is nothing more difficult to take in hand, more perilous to conduct, or more uncertain in its success, than to take the lead in the introduction of a new order of things.

—Niccolò Machiavelli (1469–1527)

Master academic advisors look beyond the present to consider what the future could be. They help students make meaning of their college experiences. They use insights received from students to become thought leaders able to review and analyze the situation to pinpoint and facilitate the changes needed to improve student persistence to completion of their goals. Leaders in change know the components of academic advising, advisors' roles in helping students make meaning, and ways the organization and delivery of academic advising affect students' abilities to set and complete their educational goals. Leaders also implement effective ways to reach across perceived divides to facilitate meaningful changes that support student success.

Reader Learning Outcomes

From studying this chapter, advisors will use knowledge gained about master academic advisors to

- understand the informational, relational, and conceptual components of academic advising;
- identify and explain organizational models of academic advising;
- recognize master advisors as meaning makers;
- know strategies for reaching across perceived divides in the academy; and
- facilitate change that enhances student persistence through graduation.

Students and advising colleagues consider Drew, an experienced academic advisor, a master of the advising craft. Each day Drew, like other master advisors, encourages "students to cultivate meaning in their lives, make significant decisions about their futures, and access the institutional resources" necessary for their success (as per the Council for the Advancement of Standards in Higher Education [CAS], 2015, p. 3). Drew knows that "when practiced with competence and dedication, academic advising is integral to student success, persistence, retention, and completion" (CAS, p. 3). Yet Drew sometimes sees the negative consequences of outdated or unclear campus policies and procedures that keep students from meeting their educational goals. Despite these insights, Drew struggles to leverage institutional knowledge and become an agent of positive campus change.

Whether facilitating change for one student or for a campus process, Drew understands the elements that influence the situation. Effective academic advising is not conducted in isolation; master advisors know that advising involves others. To effect meaningful change, advisors must reach across their institutions and professional divides to connect with others who help students "cultivate meaning in their lives" (CAS, 2015, p. 3). They bridge perceived and real divides by sharing a common language with campus constituents.

Student retention, persistence, and completion are common themes across the academy. *Student retention* refers to the "percentage of first-time bachelors (or equivalent) degree-seeking undergraduates [in 4-year institutions] from the previous fall who are enrolled in the current fall. For all other institutions this is the percentage of first-time degree/certificate-seeking students from the previous fall who either re-enrolled or successfully completed their program by the current fall" (National Center for Education Statistics [NCES], n.d.a, ¶1). *Persistence* refers to retained students making progress through their postsecondary education through completion of their program and graduation (Texas Guaranteed Student Loan Corporation, 1999; Tinto, 1988). The NCES refers to completion as the time that a student "receives a degree, diploma, certificate, or other formal award" (NCES, n.d.b, ¶34). The academy focuses on making sure students come back after their first year (retention), persist (make progress toward their goals), and complete (meet those goals). Advisors' actions help students accomplish these three benchmarks (Ross & Kena, 2012, p. 261).

Tinto (1999) noted that "students are more likely to stay in schools that involve them as valued members of the institution" (p. 5). According to Strayhorn (2014), "The moment students feel they belong, they stay in college." For many students, that moment of belonging comes in the presence of academic advisors. Working with an academic advisor significantly improves students' chances to persist (Klepfer & Hull, 2012). "The number of meetings with an academic advisor was positively linked with perceptions of a supportive campus environment. This finding was remarkably consistent across racial/ethnic groups, indicating that all student groups benefit from the advising relationship" (NSSE: National Survey of Student Engagement, 2014, p. 8).

Advisors are important to student retention, persistence, and completion because they serve as cultural navigators who teach students the language of the academy and help them acclimate to the academic environment (King, 2012; Strayhorn, 2014). Drew knows that when students understand the language used on campus and how to navigate the educational environment, their academic confidence increases. This academic confidence undergirds the self-efficacy students need for success (Strayhorn, 2014). Drew understands the importance of confidence and self-efficacy conveyed in conversations with advisees and with colleagues across campus and throughout the academy.

Components of Academic Advising

"Every profession establishes a language of practice, one that captures the important concepts and understandings shared by members of the profession" (Danielson, 2007, ¶16). Master advisors recognize that conversations about academic advising are enhanced when advisors share not just a common language but also a collective understanding of the components of advising practice. Habley (1987) divided the advising practice into three components: informational, relational, and conceptual. With information serving as the foundation for academic advising, components are built upon each other. Master advisors appreciate the role of effective relational skills in facilitating the communication needed to understand conceptual issues.

The Informational Component

The bottom of the advising pyramid in Figure 3.1 illustrates the information advisors must know to do their jobs effectively (Folsom, Yoder, & Joslin, 2015). Those new to advising use *The New Advisor Guidebook: Strategies That Teach Students to Make the Most of College* (Folsom et al., 2015), the first book in the NACADA/Jossey-Bass advisor core resource library, featuring the New Advisor Development Chart (Folsom, 2015) to document their growing knowledge base and professional development. The chart is based, in part, on the NACADA: The Global Community for Academic Advising (2014a) academic advisor competencies that include knowledge about student characteristics, career information, and the institution.

Nutt (2003) noted that much of the informational component "consists of the facts or knowledge of the institution and programs that advisors must know to correctly guide advisees through the completion of their majors and programs" (p. 10). According to Fusch and Phare (2014), 90% of advising directors address the informational component during advisor training (¶2).

Recognizing the importance of mastering institutional knowledge, seasoned practitioners can become mired in information giving. Because institutional knowledge can become an all-consuming focus, Higginson (2000) broke the informational component into four equal parts so that institutional information does not overshadow the other types of information advisors need to know: internal environment, external environment, student needs, and advisor self-knowledge (p. 304).

Figure 3.1. The advising pyramid

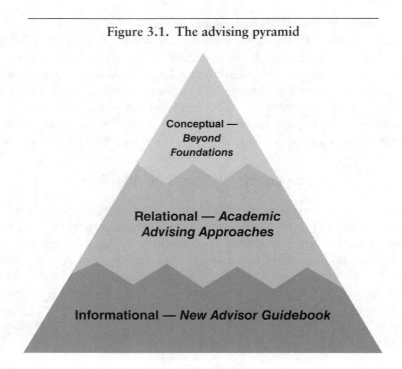

Academic advisors serve as information central for students who need clarification regarding institutional policies and procedures. Therefore, advisors must possess intimate knowledge regarding their institution's internal workings. For example, Drew regularly connects with counterparts across campus to learn about changes to programs, policies, and procedures and was instrumental in establishing a campus advising association (as per Bryant, Chagani, Endres, & Galvin, 2006).

The external information advisors must know includes that pertaining to applicable laws (e.g., Family Educational Rights and Privacy Act), policies (e.g., funding), procedures (e.g., transfer), and referral resources (e.g., legal services) both on and off campus. The external component includes national, state, or provincial legal mandates (chapter 8). For example, Drew acquired intimate knowledge of local referral networks for issues ranging from mental health counseling to internship opportunities, from drop-in child care options to food banks.

To help students succeed, Drew understands students' needs (Higginson's [2000] third informational component) and helps them make essential connections. Drew gained familiarity with new students and the issues that concern them during new student planning conferences and by connecting with new students partway through their initial academic term at the institution (as per Cloud County Community College, n.d.) to learn about new or continuous concerns (e.g., academic progress, living conditions, most challenging issues to date). Advisors who converse with students and learn about their successes and challenges can connect them with necessary support and prove crucial for students who lack other necessary support systems.

The final element of Higginson's (2000) informational component, advisor self-knowledge, mandates that advisors know themselves, including their own innate points of view and preconceptions, so that they can help others (Archambault, 2015). McClellan (2007) thinks advisor self-knowledge deserves consideration as a separate component of advising, which he termed the *personal component*.

Master advisors must develop a deep personal understanding beyond knowledge of their personal values, stressors, and levels of commitment for specific endeavors. Master advisors set personal and professional goals and monitor their growth toward meeting them (McClellan, 2007, ¶15). Whether advisor self-knowledge warrants designation as a separate component of academic advising remains debatable, but it contributes to successful advising practice. For instance, although the first family member to graduate from college, Drew recognizes that many advisees come from homes with college graduates or do not share all the characteristics identified with many first-generation students. Therefore, Drew determines students' knowledge of college terms and their understandings of institutional policies and procedures before making assumptions. Master advisors never assume.

The Relational Component

Habley's (1987) relational component encompasses advisors' actions—what they must do—to be effective. Academic advisors must connect with students. Master advisors do not rely on one advising approach when communicating with students; instead they employ different approaches as needs arise. In *Academic Advising Approaches: Strategies That Teach Students to Make the Most of College* (Drake, Jordan, & Miller, 2013) (the second book in the NACADA/Jossey-Bass advisor core resource library), the authors delineated several approaches commonly used by master advisors including (but not limited to) appreciative advising (Bloom, Hutson, & He, 2013), advising as teaching (Drake, 2013), developmental advising (Grites, 2013), self-authorship (Schulenberg, 2013), and proactive advising (Varney, 2013). Drew uses information and case studies from the *Approaches* book for professional development and to shape advising practice.

Drew routinely uses different question types (e.g., involvement, clarifying, and continuing; Drake, Hemwall, & Stockwell, 2009, p. 12) to stimulate discussions with students. Students approach advisors to discuss a variety of issues dealing with the institution, possible careers, and personal concerns. Master advisors know that student-focused conversations include discussions regarding the student's background, current situations, goals, and aspirations (Drake et al., 2009, p. 11). When conversing with students, master advisors effectively use questions to help students discover insights needed to succeed (Drake et al., 2009).

Advisors must possess the relational skills needed to successfully refer students to necessary resources. They need to know more than the relevant office and must employ a variety of methods to ensure that students make needed connections. When time allows, Drew walks the referred student to the appropriate campus resource. Although few advisors can take the time to escort students, they can effectively use technologies to make introductions and introduce the student. Drew often assists students in phoning for an appointment, helps students craft e-mails, or teaches them the scheduling software utilized by the referred resource.

Master advisors use technologies by understanding their purpose and use for student benefit (McClellan, 2007). Whether technology is used with all three of Habley's advising components or as a stand-alone component within advising practice (as suggested by McClellan, 2007), master advisors know that the effective use of technology comprises a vital part of advising practice (chapter 16).

The Conceptual Component

The top of the advising pyramid is crowned with the conceptual component, which explains the ideas that advisors must comprehend and apply to meet their advising objectives. To master the craft, everyone within the advising community must understand, value, and act upon key concepts of the field to contribute to their students and institutions as well as benefit the field and themselves. For example, advisors must grasp the ways advising is organized and delivered on their campus. They also need to act upon the need to bridge institutional divides to effect changes that help students set educational goals and persist until completion.

As campus linchpins, master advisors act upon their understanding of issues and develop into thought leaders (McClellan, 2009, ¶1) who connect with various campus and advising affiliates. Thought leaders "understand the divergent needs of the multiple constituencies that make up the advising community" (McClellan, 2009, ¶4) and act upon that knowledge. Thought leaders within the advising community include "professional [primary-role] and faculty advisors, administrators, advisor training personnel, researchers, philosophers, theorists, and students" (McClellan, 2009, ¶4).

Master advisors know their campus definition of, mission of, and vision for advising. On campuses without these three documents, thought leaders promote discussions leading to the delineation of these important statements (chapter 4). For these efforts, they consult existing institutional statements and three pillars of advising: the NACADA Statement of Core Values of Academic Advising, the Concept of Academic Advising (NACADA, 2005, 2006), and the CAS Standards (CAS, 2015). Additionally, master advisors know that a philosophy of advising for themselves and their advising units must be generated by thought leaders (NACADA, 2014c).

The three components of advising, as outlined by Habley (1987), meet in the application of skills. Advisors reach out to students before small issues grow into big problems. Seventy percent of surveyed institutions provide training in proactive advising (Fusch & Phare, 2014, ¶3). Many use materials from Varney (2013) and the links found on the NACADA Clearinghouse (NACADA, 2014d) to stimulate discussions that pinpoint key times when advisors should connect with students. Master advisors gain familiarity with the latest literature and brainstorm effective strategies for helping students explore options to problems that may hinder successful completion of their educational goals. Master advisors possess needed information (the informational component), understand the best ways to apply it (the conceptual component), and can effectively communicate with students and colleagues (the relational component) to help students reach their academic goals.

In their groundbreaking study, Klepfer and Hull (2012) identified three factors that significantly improved student persistence: learning high-level mathematics in high school, successful completion of Advanced Placement/International Baccalaureate courses, and meeting often with a college academic advisor (p. 15). "Advisors teach students how to make the most of their college experience" (Miller, 2013, ¶1) and serve as "interpreters who help students navigate their new world" (King, 2012).

Organizational Models of Academic Advising

Master advisors know that new students must learn the role advising plays in their academic success and the ways to access it. Likewise, advisors who understand the definition for and the organization of it in their unit (i.e., department or college) may not realize that advising may be defined and organized differently elsewhere within the institution and academe. Pioneers in the advising field crafted a common language to help advisors discuss advising organization and delivery to encourage meaningful conversations.

Habley (1983) suggested seven organizational models for academic advising: faculty only, shared supplementary, shared split, dual, total intake, satellite, and self-contained. While faculty only and self-contained definitively explain two types, the other five were less clear to many advisors. In 2004, Pardee updated Habley's models by suggesting three types: centralized, decentralized, and shared (¶3). However, in the decade after Pardee identified the models, many in the advising field realized that increased accountability, including the need for assessment of student learning outcomes (SLOs) and benchmarking, required focused attention on the differences in definitions of the variety of organizational models utilized in seemingly similar advising situations (e.g., departments, colleges, and campuses).

The CAS Standards for Academic Advising Programs (CAS, 2015) and assessments mandated by many accreditation agencies (e.g., The Higher Learning Commission, 2015) dictate the crafting of advising mission statements. Master advisors know that discourse on formalizing an advising mission often leads to discussions regarding definitions, institution or department philosophies, and organizational models of advising. As these discussions transpire, some master advisors focus on finding similar programs for required benchmarking; others concentrate on finding advising organizational models that best fit the student body and the institution. The conversations on organizational models, while more numerous and important than in the past, remain convoluted when structures remain dissimilar and difficult to define.

Respondents to the *2011 NACADA National Survey of Academic Advising* reported use of more than 100 different organizational models for academic advising. A majority (53.6%) indicated that advising duties on their campuses are *shared* (a term used by Habley [1987] and Pardee [2004]) in some form between primary-role and faculty advisors (Carlstrom & Miller, 2013a). With so many variations in advising models, I encouraged those discussing advising organizational models to answer four questions early in their conversations (Miller, 2013):

- o Who is advised?
- o Who advises?
- o Where is advising done (including the use of any technologies)?
- o How are advising responsibilities divided? (¶13)

Barron and Powell (2014) added a fifth question: When does advising occur? (p. 16)

Answers to these five questions provide a structure for conversations and help simplify the search for like models. Additionally, the answers help those seeking to restructure advising find the model(s) they would like to consider for adoption. Master advisors know that the choice of an advising model reveals the decisions considered and the priorities set when advising was defined, and it reflects the ways advising is currently viewed and understood at the institution. As a result of this knowledge, they recognize the importance of the model chosen when restructuring the organization of advising (Miller, 2004).

Assessment points to the effectiveness (or ineffectiveness) of any advising model, and master advisors help facilitate the assessment of their advising programs. Robbins (chapter 14) notes that assessment of advising program effectiveness hinges on the development of SLOs. McFarlane (2013) tied advising models to student success by stating,

> Results indicated statistically significant relationships between . . . advising learning outcomes and how advising is delivered, specifically, who advises students, where students are advised, how frequently students are required to see an advisor, how frequently students choose to see an advisor, and how "mandatory" advising is implemented (p. i).

When assessment results show that changes in advising or institutional procedures better facilitate the achievement of SLOs, then master advisors must reach across the institution to effect meaningful change. Keeling (2014) affirmed that meeting campuswide SLOs must drive both institutional and advising agendas.

Master Advisors as Meaning Makers

Academic advising "provides perhaps the only opportunity for all students to develop a personal, consistent relationship with someone in the institution who cares about them" (Drake, 2011, p. 10). The relationships that master advisors cultivate with students are crucial not only to their learning but also to their retention and persistence in completing educational goals (Klepfer & Hull, 2012; Tinto, 1999).

Master advisors become students' go-to people to help them answer questions that include and extend beyond academic program information, including

- o What am I?
- o Why am I?
- o Where am I going?
- o What is worth knowing?
- o What should I believe, hope for, and trust in?
- o What is the source of my joy?
- o Where am I most vulnerable?
- o What is my responsibility to others?
- o What is my vocation? (Nash & Jang, 2013, p. 4)

Advisors help students make meaning and set goals central to their education (Nash & Jang, 2013). They also help students gain self-awareness of their interests, talents, values, and priorities (Cuseo, n.d.). They enable "students to see the 'connection' between their present academic experience and their future life plans" (Cuseo, n.d., p. 13). Advisors help students broaden their perspectives, consider personal life choices, and sharpen the cognitive skills needed to make choices (Cuseo, n.d.). Master advisors use a variety of advising approaches to help students discover their potential, purpose, and passion. Master advisors also teach students "effective problem-solving, critical thinking, and reflective decision-making" (Cuseo, n.d., p. 13) as they engage students in conversations that help them make meaning and learn the skills needed to persist and complete their goals.

Advisors who simplify meaning-making conversations are central resources who "facilitate discussion and introduce pedagogies to encourage critical thinking and deep, existential reflections" (Nash & Jang, 2013, p. 7) essential for student success. With advisors, students are "heard and affirmed that their worries, concerns, hopes, and dreams are valid" (Nash & Jang, 2013, p. 7). All who advise, no matter to whom they report, help students make meaning regardless of any campus divides. When students bring forward a problem with a campus process, master advisors vet and share relevant information with those charged with making needed changes. For example, upon hearing students complain about a registration procedure for a new course that had been approved by faculty vote and administered by the registrar, Drew investigated the process, discovered the root of the problem, and met with the appropriate stakeholders in both administration and faculty to suggest a change. Follow-up corrections require participation over perceived campus divides.

Master Advisors Reach Across Divides

Thought leaders not only understand conceptual issues; they also take action. Campus leaders, including master advisors functioning as thought leaders, must remain nimble in multiple situations and collaborate to help students persist through graduation (Keeling, 2014). Silos have no place on campus; today's challenges require that no one remains static (Keeling, 2014). Few can facilitate the key cross-institutional communication as master academic advisors and their administrators.

Respondents to the *2011 NACADA National Survey of Academic Advising* indicated a range of advisor reporting channels: 57.1% reported through academic affairs, 20.6% through student affairs, 10.8% jointly through academic and student affairs, 6.9% through enrollment management, 2.3% through the registrar, 2.3% other (Carlstrom & Miller, 2013b). Regardless of the reporting line, master advisors have one foot firmly planted in the academic side of the institution and another in student affairs.

Bourassa and Kruger (2002) affirmed that on many campuses a gulf splits the distance between academic and student affairs and creates challenges for those seeking to reach across divides and become trusted and valued colleagues. The breach hinders the communication necessary to implement changes that support student success. Advisors who help students make meaning are strategically placed to know the ways the institution can better support students.

"Communication throughout the college has to become a fundamental process not an afterthought" (Shaw, 1989, p. 80). Strategically reaching across campus means creating "cross-functional, interdepartmental linkages that combine resources and expertise to address the learning needs of students" (Whitt et al., 2008, p. 236). Banta and Kuh (1998) spent two decades working with campuses to improve the quality of the undergraduate experience by creating an environment for seamless learning. They explained that any process as complex and multifaceted as improving quality "demands cooperation of the two campus groups that spend the most time with students: faculty and student affairs professionals" (p. 42).

How do faculty and primary-role advisors work across reporting lines? Strategically.

> Although some kinds of information will be more welcome from advisors who are also faculty, once nonfaculty advisors have built rapport, the same interaction can take place. The advisor who stays in the advising office does not open the lines that allow this level of communication. (Miller & Alberts, 1994, p. 44)

Master advisors who are thought leaders and meaning makers connect with colleagues across the campus not in only one or two units or departments.

Academic and student affairs partnership programs are "one means to bridge the academic, social, and affective elements of students' experiences by creating seamless environments and engaging students in their own learning" (Whitt et al., 2008, p. 236). Thought leaders who bridge institutional divides pool their perspectives on students' in-class and out-of-class experiences so "that cognitive and affective development are inextricably intertwined and . . . curricular and out-of-class activities are not discrete, independent events" (Banta & Kuh, 1998, p. 42).

Kezar (2001) found that every institution represented in one nationwide survey reportedly engaged in some form of collaboration across institutional divides (p. 41). Thought leaders identify collaborations that work on their campuses and build upon those to effect change. For instance, Kezar found that community colleges excelled in successful cross-institutional collaborations possibly because advisor training and development were also considered faculty development. Many 4-year colleges host teaching and learning centers that help those who coordinate advisor training and development activities reach all who advise. Partnerships forged for cross-institutional training opportunities create enhanced student learning (Kezar, 2001).

Factors that make the most difference to the success of collaborative efforts include levels of cooperation, staff attitudes, common goals, and personalities (Kezar, 2001, p. 44). Although Kezar's (2001) findings may contradict the literature that points to "structural changes, planning, and senior administrative/leadership support as significant to creating working partnerships" (p. 44), they should give master advisors hope for facilitating cross-campus partnerships.

A combination of cultural and structural strategies comprises the critical strategies for developing change that lead to cross-campus partnerships (Kezar, 2003). Leadership (especially the support of senior administrators) makes up the most important individual strategy to promote cross-institutional dialogue. Both structural (setting expectations, planning) and cultural strategies (engaging in cross-institutional dialogue, generating enthusiasm, creating a common vision, developing staff competencies) also facilitate collaboration (Kezar, 2003, p. 14).

At large institutions, master advisors may need specific resources and incentives to establish collaboration priorities, whereas on small campuses, they can bolster cross-campus cooperation by selecting a senior leader who sets priorities. According to Kezar's (2001) survey, community colleges may face the fewest structural obstacles in facilitating institutional collaboration; however, at institutions with more than 10,000 enrollments, structural strategies and monetary incentives were considered slightly more important than they were at other institutions (Kezar, 2001, pp. 45–48).

The most cited obstacles to cross-campus collaboration, according to Kezar's (2001) survey, related to structural and cultural concerns: lack of established goals, lack of time, faculty disciplinary ties, and faculty resistance (p. 47). Keeling (2014) pointed out that faculty members are most receptive to working with nonfaculty staff who acknowledge increased faculty stressors: achieving promotion and tenure along with the demands for teaching, research, and service. Primary-role advisors who reach out often to faculty help reduce faculty resistance to change and facilitate student learning and success.

Sanaghan and Lohndorf (2015) explained that "to engage in cross-boundary collaboration, senior leaders must be dedicated to creating opportunities for their stakeholders to make connections with each other, share best practices, problem solve and seek opportunities to leverage the time and talent of campus stakeholders" (p. 17). For example, to address the problematic course registration issue brought forward by advisees, Drew builds upon a strength: knowledge about the ways to facilitate student persistence and completion. Drew volunteers for campus committees, shows up at campus discussions, and develops senior administrative support for cross-campus collaborations. Drew's actions as a master advisor garner senior administration support vital to successful collaborations (Kezar, 2001) and help bring the student voice to administrative discussions.

Thought leaders craft discussions around the shared goal of student success through improved learning environments, retention, institutional communication, cultural trust, and campus relationships (Kezar, 2001, p. 49). According to Whitt et al. (2008), good practice for successful cross-campus partnerships

- o reflects and advances the institution's mission (p. 239);
- o embodies and fosters a learning-centered ethos (p. 240);
- o builds on and nurtures relationships (p. 241);
- o recognizes, understands and attends to institutional culture (p. 242);
- o values and implements assessment (p. 243);
- o uses resources creatively and effectively (p. 244); and
- o cultivates multiple manifestations of leadership (p. 245).

Keeling (2014) recommended that thought leaders be involved in each step of a project. Susan Campbell and Susan McWilliams (chapter 4) agree, noting that master advisors offer critical input to efforts for revisiting (or crafting where nonexistent) mission, vision, and goals for academic advising that draw upon institutional mission, vision, and goals. Administrators charged with naming committees to complete such tasks should add thought leaders who, using ideas presented by Kezar (2001), proactively reach across campus to increase student learning and completion of their educational goals.

Thought leaders demand accountability, volunteer to serve on joint cross-divisional councils or committees, and support various forms of restructuring (e.g., developing learning communities or enrollment management initiatives) that foster student persistence to completion (Kezar, 2001). Master advisors seeking to improve cross-campus collaboration (a) know their institution and the players within it, (b) focus on student learning, (c) take advantage of opportunities, (d) engage in assessments (e.g., needs as well as formative and summative program assessments), and (e) realize that partnerships require tremendous amount of work (Whitt et al., 2008, p. 247). Master advisors select a project and reach across perceived boundaries to initiate change. In committing to action, they become change agents (chapters 10 and 11).

Master Advisors Facilitate Change

Meaningful change does not occur easily. According to Moss Kanter (2003), change leaders

> know that problem solving requires collaboration across departments and divisions—not just because innovations often come from these joint projects. Changing

the dynamics requires collective commitments to new courses of action lest a local decision, taken in isolation, undermines that change. New strategies are possible when new kinds of conversations are held about combining organizational assets in new ways. (p. 8)

Because academic advising is found at the intersection of academic and student affairs (Miller & Alberts, 1994), academic advisors are often "cultural travelers" on campus (Sanaghan & Lohndorf, 2015, p. 25). Advisors who are also thought leaders move between and among the various campus groups and know those on campus who will be most helpful in realizing the envisioned change. Drew serves on cross-divisional committees and can relatively easily take the course registration issue to both a leader of the faculty senate and a person in the Registrar's office. Once these stakeholders learned of the problem students were facing in negotiating the new rule, they brokered a solution workable for all involved. How did Drew know the colleagues in the best position to implement change?

Colleagues can be divided into two categories: those ready to act and those resistant to change (Smith Jaggars, Fletcher, West Stacey, & Little, 2014). The ready-to-act category is made up of two groups. The first consists of doers with positive attitudes and who "know the system extremely well and are often turned to for creative trouble-shooting and problem solving" (Smith Jaggars et al., 2014, p. 2). To collaborate, Drew approached two individuals who belonged to this group. The second group within the ready-to-act category is comprised of team players with positive attitudes and who accomplish work best when following set procedures (Smith Jaggars et al., 2014, p. 2).

Colleagues resistant to change can also be divided into two groups: the ambivalent and the naysayers. According to Smith Jaggers et al. (2014), the ambivalent are

neither active proponents nor opponents of change, but are important to include if they play a key role in processes targeted for improvement. Those who are ambivalent often become proponents of change when exposed to student stories documenting the need for change and when they are given a role in imagining potential solutions for improvement. (p. 2)

The naysayers are "individuals with strong negative opinions about the proposed changes" (Smith Jaggars et al., 2014, p. 2). Within the naysayer group are those against all change and those skeptics O'Banion (2015) identified as curmudgeons: highly visible individuals who take pride in "thinking otherwise" (¶4). Skeptics (curmudgeons) appear to be critical of any change in which they are not intimately connected. These individuals "identify problems that lurk under the surface and that influence campus culture" (O'Banion, 2015, ¶10). Issues identified by curmudgeons often must be addressed for meaningful change to occur. Thought leaders find constructive ways to involve curmudgeons because including one of these skeptics can produce positive results for everyone (O'Banion, 2015). However, one should choose the committee's naysayer with care by looking for the curmudgeon who has campus influence but may feel unheard. When well-known doubters feel appreciated, they are less likely to criticize projects because they feel ownership in them and will more likely embrace changes that advance the identified agenda (Brown & Cregan, 2008).

Despite differences in strategies and tactics, skeptics "may become the strongest and most effective proponents once their concerns are taken into account" (Smith Jaggars et al., 2014, p. 2). As the campus sees a cynic's perceived reticence replaced by initiative, other ambivalent naysayers may take note of the project and give the proposed change a cautionary chance (Moss Kanter, 2003, p. 10). As enthusiasm is generated by a project's forward movement, others will want to be connected with it thus restoring confidence and raised expectations of others (Moss Kanter, 2003).

Change leaders utilize steps from Smith Jaggars et al. (2014) when moving forward with a project:

- o "Identify which problems could be addressed fairly quickly at minimal cost" (p. 3). Frontline staff often have the best insight into simple changes that can address the most straightforward issues.

- o Emphasize shared values.

  A fundamental shared value for most community college faculty and staff is that of student success. When communicating the need for change, leaders should consistently invoke the importance of designing processes that respond to student needs and that support their success. When leaders work to engage faculty and staff who will play a role in implementing change, they can use data on the student experience to frame the conversation and invoke these shared values. (p. 4)

- o Build a culture of trust. "The most successful collaborations are supported by an administration that 'leads by listening.'" Encourage administrators to attend team meetings. "A sense of trust and openness can also be developed among team members when confidentiality is maintained when discussing sensitive topics" (p. 4).

Steps toward meaningful change take time and administrative support. For example, new committee members should send administrators appointing the committee a personal e-mail thanking them for the committee appointment and follow up with short written updates as the group makes progress toward implementation of actions that will improve student completion (Nutt, 2014). Thought leaders know that letting top-level administrators know about progress keeps the committee's work up front and bolsters administrative support for change.

Summary

Master advisors understand the components of academic advising and the role each aspect plays in their advising practice. They know the importance of understanding, valuing, and acting upon concepts that help students make the meanings needed to bolster their academic success.

Master advisors understand that the organization and delivery of academic advising affect student persistence and completion. When they develop into thought leaders, master advisors facilitate discussions surrounding advising models and create opportunities to identify changes needed to help students meet their goals.

Academic advisors, with one foot firmly planted in academics and the other in student affairs, have a unique place in the institution and provide a perspective increasingly valued in the conversations about student persistence to completion. Advisors who become change leaders utilize a variety of strategies to reach across institutional divides for facilitating needed change. Master advisors, like Drew, know that identifying, articulating, and implementing needed change is not easy. However, their efforts can be rewarded when more students make meaning of their college experience and persist in completing their educational goals.

Aiming for Excellence

Components of Academic Advising

o Discuss with colleagues pieces of little-known institutional information that upon revelation would make the biggest difference to students and other advisors. Then brainstorm ideas for creating access to these nuggets of information.

o Read a chapter in *Academic Advising Approaches: Strategies That Teach Student to Make the Most of College* (Drake et al., 2013) and then discuss with colleagues ways to incorporate the highlighted strategies into advising practice.

o Find the definition for campus advising or a mission statement and discuss them with colleagues. Specifically, address the ways current advising practice mirrors (or not) the definition or mission. If neither a definition nor a mission statement exists, discuss the elements to include in drafting a definition and mission statement.

o Refer to the Question Types resources on the Communication and Listening page of the NACADA Clearinghouse (2014b) and answer the following questions:

o What questions build relationships with advisees? For example, what inquiry leads to discovery of students' backgrounds? Their goals? Gaps in their knowledge about the institution?

o What tips, based upon the question types, would you suggest to colleagues to help them craft academic advising questions that elicit enlightening responses?

o Read chapter 6 by Karen Archambault and discuss with colleagues the ways in which advisors' personal backgrounds differ from those of their students.

o Discuss whether, like McClellan (2007), advisors believe that understanding their own personal backgrounds should be considered a stand-alone component of advising? Why or why not? What preconceived notions (conscience or unconscious biases) does each advisor bring to advising conversations?

o Do you agree with McClellan (2007) that technology should constitute a stand-alone component of academic advising? Which of the technologies currently used are the most helpful? Which are the least effective? What other technologies would be helpful to advising practice?

Organizational Models of Academic Advising

o Answer the five questions regarding the structure and delivery of advising: Who advises? Who is advised? Where is advising done? How are advising responsibilities divided? (Miller, 2013) and When is advising done? (Barron & Powell, 2014). Does your campus use a single advising model or do several advising organizational models exist on campus?

o Determine the benchmarks used at the institution (e.g., campuses used for assessment comparisons). How does the advising structure compare at your institution to the organizational models used on the benchmark campuses? What aspects of other models would help make advising more effective on your campus?

o Read the Klepfer and Hull (2012) study that delineates three predictors of student success: advising, completion of higher math, and passing AP/IB courses. Does academic advising practice or organizational structure dissuade students from persisting to completion? What (if anything) needs to change in the ways advising is accessed and delivered to correct the problems?

o Where advising is a shared responsibility, how do advisors communicate and learn about practice? Do advisors share a common philosophy about practice? Should they?

o If changes need to be made to the current advising organizational model, use Miller's (2004) 16 factors for (re)structuring academic advising to start conversations about the current status of academic advising on your campus.

Making Meaning

o What strategies are most effective for helping students determine their own values?

o How do you help students discover their potential, purpose, and passion? What activities are the most effective?

o Take a look at the NACADA Clearinghouse goal-setting resource. Which goal-setting strategies have you used? Select a strategy new to you and try it with students. Reflect on the approach that worked especially well with students.

o Choose one of the articles in the Joe Cuseo collection at the University of Wisconsin Colleges (2015) web site of academic resources as a common reading. Discuss with colleagues the insights learned from the featured topics.

o Discuss with colleagues the institutional insights you have learned from students and identify those insights best shared with administration. Determine a way to articulate the insights to facilitate needed changes.

Reaching Across Divides

o Identify thought leaders who consistently reach across campus barriers to accomplish initiatives or effect change. Invite those individuals for coffee and discuss ways they facilitate cross-campus conversations.

o Volunteer to serve on a campus committee or task force that is outside your typical duties or area of expertise. Use the opportunity to garner different perspectives regarding campus issues.

o Revisit the mission, vision, and goals of academic advising. How is academic advising defined on your campus? If it is time to write or revise these statements, form a committee using strategies suggested in this chapter.

o Enlist assistance from a senior administrator known for reaching across campus. Ask that administrator to address an advisor training session or task force meeting to discuss successful strategies for working across campus culture divides.

o Hold a brown bag lunch to discuss the Klepfer and Hull (2012) study and how campus entities can work together to facilitate student success.

Facilitating Change

o What student (and institutional) needs are currently met by the current advising system? What needs are not being met? Look at Miller's (2004) 16 factors to consider when (re)structuring academic advising and discuss issues identified with your colleagues.

o What problems can be addressed fairly quickly at minimal cost?

o Select one issue that needs to change on your campus. Ask individuals who can make the change happen to formulate plans.

o Identify colleagues who are ready to act and who are resistant to change.

o Identify skeptics whose opinions hold the most sway on campus. What can be said or done to bring at least one of these skeptics on board for your project?

o Read chapter 10 by Chrissy Davis Jones on leading from your position. What strategies will help you facilitate changes?

o Construct a plan to facilitate change and present it to an administrator whose backing will be influential.

Assessment Strategies

o Ask readers to identify the categories of Reader Learning Outcomes described within the chapter that interested them the most.

o Choose at least one Aiming for Excellence activity related to reader's named favorite topics. Facilitate implementation of the activity with readers, and together identify at least three possible changes that can result from completing the activity. Follow up three and six months later to determine the progress that has been made.

o Determine if change followed from the activity chosen. If changes have been made, assess whether they led to positive outcomes and determine other plans that may stimulate further positive action.

References

Archambault, K. L. (2015). Developing self-knowledge as a first step toward cultural competence. In P. Folsom, F. Yoder, & J. E. Joslin (Eds.), *The new advisor guidebook: Mastering the art of academic advising* (2nd ed.) (pp. 185–202). San Francisco, CA: Jossey-Bass.

Banta, T. W., & Kuh, G. D. (1998, March-April). A missing link in assessment: Collaboration between academic and student affairs professionals. *Change: The Magazine of Higher Learning*, 40–46.

Barron, K. E., & Powell, D. N. (2014). Options on how to organize and structure advising. In R. L. Miller & J. G. Irons (Eds.), *Academic advising: A handbook for advisors and students. Volume 1: Models, students, topics, and issues.* Retrieved from http://www.teachpsych.org/Resources/Documents/ebooks/advising2014Vol1.pdf

Bloom, J. L., Hutson, B. L., & He, Y. (2013). Appreciative advising. In J. K. Drake, P. Jordan, & M. A. Miller (Eds.), *Academic advising approaches: Strategies that teach students to make the most of college* (pp. 83–99). San Francisco, CA: Jossey-Bass.

Bourassa, D. M., & Kruger, K. (2002). The national dialogue on academic and student affairs collaboration. *New Directions for Higher Education, 2001*(116), 9–38. doi:10.1002/he.31

Brown, M., & Cregan, C. (2008). Organizational change cynicism: The role of employee involvement. *Human Resource Management, 47*(4), 667–686.

Bryant, R., Chagani, A., Endres, J., & Galvin, J. (2006). *Professional growth for advisors: Strategies for building professional advising networks.* Retrieved from http://www.nacada.ksu.edu/Resources/Clearinghouse/View-Articles/Building-professional-advising-networks.aspx

Carlstrom, A. H., & Miller, M. A. (Eds.). (2013a). Advising models [Table 5.1]. *2011 NACADA national survey of academic advising* (Monograph No. 25). Manhattan, KS: National Academic Advising Association. Retrieved from http://www.nacada.ksu.edu/Portals/0/Monographs/nat%20survey%20upload%20docs/Chapter%205%20tables%20final%20jv.pdf

Carlstrom, A. H., & Miller, M. A. (Eds.). (2013b). Reporting lines [Table 14.1]. *2011 NACADA national survey of academic advising* (Monograph No. 25). Manhattan, KS: National Academic Advising Association. Retrieved from http://www.nacada.ksu.edu/Portals/0/Clearinghouse/M25/rebuilt_chap14final.pdf

Cloud County Community College. (n.d.). *New student planning conference [handout].* Retrieved from http://www.nacada.ksu.edu/portals/0/Clearinghouse/Links/documents/New-Student-Planning-Conference.pdf

Council for the Advancement of Standards in Higher Education. (2015). *Academic advising programs.* Retrieved from http://standards.cas.edu/getpdf.cfm?PDF=E864D2C4-D655-8F74-2E647CDECD29B7D0

Cuseo, J. (n.d.). *Academic advisement and student retention: Empirical connections &* *systemic interventions.* Retrieved from http://cpe.ky.gov/NR/rdonlyres/6781576F-67A6-4DF0-B2D3-2E71AE0D5D97/0/CuseoAcademicAdvisementandStudent RetentionEmpiraclConnectionsandSystemicInterventions.pdf

Danielson, C. (2007). *Enhancing profession practice: A framework for teaching* (2nd ed.). Retrieved from http://www.ascd.org/publications/books/106034/chapters/ The-Framework-for-Teaching@-An-Overview.aspx

Drake, J., Hemwall, M., & Stockwell, K. (2009). *A faculty guide to academic advising.* Manhattan, KS: National Academic Advising Association.

Drake, J. K. (2011, July-August). The role of academic advising in student retention and persistence. *About Campus, 16*(3), 8–12.

Drake, J. K. (2013). Advising as teaching and the advisor as teacher in theory and in practice. In J. K. Drake, P. Jordan, & M. A. Miller (Eds.), *Academic advising approaches: Strategies that teach students to make the most of college* (pp. 17–32). San Francisco, CA: Jossey-Bass.

Drake, J. K., Jordan, P., & Miller, M. A. (Eds.). (2013). *Academic advising approaches: Strategies that teach students to make the most of college.* San Francisco, CA: Jossey-Bass.

Folsom, P. (2015). The new advisor development chart. In P. Folsom, F. Yoder, & J. E. Joslin, (Eds.), *The new advisor guidebook: Mastering the art of academic advising* (2nd ed.) (pp. 19–35). San Francisco, CA: Jossey-Bass.

Folsom, P., Yoder, F., & Joslin, J. E. (Eds.). (2015). *The new advisor guidebook: Mastering the art of academic advising* (2nd ed.). San Francisco, CA: Jossey-Bass.

Fusch, D., & Phare, C. (2014). *Survey report: Training academic advisors.* Retrieved from http://www.academicimpressions.com/news/survey-report-training-academic-advisors

Grites, T. J. (2013). Developmental academic advising. In J. K. Drake, P. Jordan, & M. A. Miller (Eds.), *Academic advising approaches: Strategies that teach students to make the most of college* (pp. 45–59). San Francisco, CA: Jossey-Bass.

Habley, W. R. (1983). Organizational structures for academic advising: Models and implications. *Journal of College Student Personnel, 24*(6), 535–540.

Habley, W. R. (1987). Academic advising conference: Outline and notes. *The ACT National Center for the Advancement of Educational Practices* (pp. 33–34). Iowa City, IA: ACT. Retrieved from www.nacada.ksu.edu/Portals/0/Clearinghouse/advisingissues/documents/ AcademicAdvisingConferenceOutlineandNotes.pdf

Higginson, L. C. (2000). A framework for training program content revisited. In V. N. Gordon & W. R. Habley (Eds.), *Academic advising: A comprehensive handbook* (pp. 298–306). San Francisco, CA: Jossey-Bass.

The Higher Learning Commission. (2015). *The criteria for accreditation and core components.* Retrieved from https://www.ncahlc.org/Criteria-Eligibility-and-Candidacy/ criteria-and-core-components.html?highlight=WyJwcm9ncmFtIiwibWlzc2lvbiIsInN0Y XRlbWVudCIsIm1pc3Npb24gc3RhdGVtZW50Il0=

Keeling, R. (2014, November 10). *Public director oral report to the Council for the Advancement of Standards.* Alexandria, VA.

Kezar, A. (2001). Documenting the landscape: Results of a national study on academic and student affairs collaborations. In A. Kezar, D. Hirsch, & C. Burack (Eds.), *Understanding the role of academic and student affairs collaboration in creating a successful learning environment* (New Directions for Higher Education, No. 116) (pp. 39–52). San Francisco, CA: Jossey-Bass.

Kezar, A. (2003). Achieving student success: Strategies for creating partnerships between academic and student affairs. *NASPA Journal, 41*(1), 1–22.

King, N. (2012, June 24). *Academic advising: Past, present and future.* Presentation made at the NACADA Summer Institute, Austin, TX.

Klepfer, K., & Hull, J. (2012). *High school rigor and good advice: Setting up students to succeed.* Retrieved from http://www.centerforpubliceducation.org/Main-Menu /Staffingstudents/High-school-rigor-and-good-advice-Setting-up-students-to-succeed/ High-school-rigor-and-good-advice-Setting-up-students-to-succeed-Full-Report.pdf

Machiavelli, N. (2015). *The prince.* Retrieved from http://www.constitution.org/mac/ prince06.htm (original work published 1532)

McClellan, J. (2009). Thought leaders wanted: What each of us must do to advance the field of academic advising. *Academic Advising Today, 32*(4). Retrieved from http://www. nacada.ksu.edu/Resources/Academic-Advising-Today/View-Articles/Thought-Leaders- Wanted-What-Each-of-Us-Must-Do-to-Advance-the-Field-of-Academic-Advising.aspx

McClellan, J. L. (2007). *Content components for advisor training: Revisited.* Retrieved from http://www.nacada.ksu.edu/Resources/Clearinghouse/View-Articles/Advisor-Training- Components.aspx

McFarlane, B. L. (2013). *Advising structures that support student success* (Unpublished dissertation). Portland State College, Portland, Oregon. Retrieved from http://pdxscholar. library.pdx.edu/cgi/viewcontent.cgi?article=2043&context=open_access_etds

Miller, M. A. (2004). *Factors to consider when restructuring academic advising.* Retrieved from http://www.nacada.ksu.edu/Resources/Clearinghouse/View-Articles/(Re) Structuring-academic-advising.aspx

Miller, M. A. (2013). *Structuring our conversations: Shifting to four dimensional advising models.* In A. H. Carlstrom & M. A. Miller (Eds.), *2011 NACADA national survey of academic advising* (Monograph No. 25). Manhattan, KS: National Academic Advising Association. Retrieved from http://www.nacada.ksu.edu/Resources/Clearinghouse/ View-Articles/Structuring-Our-Conversations-Shifting-to-Four-Dimensional-Advising- Models.aspx

Miller, M. A., & Alberts, B. (1994). Developmental advising: Where teaching and learning intersect. *NACADA Journal, 14*(2) 43–45.

Moss Kanter, R. (2003, June). Leadership and the psychology of turnarounds (Reprint R0306C). *Harvard Business Review.* 3–11. Retrieved from http://www.schoolturnaroundsupport.org/ sites/default/files/resources/HBR%20-%20Kanter%20Leadership%20and%20the% 20Psychology%20of%20Turnarounds%202003%20(2).pdf

NACADA: The Global Community for Academic Advising (NACADA). (2005). *NACADA statement of core values of academic advising.* Retrieved http://www.nacada.ksu.edu/ Resources/Clearinghouse/View-Articles/Core-values-of-academicadvising.aspx

NACADA. (2006). *NACADA concept of academic advising*. Retrieved from https://www.nacada. ksu.edu/Resources/Clearinghouse/View-Articles/Concept-of-Academic-Advising.aspx.

NACADA. (2014a). *Academic advisor competencies*. Retrieved from http://www.nacada.ksu. edu/Resources/Clearinghouse/View-Articles/Academic-advisor-competencies.aspx

NACADA. (2014b). *Communication & listening skills resources*. Retrieved from http://www. nacada.ksu.edu/Resources/Clearinghouse/View-Articles/Communication--listening-skills-resources.aspx

NACADA. (2014c). *Personal advising philosophy examples*. Retrieved from http://www. nacada.ksu.edu/Resources/Clearinghouse/View-Articles/Personal-advising-philosophy-examples.aspx

NACADA. (2014d). *Proactive (intrusive) advising resource links*. Retrieved from http://www. nacada.ksu.edu/Resources/Clearinghouse/View-Articles/Proactive-(intrusive)-advising-resource-links.aspx

Nash, R. J., & Jang, J. J. J. (2013, September-October). The time has come to create meaning-making centers on college campuses. *About Campus, 18*(4), 2–8.

National Center for Education Statistics (NCES). (n.d.a). *Integrated postsecondary education data system glossary*. Retrieved from http://nces.ed.gov/ipeds/glossary/index.asp?id=772

NCES. (n.d.b). *Integrated postsecondary education data system glossary, C*. Retrieved from http://nces.ed.gov/ipeds/glossary/?charindex=C

NSSE: National Survey of Student Engagement. (2014). *Bringing the institution into focus: Annual results 2014*. Retrieved from http://nsse.iub.edu/NSSE_2014_Results/pdf/ NSSE_2014_Annual_Results.pdf

Nutt, C. L. (2003). Creating advisor-training and development programs. In *Advisor training: Exemplary practices in the development of advisor skills* (Monograph No. 9) (pp. 9–16). Manhattan, KS: National Academic Advising Association.

Nutt, C. L. (2014, December). From the executive director: Waiting for the future or preparing for the future? *Academic Advising Today, 37*(4) Retrieved from http://www. nacada.ksu.edu/Resources/Academic-Advising-Today/View-Articles/From-the-Executive-Director-Waiting-for-the-Future-or-Preparing-for-the-Future-.aspx

O'Banion, T. (2015, April 3). *In defense of curmudgeons*. Retrieved from https://www. insidehighered.com/views/2015/04/03/essay-thoughts-community-college-curmudgeons-and-how-engage-them

Pardee, C. F. (2004). *Organizational structures for advising*. Retrieved from http://www. nacada.ksu.edu/Resources/Clearinghouse/View-Articles/Organizational-Models-for-Advising.aspx

Ross, T., & Kena, G. (2012, August). *Higher education: Gaps in access and persistence study*. Retrieved from https://nces.ed.gov/pubs2012/2012046.pdf

Sanaghan, P., & Lohndorf, J. (2015, March). *Collaborative leadership: The leadership stance*. Retrieved from http://issuu.com/academicimpressions/docs/0315-collaborative-lead-md_62e5111ca4256f?e=8028828/11923932#search

Schulenberg, J. K. (2013). Academic advising informed by self-authorship theory. In J. K. Drake, P. Jordan, & M. A. Miller (Eds.), *Academic advising approaches: Strategies that teach students to make the most of college* (pp. 121–136). San Francisco, CA: Jossey-Bass.

Shaw, R. (1989). Telling the truth, warming the heart: The future of student development in the community college. In W. Deegan & T. O'Banion (Eds.), *Perspectives on student development* (pp. 73–84). San Francisco, CA: Jossey-Bass.

Smith Jaggars, S., Fletcher, J., West Stacey, G. & Little, J. (2014). *Simplifying complexity in the student experience: Using data.* Retrieved from http://ccrc.tc.columbia.edu/media/k2/attachments/simplifying-complexity-using-data.pdf

Strayhorn, T. L. (2014, October 9). *Academic advisors: Cultural navigators for student success.* Keynote address, NACADA annual conference, Minneapolis, MN.

Texas Guaranteed Student Loan Corporation. (1999, March). *Retention and persistence in postsecondary education: A summation of research studies.* Retrieved from https://www.tgslc.org/pdf/persistence.pdf https://www.tgslc.org/pdf/persistence.pdf

Tinto, V. (1988). Stages of student departure: Reflections on the longitudinal character of student leaving. *The Journal of Higher Education, 59*(4), 438–455. doi: 10.2307/1981920

Tinto, V. (1999). Taking retention seriously: Rethinking the first year of college. *NACADA Journal, 19*(2), 5–9.

University of Wisconsin Colleges. (2015). *Academic resources.* Retrieved from http://www.uwc.edu/employees/academic-resources/esfy/seminar

Varney, J. (2013). Proactive advising. In J. K. Drake, P. Jordan, & M. A. Miller (Eds.), *Academic advising approaches: Strategies that teach students to make the most of college* (pp. 137–154). San Francisco, CA: Jossey-Bass.

Whitt, E. J., Elkins Nesheim, B., Guentzel, M. J., Kellogg, A.H., McDonald, W. M., & Wells, C. A. (2008). "Principles of good practice" for academic and student affairs partnership programs. *Journal of College Student Development, 49*(3), 235–249. Retrieved from http://www.education.uiowa.edu/docs/default-source/crue-publications/Whitt_Nesheim_Guentzel_Kellogg_McDonald_Wells_2008.pdf?sfvrsn=0

4

DEFINING ACADEMIC ADVISING

CONCEPTS AND CONTEXTS FOR PRACTICE

Susan M. Campbell and Susan McWilliams

If you don't know where you are going, you might wind up someplace else.

—Yogi Berra (1925–2015)

Definitions of *academic advising* are generated in institution-specific contexts. Therefore, effective advising programs and practices reflect a particular institution's values and corresponding statements of vision, mission, goals, and objectives. Master advisors align their values and philosophies with institutional advising visions and practices. In this chapter, we address the ways statements of vision, mission, objectives, and outcomes reflect elements of the pillars of academic advising and how each becomes a foundational element of the role and philosophy of a master advisor. We provide examples of academic advising program statements as well as academic advisor philosophies. We encourage reflection upon academic advising as a high-impact practice with the potential to positively affect student learning and overall success in college.

Reader Learning Outcomes

From studying this chapter, advisors will use knowledge gained about the context and concepts of advising, including incorporation of the three pillar documents, to

- o clarify the importance of advising values and definitions at the individual and institutional levels;

- o understand the alignment of institutional vision and mission, academic program objectives, and statements of advising vision and mission as well as goals and outcomes;

- o identify advising practices consistent with an advising vision and related goals and outcomes; and

- o connect an advisor's (including one's own) role and philosophy to the institutional vision for advising and related goals and outcomes.

The literature has continually affirmed the importance of effective academic advising to student retention and success nationally and internationally (Allen & Smith, 2008; Applegate, 2012; Bean & Kuh, 1984; Pascarella, 1980). In addition, to inform the field and improve the global practice of academic advising, the research agenda of NACADA: The Global Community for Academic Advising has encouraged close examination of advising and advisor effectiveness. Regardless of whether advising is offered through centralized or decentralized organizational models, delivered by faculty or primary-role advisors, or called *advising* (United States) or *personal tutoring* (United Kingdom), academic advising remains one of the only institutional activities in which students have the opportunity to connect one-to-one with an individual concerned about their educational, career, and life goals (Habley, 1994). The promise of this individualized connection has propelled academic advising as an important strategy in any institutional retention effort (Tinto, 2012).

As with other teaching and learning processes, no one-size-fits-all academic advising program can be designed, nor does a single, uniform definition apply to this important responsibility. Over the years, many have attempted to define academic advising, adding to the myriad definitions that have emerged over time to contribute to the complexity of communication (NACADA, 2014).

Successful advising programs and practices reflect individual institutional contexts, cultures, and structures. The pillars of academic advising—The NACADA Concept of Academic Advising (NACADA, 2006), the NACADA Statement of Core Values of Academic Advising (NACADA, 2005a, 2005b), and the Council for the Advancement of Standards in Higher Education (CAS) (2015a) Standards for Academic Advising Programs—guide and inform effective advising programs and practices. However, they must be interpreted through the lens of an institutional context to be meaningful; therefore, they do not stand as the only resources for creating programs and practices.

On campuses with stakeholders seeking to effect meaningful programs, an operational definition of academic advising emerges. This theoretically and institutionally grounded specification serves as the basis for statements of vision, mission, goals, and program objectives that further codify the values, philosophies, approaches, and central purposes of academic advising. These statements anchor the academic advising program, communicate program purpose to the institution, and provide the framework for assessable student learning and advising delivery outcomes (Campbell, 2008). When intentionally and collaboratively constructed, these statements offer a collective understanding of academic advising, and more important, they set the expectations for academic advising contributions to student learning. The master advisor uses these expectations to guide practice.

A definition of advising and an advising program must be tied to institutionally defined mission and vision as well as related goals and outcomes. Collaboration is necessary to establish legitimacy, and because of increasing internal and external calls for accountability, to ensure that the advising enterprise is defined from within, rather than outside, the academy. Stakeholders, including master advisors, must address the central issue, which is not about identifying a single definition of academic advising but about determining the relationship between the institutional context, the local definition and philosophy of academic advising, and the desired outcomes for student learning.

Informing Practice: The Three Pillars

A symbiotic relationship between the academic advising program vision and mission as well as goals, objectives, and outcomes and an advisor's philosophy, principles, and practices characterize effective programs and master advisors. The advising program and advisor practice should reflect and inform the theoretical underpinnings and values of each other.

The master advisor's philosophy serves as an interpretive lens for reflection and improvement of practice. To be sure, the complexity of higher education, the personal nature of academic advising roles, and the diversity of ways in which students learn, grow, and develop make contemplation and refinement of practice challenging. Yet, a master advisor also possesses the tools necessary—The NACADA Statement of Core Values of Academic Advising, the NACADA Concept of Academic Advising (NACADA, 2005a, 2005b, 2006), and the CAS Standards for Academic Advising Programs (CAS, 2015a)—to guide the development of effective institutional programming and individual practice (chapter 18). Institutional definitions of academic advising emerge from these pillar of advising documents and are shaped by the nuanced cultural and structural characteristics of a particular campus (i.e., the campus core values and organizational structure). These definitions are translated into practice through the philosophies enacted by individual academic advisors.

NACADA Statement of Core Values of Academic Advising

Values, by definition, reflect beliefs about issues of perceived importance that guide and ensure the integrity of practice. A code of ethics specifies the values and beliefs that guide behavior. Many in the academic advising profession use the NACADA Statement of Core Values of Academic Advising (hereafter, NACADA Core Values) as their ethical compass. The NACADA Core Values statement provides three levels of explication: an introduction (NACADA, 2005c), a declaration (NACADA, 2005a), and an exposition (NACADA, 2005b). Each level adds specificity to the other, ultimately focusing on advising practices as they relate to each core value. As with the other pillar documents, the NACADA Core Values document acknowledges higher education complexities and cautions against adopting the language as written in toto. Rather, to be effective, master advisors need to review the value statements in light of their own institutional context, culture, clientele, and individual values and beliefs.

The NACADA Core Values apply to both programs and individual practice. For example, from a programmatic perspective, they "affirm the importance of advising within the academy and acknowledge the impact that advising interactions can have on individuals, institutions, and society" (NACADA, 2005c, ¶2). From an individual perspective, the NACADA Core Values "are the reference points advisors use to consider their individual philosophies, strengths, and opportunities for professional growth" (¶5).

The guiding principles of the NACADA Core Values (NACADA, 2005a) speak to personal and programmatic integrity and accountability by stipulating that all advisors (and thus all advising programs) are responsible

o to the individuals they advise (¶1–3). Every one in academic advising programs takes collective and individual responsibility to understand the unique backgrounds and perspectives of advisees while facilitating a supportive, trust-based, educational process through which students learn, grow, and develop as citizens in a democratic society.

o for involving others, when appropriate, in the advising process (¶4). Academic advising is best approached from a holistic perspective. The Jesuit tradition of cura personalis applies to practice; that is, the health of the individual goes beyond the health of the mind, and "talents, abilities, physical attributes, personalities, desires, hearts, faith, and minds are all equally worthy of care and attention" (Otto, 2013, ¶2). This concept also suggests the improbability that any individual possesses all the skills necessary to address the needs of all students.

o to their institutions (¶5). Academic advising programs and advisors are integrated in the larger institutions such that advisors must understand the boundaries for their actions, maintain collegial relationships with others, and appreciate the consequences of their actions or inactions.

o to higher education (¶6). Academic advising, as an essential component of higher education, must inspire advisors to value the diversity of institutions and students as well as appreciate the myriad ways advising and advising programs support the educational achievement of students.

o to the broader educational community (¶7). As the interpreters of institutional culture and values, advisors serve as role models within the academy. In addition, through building relationships with the surrounding community, they create seamless connections of support for students, whose lives extend beyond campus boundaries.

o for conducting professional practice and undertaking personal development (¶8). Increasingly, academic advising embodies a community of scholars and of learners. The profession mandates a sharing of knowledge and practices that benefit students.

CAS Standards for Academic Advising Programs

"CAS, a consortium of professional associations in higher education, promotes the use of its professional standards for the development, assessment, and improvement of quality student learning, programs, and services" (CAS, 2015c, ¶1). These international standards serve as guides for institutions to use in auditing areas that support student development, and they provide a needed framework to develop programs and align them with prevailing best practices. The CAS Standards demonstrate internal and external accountability and legitimacy. The specific set of Standards for Academic Advising Programs (CAS, 2015a) does not prescribe existing or ideal advising unit organization; institutional leadership makes these decisions. The CAS Standards identify critical areas for reflection, evaluation, and consideration in the organization and delivery of academic advising. The 12 major sections of the CAS Standards offer guidance relevant to all advising programs regardless of specialty of focus. These sections, called *parts*, include mission; program; organization and leadership; human resources; ethics; law, policy, and governance; diversity, equity, and access; institutional and external relations; financial resources; technology; facilities and equipment; and assessment and evaluation (CAS, 2015a).

The relationship between the NACADA Core Values (2005a) and the CAS Standards is reflected in the CAS (2015a) Standard (Part 2): The academic advising program must be

- o intentionally designed;
- o guided by theories and knowledge of learning and development;
- o integrated into the life of the institution;
- o reflective of developmental and demographic profiles of the student population;
- o responsive to the needs of individuals, populations with distinct needs, and constituencies;
- o delivered using multiple formats, strategies, and contexts; and
- o designed to provide universal access (p. 6).

In addition, the academic advising program must act in concert with other campus units; the CAS Standards demand collaboration that supports student learning and development. In general, the academic advising program and the delivery of academic advising must be conceptually grounded, responsive to the diversity of the institution and students, and viewed as an important activity that supports learning and development.

Of critical importance, the most intense focus is directed toward student learning and development outcomes as represented in the CAS (2015b) domains of learning and development:

- o knowledge acquisition, integration, construction, and application;
- o cognitive complexity;
- o intrapersonal development;
- o interpersonal competence;
- o humanitarianism and civic engagement; and
- o practical competence (p. 5).

These domains capture and expand upon contemporary views of the outcomes of higher education as generally directed to cognitive maturity, integrated identity, and mature relationships (Baxter Magolda & King, 2004). In addition, these CAS domains correspond to national best practices regarding the essential learning outcomes of a liberal education (Association of American Colleges & Universities, 2015). Each of the six CAS domains features a set of associated dimensions that clarify the intention of the more broadly framed domain and provide direction for the development of accessible student learning outcomes. Finally, the CAS domains and dimensions are accompanied by examples to further support assessment of learning. Table 4.1 provides an excerpt from the CAS (2015b) learning and development outcomes.

Table 4.1. CAS learning and development outcomes

Student Outcome Domain	Dimensions of Outcome Domains	Examples of Learning and Development Outcomes
Knowledge acquisition, construction, integration, and application	Understanding knowledge from a range of disciplines	Possesses knowledge of one or more [specific] subjects
	Connecting knowledge to other knowledge, ideas, and experiences	Accesses diverse sources of information such as the Internet, text observations, and data bases
Cognitive complexity	Critical thinking	Identifies important problems, questions, and issues
	Reflective thinking	Applies previously understood information, concepts, and experiences to a new situation or setting
Intrapersonal development	Realistic self-appraisal, self-understanding, and self-respect	Assesses, articulates, and acknowledges personal skills, abilities, and growth areas
	Identity development	Integrates multiple aspects of identity into a coherent whole
Interpersonal competence	Meaningful relationships	Establishes healthy, mutually beneficial relationships with others
	Interdependence	Seeks help from others when needed and offers assistance to others
Humanitarianism and civic engagement	Understanding and appreciating cultural and human differences	Understands one's own identity and culture
	Global perspective	Understands and analyzes the interconnectedness of societies worldwide
Practical competence	Pursuing goals	Sets and pursues individual goals
	Communicating effectively	Conveys meaning by writing and speaking coherently and effectively in a way that others understand

Note. CAS (2015c), pp. 3–4. Adapted with permission.

Clarity is perhaps the most significant CAS contribution to academic advising. It is offered in the domains, dimensions, and the examples, which further ground academic advising as an integral part of teaching and learning. In this regard, the CAS (2015a) Standards for Academic Advising support and highlight the NACADA Concept of Academic Advising (NACADA, 2006). Furthermore, by guiding institutionally defined advising learning outcomes, the CAS (2015a) Standards help master advisors respond to the national agenda on assessment (chapters 14 and 15).

NACADA Concept of Academic Advising

The NACADA Concept of Academic Advising (2006) (hereafter, NACADA Concept of Advising) gives master advisors a conceptual framework for the overall program as well as for the development of an individual philosophy of advising. It affirms the perspective of advising as teaching with a curriculum, a pedagogy, and a set of learning outcomes for students. The NACADA Concept of Advising further explicates the meaning of each teaching element as it relates to academic advising. While confirming the contextual and individual nature of the design and delivery of academic advising, the NACADA Concept of Advising reinforces academic advising as a holistic and developmental process that requires collaborative approaches to facilitate and support student success toward goal achievement. In many ways, the NACADA Concept of Advising serves as the vehicle through which both the NACADA Core Values (2005a, 2005b, 2005c) and the CAS Standards (2015a) are realized. All three, as the pillars of advising, establish the conceptual and theoretical basis of effective academic advising practice.

Grounding and Guiding Academic Advising: The Advising Program

Planning in higher education, as both art and science, depends on context and thus no single model applies (Rowley, Lujan, & Dolence, 2001, p. xv). In fact, "to be successful, planning must . . . adapt to local, specific conditions and to the temper of the times" while incorporating traditional fidelity as well as addressing environmental forces and stakeholder interests (Keller, 2007, p. 61). Therefore, mission statements need to reflect the present and the future such that their formulation requires dialogue among constituents (Campbell, 2008; Keller, 2007; Rowley et al., 2001). In the process of developing effective vision, mission, goal, and program objective statements, collaborators engage in the reflection, dialogue, and analysis processes that promote a collective commitment to mutual goals for advising (Campbell, 2008).

As first explained in *Academic Advising: A Comprehensive Handbook* (Gordon, Habley, & Grites, 2008),

> The vision, mission, goals, and program objectives for academic advising serve a number of key purposes. . . . They anchor the advising program, forming the foundation from which activities and initiatives are derived and guided. . . . The vision, mission, goals, and program objectives therefore play important roles in communicating the

purpose and intentions of academic advising to internal and external audiences—
that is, the campus community and the community at-large. . . . [These statements]
frame action and guide the design of intentionally sequenced educational opportunities to support desired student learning and development outcomes. (Campbell, 2008,
pp. 230–231)

Well-crafted statements of vision, mission, goals, and program objectives also
inform assessment (chapters 14 and 15) and help master advisors intentionally direct
initiatives and practice. They serve as anchors that keep plans moored to measurable
and communicable outcomes and thus keep advising programs from becoming
embodiments of disparate, singular, and anecdotal ideas.

The Interrelation of Vision, Mission, Goals, and Program Objectives

To ensure that the statements of vision, mission, goals, and program objectives for
advising reflect more than good intentions (Drucker, 1992, p. 4), master advisors
must understand the interrelationships of these critical guiding documents and their
connections to the central purpose and mission of the institution. The CAS Standards
affirm this point. Figure 4.1 depicts, in elementary form, the interrelational nature of
the vision, mission, goal, and program objective statements. It illustrates the multidi-
rectional ways in which each level influences and is influenced by the others. Each
level needs to be integrated with the level above it, and all activities are derived from
and are informed by the institutional statements of mission, goals, and objectives. In
situations in which actions do not correspond to any of the levels, master advisors
and other leaders should question the efficacy of the initiative or the applicability of

---

Figure 4.1. Relationship between institutional, school, college, and division with program mission

Note. Reprinted by permission. From S. Campbell, p. 233, in V. N. Gordon,
W. R. Habley, & T. J. Grites (Eds.), *Academic Advising: A Comprehensive
Handbook* © 2008 by Jossey-Bass.

the guiding statements for the advising program. All programs must align with the critical statements that reflect institutional mission.

As the relationship among the articulated vision and mission as well as goals and objectives at various institutional levels must be evident, so must the relationship characterize advising programs. By design, the most influential statements or components are

- contextual,
- interrelated,
- in deductive and inductive relationship, and
- used for measuring strategies and actions. (Campbell, 2008, p. 233)

The contextual nature of the key statements—vision and mission as well goals and program objectives—cannot be overemphasized; no single version applies to all academic advising programs (Drucker, 1992, 2003; Habley, 2005; Keller, 2007; Rowley et al., 2001; White, 2000). Institutional, environmental, and campus cultural differences make a uniform approach impossible, impractical, and undesirable. Therefore, the conversations among key stakeholders most effectively drive the appropriate statements and practices.

Figure 4.2 depicts the dynamic interrelationships between the four key statements. Each mirrors, in a general way, the broader relationship among organizational levels within the institution. The triangle in Figure 4.2 also "illustrates the deductive and inductive nature of mission, goals, and program objective statements" (Campbell, 2008, p. 233). Statements of vision, mission, goals, and program objectives should lead to

Figure 4.2. Relationship among statements of vision, mission goals, and program objectives

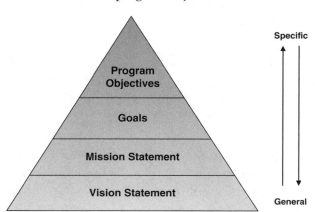

Note. Reprinted by permission. From S. Campbell, p. 234, in V. N. Gordon, W. R. Habley, & T. J. Grites (Eds.), *Academic Advising: A Comprehensive Handbook* © 2008 by Jossey-Bass.

the development of learning opportunities that support achievement of desired student learning and development outcomes; that is, they should affect advising practice, which is assessed to support improvement and mission achievement.

In reality, the relationship among statements of vision, mission, goals, and program objectives looks much more complex than the arrows in Figure 4.2 suggest. The components of vision and mission as well as goals and objectives are nested within each other rather than stacked on top of each other. This nesting captures the depth and breadth of the relationship.

Statements of Vision, Mission, Goals, and Program Objectives

Statements of vision, mission, goals, and objectives present a common language for use in the development of successful advising programs (Campbell, 2008, p. 234). A contextual and institution-specific language remains essential to the development of a shared understanding and definition of academic advising. Excerpts, including a combination of tables featured in Table 4.2, from *Academic Advising: A Comprehensive Handbook* (Gordon et al., 2008), summarize the key features for each of the elements and the ways each informs the outcomes for student learning and development.

> **Vision Statements.** The prelude to a mission statement is a statement of vision. Essentially a vision is "a mental model of a desirable or idealistic future for an organization" (Nanus, 2003, p. 356). Vision statements are inspirational and ambitious, but they are also contextual and should be grounded by information about the environment and the distinctive character of the organization and what it is able to achieve (Nanus, 2003). (Campbell, 2008, pp. 234–235)

> **Mission Statements.** In contrast to vision statements, *mission statements* [emphasis in the original] articulate purpose and direction. Value-laden, mission statements provide focus for action, guidance to the future, and inform immediate action. Mission statements are the "roadmap" to one's vision and are, like vision statements, future-oriented. (Campbell, 2008, p. 235)

As a general rule, mission statements are realistic, concise, explicit, and understandable. As Habley (2005) emphasized, the mission statement for academic advising serves as both an umbrella and a window. It covers the delivery of services and provides a view for practitioners to see their work as it fits within the unit and the institution.

> **Goal Statements.** Simply put, goal statements are expressions of the desired future state or "aims" of the organization or program and are based on the mission statement. . . . When goals are met, the mission is achieved; students are engaged in learning; the advising program promotes students' academic success and fosters students' personal and intellectual growth. Drucker (2003) indicates that goals should be clearly defined . . . and that from the goals, the strategies and actions . . . and results . . . should be . . . identified. (Campbell, 2008, p. 238)

Table 4.2. Summary of vision, mission, goals, and program objectives statements from Campbell (2008)

Statement Definition	Example	Key Features
Vision statements reflect the aspirations of what academic advising can be on a campus. It represents a desired or ideal future. (p. 235)	". . . aspires to be a vehicle of student success, an integral and vibrant component of a campus-wide commitment" (University of Louisville, 2015).*	Represent a desired future state [Are] inspirational [Are] ambitious yet realistic Generate enthusiasm Generate commitment to direction and purpose (p. 235)
Mission statements reflect the purpose of academic advising on the campus and serve as the roadmap to achieving the vision and affirming values. (p. 236)	"Academic Advising at the University of Louisville, in partnership with the campus-community, empowers students to develop and realize a plan for academic and career success" (University of Louisville, 2015).*	Identif[y] purpose [Are] consistent with institutional mission [Are] long-range [Are] clear and concise [Are] repeatable [Are] general in nature (p. 236)
Goal statements are long-range expressions of the desired future state of the organization or program. If met, they express what the organization would look like if the mission was achieved. (p. 239)	o Engage students in learning o Promote students' academic success o Foster students' personal and intellectual growth (p. 239)	Represent the aims of the advising program Are long range Are clear Provide guidance for action Are general in nature, although more specific than the mission [statement] (p. 239)
Program Objectives articulate, in a general way, the expectations regarding how academic advising is delivered and what students are expected to demonstrate they know and can do. (p. 240)	o To develop intentional partnerships where academic advisors are appropriately accessible, and knowledgeable; where academic advisors use their expertise to guide and facilitate student educational and life decision-making processes, and where students share responsibility for advising. o To offer a collective, collaborative process that makes use of appropriate University resources to support student responsibility for their learning and success. (p. 240)	Specify the intentions of the academic advising program for student learning and advising delivery Reveal, in a general way, expectations for student learning. Inform and guide the development of student learning outcomes and advising delivery outcomes Are general in nature, although more specific than goals [statements] (p. 240)

Note. Adapted by permission. From S. Campbell, pp. 235, 236, 239, and 240, in V. N. Gordon, W. R. Habley, & T. J. Grites (Eds.), *Academic Advising: A Comprehensive Handbook* © 2008 by Jossey-Bass. *New examples, not shown in the original, used with permission.

Program Objectives. Program objectives "identify content or learning parameters—what students should learn, understand, or appreciate as a result of their studies" (Maki, 2004, p. 61). . . . In general, at the program objective level, the interest is in continuing to develop the overall portrait of the academic advising program to anchor it and to communicate the programmatic intentions to internal and external communities. (Campbell, 2008, p. 239)

Master advisors, as part of the planning team, help discern appropriate measurements of the strategies and actions as derived from the outcomes identified for student learning and development. These measures provide the evidence with regard to the achievement of outcomes (chapters 14 and 15). In much the same way that the pillars of academic advising inform the statements of vision, mission, goals, and objectives for an advising program, the list of CAS (2015b) student learning and development outcomes should be used to frame advising outcomes.

Contextualizing Academic Advising: Philosophy

Outcomes reflect the valued component of an academic advising program and the theory that guides advising practice. All advisors, but particularly master advisors, enact their personal philosophies in their interactions with students and others in academe. In addition to the theories that advisors learn and apply, the NACADA Concept for Advising, NACADA Core Values, and the CAS Standards (CAS, 2015a; NACADA, 2005a, 2005b, 2005c, 2006) also inform these philosophies as well as align with the statements of vision, mission, goals, and objectives of the academic advising program. Because they are enacted through practice, collective personal advising philosophies influence the ongoing evolution of the advising mission and vision as well as the related goals, objectives, and outcomes.

Effective practices provide guidance to practitioners in the development of advising philosophies. Freitag (2011) provided an overview of the development of advising philosophies, noting that they reflect both the institutional context and address the personal and equally (if not more) important questions of "Why am I an academic advisor? How do I make a difference in the lives of students and colleagues?" (¶12)

Although a personal endeavor, successful advising practice is informed by the institutional context and culture. Effective academic advising practice is guided by a code of ethics that reflects values and beliefs regarding the profession. It also embodies a personal philosophy that structures and directs interactions with students and provides a trajectory to long-term career goals (Dyer, 2007; Freitag, 2011).

Freitag (2011) suggested that personal philosophies regarding academic advising are revealed in ways advisors enact their roles. He argued for intentionality in the development of a personal philosophy of academic advising, describing it as a way to provide insight into one's "methods and interactions with students. . . . It enables her [sic] to be a better advisor" (p. 1). Freitag's article offers a discussion of the components—such as advising approach and theoretical framework as well as areas of interest for professional development and career aspirations—as they apply to a personal philosophy of academic advising.

The components of a personal philosophy of academic advising mirror those for academic advising programs in that both express values, beliefs, and predispositions altered, over time, through experience in the profession. The personal vision, mission, goals, and objectives form the roles of the master advisor.

Advising as a High-Impact Practice

Research on the effects of academic advising on student success continues to expand. Is it time to synthesize findings and point to new research directions that would frame academic advising as a high-impact practice? The 2015 National Survey of Student Engagement suggested that high-impact practices "share several traits: They demand considerable time and effort, facilitate learning outside of the classroom, require meaningful interactions with faculty and students, encourage collaboration with diverse others, and provide frequent and substantive feedback" (¶1).

These high-impact traits fundamentally describe effective academic advising practice. Furthermore, beyond the classroom experience, whether on-site or in virtual space, academic advising is offered to all students at every college or university. How would aligning and defining academic advising as a high-impact practice affect the college experience for students and communicate the value of advising to them and to others? These questions are ripe for consideration, and the answers to them may lie in future research and ideas that master advisors, as thought leaders, will be expected to undertake and encourage.

Implications for the Master Advisor

Throughout this chapter, we have emphasized the contextual and institution-specific nature of academic advising definitions as well as the importance of the pillars of advising to inform advising and shaping practice. We also highlighted the role of an individual's advising philosophy as a guide for practice.

The master advisor is also a master translator who uses philosophy to inform practice and align it with the profession as well as with institutional goals and values. Advising practice needs to reflect the teaching and learning that characterize all of higher education. In fact, master advisors make advising as teaching and learning their lived paradigm. Lowenstein (2005) reinforced this emphasis in his expansion on the early work of Crookston (1972/1994/2009), suggesting that a philosophy of advising as teaching requires application of a learning-centered paradigm. The advisor-as-teacher philosophy, according to Lowenstein (2005), transforms the advising relationship from coaching to supporting meaning making:

> An excellent advisor does the same for the student's entire curriculum that the excellent teacher does for one course. . . . Learning transpires when a student makes sense of his or her overall curriculum just as it does when a person understands an individual course, and the former is every bit as important as the latter. In fact, learning

in each individual course is enhanced by the learning of the curriculum, and thus may continue long after the course has been completed. (p. 69)

Lowenstein (2000, 2005) argued that when advising is teaching, advisors help students make meaning of the curriculum (for both their major and general education) in a transformative way. For advising to be teaching and learning, an equal emphasis needs to be placed on student learning as on advising approaches; the active learning of the advisee needs to be the key objective for advising.

In practice, if the advising-as-teaching framework is updated to comport with broader educational values regarding student learning, then advising outcomes that capture the active, informed, purposeful, and self-reflective decision-making behaviors of the advisee can be identified. In such a future, the master advisor's values might shift from advising as teaching to advising as teaching and learning, making the efforts learner centered. In this scenario, advising outcomes shift from the barebones description of "understands the curriculum" to a heartier specific statement of intention: "selects learning experiences that enhance his or her achievement of the program's objectives." This vision inspires the way a conceptual and contextual definition of academic advising informs practice and evolves over time. The master advisor, ever cognizant of institutional culture and grounded in the profession, articulates a developed philosophy of academic advising as enacted through a practice that places the student in the center of the institutional universe.

Aiming for Excellence

- o Assess your level of understanding by completing the following statements:
  - o The primary difference between vision and mission statements is . . .
  - o The pillars of academic advising inform advising programs and practice in a number of ways, including (list as many as possible) . . .
  - o Advisors enact their personal advising philosophies through
    _____.
  - o The advisor-as-teacher philosophy means that the advising relationship focuses on_____.
- o If the institution has defined an advising mission and vision and also has developed goals and program objectives, convene advisors to review them in relation to the overall institutional mission and vision statements. Specifically,
  - o compare the broader institutional mission and vision statements to the mission and vision statements for academic advising to identify areas of alignment and misalignment, and
  - o identify strategies for addressing any misalignments and for creating practices that take advantage of and highlight the alignments.

o If the institution does not have an identified mission and vision or no program objectives have been created for academic advising, use Table 4.2 to draft them. Specifically,

  o collaborate with academic advisors and other stakeholders and review examples of other institutions' mission and vision statements as well as program objectives.

  o identify key ways the studied statements do and do not fit with the local context and then draft preliminary statements of mission, vision, and program objectives based on identified areas of commonality between the benchmarked institutions and your own institutional situation.

o Review existing assessment data on advising effectiveness at the institution and identify key gaps or shortcomings. Based on your findings, name aspirations to inform the creation or revision of advising mission and vision and related program objectives.

o Host a brown bag lunch for academic advisors and instructors of first-year seminars, orientation courses, or other critical introductory programs. Discuss stated learning objectives for such courses in relation to institutional advising objectives and identify areas of common focus. Look for strategies that mutually support student achievement of shared outcomes.

o Encourage advisors to draft an advising philosophy and definition of his or her role as an advisor. Share and review the statement in a meeting. Review themes and practices as they relate to existing or needed advising program objectives.

References

Allen, J. M., & Smith, C. L. (2008). Importance of, responsibility for, and satisfaction with academic advising: A faculty perspective. *Journal of College Student Development, 49*(5), 397–411.

Applegate, J. L. (2012). Graduating the 21st century student: Advising as if their lives (and our future) depended on it. *NACADA Journal, 32*(1), 5–11.

Association of American Colleges & Universities. (2015). *Liberal education and America's promise.* Retrieved from https://www.aacu.org/leap

Baxter Magolda, M. B., & King, P. M. (2004). *Learning partnerships: Theory and models of practice to educate for self-authorship.* Sterling, VA: Stylus.

Bean, J. P., & Kuh, G. D. (1984). The reciprocity between student-faculty informal contact and academic performance of university undergraduate students. *Research in Higher Education, 21*(4), 461–477. doi:10.1007/BF00992637

Campbell, S. M. (2008). Vision, mission, goals, and program objectives for academic advising programs. In V. N. Gordon, W. R. Habley, & T. J. Grites (Eds.), *Academic advising: A comprehensive handbook* (2nd ed.) (pp. 229–241). San Francisco, CA: Jossey-Bass.

Council for the Advancement of Standards in Higher Education (CAS). (2015a). *Academic advising programs.* Retrieved from http://standards.cas.edu/getpdf.cfm?PDF=E864D2C4-D655-8F74-2E647CDECD29B7D0

CAS. (2015b). *Learning and development outcomes*. Retrieved from http://standards.cas.edu/getpdf.cfm?PDF=D87A29DC-D1D6-D014-83AA8667902C480B

CAS. (2015c). *Mission, vision, and purpose*. Retrieved from http://www.cas.edu/content.asp?contentid=142

Crookston, B. B. (2009). 1994 (1972): A developmental view of academic advising as teaching. *NACADA Journal, 29*(1), 78–82. (Reprinted from *Journal of College Student Personnel, 13*, 1972, pp. 12-17; *NACADA Journal, 14*[2], 1994, pp. 5–9)

Drucker, P. F. (1992). *Managing the nonprofit organization: Principles and practices*. New York, NY: HarperCollins.

Drucker, P. F. (2003). "What is our mission?" In J. M. Kouzes (Ed.), *Business leadership: A Jossey-Bass reader*. San Francisco, CA: Jossey-Bass.

Dyer, A. N. (2007). Advisement philosophy. In P. Folsom (Ed.), *The new advisor guidebook: Mastering the art of advising through the first year and beyond* (Monograph No. 16) (pp. 47–48). Manhattan, KS: National Academic Advising Association.

Freitag, D. (2011). *Creating a personal philosophy of academic advising*. Retrieved from http://www.nacada.ksu.edu/Resources/Clearinghouse/View-Articles/Personal-philosophy-of-academic-advising.aspx

Gordon, V. N., Habley, W. R., & Grites, T. J. (Eds.). (2008). *Academic advising: A comprehensive handbook*. San Francisco, CA: Jossey-Bass.

Habley, W. R. (1994). Key concepts in academic advising (*Summer Institute on academic advising session guide*, p. 10). Manhattan, KS: NACADA: The Global Community for Academic Advising. Retrieved from www.nacada.ksu.edu/Resources/Clearinghouse/View-Articles/Advising-and-Retention-Quotes.aspx

Habley, W. R. (2005). *Developing a mission statement for the academic advising program*. Retrieved from http://www.nacada.ksu.edu/Resources/Clearinghouse/View-Articles/Academic-advising-mission-statements.aspx

Keller, G. (2007). The emerging third stage in higher education planning. *Planning for Higher Education, 35*(4), 60–64.

Lowenstein, M. (2000, April 14). Academic advising and the "logic" of the curriculum. *The Mentor, 2*(2). Retrieved from https://dus.psu.edu/mentor/old/articles/000414ml.htm

Lowenstein, M. (2005). If advising is teaching, what do advisors teach? *NACADA Journal Volume, 25*(2), 65–73.

Maki, P. L. (2004). *Assessing for learning: Building a sustainable commitment across the institution*. Sterling, VA: Stylus.

NACADA: The Global Community for Academic Advising (NACADA). (2005a). *NACADA statement of core values of academic advising: Declaration*. Retrieved from https://www.nacada.ksu.edu/Resources/Clearinghouse/View-Articles/Core-values-declaration.aspx

NACADA. (2005b). *NACADA statement of core values of academic advising: Exposition*. Retrieved from http://www.nacada.ksu.edu/Resources/Clearinghouse/View-Articles/Core-values-exposition.aspx

NACADA. (2005c). *NACADA statement of core values of academic advising: Introduction*. Retrieved from http://www.nacada.ksu.edu/Resources/Clearinghouse/View-Articles/Core-values-of-academic-advising.aspx

NACADA. (2006). *NACADA concept of academic advising*. Retrieved from http://www. nacada.ksu.edu/Clearinghouse/AdvisingIssues/Concept-Advising.htm

NACADA. (2014). *Definitions of academic advising*. Retrieved from http://www.nacada.ksu. edu/Resources/Clearinghouse/View-Articles/Definitions-of-academic-advising.aspx

Nanus, B. (2003). Where tomorrow begins: Finding the right vision. In J. M. Kouzes (Ed.), *Business leadership: A Jossey-Bass reader*. San Francisco, CA: Jossey-Bass.

National Survey of Student Engagement. (2015). *High impact practices*. Retrieved from http://nsse.indiana.edu/html/high_impact_practices.cfm

Otto, A. (2013, August 15). *Cura personalis* [web log]. http://www.ignatianspirituality. com/16996/cura-personalis.

Pascarella, E. T. (1980). Student-faculty informal contact and college outcomes. *Review of Educational Research*, *50*(4), 545–595.

Rowley, D. J., Lujan, H. D., & Dolence, M. G. (2001). *Strategic change in colleges and universities*. San Francisco, CA: Jossey-Bass.

Tinto, V. (2012). *Completing college: Rethinking institutional action*. Chicago, IL: Chicago University Press.

University of Louisville. (2015). *Undergraduate advising: About academic advising at UofL*. Retrieved from http://louisville.edu/advising/about

White, E. R. (2000). Developing mission, goals, and objectives. In V. N. Gordon & W. R. Habley (Eds.), *Academic advising: A comprehensive handbook* (pp. 180–191). San Francisco, CA: Jossey-Bass.

5

DEFINING STUDENT SUCCESS

Stephen O. Wallace and Beverly A. Wallace

To live is to choose. But to choose well, you must know who you are and what you stand for, where you want to go and why you want to get there.

—Kofi Annan (1997)

Student success is one of the hottest topics in higher education; however, different stakeholders embrace various meanings of student success. In this chapter, we outline the ways popular definitions of student success, the completion agenda, and economics influence expectations for advising practices. Prominent productivity- and institutional-centered definitions measuring student success, typically in terms of retention and graduation rates, offer helpful guidance in some ways but may exclude some of the most important aspects of success. We highlight the important role that academic advisors fill as partners in student success, offer strategies practitioners can use to cultivate a learning environment that fosters student success, and provide tips on advising for student success that balances the needs of various stakeholders.

Reader Learning Outcomes

From studying this chapter, advisors will use knowledge gained about student success to

o articulate or formulate definitions of student success from the perspective of the advisor, advising unit, student, and institution;

o identify the people targeted by success measures based on personal, unit, and institutional definitions;

o recognize potential conflicts between personal and institutional definitions of student success and create a strategy to manage it;

o design a plan that aligns advising responsibilities to the student and the institution with the NACADA Statement of Core Values of Academic Advising (NACADA: The Global Community for Academic Advising [NACADA], 2005);

o balance the responsibilities to the advisee and to the institution; and

o base practice upon the assessment of student needs and institutional expectations.

A Dilemma Faced by Academic Advisors

"Did I do the right thing?" the advisor asks after supporting a student's decision to transfer to another institution. The advisor's inner struggle and question demonstrate a dilemma inherent in the practice of academic advising in higher education. Quality academic advising is a dynamic, multidimensional process built upon a partnership of diverse stakeholders. Academic advisors often function at the crossroads of differing, and sometimes conflicting, definitions of advising and expectations for advisors. Most of the stakeholders share a common desired outcome—student success—and many academic advisors are placed on the front lines to ensure students succeed. Advisors held accountable for student success must embrace the definition of the success they encourage; however, just as advisors and administrators invoke differing definitions of academic advising, stakeholders embrace various meanings of student success. Therefore, the answer to the advisor's question regarding the appropriateness of advice (or practice) depends upon the person providing the response.

To be effective, advisors must acknowledge and appreciate the voices of an array of stakeholders—external agencies, those within the institution, parents, employers, students, and others as assigned by the student—who may hold differing expectations for advisors and definitions of student success. Academic advisors must determine the definitions and the commensurate measures of student success that take precedence at their institutions. They also need to understand the ways these definitions affect their work with students. At times, competing interests may contribute to an inner conflict that advisors must learn to manage.

Neither a one-size-fits-all definition of student success nor a prescribed model for the practice of advising guarantees student success. Rather, in this chapter, we hope to stimulate ongoing discussions on the definitions of student success, influences that shape those definitions, and expectations of stakeholders that affect the practice of advising. To advance this discourse, we identify some of the most influential voices that have shaped popular ways of thinking about student success and examine some ways these understandings affect advising practices. Specifically, we highlight the important role that academic advisors fill in cultivating a learning environment that fosters student success.

We were inspired to broaden this inquiry based on an observation we find curious: Among the diverse voices that lead the ongoing discussions and debates about student success and shape institutional policies, few come from students. Therefore, in this chapter we include input from students as they discuss their perceptions of student success and provide descriptions of the influences that shaped those meanings.

We encourage readers to reflect upon and draw their own answers to three critical questions, from relatively simple to complex, that can confound clear-cut answers to questions of practice:

1. What is the definition of student success at my institution?
2. Through the various definitions, whose success is being defined?
3. How should advisors respond when their definitions of student success differ from those of institutional personnel or other stakeholders who influence practice?

Student Success—Everyone Is Talking About It

Student success is among the hottest topics in higher education. It is recognized as a political platform that drives federal and state legislation at one level and institutional strategies and practices at another. Leveille (2006) noted:

> Educational institutions will continue to feel the pressure and demands for accountability. Control of costs, elimination of duplication (and, in some cases, unique options perceived to be too costly), and evidence of other efficiencies are the focus for legislatures and higher education regulating and coordinating agencies. Similarly, demands for greater productivity in higher education will continue to be heard with greater frequency than at any time in the past. (p. 5)

This prediction became federal policy when President Obama (2013) pushed for major changes in the accountability system for higher education. He called on Congress to consider value, affordability, and student outcomes in making determinations about the colleges and universities that will receive access to federal student aid. Specifically, he proposed that institutions incorporate measures of value and affordability into the existing accreditation system or establish a new, alternative system of accreditation that provides pathways for postsecondary institutions to receive federal student aid based on performance and results.

Current accountability models are based on the goal that education provided by postsecondary institutions meets acceptable levels of quality. Specifically, institutions must demonstrate strategies, programs, and services that satisfy determined standards of excellence that include assessment of student retention and student learning outcomes (see, e.g., Higher Learning Commission, 2010; Middle States Commission on Higher Education, 2015). To achieve these standards, student success is publicly proclaimed as a core value of institutions of higher education, and enormous amounts of time, energy, and institutional resources are invested in student success initiatives. Campuses establish divisions of student success, operate centers for student success staffed by student success professionals, deliver student success programs, and teach student success courses. All of these investments are targeted at a primary, desired outcome: student success. However, the definition of student success differs among institutions.

In support of the desired outcome, educational researchers engage in ongoing studies to identify the most effective student success strategies, and advising tools that employ intricate, analytic, data-mining techniques are designed to predict and promote student success. These tools are used to analyze the students' profiles, institutional programs, and course data. They provide information for matching a student's talents with programs of study that offer the greatest opportunity for that individual to achieve academic success.

The topic of student success has generated an abundance of research and literature. For example, the commissioned report for the National Symposium on Postsecondary Student Success, *What Matters to Student Success: A Review of the Literature* (Kuh, Kinzie, Buckley, Bridges, & Hayek, 2006) includes over 875 references. In addition, researchers and practitioners meet at professional conferences to discuss, define, and promote the topic of student success.

Much of the existing research and discussion focuses on identifying variables consistently related to student success. Kuh and Hu (2001) highlighted student engagement with faculty; Pike and Kuh (2005) described environmental and instructional variables, such as collaborative practices in and out of the classroom, as important correlates of students' success. Pascarella, Pierson, Wolniak, and Terenzini (2004) conducted a longitudinal study that showed a clear advantage for students with at least one parent who has attended college. Pike and Kuh (2005) also found evidence that second-generation status positively affected college students. The research highlights the complex nature of student success and various variables—cognitive, metacognitive, personality, and demographic—associated with student success.

In development programs across the nation, advisors are trained on ways to facilitate student success. In addition, numerous authors claim to have found the formula that guarantees student success: for example, articles, such as "88 Surefire Tips for Succeeding in College" (2013) and books with titles such as *The Secrets of College Success* (Jacobs & Hyman, 2013), which reveals over 800 tips, tricks, and strategies, and *College Success: What It Means and How to Make It Happen* (McPhearson & Schapiro, 2008). If these tips, tricks, and strategies lead to college success, why is everyone still debating how to make it happen?

The following questions to the purveyors of the success formula will perhaps yield the most useful answers: "What are you guaranteeing? What is your definition of student success?" In many publications and typical conversations, authors define student success in terms of academic achievements: good grades, persistence from semester to semester, transfer into a baccalaureate program, and timely graduation. However, as the literature review by Kuh et al. (2006) noted, student success defies simple academic measures, and a variety of definitions can be appropriately ascribed to it.

Federal and state policymakers, institutional administrators, faculty members, students, and parents demand student success and place academic advisors on the front lines to actualize it. The NACADA Statement of Core Values (NACADA, 2005) is based on the belief that students can be successful, and it makes clear that academic advisors act as partners in student success. Educators, policymakers, and other stakeholders have long debated the best ways to promote student success and measure the level to which the student attains it, but no consistent definition of student success has emerged. To build strong advising partnerships, advisors must acknowledge and appreciate the definitions and expectations of a diverse array of stakeholders.

Student Success: The Goal of the Completion Agenda

Throughout U.S. history, higher education has been valued as a public good and partially financed through federal and state funds. A portion of the funding has hinged on achievement of externally imposed measures of accountability, which supply evidence that the investments produced desired outcomes. Until recently, the primary performance indicators focused on issues of access and were measured by criteria such as the number of full-time-equivalent students enrolled at the beginning of a semester. This model produced an array of strategies to open access and increase enrollments in colleges and universities. However, according to a College Board report (Lee & Ransom, 2011), despite increased higher education enrollments, degree completion rates have not kept pace, especially among young men of color, who are more likely to drop out of high school, less likely to gain access to college, and less likely to complete college than their female counterparts. Thus, the alarm has been sounded: America is losing the prestige of being the most educated nation in the world.

The intensity of current political and public interest on the subject of student success was stoked by President Obama's American graduation initiative (The White House Office of the Press Secretary, 2009) and the vow that America will regain the status of being the world's leader in producing college graduates by 2020. This proclamation came after the College Board (2008) reported that the United States ranked 12th in the world in terms of college graduation rates: 40.4% of people aged 25 to 34 years earned a minimum of an associate's degree. In recent trends, approximately two of every three students enroll in a college or university within one year of high school graduation, but to reach President Obama's proposed college completion goal, the total number of degrees granted between 2010 to 2020 must increase by as many as 13.4 million (Santiago, 2010).

In response to the political mandate for colleges and universities to produce more graduates, the completion agenda has become a driving force in higher education. The intent of the effort is expressed in the pledge of the American Association of Community Colleges (2015):

> We affirm the need for a dramatic increase in the number of Americans with postsecondary degrees and certifications to fulfill critical state and national goals. With the "completion agenda" as a national imperative, community colleges have an obligation to meet the challenge while holding firmly to traditional values of access, opportunity, and quality. (¶1)

The completion agenda is also promoted by public and private enterprises. The Bill & Melinda Gates Foundation (n.d.) established a postsecondary success team committed to advocating for strategies that dramatically increase the number of young people who obtain postsecondary degrees or certificates with labor-market value, and it has made ambitious investments to ensure that all students receive the opportunity to earn a high-quality education. In addition to the college ready initiative, the foundation funds programs such as Completion by Design (2015) that work with community colleges to significantly increase completion and graduation rates for low-income students. NACADA has partnered with the Bill & Melinda Gates Foundation on the Momentum Challenge on Academic Advising (Scott, 2013).

Conceived as an initiative in 2004 by the Lumina Foundation (2013) and seven founding partner organizations, Achieving the Dream (2015) leads a comprehensive nongovernment reform movement for community college student success. In 2009, the Lumina Foundation (2013) released Goal 2025, a strategic plan based on the goal that 60% of Americans obtain a high-quality postsecondary degree or credential by 2025. The plan places emphasis on the quality of student learning outcomes that provide pathways to further education and employment. Initiatives link, to the point of equating, student success with graduation and career success. Of course, without a consensus on the definition of student success, can any stakeholder adequately define career success? Can the definition of one be used to validate the other?

Completion initiatives, whether motivated by political agenda or public interest, share a commitment to improve the quality of the American higher education system and to increase the level of educational attainment for all students, especially those from underrepresented populations. The underlying assumption that drives the completion agenda appears to be based on the role of higher education in providing a skilled workforce for the U.S. economy, which commensurately promotes economic growth, keeps America competitive worldwide, and serves as a vehicle of social mobility. In this framework, student success is assessed in terms of graduation rates and social productivity.

A report by the American Federation of Teachers (2011) suggested that in the current trend of dwindling public resources, the policy debate has shifted from access to a focus on measurable outputs, including high persistence and graduation rates, especially among minority and underrepresented populations. This emphasis has given rise to various scorecards that measure institutional progress and programs that focus on student success. For example, the Student Success Scorecard, established by the California Community Colleges Chancellor's Office (2013), tracks student success at all 112 state-sponsored community colleges. Other initiatives, such as Access to Success (The Education Trust, 2014), have been launched with goals to cut the college attendance and graduation gaps between majority and low-income as well as minority students in half by 2015. However, The Education Trust report (2014) *Access to Success: How Far Have We Come?* notes that the gap in goals has not been closed. These initiatives measure student success in terms of graduation rates, illustrating a shift in policy that aligns external funding with institution and student performance such that diplomas translate into institutional dollars.

Student Success: A Goal of Institutional Planning

The Fall 2007 edition of *Together*, the official gazette of the Hispanic Educational Telecommunications System, focused on the importance of student success as the starting point in institutional planning. Acknowledging that student success, as a core value, should drive all institutional commitments and initiatives, many policymakers write student success into institutional mission statements and academic master plans. They designate resources to produce desired outcomes and create institutional offices and systems to measure and report student success. These institutional reports affect levels of external funding and shape public images.

What Is Measured?

Plenty of institutional programs facilitate student success; however, that success is not clearly defined, and assessment strategies of these initiatives generally focus on program rather than student outcomes. In the absence of a standardized definition, some prominent meanings of student success, as ascribed by postsecondary institutions, can be deciphered through reviews of institutional web sites. We randomly selected the featured statements with no intention to identify any single institution or degrade any perspective on student success; instead, they illustrate the complexity of student success as discussed in higher education and the institutional commitments to achieve it.

o The University of Kansas (2009) extolls a student success mission statement that highlights student success as an institutional program. The statement reveals a holistic description of desired program outcomes but does not provide a definition of student success:

Student Success at the University of Kansas provides services and programs that are essential to the intellectual, cultural, physical, social and moral development of students. Student Success encourages students to realize their potential as individuals and as prepared, enlightened, responsible members of an increasingly complex and diverse global society. As a partner in the educational process at a comprehensive research and teaching university, Student Success is vital to the institution's mission to serve as a center for learning, scholarship and creative endeavor. (University of Kansas, 2009, ¶1)

o The Student Success Center at the University of South Carolina (n.d.) reveals a popular programmatic approach to promote student success. Various specialized areas of assistance are identified that each target student success:

engagement coaching, tutoring, and transfer-student advising as well as supplemental instruction and academic progress, among others. However, the description leaves unclear the goal: Do these services lead to higher grades? Speedier time to graduation? Higher graduation rates? Better decisions? Something else entirely?

Some institutional statements and initiatives reveal student success in institutional parlance:

- o "Find out how Georgia State's [2014] student success programs are helping raise graduation rates" (¶1).

- o "Our services are designed specifically with you (and your goal to graduate from MSU) in mind" (Montana State University, n.d., ¶2).

- o "Our efforts focus on empowering individuals to become interdependent, self-directed lifelong learners. The Department provides a variety of services, resources and tools to enable individuals to pursue educational goals." (River Valley Community College, 2015, ¶1)

- o "The Springfield Technical Community College Student Success Center is designed with the student's success in mind. We will seek to provide each individual the chance to overcome obstacles and to be successful in accomplishing their individual goals." (Springfield Technical Community College, n.d.)

A commentary in the *The Chronicle of Higher Education* (Pennington, 2012) carried the provocative title, "For Student Success, Stop Debating and Start Improving." The title seems to imply that student success carries a universal meaning such that any dissent on the matter has been settled and that educators and student affairs must get down to the business of making it happen. The article features the subheading "Give students more-structured academic programs that accelerate their progress toward degrees" (¶11). Although the importance of student success to institutional success is clearly established, the question remains: Which one drives the other?

Whose Success Is Defined and Measured by Established Benchmarks?

The effectiveness of program strategies and student interventions is typically assessed by the impact they have on the attainment of institutional persistence and graduation goals. Without question, student success is embedded in such measures; however, retention and graduation rates are more accurately understood as indicators of institutional outcomes. In many cases, success initiatives are described in terms of student success when, in fact, they measure institutional effectiveness.

Retention, persistence, and graduation measure institutional outcomes and not student experiences, yet they have become the benchmarks used to drive institutional planning and assessment as well as to define and measure student success. Why? Student success and institutional success are codependent by nature: Institutions cannot have one without the other. Furthermore, stakeholders in these institutions know they are measuring economic outcomes, which drive institutional planning, strategies, and interventions, as well as determining the benchmarks for student success.

In the fierce competition for performance funding and other external monies, administrators of higher education institutions understand that retention and graduation rates carry the weighted points on the imposed scorecards. With rising expenses and fewer taxpayer dollars to cover them, institutions of higher education must heavily rely on retaining the students they recruit. Because effective retention begins with recruitment, Kuh et al. (2006) noted that consumerism strategies drive many institutional practices. Many colleges and universities market their admissions approach to recruit the right "customers." Administrators employ elaborate algorithms to identify those students best predicted to succeed (graduate) at their institution, and they enact strategic policies to alleviate concerns about the substantial investment of time and money made by students and parents at the institution.

The Chancellor of the California State University system signed an executive order that requires students to pay student success fees to support the promise of more classes and programs as well as improved graduation rates (The California State University Office of the Chancellor, 2013). Improved graduation rates are stated as the goal, and most would agree that more academic opportunities and support services are needed; however, the practices based on these premises raise several important questions that add to the dialogue on student success: Do improved graduation rates equate to student success? Can students be promised success? If students pay a fee, are they entitled to a product?

Retaining and graduating tuition-paying, fee-generating students translate into the dollars necessary to maintain the institutional budget and keep the classroom doors open. Besides tuition monies, postsecondary institutions lose other needed sources of revenue when students withdraw before graduation, such as room and board fees as well as alumni contributions; students who are not retained are also more likely to default on their student loans (Cuseo, 2010). From an institutional perspective, student success, meaning high retention and graduation rates, produces a desired outcome: fiscal stability. Generating revenue is not a bad goal. It is an essential goal. However, these institutional objectives are not student objectives.

Success: The Dream for Many Students

In most of the ongoing debates to define student success, a critical voice is often neglected—that of the student. Little attention has been paid to students' ideas of success. The definition of success varies among college students depending on their unique lived experiences, needs, and goals. Students approach the process of defining success with a stock of knowledge gained through past experiences, interactions, and expectations. To understand student success as interpreted by students, scholars must examine the formation and structure of those lived experiences and future intentions that give meaning to student expectations.

The meaning of college success to students who met the federal guidelines of *at risk* and attended a predominantly White university in the American South was investigated (Wallace, 2000). Through a series of focus groups and individual interviews, participants reflected upon the factors they thought would define their college experience as a success. The responses demonstrated that students interpret success in various ways.

In the study (Wallace, 2000), at-risk students talked about college success in terms of academic achievements and personal accomplishments. Graduation was the common goal for this group of students. Perhaps one student summed up the feelings of many others when she said, "Success will come when I can look back and say that I basically worked my butt off and got a degree" (p. 152).

In an interesting finding, the perspectives on student success differed between majority and minority student participants from the host university (Wallace, 2000). Whereas most of the majority students stated that success was measured by the level of their academic accomplishments, such as "graduate with honors" or "graduate in four years," many minority students identified success by levels of personal satisfaction. For some who grew up believing that they would never attend college, admittance defined the measure for success. Other minority students talked about personal growth and development: "Being better than I was when I came here" (p. 151).

In a popular response, students in the study referred to college success as a means of securing employment: "graduating and moving on to a job" (Wallace, 2000, p. 150). The respondent added, "You won't be successful if you go through school and get out there and don't get a job. That's just a waste of four years."

One of the study participants (Wallace, 2000), Andrew, an African American, came from the county rated as the economically and educationally poorest in the state. He had maintained a B GPA at a high school ranked at the bottom in the state. Because his ACT scores (composite 19, math 17) were below the university's standards, he was admitted on a conditional basis. During his first semester, he was recruited into the university's computer engineering major through a minority student enrollment initiative. Andrew recognized his inadequate high school preparations and took various academic skills development courses at the university to improve his academic deficits. However, he remained on academic probation due to failing prerequisite math and chemistry courses. Based upon his academic performance, his academic and career advisors suggested that he change his college major and career choice.

Andrew explained that he attended college due to his sense of responsibility to his family and community. He felt that all of those who could not enroll in college were at the university with him, and he refused to give up his dream. He defined success as persistence: "A student should have goals in mind, understanding that they may not be reached, but will still be successful for taking a step toward its accomplishment." He continued, "There will be times where students face hardships, but should remember to continue their perseverance and that a grade at the end of a course is not a measure of success" (p. 151). For Andrew, not giving up and not losing hope, not necessarily academic progress, described the measures of his success. He was eventually academically dismissed.

In a similar study on student success, Gonsalves and Vijaya (2008) asked students at a public, 4-year college in the American Northeast to complete the statement, "I will know that my college experience is a success when. . . ." Although the characterizations of success primarily referred to graduation from college and getting a good job, some students in upper divisions offered reflective responses: "I can look back and honestly say that I am a better, more rounded person due to my experiences here," and "I have become a more involved and productive member of society and can thankfully say that college has helped me to succeed" (¶11). The authors also noted the relatively high number of students who mentioned happiness as a criterion for measuring success.

Some students perceived that attending college will provide the opportunity to pursue a life better than the one they were living, and many expressed motivation to attend college by the lure of perceived benefits, such as satisfying high-paying jobs or happy lives. However, many students from all backgrounds fear that their dreams will not come true. The findings of these studies cannot be generalized to all student populations, but they do give insight into the complex process of defining student success. The meanings differ among students and may be influenced by racial background, socioeconomic status, and educational experiences. Additional research for identifying the factors that influence student definitions of success would prove a worthy endeavor.

An Authentic Definition of Student Success

The various stakeholders' demands for evidence of student success in postsecondary education contribute to the multiple definitions of success. With divergent understandings of the term, can an authentic definition of student success be crafted? Does the definition of student success belong to each stakeholder? If the definition is individualized by each student, how can researchers design measurements of it? Even if student success and institutional success were deemed synonymous, a singular definition would remain elusive because of the diversity of higher education institutions in terms of size, mission, location, and the personal, academic, and career goals of the students who enroll.

The title of this section was based on an article by Harrell and Holcroft (2012), members of the Academic Senate for California Community Colleges. They argued that although attempts to design metrics and scorecards to measure student success help guide programs, these measures exclude some of the most important aspects of success, such as transitioning to new academic and social communities, developing sound academic and career goals, and ultimately, becoming lifelong learners. A significant yet often overlooked element of success—perhaps because it is abstract, subjective, and nonquantifiable—is student learning. Higher education accreditation agencies now expect institutions to show evidence that students are learning in their educational experiences; however, these agencies do not address the important question: Who defines and assesses authentic learning?

Student learning outcomes are used in the assessment of the teaching–learning process to measure the extent that students fulfill course and program objectives, and they provide guided metrics to assign course grades. However, learning outcomes cannot be used to adequately measure student success because students' intended outcomes for a course may differ from those of the instructor, institution, or external evaluator. Student success is multidimensional with student learning being only one possible component.

Can success be reduced to one standard? Prominent definitions tend to measure student success in terms of retention and graduation rates. However, Harrell and Holcroft (2012) pointed out that not every student who enters a college or university seeks a certificate, degree, or transfer to another institution. In fact, students attending 2-year institutions, in particular, pursue a range of goals. In addition to those earning associate's degrees or transferring to 4-year colleges, some want job training, specialized classes that advance career opportunities, or acquisition of a skill for personal fulfillment (e.g., proficiency in a foreign language or improvement of artistic skills). Harrell and Holcroft offered two examples that challenge the notion that student success culminates in diplomas (¶2-3): One student leaves before earning a certificate because his course work allowed him to secure a permanent full-time position in his field, and a mother of two takes a single class to improve skills that helped her secure a job promotion. One sought a certificate but left without it to follow the greater dream, and the other held no aspirations for a degree or certificate but earned the promotion she sought.

Those who assess outcomes based on popular institutional definitions may not agree that the two students in the Harrell and Holcroft (2012) example demonstrate success because neither met persistence and graduation goals as defined by many institutions. However, the students in these cases would likely disagree with the institutional evaluators: They both met their personal goals. In cases featuring conflicting objectives, whose definition of success should be embraced?

In his remarks at the Faculty Resource Network National Symposium, Patrick Love (2008) shared his perspective on student success:

> A student succeeds when she or he constructs a vision of her or his future, charts possible paths to that future, and takes steps along that path. To create such a vision students must recognize both the need to create their own future and their active role in that process. Students need to be or become aware, conscious, and intentional in their journey. Overall, student success is about learning and learning is about discovering, dreaming, creating, and achieving. (¶3)

Harrell and Holcroft (2012) concluded their argument with the following:

> The truest definition of student success is determined by the goals and personal situation of each individual student. For this reason, no single comprehensive statement

or simple set of metrics can offer a complete and meaningful picture of the many ways in which our students succeed every year at all of our colleges. (¶8)

According to this statement, no one-size-fits-all definition adequately characterizes student success. Stakeholders at each institution must create a definition that captures the uniqueness of their campus and students. Rather than allow others to determine this definition, academic advisors must take the lead in the conversation about success at their institutions.

Student Success Definitions: Implications for Academic Advisors

Academic advising plays an integral role in fulfilling the mission of higher education institutions of all types. It is delivered by diverse individuals within various environments; however, all academic advisors face the intense challenge of delivering quality services that are responsive to the specific contexts of their institutions and the changing needs of students. Academic advisors often must function at the crossroads of differing, and sometimes conflicting, definitions of student success. At times, they may struggle with inner conflicts and moral dilemmas in deciding whose definition and what measures of student success take precedence at their institution. Advisors must remain aware of the way popular definitions of student success and the subsequent expectations for advisors affect their work with students. To be effective, advisors must balance their responsibilities to the students they advise (NACADA Core Value 1) and to the institutions they serve (NACADA Core Value 3) (NACADA, 2005, ¶1–3, 5).

Productivity-Centered Definitions

Definitions that equate student success with desired production outputs, such as retention and graduation, are called *productivity centered* and are found prominently in government- and industry-directed initiatives. Completion agenda efforts to make college more affordable to students in all income brackets, better prepare students for college, assist students in completing their programs of study, and help students with the transition from college life to career life are welcomed by the higher education community as well as parents and students. Demands for accountability can improve the quality of institutions of higher education, but how do these appeals affect academic advising practices and the expectations placed on advisors?

When colleges and universities are driven to produce more graduates, and the number of graduates is linked to needed performance-funding dollars for institutions, the number of diplomas granted becomes highly important to administrators— the higher the number, the better. Advisors are often given the responsibility to keep the student pipeline flowing from enrollment to a speedy graduation. Use of this framework can lead to products that are more valued than the process. Retention and graduation rates are used to assess not only institutional outcomes but also measure advisor effectiveness.

Many academic advisors who are expected to meet these ambitious institutional goals lack the opportunity to engage in meaningful proactive advising-related topics other than scheduling, course grades, or graduation. Two common practices contribute to the pilfering of precious time that could be devoted to other student concerns: schedules packed with back-to-back 15 to 30 minute appointments and students who come to appointments unprepared to maximize the limited appointment time. Rather than develop a close student-advisor relationship, advising sessions often become a perfunctory process of answering questions, creating schedules, explaining institutional policies, and keeping students on track for the semester.

In productivity-centered environments, advisors are expected to provide customer satisfaction. In this consumerist perspective, students and parents are viewed as end users of colleges and universities. Because they pay tuition, they are entitled to receive the direct benefits of their purchase. Some advisors are evaluated based on the levels of student satisfaction rather than the student learning outcomes for academic advising (chapter 14). Stakeholders are motivated to foster this paradigm based on the premises that satisfied customers will contribute to the graduation rate and financial stability of the institution and that dissatisfied customers will take their business and tuition dollars elsewhere.

Should academic advisors pander to student and parent demands for customer satisfaction? In the quest for customer satisfaction, should institutions and advisors operate from a Burger King have-it-your-way mentality? At some point, advisors must assist all stakeholders in understanding that tuition dollars do not buy guaranteed success, but they open doors to opportunities for success. Student success is not an entitlement purchased by tuition dollars; instead, it is an earned achievement, and academic advisors partner with students (and parents when appropriate) to help them evaluate and capitalize on the opportunities available. Quality academic advising is transformative, not transactional (Lowenstein, 2014).

Institution-Centered Definitions

Not only are institutions of higher education committed to provide a pool of literate and trained workers who will promote economic development but they also depend on the revenue from students to keep their doors open; that is, students equal revenues. Confronted with difficult economic realities, many postsecondary institutions prioritize self-preservation, and many decisions that shape policies and procedures are driven by budgets and resources. At some institutions, economic-driven policies have resulted in various institutional practices that affect the work of advisors with students, including advisor accountability for student persistence and graduation rates.

Whose interest is served by recruitment policies that offer students the promise of fields of study that do not exist at the institution? Who benefits from forcing students to declare majors before they are developmentally ready to make such decisions? Who gains when course offerings are restricted to channel students into classes with low enrollments? Such practices may make perfect sense from a resource management perspective, but to whom does the educational experience belong: the institution or the student?

Academic Advisors as Partners in Institutional Success

Advisors work in many types of higher education institutions and abide by the specific policies, procedures, and values of the department and institution for which they work (NACADA, 2005, ¶3). Therefore, the institutional definition of student success shapes the role of academic advising and expectations placed upon advisors. At times, the institutional definition of success and imposed advising expectations may differ from the understanding and role as perceived by the advisor. How should the advisor respond when faced with such a professional dilemma that is often rooted in the advisor's personal value system? (chapter 7)

In the face of such quandaries, some fight the system or take to flight. However, in a more positive approach, advisors realize the unique role they can play in cultivating a campus ethos that offers students the greatest opportunities to achieve their desired successes. Because of the nature of their practice, advisors often develop a broad understanding of the institutional culture, needs of the students, and availability of resources to assist students in achieving their goals. Based upon this insight, advisors can assist students in assessing the best ways the institution can facilitate progress toward their educational goals. Advisors can also promote a greater understanding of students among others at the institution.

Academic advisors should take a prominent role in the assessment of the current institutional definition of student success and the programs, policies, and procedures used to enhance student success. However, these same advisors need to recognize that navigating this challenge can lead the well intentioned into a political minefield; therefore, respected master advisors with political savvy and security in their positions should take the lead in negotiating any new terms of success and related programs. Tenured faculty advisors recognized as master advisors can speak on behalf of students regardless of institutional pressure (chapters 3 and 10).

In the current economic environment of competition for shrinking institutional resources, support for academic advising programs is often determined by assessments of the value of advising to fulfill institutional mission and goals. Advisors must establish the value and worth of their practices and programs with accurate collection of data that show support for the institutional mission and definition of student success. Although the extent that advising contributes to retention and graduation rates remains difficult to show, data on the number of advising sessions conducted as well as the number of students who register for the upcoming semester during the initial registration period, persist from semester to semester, and graduate within four years provide useful support.

Furthermore, advising administrators should conduct assessment activities in addition to student satisfaction surveys. Specifically, they should identify and assess learning outcomes for advising (chapter 14) and report the data to senior administrators through the proper channels. In addition, master advisors should demand a presence and a voice during discussions of student success, institutional policies that affect students' experiences, and allocation of resources. Also, advisors can embrace the power of students' voices to advance the agenda that most benefits advisees. (How many flavors of ice cream have been added to dining halls because students stood up and demanded it?)

Advisors as Partners in Student Success

Academic advisors are among the greatest resources for student success. Quality advising is driven by the belief that students can be successful and involves more than provision of accurate information and assistance with course schedules. Effective advisors support the context in which students can dream, explore, discover, and develop. They advise students to design meaningful goals consistent with their interests and abilities so they can realize their aspirations. Advisors help students develop their own definitions of success and support their assessments and refinements to those definitions. When institutional circumstances interfere with students' success, advisors act as advocates, serving as mediators and facilitators who leverage their specialized knowledge and experience to help students remove obstacles in the path to success. Advising for student success reflects the heart of the NACADA (2005) Core Values of Academic Advising.

Advising for Student Success

When developing strategies to advise students for success some advisors put the cart before the horse. In these cases, advising sessions quickly turn to discussions about tips on how to be successful and how to develop techniques and skills to achieve success. Students leave college with action plans, great expectations, and high hopes for using their magical wand for creating happiness. However, many never reach the destinations of their dreams because they have skipped two crucial considerations in their pursuits of success. Every successful expedition, whether taken for a family vacation, in pursuit of a career, or while earning a college degree, begins with a sense of purpose. In addition, every person who successfully reaches their destination plans the journey.

Without a Reason, Nothing Makes Sense

The most important question that students should consider at the beginning of their educational journeys is not, "What do I want to be for the rest of my life?" or "What should I choose as a major?" Rather, students should reflect upon the reasons they want to be in college. Advisors can assist students by asking questions that encourage lucid reasoning: "What influenced you to make the decision to come to college?" and "What does being a college student mean to you?" Answers to these questions describe the student's essential definition of success.

Most new students can readily list benefits they hope to achieve by graduating from college, but few have attempted to reflect critically on the reason they seek the aforementioned benefits. Furthermore, the stated reason must not be imposed by other stakeholders; it must come from the student. Not everyone goes to college for the same reasons, but the reasons for going to college may be equally good. Some go to college because they think the degree is the ticket to a high-paying job. Some feel pressured to seek a college education. Some enjoy studying and learning. Others cannot think of anything else to do (it is better than living at home in their parents' basement). A few plan to party until the financial aid runs out.

Students need to understand that their motivation will affect their experiences in college. Without a reason to attend, the process of earning an education makes no sense.

Aim at Nothing: Hit It Every Time

Every successful journey is based on a destination that keeps the traveler moving forward. After discerning the reasons for a decision, students should consider the potential benefits of their actions, and advisors can assist by asking: "What do you hope to gain by attending college?" Advisors can encourage students to think deeply and to assess their initial goals by asking follow-up questions such as "When did this goal first become important to you?" "Why is this goal of value to you?" "What skills, behaviors, and attitudes do you need to develop to achieve this goal?"

At this point, some students struggle with conflicting interests between their perceptions of the actions they should take and those they want to pursue. They may express this dilemma in the following way: "My parents insist that I major in business so that I can get a good job, but I am really interested in art." In addition to paying college expenses, parents and other outside stakeholders want their student to succeed, and many parents define success as graduating and securing a good-paying job as a means to be self-supporting. In some cultures, student success is the family's success. Although college students should appreciate the viewpoint of those who care about their future, at some point they must define success for themselves. It is the student's journey, and it is the student's success.

To avoid the cost of taking unneeded courses, extending graduation, and accumulating lost opportunities, students should explore and discover an appropriate program of study as early as possible. However, students also need to recognize that as they change during the journey through college, their reasons for persisting and the goals they seek may also evolve.

Advisors help students take ownership of their definitions and pursuits of success. They encourage them to choose the journey not by prescribing the path the student must take, but by helping them develop expertise in reflecting upon their own goals and the influences that shape those goals. They ask students to assess their interests, skills, and values, and they suggest that advisees adjust their goals as appropriate. The ultimate, desired outcomes in this advising process do not necessarily culminate in graduations or high-paying jobs; rather they are reflected in students' abilities to create their own definitions of success and subsequently assume command of their successes.

Just as they must proficiently assist students in defining and taking ownership of their successes, advisors also must develop strategies for helping students who fail to achieve their desired outcomes. Advisors must resist both the temptation to assign their own interpretations to the students' experiences and the urge to fix the problem. Instead, they should teach students the process of assessing the situation and getting on track so that resolution of the issues becomes a positive growth experience for students. The advisor-assisted problem-solving process includes the following phases:

1. Assist the student in reexamining answers to the most important questions. Why are you in college at this time? What does being a college student mean to you? What do you hope to achieve by being in college? Now that you have some experience in college, what does student success mean to you? How will you know if you achieve the successes you desire? At this point in your college experience, would you consider yourself a successful student? Why or why not? Encourage the student to compare current answers to those previously given to these questions. Ask the student to explain the reasons for any changed answers.

2. Help the student identify the possible contributors to the setback in achieving the desired goals. Explore possible factors by inquiring about the nature of the problem: Did this problem happen once, or is it a recurring or long-term issue? Determine whether the dilemma represents a larger issue: Are the student's reasons for being in college or the desired outcomes unreasonable or based on faulty decision making? Is the institution a good fit for the student? Consider the student's personal attributes: Is the student's set of personal and academic skills adequate for the chosen field of study? Has the student demonstrated the motivation and commitment required to reach his or her goals?

3. Encourage the student to develop an action plan for recovering from a disappointment. The student must take ownership of this part of the process and should consider addressing goals and motivation: What will it take to get from where I am to where I want to be? What am I willing to do to achieve the successes I desire? The advisor can aid the student in identifying specific actions and available resources that may support achievement of the desired outcomes, such as schedule regular tutoring; meet with professors; retake courses with grades lower than C; complete a career interest inventory to identify occupations of interest; investigate other options for programs of study; reduce work and outside-of-class commitment times.

4. Collaborate with the student to design a time line for executing each action and an accountability system to check the student's progress. The critical part of any action plan is executing it.

5. Honestly inform the student of the risks of failure. Advisors may also need to explain that recovery does not culminate in a single action, but is a process. Furthermore, they should advise that, at times, the recovery plan, in whole or in part, may need to be repeated.

Case Study: What Is Wrong With This Picture?

Advising for student success involves protecting students from institutional policies and personal decisions that may lead to failed outcomes. A popular feature in children's magazines asks the reader to discover the image that does not fit with the others in an illustration. We emulate the exercise with the following scenario and ask the reader: What is not right with this picture?

Shonda is an incoming freshman who graduated from a low-ranked inner-city high school. She confirmed her admission late and did not attend the university's new student summer orientation, which offers advice and assistance in registering for first-semester courses; for those who cannot attend orientation, personnel in one of the administrative offices prepare the class schedule without consulting the student.

Shonda wants a nursing career because she enjoys helping people. Although the university does not offer a nursing or pre-nursing program, Shonda was assured she could pursue other paths at the institution to achieve her goal. She was admitted as an undeclared student with a science interest. Without consultation with Shonda, the scheduler assigned her 18 credit hours that consisted of the following classes:

o Biology 101, Principles of Biology, a required course for health science majors that has one of the highest failure rates on the campus. The Biology Department strongly recommends that students have strong science and math backgrounds before attempting the killer course, but does not restrict registration.

o History 105, History of Western Civilizations, a required skills course in the general education program that has the reputation of being extremely reading and writing intensive; it also has a high failure rate.

o English 250, Culturally Diverse Literature, another course that satisfies a general education requirement and is reading intensive with a high failure rate.

o Political Science 101, World Politics, a general education requirement and reading intensive.

o Music 121, Music Appreciation, which features opera and music theater and satisfies a general education requirement.

o Military Science 190, Basic Military Science, an elective.

Shonda was concerned about the music course because she had no music background and no interest in the course. Because first-semester students are not allowed to self-adjust their schedules, she called an advisor to inquire about dropping the music class.

Although Shonda's schedule met the institution's guidelines and expectations for students with a science interest, when Shonda made the drop request, the advisor reviewed her high school transcript, SAT scores, and institutional placement testing results. Shonda's SAT composite score of 880 met admissions requirements, but her math test score fell significantly below the cutoff for developmental classes, and she had not taken the math placement test. She had completed the required English-writing placement test, but the score had not been posted. Based on her SAT verbal score, she narrowly avoided a mandated developmental reading course. During the conversation with Shonda, the advisor discovered that she had not taken any advanced mathematics courses in high school and that she had not taken any math or science courses in her senior year. What can the advisor do to increase Shonda's opportunities for success?

Important desired outcomes from the advising process include student assumption of ownership over their own successes and development into well-rounded individuals. According to NACADA (2005) Core Value 1, advisors are responsible to the individuals they advise, and they become partners in students' successes by assisting them in transitioning to new academic and social communities. Advisors help students develop and reinforce realistic self-perceptions and use this information in mapping their personal, academic, and career futures. Advisors encourage self-reliance and support students as they strive to make informed and responsible decisions, set realistic goals, and develop lifelong learning and self-management skills. Furthermore, they encourage students to become responsible for their own successes (and failures).

Advisors must take care not to measure student success according to institutional, or their own, definitions; rather, they must seek an understanding of each student's perceptions of success and assist the student in recognizing the internal and external influences that shape the meanings of those definitions. Although students map their own paths, they need assurance that they do not travel alone on the journey.

Student Success Is Everyone's Success

A variety of stakeholders take interest in student success in postsecondary education. Student success has been the subject of ongoing debates among policy makers, educators, students, parents, and others, which has generated an abundance of literature. In spite of all of the attention, agreement on an authentic definition has eluded the higher education community and stakeholders. Student success is defined according to the institution, mission, student population (including their needs), and campus culture. To effectively meet the needs of their institutions and students, advisors must develop quality partnerships with a diverse array of stakeholders.

Business and industry rely on an educated and skilled workforce to remain creative and competitive and to advance economic growth. Parents are committed and invested in the overall well-being of their children. Students seek the knowledge and preparation they need for the lives they desire. Postsecondary institutions provide educational services that foster personal, academic, and career development. Of all these interested parties, academic advisors are in the best position to help bring to fruition these multiple goals.

"Did I Do the Right Thing?"

Conscientious advisors ask themselves, sometimes frequently, "Did I do the right thing?" The answer depends upon who answers it. In the scenario that introduced this chapter in which the student's decision to transfer to another institution that offered her desired major was supported by her advisor, the institutional answer is decidedly "No," because every student who leaves reflects negatively on retention and graduation goals. The student's parents might answer, "No," if the new institution is more expensive and takes their student farther away from home. The student might answer, "Yes. The advisor did the right thing in assisting me to make a critical decision that is in my best interest."

In the midst of clashing voices and demands, academic advisors must determine whose definition (interest) takes precedence. In meeting a variety of expectations, advisors must stay strong and remain confident so they can hear and honor the voices of all stakeholders, serve as ambassadors for their institutions, advocate for students, and act as agents of institutional change.

Aiming for Excellence

- o What is your definition of student success?
  - o Whose success is measured by your definition?
  - o Identify the theories that inform your perspective on student success.
  - o Assess the best practices you employ that promote student success.
  - o Periodically review your philosophy in light of institutional and student needs.
- o What is the definition of student success in the advising unit or academic department?
  - o Carefully read and dissect the statements on advising mission, responsibilities for advisors, and expectations for advisees. Do these statements focus on student success?
  - o Facilitate advisor discussion groups on the topic of student success.
- o How do students describe their own success?
  - o During advising sessions, prompt students to explain their idea of success.
  - o Ask students the reasons they are in college and their goals for their college experience; document responses for continuing discussions.
- o What is the definition of student success at your institution?
  - o Whose success is measured by the institutional definition?
  - o Carefully read and dissect the institution mission statement; highlight sections of the institution's strategic plan for student success.

o Facilitate cross-campus discussions among administrators and faculty members on the topic of student success.

- Select a conflict that will likely affect advising practices and design a strategy to manage it.
- Delineate your responsibilities based on your advising role at the institution.
- Identify institutional expectations for advising outcomes.
- Review NACADA (2005) Core Values 1 and 3, which address advisors' responsibilities to advisees and to their institutions. Respond to the following questions:
    - How does your definition of student success and description of your responsibilities exemplify the NACADA Core Values?
    - Do institutional expectations for advising outcomes demonstrate the NACADA Core Values of Academic Advising?
    - How can the roles of advisor and institutional expectations be better aligned with NACADA Core Values?
- Use the case of Shonda to complete the following exercises:
    - Identify Shonda's personal and student characteristics.
    - Assess the institutional response to Shonda.
    - Create a strategy to assist Shonda.

References

88 Surefire tips for succeeding in college. (2013). Retrieved from http://oedb.org/library/college-basics/88-surefire-tips/

Achieving the Dream. (2015). *Helping more community college students succeed.* Retrieved from http://achievingthedream.org/

American Association of Community Colleges. (2015). *College completion challenge: A call to action.* Retrieved from http://www.aacc.nche.edu/About/completionchallenge/Pages/default.aspx

American Federation of Teachers. (2011). *Student success.* Retrieved from http://www.aft.org/position/student-success

Annan, K. A. (1997, June 6). *Commencement address: Massachusetts Institute of Technology.* Retrieved from http://news.mit.edu/1997/annansp

Bill & Melinda Gates Foundation. (n.d.). *College ready.* Retrieved from http://collegeready.gatesfoundation.org/

California Community Colleges Chancellor's Office. (2013). *Student success scorecard.* Retrieved from http://scorecard.cccco.edu/scorecard.aspx

The California State University Office of the Chancellor. (2013, June 18). *Academic excellence and student success fee* [Executive Order 10860]. Retrieved from www.calstate.edu/eo/EO-1086.html

College Board. (2008). *Coming to our senses: Education and the American future.* Retrieved from http://professionals.collegeboard.com/profdownload/coming-to-our-senses-college-board-2008.pdf

Completion by Design. (2015). *Completion by design.* Retrieved from http://completionbydesign.org/

Cuseo, J. (2010). *Fiscal benefits of student retention and first-year retention initiatives.* Retrieved from http://www.ohio.edu/fye/upload/retention-fiscal-benefits.pdf

The Education Trust. (2014). *Access to success: How far have we come?* Retrieved from http://edtrust.org/wp-content/uploads/2013/10/dc-a2s-edtrust.final_.pdf

Georgia State University. (2014). *Student success: Crushing the odds.* Retrieved from http://success.students.gsu.edu/

Gonsalves, S. V., & Vijaya, R. (2008). *First year students, definitions of success.* Retrieved from http://www.nyu.edu/frn/publications/defining.success/Gonsalves.Vijaya.html

Harrell, K., & Holcroft, C. (2012). *Searching for an authentic definition of student success.* Retrieved from http://www.asccc.org/content/searching-authentic-definition-student-success

Higher Learning Commission. (2010). [Home page]. Retrieved from http://www.ncahlc.org/

Jacobs, L., & Hyman, J. (2013). *The secrets of college success.* San Francisco, CA: Jossey-Bass.

Kuh, G. D., & Hu, S. (2001). The effects of student-faculty interaction in the 1990s. *The Review of Higher Education, 24*(3), 309–332.

Kuh, G. D., Kinzie, J., Buckley, J. A., Bridges, B. K., & Hayek, J. C. (2006). *What matters to student success: A review of the literature.* Retrieved from http://nces.ed.gov/npec/pdf/Kuh_Team_Report.pdf

Lee, J. M., & Ransom, T. (2011). *The educational experience of young men of color: A review of research, pathways and progress.* Retrieved from http://media.collegeboard.com/digitalServices/pdf/advocacy/nosca/nosca-educational-experience-young-men-color-research.pdf

Leveille, D. E. (2006). *Accountability in higher education: A public agenda for trust and cultural change.* Retrieved from http://www.cpec.ca.gov/CompleteReports/ExternalDocuments/Leveille_Accountability.20.06.pdf

Love, P. (2008, November). *Diverse perspectives on student success.* Presented at the Faculty Resource Network National Symposium, San Francisco, CA. Retrieved from http://www.nyu.edu/frn/publications/defining.success/Love.plenary.html

Lowenstein, M. (2014, August 12). Toward a theory of advising. *The Mentor: An Academic Advising Journal.* Retrieved from http://dus.psu.edu/mentor/2014/08/toward-a-theory-of-advising/

Lumina Foundation. (2013). *Goal 2025.* Retrieved from http://www.luminafoundation.org/goal_2025

McPhearson, M., & Schapiro, M. O. (2008). *College success: What it means and how to make it happen.* New York, NY: College Board.

Middle States Commission on Higher Education. (2015). *Middle States Commission on Higher Education.* Retrieved from http://www.msche.org/

Montana State University. (n.d.). *Student success resources*. Retrieved from http://www.montana.
    edu/success/

NACADA: The Global Community for Academic Advising. (2005). NACADA statement of
    core values of academic advising: Declaration. Retrieved from http://www.nacada.ksu.
    edu/Resources/Clearinghouse/View-Articles/Core-values-declaration.aspx

Obama, B. (2013). *The President's plan for a strong middle class & a strong America*.
    Retrieved from https://www.whitehouse.gov/sites/default/files/uploads/sotu_
    2013_blueprint_embargo.pdf

Pascarella, E. T., Pierson, C. T., Wolniak, G. C., & Terenzini, P. T. (2004). First-generation
    college students: Additional evidence on college experiences and outcomes. *The Journal
    of Higher Education, 75*(3), 249–284.

Pennington, H. (2012, April 12). *For student success, stop debating and start improving*.
    Retrieved from http://chronicle.com/article/For-Student-Success-Stop/131451/

Pike, G. R. & Kuh, G. D. (2005). First- and second-generation college students: A comparison
    of their engagement and intellectual development. *The Journal of Higher Education,
    76*(3), 276–300.

River Valley Community College. (2015). *Student Success Center*. http://www.rivervalley.edu/
    academics/student-success-center

Santiago, D. (2010). *Ensuring America's future: Benchmarking Latino college completion to
    meet national goals: 2010 to 2020*. Retrieved from http://www.edexcelencia.org/
    research/benchmarking-latino-college-completion

Scott, P. (2013, September 18). *Gates Foundation, NACADA to discuss academic advising.
    Kansas State University*. Retrieved from http://www.k-state.edu/today/announcement.
    php?id=9976

Springfield Technical Community College. (n.d.). *Student success center*. Retrieved from
    http://www.stcc.edu/success/

Together: The Official Gazette of the Hispanic Education Telecommunications System.
    (2007). *Defining student success: The starting point to institutional planning*. Retrieved
    from http://hets.org/wp-content/uploads/2011/11/4.pdf

University of Kansas. (2009). *Student success mission statement*. Retrieved from http://www.
    vpss.ku.edu/missionstatement.shtml

University of South Carolina. (n.d.). *Student success center*. http://www.sa.sc.edu/ssc/

Wallace, S. O. (2000). *Meaning-establishment and meaning-interpretation in the experiences
    of "at-risk" college students making academic decisions* (Doctoral dissertation).
    Retrieved from ProQuest Dissertations and Theses database. (UMI No. 9996507)

The White House Office of the Press Secretary. (2009, July 14). *Remarks by the President on
    the American graduation initiative*. Retrieved from http://www.whitehouse.gov/
    the_press_office/Remarks-by-the-President-on-the-American-Graduation-Initiative-
    in-Warren-MI/

6

KNOWING AND REACHING STUDENTS

Karen L. Archambault

We need to give each other the space to grow, to be ourselves, to exercise our diversity. We need to give each other space so that we may both give and receive such beautiful things as ideas, openness, dignity, joy, healing, and inclusion.

—Max de Pree (1987)

Although students have always been complex individuals, each with his or her own behaviors and characteristics, modern students bring uniquely complex backgrounds and experiences to their campuses and their advisors. In particular, master advisors responsible for the training and development of their peers must possess the skills to support these student needs effectively. To undertake this responsibility successfully, they need to apply a wide variety of theoretical frameworks. Case studies offer the practice necessary to expand the skill set of master advisors to work more effectively with students, to advocate for students across campus, and to support advisor training and development programs.

Reader Learning Outcomes

From studying this chapter, advisors will use knowledge gained about complex student identities and cultural competence to

- o understand multiple identities and how they affect interactions with students,
- o expand knowledge of theories related to social identity,
- o develop a framework for understanding and evaluating cultural differences,
- o evaluate case studies to determine ways identity and background influence the needs of students, and
- o utilize knowledge of diversity in advising and advisor training.

Regardless of the campus on which they work, many new advisors visualize the advisee as the stereotype often applied to a residential student at brick-and-mortar institutions: prepared for college from their recent high school attendance and participating full-time in college with the financial and personal support of parents. However, fewer college students fit this pattern than in the past (Institute of International Education, 2014; National Center for Education Statistics [NCES], 2014, 2015). Many hold racial, gender, religious, socioeconomic, or other identities incongruent with the stereotype or with the advisor. Students commuting to community college campuses, returning adults taking classes online, underprepared first-generation students with little familial support, and others managing multiple priorities, including work and family, may enjoy few emotional or financial resources.

In *The New Advisor Guidebook: Mastering the Art of Academic Advising* (Folsom, Yoder, & Joslin, 2015), I posited that new advisors could streamline their interactions—with students with whom they identify as well as with those from whom they differ—by utilizing five standard questions (Archambault, 2015):

- o How does the student's experience differ from my own?
- o Am I making assumptions about this student based upon both visible and invisible areas of diversity?
- o How do my assumptions about all students on this campus seem to fit or not fit this student?
- o What student characteristics contribute to academic successes or challenges?
- o What types of support does this student (and this campus) possess to address specific areas of diversity that he or she represents? (pp. 189–191)

For the new advisor, these questions assist in initiating conversations with students; they focus on understanding the challenges a student may face. They serve as a foundation, not an end point, in student interactions.

Master advisors use a greater range of skills in the tool kit from which they draw. Acknowledgment of difference may be sufficient to assist an individual student in a single meeting, but master advisors recognize their broad role on campus, which includes individual interactions and extends to reflect responsibilities beyond the advising office. Advising relationships with students often become uniquely permanent, especially when master advisors respond to students' needs holistically. Master advisors not only require a strong skill set to identify the needs of students but they must also impart these skills to new staff.

Higginson (2000) argued that advisors require a range of knowledge and skills to perform their roles, and they gain the needed information from the institution catalog or web site as well as through awareness of self and of the student. In this chapter, I challenge master advisors to develop skills that benefit many students with whom they interact, including those who present diverse backgrounds. I also encourage them to use these skills as advocates of diversity across campus and as promoters of effective advisor-training outcomes.

After reviewing the social identity theories that describe specific student characteristics, I explain additional theories that master advisors may consider in addressing multiple levels of identity. I also present models that focus on additional complexities students may present. The chapter concludes with case studies that encourage closer inspection of theory as advisors consider a variety of student identities and the salience of each in specific situations.

Revisiting Identity Theories

As master advisors know from experience, college students are not homogeneous. Enrollees include students of various racial, ethnic, and socioeconomic backgrounds as well as transfer and international students, military veterans, students with disabilities, returning adults, and those first in their families to pursue higher education (Institute of International Education, 2014; NCES, 2014, 2015). Master advisors remain well informed about their own institution, specifically the racial, ethnic, religious, socioeconomic, and other demographic profiles associated with specific student needs. Master advisors also draw on various theories and theoretical frameworks to assist these students and the less experienced advisors in their units. Of special note, theories such as those Peggy Jordan describes in chapter 2 reflect the many identities with which students arrive on campus, including those that add to the racial, ethnic, and cultural diversity of postsecondary institutions. Advisors must know certain, essential diversity theories (Archambault, 2015; Jordan, 2015): Atkinson, Morten, and Sue's (1998) minority identity model, suggesting that those in racial or cultural minorities begin to conform to the majority culture, withdraw from that culture, and eventually find balance between the dominant culture and all aspects of their own heritage; theories for lesbian gay bisexual and transgender identities, such as D'Augelli's (1994) model, which suggests development as a process, rather than as linear stages, that needs to occur both individually and within communities of support; and ethnic development, such as Torres, Howard-Hamilton, and Cooper's (2003) Hispanic identity model. These theories add to a meaningful understanding of students; as Torres et al. (2003) argued, without this knowledge of identity, the likelihood of a communication gap grows, challenging the ability of primary-role and faculty advisors to effectively interact with their students.

Theories for Multiple Identities

Identity theories promote understanding of student characteristics that may differ from an advisor's own experience. Although these theories guide practice, master advisors recognize that students are composed of multiple identities that exist simultaneously and prevail to different degrees at various times in the student's experience.

A former Marine attending college as a result of the GI Bill might identify as female, a parent of two young children, and an honors transfer student. She may also identify as transgender, African American, and Christian, and may need assistance with a learning disability. Like all human beings, this student is complex—more than the proverbial sum of single-identity parts. In an advising session, this student may require assistance related to one or many of these identities, and the need may shift from one advising interaction to the next. For example, in one session, this student may struggle with school-life balance common to many trying to raise children while pursuing higher education, while in another appointment, she may express academic and financial concerns caused by incongruence in course work between institutions and the limits of GI Bill funding.

An advisor who sees only the student's racial or ethnic identity would fail to appropriately address all the needs of this student; however, a mindful advisor may uncover that the academic challenge results from discrimination experienced due to the identity statuses of this student. To address this complicated situation, a master advisor recognizes the many components that comprise the whole of the student and uses a multifaceted approach to address her concerns. The ability to shift between approaches and to recognize the student's needs, rather than those of the advisor, marks a culturally competent professional.

Evans (2012) referred to the presentation of many characteristics by a single individual as a *tapestry*, (¶2) and describes the need to weave each individual feature into a complete, visualized whole. As each student is a culmination of many experiences and attributes, master advisors have learned to see the identities and needs that resonate with the student. Therefore, they utilize theories based upon the identities as the student perceives them not as the reflection of an advisor's beliefs about them.

In addition to utilizing individual theories, master advisors—particularly those responsible for training—have expanded their repertoire to additional social identity theories and multifaceted frameworks through which to understand cultural differences of students. Master advisors recognize that students interact in ways that reflect more than a compilation of their individual characteristics; instead, they know that each student demonstrates many characteristics enhanced through personal and societal experiences. These combined experiences are derived from personal, lived experiences, the lives of families and communities, and society at large. Pratt-Johnson (2006) referred to the need for educators to think of culture as multidimensional—an onion with hidden layers or an iceberg with submerged, undetectable portions. Master advisors feel the impact of the unseen as they uncover all aspects of the learner's experience. In other words, the student may bring experiences not immediately visible to the advisor or even to the student; the master advisor has developed expertise at uncovering this hidden, but essential, information.

Theories on Racial, Biracial, and Multiethnic Identity

With changing demographics on college campuses (NCES, 2014, 2015), advisors must learn about the latest theories related to Black and biracial identity and adult learning theory to offer successful advising and training. New theories may assist advisors in gauging the students' experiences and identities as they enter the advising interaction. Cross's (1971) theory of Nigrescence forms the foundation of identity theory specific to African Americans; he argued that the process of *becoming Black* psychologically involves the movement of the individual from a viewpoint of being ignorant about one's culture to one that culminates in full acceptance and advocacy. Specifically, the person initially favors the majority culture (largely resulting from a lack of exposure to Black culture) through immersion in Black culture, in which the individual may demonstrate (or may be perceived as having) anti-White sentiment, and evolves until a fully formed identity encourages focus on social change and justice. In an updated work, the theorist, with coauthor Fhagen-Smith, reconceptualized the model with a life span focus (Cross & Fhagen-Smith, 2001). In traditional-aged college students, the process varies depending upon prior experiences, but the person may or may not view race as important.

Poston (1990) addressed biracial identity development through a five-stage model. In the first stage, an individual's initial identity is essentially neutral; that is, it does not depend upon ethnicity. In the second stage, individuals connect with one race as determined not only by a personal choice but also by the social support and status associated with each of the races. In the third stage, an individual may feel a sense of self-hatred, confusion, and guilt due to a perception of needing to choose one race over the other. Prior to the final step of full integration, a person begins to appreciate multicultural identity and the diversity it represents. College students may be facing the confusion or self-hatred inherent in this process, or they may rebel against the suggestion that they are of one race or the other.

In Root's (1990) theory of multiracial and multiethnic identity development, the person moves from passive to active attempts to resolve the potential turmoil created by a multiethnic identity. Specifically, the individual first recognizes the assignment of an identity by others; however, the tie of this person to this socially appointed identity, even if positive, remains fragile. As the individual attempts to identify with both racial groups, the features of a single group seem more salient to the person, and in the end, the individual embraces a biracial identity. Root pointed out that teens, in particular, may not feel a sense of belonging to any particular social group, and the resolution process may especially challenge Americans who live in relatively less diverse neighborhoods where few people identify with more than one racial or ethnic heritage. Renn (2008) argued that students who feel excluded by those associated with individual races or ethnicities may opt out of identification with any race.

The various development pathways described by theorists challenge advisors, who must identify the ways a student is integrating into the campus community as assimilation relates to the student's association with ethnic and racial identity. The master advisor does not impose an identity onto the student; the student must disclose it. However, the advisor may seek additional information from the student, including that related to activities, social interactions, or interests, to understand the person's self-identity.

Adult Learning Theory

Adult learning theory marks distinct differences between approaches to learning of adults and their younger counterparts (Knowles, 1990). Although most college students are legal adults, current adult learning theories apply to nontraditional-aged students with multiple responsibilities other than student. Knowles (1990) suggested that educators of adult students can make certain assumptions: Adults may become increasingly more self-directed and use their experiences as a resource for learning; their readiness to learn depends upon their need to use the knowledge to satisfy their life roles; their motivation is internalized rather than focused on meeting external goals (such as fulfilling the wishes of a parent). Adult students tend to home in on problems instead of content. Because they want to know the reasons for phenomena, they typically do not accept knowledge or learning at face value.

For master advisors, the learning theory unique to adults translates into a shift of methods and approaches. While a traditional student might take a course because it sounds interesting, an adult may choose one that applies to a life circumstance or career concern. Advisors should acknowledge that adults expect to partner in the advising process and bring experiences and backgrounds to advising sessions in more cognizant ways than most traditional-aged students. Master advisors designing training experiences consider the way advisors model experiences that emphasize utilization of prior knowledge, allow adult students to make mistakes, and encourage exploration while receiving guidance.

Frameworks for Multicultural Interactions

While identity theories benefit educators of students, the master advisor is best served when the theories are supplemented by additional frameworks that encourage consideration of multiple characteristics of a student. For example, stereotype threat (Steele, 1997) explains the impact of preconceived bias on academic performance, and descriptions of cultural differences in communication (Pratt-Johnson, 2006) assist advisors in understanding the intricacies involved in overcoming cultural barriers.

Recognizing Stereotype Threat

Steele and Aronson (1995) defined stereotype threat as the feeling that an action may confirm a negative stereotype for a group to which the individual belongs. Steele (1997) argued that stereotype threat may keep students from reaching their highest potential levels of achievement—not because they are incapable—but because they fear failure. The individual imagines that personal failure will justify a societal belief in the stereotype. For example, a woman in advanced math or science may fear that failure to earn high grades will encourage others to view all women as deficient in math and science. In contrast, recognizing that a man's failure in a science or math class would likely be attributed to him, a woman facing stereotype threat perceives (internally and often without conscious knowledge) that her shortcomings will support the stereotype that women are incapable of succeeding in the fields of math and science. The internalized anxiety caused by stereotype threat creates further stress for students that may make them less likely to achieve in the area associated with the stereotype.

Steele (1997) argued that stereotype threat exists for high-achieving African American students struggling academically; these students may feel that failure will justify or rationalize the beliefs of those who stereotype students of color as less capable of academic success than White students. A similar, converse stereotype threat can manifest in students who do not fit a positive stereotype. For example, Asian American students who struggle in math may feel additional pressure in testing environments because they worry about failing to live up to the stereotype of an infallible minority.

Certainly underrepresented students, including Black, Hispanic, and biracial students, may feel that they represent all those who share their racial or ethnic identity, especially on the campus of a predominantly White institution. Some students may not express their anxiety, but master advisors recognize it when capable students seem to be underachieving. Students from diverse backgrounds may believe that they must demonstrate perfection in action and skill to defend against others with prejudices, but many also feel ill equipped to speak for the experience of all who share their race, ethnicity, or skin color.

New college students, as members of various groups, may face stereotype threat. For example, an underprepared community college student may fear being seen as vulnerable and therefore not ask for help. Similarly, transfer students may worry about appearing inferior to their native counterparts, and adult students may anticipate being discovered as inherently less skilled than their counterparts who have recently received formal education.

In addition, first-generation students may carry the expectations of a family who has not been successful at navigating educational environments; as a consequence, they may demonstrate fear of fulfilling an ill-fated legacy (Steele, 1997). Students with disabilities may face stereotype threat based upon fear of demonstrating a lack of intelligence or even appearing stupid. They differ from others who experience stereotype threat because most do not necessarily consider themselves as representative of all students with disabilities; nonetheless, they do not want to encourage negative stereotypes about people with disabilities.

Communicating Across Cultural Barriers

Whether working with students who represent racial, ethnic, or religious diversity or working with immigrant or international students, master advisors recognize cultural barriers, and they know that their own culture informs communication that may hinder advising progress with students from another culture. Pratt-Johnson (2006) suggested that educators require a familiarity with broad distinctions among cultures. For advisors, such awareness advances communication among people from other cultures and aids in recognizing the needs of students. Pratt-Johnson referred to five distinct ways cultures differ that affect practice: the acquisition of information, resolution to questions, nonverbal cues, learning styles, and conflict resolution.

First, the manner in which people acquire information varies by culture. For example, many Westerners learn that information is garnered through educational sources and research, but other peoples place more value on the information gathered from oral traditions, through elders, or from experiencing religious rites or spirits. Master advisors know that the emphasis upon academic knowledge may not resonate with all students in the same way.

Second, because values and beliefs differ, the manner in which questions are resolved also differs. Pratt-Johnson (2006) presented a simple but fascinating example: When presented with a life-threatening situation in which an individual can save only one among a child, parent, and spouse, members from Western cultures are inclined to save the spouse or child, valuing the relationship with the spouse or the future potential of the child; however, those of Asian descent are inclined to save the parent, believing that their relationship is irreplaceable and that they owe a parent a debt that must be, if necessary, repaid with a child's life (¶8-12). An advisor without cultural competence might push or pressure an advisee to make decisions based upon the advisor's own values, such as exertion of independence as often valued among Americans, while the advisee may pay greater deference to family than independence. For example, as Galinova and Giannetti (2014) suggested, many Chinese parents pressure their children to be successful, which weighs heavily on students; this sense of obligation is made more profound by family relationships in which respect for authority and elders is emphasized. Master advisors understand cultural values as an essential consideration when helping students with decision making.

Third, people from different cultures use nonverbal communication and symbols differently. As Rugsaken (2006) described, people offer unique hand gestures, facial expressions, and angles of the feet to suggest emotions. Smiling or making direct eye contact, for example, may be construed as signifying attentiveness or happiness among most Americans, but in other cultures, that behavior might signify a lack of appropriate respect or seriousness. Symbols of religious significance in one culture may be perceived as unimportant or offensive in another. A new advisor working with a first-year student, for example, might interpret a student with a solemn disposition as unhappy and may assume that the student has not integrated into campus life well; instead, a master advisor recognizes that the student is demonstrating the seriousness with which he or she approaches studying. Similarly, failing to understand the value or importance of a cultural symbol, an unaware advisor may dismiss a significant belief of the student. For example, an article of clothing, such as a head cover, may carry cultural or religious meaning to the student but seem a trivial fashion custom to an advisor who has yet to develop cultural competence.

Fourth, learning profoundly differs between cultures. In Western cultures, educators encourage learning from classmates and self-discovery, but teachers in other cultures expect recognition as the authority and primary holder of knowledge (Pratt-Johnson, 2006). Western institutions offer venues for students to craft their own learning opportunities and take responsibility for them. Some instructors act as a learning coach. However, students from instructor-dominated learning models may struggle, not from lack of content knowledge but because an instructor emphasizes group work or participation. In addition, an appreciation or promotion of challenges to authority runs counter to some students' learning paradigm. Master advisors recognize that students may seek wisdom from advisors and reluctantly engage in the investigation process that often undergirds a meaningful advising session.

Pratt-Johnson (2006) pointed to cultural differences in dealing with conflict. Many in the West value a direct approach in resolving disagreements, but those with other cultural lenses may view open conflict as questioning authority or as a means to embarrass another person. A master advisor working through conflict with a non-Western student—whether the disagreement involves the advisor or not—considers alternative ways of resolving the situation instead of aggressively seeking a direct resolution. A master advisor knows that a student is trying to work through issues with a faculty member or a parent and offers guidance that the advisee can embrace and execute. A student uncomfortable addressing conflict directly may nod approvingly to the advisor's suggestion and never execute the plan or act in an opposite manner. Rather than behaving defiantly, this student may be acquiescing in the presence of the advisor to avoid the appearance of challenging the advisor's authority.

International students face unique challenges dependent upon their country of origin, and any of the cultural differences presented by Pratt-Johnson (2006) may apply to them. Some students may question the sources of learning and not respect academic sources as much as their ancestral sources of wisdom. Others, particularly those who honor the opinions of elders more than their own, may struggle in negotiating American values, such as independent decision making.

Although directed with international students in mind, Pratt-Johnson's (2006) framework applies to groups whose cultural background may not comport with the major influence at the university. For example, transfer students may face challenges in their ways of learning within campus cultures; one campus may feature lectures and the teacher is considered the expert, but another may emphasize group work or student-driven research.

First-generation college students, depending upon family background, may also experience cultural dissonance in communication. For example, a student from a family that prizes wisdom handed down from generation to generation over knowledge gained in classroom settings may experience cultural challenges not unlike those faced by international students (Pratt-Johnson, 2006). In addition, some students express a limited understanding of postsecondary education. They matriculate unprepared for the complexity of learning that they encounter at the university. For example, some students expect information to be handed to them like it was in high school and not fully engage in the education process because they do not understand their role in the process. Furthermore, if the family of origin values education solely as a means of achieving high levels of income, the student may fail to see the purpose and value of general or core education; they do not necessarily see the connection between this broad education and the career or profession they hope to secure upon graduation.

Advanced Practice

When advisors better understand the many theories and approaches appropriate to assist the complex identities that students present, they consider ways to elicit from students the most salient identities for a given situation. As with the former Marine returning to school, students present unique needs at various times, and master advisors invoke the appropriate skills to guide them. Evans (2012) suggested that students continually evolve with emerging identities; that is, they do not simply present as people formed in the past. Master advisors model acceptance toward those from diverse backgrounds and assist them in integrating their multiple identities into a coherent whole.

Case Studies

Four case studies apply theoretical constructs on identity formation and evolution. Master advisors recognize that, unlike those featured in these case studies, their students come with multidimensional characteristics of race, ethnicity, age, educational experience, country of origin, and a lifetime of lived experiences that may affect the manner in which the student evaluates his or her diversity.

Case Study 1: Getting the Most From College

The Advising Interaction.   Ronaldo meets with Sienna, who arrived on campus the prior term as a transfer student from a community college. Ronaldo has known Sienna for several terms because he serves as the transfer liaison to Sienna's former institution. An excellent student, Sienna was awarded Phi Theta Kappa honors while at her community college despite a 10-year break from education after high school. She shows great promise in her first term as a pre-law student. During her community college days, Sienna had completed many of her classes online so that she could manage both her education and responsibilities with her family, including her husband of 10 years and her two small children. However, Sienna says that now that she has transferred, she wants a more comprehensive college experience.

Applying Theory.   In addition to her race and ethnicity not discussed in this study, Sienna presents as a returning adult and a transfer student. As an adult student, Sienna likely appreciates the applicability of her education, but Ronaldo may still need to explain the degree requirements as they apply to Sienna's aspirations (Knowles, 1990). In considering adult learning theory, Ronaldo treats Sienna's past experiences as valuable. Her prior learning includes time at the community college, but Ronaldo also values her experiences during her break after high school (Knowles, 1990). In addition, Ronaldo is prepared to help Sienna with any stereotype threat associated with being a transfer and an adult student (Steele, 1997). Due to internalized negative messages, Sienna may struggle in upper level course work.

Ronaldo refers Sienna to campus activities that keep her academically focused while giving her the ability to apply her education in hands-on settings or experiences. In addition, Ronaldo assists Sienna in seeing potential challenges ahead as surmountable. He recognizes that she may rely on past experiences to frame her future (Knowles, 1990), and because she has limited experience with the workload or expectations of upper level courses, Ronaldo explains ways to use her prior knowledge as a springboard for future success. Although Sienna may express concerns about being underprepared, as per stereotype threat, Ronaldo utilizes her interest in involvement to introduce her to those who disprove the stereotype so Sienna can witness their positive behaviors and related success in action.

Case Study 2: Learning a New Culture

The Advising Interaction. For the past two terms, Quentin has been advising Jiang, an international student from China. Jiang is majoring in chemistry, a field in which he obviously struggles, as shown in his poor grades from prior and current classes. When Quentin asks about his academic struggles, Jiang says, "I will try harder" and declares that he will be successful like his chemist father. When Quentin gently suggests that perhaps another major, such as psychology, in which Jiang earned a perfect GPA and received recommendations for a special project from his professor, may suit him better than chemistry, Jiang replies, "Psychology is only for fun. It would not be a good major for me." When Quentin asks if Jiang has sought assistance from a study group or in the chemistry learning labs, Jiang drops his head and replies: "I will work on remembering more of the details that the professor gives in the lecture."

Applying Theory. Jiang's reaction may reveal simple embarrassment by his poor performance, but Quentin considers the cultural context within which Jiang may evaluate his own performance. Perhaps Jiang fears failing to meet his family's expectations. Quinten understands that Jiang receives funding based on remaining a chemistry major, and he also knows the cultural implications for Jiang of leaving the field of his father and making his own path. Although independence may be valued by Westerners, many in Asian cultures place great importance on family expectations (Pratt-Johnson, 2006). Jiang may feel significant stress about disappointing his family (Galinova & Giannetti, 2014). Also, Jiang's lack of interest in seeking assistance from fellow students may represent cultural beliefs about learning; specifically, the source of knowledge is the expert, not high-achieving counterparts (Pratt-Johnson, 2006). Finally, Jiang may experience stereotype threat generated by failing to demonstrate the academic skills typically identified with his culture.

Quentin knows that Jiang will not respond to lectures about fears and expectations carried from his cultural background; instead, Quentin acknowledges that Jiang's decisions are influenced by the needs and expectations of his family, and he tells Jiang that he values the family role in decision making and asks Jiang to elaborate on their involvement in Jiang's academic choices. With this approach, Quentin provides Jiang with options for future success without negating the influence of his family. Jiang may also benefit from referrals to resources that will reinforce his cultural identity, such as an international student group, that features academic or scientific extracurricular activities, not as distractions, but as positive ways to apply learning (Galinova & Giannetti, 2014). Although these supports may not guarantee Jiang's success in chemistry, domestic resources may help him process his academic needs without denying his cultural background.

As Quentin makes these suggestions, he notes Jiang's deferent body language, but knows that it does not necessarily represent a lack of engagement. He realizes that Jiang is likely looking for Quentin to serve as an authority, prescribing action, rather than as a guide suggesting alternatives (Galinova & Giannetti, 2014). In addition, Quentin marshals other resources on campus. He calls a colleague at the campus international center to partner in sharing resources and helping Jiang negotiate his decisions with respect to his culture and his strengths.

Case Study 3: Providing Professional Guidance

The Advising Interaction.   As director of her advising unit, Aisha serves as her college's representative on the university retention team. At the monthly meeting, the group discusses a first-generation biracial freshman named Derek who resides in a living–learning community focused on supporting first-generation students and empowering students from various racial and cultural backgrounds. Several faculty members brought Derek's situation to the attention of the retention group. Apparently, Derek does not participate in class and appears withdrawn. One of the faculty members remarked, "I do not believe I have ever heard Derek say a single word in class."

Nathan, one of the newest on Aisha's staff, has been advising Derek. His notes suggest that Derek has expressed frustration with his classes, saying, "If these professors are so smart, they would teach and explain things instead of making me teach myself." Nathan noted his suggestions that Derek attend faculty office hours, but he sees no evidence that Derek has followed this advice. In contrast to Nathan's observation, the resident assistant in the living–learning community shares that Derek seems fully engaged socially. Her only concern about Derek is recorded in a note from early in the term when he responded in a "somewhat aggressive manner" when a floor mate mentioned Derek's heritage; however, when the resident assistant confronted him about this perceived negative interaction, Derek apologized and stated that he "forgot where he was for a moment." The retention group suggests that the faculty concerns be handled in an advising meeting because the primary concerns regard Derek's academic performance.

Applying Theory.   Because she uses Derek's challenges as an educational experience for Nathan, Aisha guides Nathan to consider Derek's experiences as both a first-generation and a biracial student because both characteristics seem to have manifested in Derek's college experiences to date. Aisha points to Pratt-Johnson (2006) and encourages Nathan to see Derek's possible cultural disconnect about knowledge acquisition. Nathan recognizes that neither Derek nor his parents have experience with college, and he speculates that Derek may expect information to be delivered as it was in high school. Aisha points out that Derek may also fear being discovered by others as not belonging in college, and Nathan confirms Derek's hesitancy to see his faculty members outside the classroom. When they discuss possible stereotype threat, Nathan suggests that Derek may feel that admitting the need for help will confirm that he (and his family) is not college material. Aisha reminds Nathan about the informational resources that can assist Derek, but she also recognizes that Nathan may not yet have the fully developed relational skills for appropriately referring Derek in a manner that holds him accountable or for discussing sensitive issues (Higginson, 2000). Aisha suggests that Nathan seek help from her or another seasoned advisor when confronted with difficult situations that may surface with advisees. She also discusses biracial identity development with Nathan and encourages him to evaluate Derek for signs of his needs; for example, Derek may need greater exposure to those with similar backgrounds.

Case Study 4: Identifying Wellness Issues

The Advising Interaction.   After six years in the U.S. Army, Brooks returned from active duty this past summer and in the fall immediately began classes at the local state university. Rose, the designated primary advisor for military veterans on campus, facilitates a group advising session for service personnel experiencing academic difficulty.

Brooks grew up in Rose's neighborhood and had been friendly with her sons prior to leaving home to join the military. However, Rose's delight at seeing his name on the roster turns to concern when Brooks replies to inquiries about how the first term has been going with "Fine, ma'am, just fine." As she presses him regarding any challenges he may be experiencing to determine assistance that might benefit him, Brooks agrees to every suggestion and grows combative with another veteran who seems to question Rose as an authority. At the end of the meeting, Brooks apologizes and confides that he sometimes gets "worked up," probably as a result of a diagnosis of post-traumatic stress disorder (PTSD).

Applying Theory.   Rose initially remembered Brooks as sharing much of the same neighborhood life as her sons, but she quickly realizes that his time in the military likely shifted his cultural framework for interactions. His views of authority, communication style, and the manner of perceiving and handling conflict have likely been further shaped by the cultural norms he experienced in the military (Pratt-Johnson, 2006). Rose sees that Brooks views her as an authority figure and may be hesitant to disagree with her; specifically, his view of conflict resolution may mean that he looks to her for direction rather than options. As an adult student, Brooks also likely sees education through the lens of his prior experience; however, challenges in aligning his military experience with academic course work may further complicate his pursuit of a meaningful education (Knowles, 1990). Although Rose will encourage Brooks to be self-directed (as may be most comfortable for him as an adult student with life experience), she may need to guide him more actively than adults inexperienced in the military hierarchy; that is, while recognizing his current need for an authority figure, Rose encourages Brooks to embrace his autonomy (Knowles, 1990; Pratt-Johnson, 2006).

In addition, the revelation about navigating through PTSD complicates his situation, and Rose knows that the office of disability services may offer accommodations as appropriate. In her capacity as the advisor for military veterans, Rose knows that personnel in the disabilities office effectively interface with veterans. However, on another campus the veterans' group may be isolated on campus such that students like Brooks may fear being typecast as shell-shocked by those with limited exposure to PTSD (Steele, 1997). Rose accesses her relationships with the formal veterans' organization on campus to find a peer advisor or student leader whose background mirrors that of Brooks.

Summary

Every master advisor provides high-quality guidance to every student. With the changing nature of enrollment in colleges and universities, master advisors not only identify the background of the students but also understand the ways this background influences each student's future at the institution. They also know the institutional resources available to support diversity. While the catalog and other support materials meet the informational needs for advising, master advisors demonstrate a greater level of knowledge and skill in both the conceptual and relational aspects of advising (Higginson, 2000).

Considering a student's needs, particularly with regard to issues of diversity, requires extensive knowledge and a conscious and careful sensitivity to students' development. Because students' multifaceted characteristics add to more than the sum of all their features and experiences, master advisors skillfully navigate tenuous waters and disseminate this information across campus. They serve as ambassadors and allies for the students integrating into the larger, complex campus culture.

Aiming for Excellence

o Consider the demographics of students on your campus and how stereotype threat might apply specifically to these populations. Discuss within your advising unit.

o With the staff of the center for international students, discuss the common cultures among international students. Consider how different advising approaches may apply to students from countries other than the United States.

○ Visit with a military veterans' group on campus or in the community. Discuss the experiences that they bring to the campus, and with the veterans and the team members advising veterans, discuss preconceived notions about members of the armed forces and veterans to determine the best ways to advise them.

○ Using one of the case studies from this chapter, develop a training activity for new advisors. Consider ways the unique characteristics of the campus or students (e.g., distance, commuters) might influence the interaction used or results found for the case study.

○ Consider the five questions on bias proposed in the first part of this chapter (Archambault, 2015). What additional questions might you ask to probe the needs of students from underrepresented groups? What inquiries might bring your conversation to a higher level—to move from recognition to understanding?

References

Archambault, K. L. (2015). Developing self-knowledge as a first step toward cultural competence. In P. Folsom, F. Yoder, & J. E. Joslin (Eds.), *The new advisor guidebook: Mastering the art of academic advising* (2nd ed.) (pp. 185–201). San Francisco, CA: Jossey-Bass.

Atkinson, D. R., Morten, G., & Sue, D. W. (1998). *Counseling American minorities: A cross-cultural perspective* (5th ed.). Boston, MA: McGraw-Hill.

Cross, W. E., Jr. (1971, July). The Negro-to-Black conversion experience. *Black World, 20*, 13–27.

Cross, W. E., & Fhagen-Smith, P. (2001). A life-span developmental model of racial identity. In C. J. Wijeyesinghe & B. W. Jackson (Eds.), *Reflections on racial identity development: Essays on theory, practice and discourse* (pp. 243–270). New York, NY: New York University Press.

D'Augelli, A. R. (1994). Identity development and sexual orientation: Toward a model of lesbian, gay, and bisexual development. In E. J. Trickett, R. J. Watts, & D. Birman (Eds.), *Human diversity: Perspectives on people in context* (pp. 312–333). San Francisco, CA: Jossey-Bass.

de Pree, M. (1987). *The art of leadership*. New York, NY: Doubleday.

Evans, M. (2012). *Multiple identities*. Retrieved from http://counseling.uoregon.edu/TopicsResources/ParentsFamily/HelpfulArticles/MultipleIdentities.aspx

Folsom, P., Yoder, F., & Joslin, J. E. (Eds.). (2015). *The new advisor guidebook: Mastering the art of academic advising* (2nd ed.). San Francisco, CA: Jossey-Bass.

Galinova, E., & Giannetti, I. (2014). *Advising international Chinese students: Issues, strategies, and practices*. Manhattan, KS: NACADA: The Global Community for Academic Advising.

Higginson, L. C. (2000). A framework for training program content revisited. In V. N. Gordon & W. R. Habley (Eds.), *Academic advising: A comprehensive handbook* (pp. 298–306). San Francisco, CA: Jossey-Bass. Retrieved from https://www.nacada.ksu.edu/Portals/0/Clearinghouse/documents/2000-Higginson-Informational-Components.pdf

Institute of International Education. (2014). *Fast facts: Open door report.* Retrieved from
    http://www.iie.org/~/media/Files/Corporate/Open-Doors/Fast-Facts/Fast-Facts-2014
    .ashx?la=en

Jordan, P. (2015). Effective communication skills. In P. Folsom, F. Yoder, & J. E. Joslin
    (Eds.), *The new advisor guidebook: Mastering the art of academic advising* (2nd ed.)
    (pp. 213–229). San Francisco, CA: Jossey-Bass.

Knowles, M. (1990). *The adult learner: A neglected species.* Retrieved from ERIC database.
    (ED084368)

National Center for Education Statistics (NCES). (2014). *Characteristics of postsecondary
    students.* Retrieved from http://nces.ed.gov/programs/coe/indicator_csb.asp

NCES. (2015). *Digest of education statistics: 2013.* Retrieved from http://nces.ed.gov/
    pubsearch/pubsinfo.asp?pubid=2015011

Poston, W.S.C. (1990). The biracial identity development model: A needed addition. *Journal
    of Counseling and Development, 69,* 152–155.

Pratt-Johnson, Y. (2006). Communicating cross-culturally: What teachers should know. *The
    Internet TESL Journal, XII* (2). Retrieved from http://iteslj.org/Articles/Pratt-Johnson-
    CrossCultural.html

Renn, K. A. (2008). Research on biracial and multiracial identity development: Overview and
    synthesis. *New Directions for Student Services, 2008*(123), 13–21.

Root, M. P. P. (1990). Resolving "other" status: Identity development of biracial individuals.
    Women and Therapy, 9, 185–205.

Rugsaken, K. (2006). *Body speaks: Body language around the world.* Retrieved from http://
    www.nacada.ksu.edu/Resources/Clearinghouse/View-Articles/body-speaks.aspx

Steele, C. M. (1997). A threat in the air: How stereotypes shape intellectual identity and
    performance. *American Psychologist, 52*(6), 613–629.

Steele, C. M., & Aronson, J. (1995). Stereotype threat and the intellectual test performance of
    African-Americans. *Journal of Personality and Social Psychology, 69,* 797–811.

Torres, V., Howard-Hamilton, M. F., & Cooper, D. L. (2003). *Identity development of diverse
    populations: Implications for teaching and administration in higher education* (ASHE-
    ERIC Higher Education Report 29, No. 6). Retrieved from http://spot.pcc
    .edu/~rsuarez/rbs/school/EPFA%20520/Identity%20development.pdf

7

ADVANCED ADVISING PRACTICE

BECOMING A MASTER ADVISOR

Marc Lowenstein and Jennifer L. Bloom

The master has failed more times than the beginner has ever tried.

—Stephen McCranie (2015)

Master advisors are not distinguished by the length of time they have worked in the field but by the way they perceive and approach their work. They do not see themselves as cooks following step-by-step recipes to complete a job, but as master chefs who rely on experience, wisdom, and creativity along with lifelong learning to experiment, take risks, and explore. This perspective informs their work with students, their manner of addressing the ethical challenges that arise, their approach to inevitable adversity, and their career paths. Having enjoyed the rewards of advanced advising practice, they seek to model it for peers and students.

Reader Learning Outcomes

From studying this chapter, advisors will use knowledge gained about becoming a master advisor to

o identify best practices that distinguish an employee who advises from a master of the craft,

o explain ways that commitment to lifelong learning contributes to development of master advisors,

o describe the creative approaches to ethical challenges that distinguish master advisors from a person merely following a set of instructions,

o apply the nine principles for ethical decision making to case studies and daily advising practice,

o reframe adversity to delineate options for handling perceived threats and challenges, and

o understand the importance of modeling best practices to colleagues and students.

What distinguishes advanced advising practice? What differentiates a master from an emerging advisor? To answer these questions, we compare the differences between emerging and master advisors to the differences between a short-order cook and an accomplished chef. The short-order cook carefully follows a recipe card written by someone else while the master chef takes risks and relies on experience, improvisation, and ingenuity to create bold masterpieces from ordinary ingredients. Similarly, emerging advisors follow defined steps and use proven elements to guide their work with students, whereas advanced master advisors find their greatest rewards in unscripted innovation. Exciting and rewarding ventures in life are typically achieved through exploration and risk taking, and recipe followers may not take advantage of such opportunities.

Although advisors must follow rules or recipes often, master advisors use their creativity and expertise to evoke the best in each of their students and handle with agility problems as they arise. Master advisors see their work as too complex to fit on a recipe card, and they facilitate students' intellectual growth by engaging them in meaningful conversations about their life, career, and educational goals. They help students discover the connections between their learning in and out of class and challenge their assumptions about the connection between majors and careers. Although most advisors engage students this way, master advisors see these higher order discussions as central to the purpose of their work.

Chefs and master advisors are artists—and like all artists—they sometimes fail to create a masterpiece. Although they bring a great deal of judgment and wisdom to bear, they often traverse unexplored territory and take risks. A cook will not become a chef simply by following recipes, and similarly an advisor will not become a master advisor without learning, growing, and experimenting. Although it is tempting to think that a recipe can be followed, and voilà, a master advisor emerges, an advisor must receive some basic ingredients and a bit of inspiration before donning a chef's hat and creating an amazing career. We assert that the fundamental elements for becoming a master advisor include a commitment to lifelong learning, an alertness to ethical issues and the possible ways to address them, the use of strategies for creatively addressing adversity when it arises, and the consistent modeling of all of these characteristics to students and colleagues.

Committing to Lifelong Learning

Socrates made the point, "The more you know, the more you realize you know nothing." Master advisors recognize the need to continue learning throughout their careers. All advisors demonstrate knowledge regarding such matters as institutional policies and curricula, but once they have acquired and applied such knowledge, master advisors can turn their attention to continuing their own intellectual growth.

Why Do Master Advisors Pursue Lifelong Learning?

Master advisors must commit to being lifelong learners to accommodate change. Because students quickly adapt technology to communicate with others, changes created by technological advances may particularly challenge advisors (chapter 16). In addition, changing administrative information technology systems that institutions adopt can challenge (and frustrate) master advisors who had been comfortable using previous systems. However, advising administrators advocating for change will expect all advisors to adapt to changes, so efforts to learn and overcome challenges of technology do not distinguish master advisors from emerging advisors.

Master advisors deal with change both at the institution and in higher education. Due to current and impending economic, social, and political forces from outside academe, many institutional stakeholders must reconsider and change academic missions, administrative structures, or priorities. Advisors primarily focused on their day-to-day duties may be oblivious to changes within higher education, but master advisors know that these developments may affect their work and may create both threats and opportunities for their units. Not the least of these, changes in the forces acting on new generations of students affect their motivations, responses to educational inputs, and levels of engagement as well as their readiness to learn. Master advisors stay abreast of these developments and carefully consider their possible impact.

Master advisors do not see themselves—nor expect others at their institutions to see them—as administrative support personnel whose primary role culminates in student registration and graduation as per their educational plans; rather, they aspire to be involved and heard when matters of academic policy, curriculum, graduation requirements, and student success are discussed. Keeping informed about trends and issues positions them to earn the attention and respect of administrators and faculty members; therefore, as faculty members must engage as lifelong learners to retain the respect of colleagues and institutional leadership, so must master advisors.

Master advisors always show intellectual curiosity. They realize that they do not know the source of the next interesting idea. They take responsibility for finding or creating the relevance of the groundbreaking ideas they encounter to their advising practice.

In fact, master advisors realize that students provide a key, if unrecognized, source of daily knowledge. Few on campus have a better pulse on the life of the campus than academic advisors. This knowledge can be extremely valuable to upper level administrators seeking to increase student success. Master advisors remain open to learning from and being inspired by students' stories and experiences.

What Do Master Advisors Seek to Learn?

Master advisors seek to learn about matters that range from specific, concrete information to general, abstract ideas. Particularly when learning about practical matters, master advisors keep abreast of important trends and issues both inside and outside higher education. When addressing transcendent issues, master advisors take part in the ongoing discussion of the theory and philosophy of advising. They know that theoretical issues lead to practical consequences; that is, an advisor's ideas about the purpose of advising will affect his or her practice and organization, assessment, and evaluation. Master advisors use a well-articulated philosophy of advising to make a case to administrators about the importance of advising. They also show interest in issues about the purposes of higher education, in general, and the role that good advising can play in ensuring that academe meets purported goals.

Master advisors also keep informed about developments in other student-focused functional areas (e.g., financial aid, student conduct) at educational institutions (including the K-12 sector that prepares students for college); public policy changes; and changes in the local, national, and world economies. Master advisors seek new ideas about time management as well as communication and learning theories.

How Do Master Advisors Engage in Lifelong Learning?

The commitment of master advisors to continuous learning permits them to swiftly assimilate, evaluate, and place into context new information. It also helps them create their own personal learning infrastructure, which we call the *framework* master advisors use to structure their practice. This framework includes ethical ideals and principles, values, theories, key words and concepts, analytical and critical thinking skills, and habits. Master advisors continuously question the veracity of the information they encounter and actively dig beneath the surface of readings to connect the ideas in an article to their students, institutions, or careers.

A personal learning infrastructure is constructed over time and with contributions from many sources. For usefulness, it must provide a modicum of stability, but continual change demands that master advisors remain flexible and responsive as they update and revise their knowledge and their fundamental ideas. Sometimes a novel event or new information is so startling that it necessitates reconsideration of cherished beliefs. Master advisors know cataclysms happen. Flexibility comes from a lifelong commitment to learning.

Where Do Master Advisors Pursue Lifelong Learning?

Master advisors are familiar not only with the most recent advising resources but also some of the classic articles and books that have helped inform the advising field. However, to see their work in full context and to act as effective advocates for advising on campus, master advisors must not only keep up with the advising literature but must also pay attention to the broader educational issues of interest to faculty leaders and top administrators; therefore, they seek to read about important issues of the times: "Scholar-practitioners read what their well-informed colleagues, provosts, and presidents read" (Bloom & Lowenstein, 2013, p. 2).

Information and ideas on higher education topics appear in books, periodicals, newspapers, and other print and online media sources, including *The Chronicle of Higher Education*, *Inside Higher Education*, and *Change*. Master advisors not only read but they also join reading groups online or in-person where members reflect on the impact of their reading on their lives and careers.

Master advisors attend and engage in professional development sessions and conference presentations. In addition, they regularly seek to present their work at conferences and in written articles. Whether their work is accepted for presentation or publication, master advisors know that articulating and defending their ideas with precision and cogency, as required for conference proposals and article submissions, encourages them to think critically on the subject matter. The feedback on their published or presented work provides a valuable stimulus for further thought, improvement, and learning.

Barriers to Lifelong Learning

The quest to become a lifelong learner is both rewarding and daunting. Some may point to time constraints as the biggest barrier to staying abreast of current events and emerging literature. Many advisors shoulder heavy workloads that may discourage them from becoming engaged learners. However, in general, people make time for activities and ideas important to them. Master advisors consider learning important enough to make time for it. Additionally, when the hectic workday prohibits time to read and learn, advisors can spend free time away from the office or use breaks between appointments to read, reflect, and write.

Fear places another formidable barrier to lifelong learning. An advisor may feel intimidated by the idea of serving as an authority on a topic. Advisors may feel anxious about failing to assimilate the magnitude of available information and may dread potential rejection of submitted conference presentation abstracts or articles for publication. Master advisors may also grapple with these real, understandable fears. Although no magical solution can banish the angst, advisors who acknowledge it can keep focused on the benefits of lifelong learning. In the face of fear, some may cite lack of time or make other excuses for reluctance to engage in learning. An advisor who perseveres will ultimately find sufficient rewards to counter any frustrations and disappointments, thus reducing the fear of failure over time.

In this chapter, we argue for advisor commitment to lifelong learning. For a fuller and more specific exploration, including concrete strategies for implementation, see chapter 13.

Approaching Ethical Dilemmas

At any level of experience, advisors want to conduct themselves in an ethical manner. Master advisors deliberate ethical problems in a more complex way than demonstrated by emerging practitioners.

Most people think systematically about ethics when they experience problematic or troubling encounters. They may experience some variation of the following situations:

- They witness a behavior or dialogue that seems inappropriate, but have difficulty articulating the exact nature of the problem. For example, an advisor overhears a colleague telling a student to avoid taking a course from a particular professor. The advisor feels uncomfortable with this recommendation, but cannot cite with certainty any general rule of ethics being violated.

o They sense a strain between their ideas about right and wrong and their own self-interest. For example, an athletics advisor knows that student-athletes are enrolled in fictitious classes but fears that reporting this practice to administration could result in dismissal from the job.

o They are puzzled because two values or ideals to which they feel committed seem to conflict with one another. For example, an advisor experiences a conflict when an institutional imperative to facilitate student retention and expeditious progress toward graduation is pitted against a student's legitimate need to take a lighter load or stop out for a time.

People who wish to act ethically typically access resources, such as religious beliefs or the views of a favorite author, to help guide them. Specifically, advisors may look to The Statement of Core Values of Academic Advising (NACADA: The Global Community for Academic Advising, 2005).

In this chapter, we focus less on the sources advisors should use for ethical decisions and more on ways they use those sources. The most important point is that no set of rules, codes, or values can be used to resolve the most difficult ethical dilemmas that experienced advisors face. Just as master advisors cannot follow a simple recipe for dealing with every student situation, they also cannot practice cookbook ethics.

Important values such as honesty, promise keeping, fairness, helpfulness, and respect should characterize advisors' interactions, but they do not yield a recipe for solving ethical problems because they often stand in conflict with each other. One can imagine scenarios—in advising or other endeavor—in which keeping a promise to one person may require withholding some information from another.

To help advisors reflect on their own process for dealing with ethical issues, Lowenstein (2008) posited nine principles to help advisors consider the most appropriate course of action:

1. Seek to enhance the student's learning whenever possible.
2. Treat students equitably.
3. Enhance the student's ability to make autonomous decisions.
4. Advocate for the student.
5. Tell the truth (to advisees and to others).
6. Respect the confidentiality of communication with the student.
7. Support the institution's educational philosophy and policies.
8. Maintain the credibility of the advising program.
9. Accord colleagues appropriate professional courtesy and respect. (pp. 41–43)

These ideas do not represent formal ethical statements advocated by any agency, and advisors may find them deficient and prefer different formulations. However, they serve as starting points for advisors' own thinking. Master advisors will develop their own personal views of ethical advising. They find that whatever principles they adopt or create cannot resolve all the problems encountered or answer all the questions posed; that is, they will need to learn the art of ethical problem solving. This art consists of balancing one principle against another in cases in which principles seem to conflict and finding a course of action that does the least harm to the advisor's beliefs. Often this is not an easy task.

Case Study: Conflicting Ethical Principles

Advisor Kai tries to follow Lowenstein's (2008) nine principles of ethical behavior but faces a challenge when advisee Taylor comes to the pre-graduation advising appointment in a panic. Taylor claims, "I just found out I need a math course to graduate this spring! I completely forgot to take it!" Kai suspects that Taylor intentionally avoided this general education requirement; in fact, Taylor seems to have chosen an English major partly to avoid as much math as possible. Regardless of the cause of the error, students cannot take the class or arrange independent study this late in the semester. This reality does not upset Kai, who thinks such avoidance stratagems are fraudulent because they do not promote student learning (Principle 1).

Taylor asks to submit an appeal for an exception to the degree requirement. Kai knows that Taylor has the right to submit an appeal, and moreover, the dean who adjudicates such appeals dislikes the math requirement and recently granted a similar appeal from another student, Armani. What should Kai do?

Case Study: Response

Kai feels obligated to answer Taylor's question truthfully (Principle 5) and embraces the role of advocate (Principle 4), but also recognizes that the decision to appeal lies with Taylor alone (Principle 3). Furthermore, Kai questions the fairness of the situation: "What about treating students equitably? If Armani escaped the requirement," Kai honestly admits, "Taylor should be able to submit an appeal as well."

Kai has difficulty with the appeal but sees both sides of this situation. On one hand, should Taylor face an unfair disadvantage when Armani did not? On the other hand, hundreds of students meet the requirement every year, even if they are just as reluctant as Taylor to take the class. Kai wants to be equitable, but thinks it may be more important to be fair to the majority of students required to complete the math course than to Armani.

Believing that Taylor would benefit from learning more math (and from bolstered confidence in completing the class), Kai sees particular relevance in Lowenstein's (2008) Principles 1 and 7, believing that Taylor would benefit from learning more math and that advisors have a duty to support institutional policy, even the one that Taylor wants to avoid.

No recipe or sure-fire algorithm exists for resolving this conflict of principles. Instead, Kai must find a compromise that violates as few closely held principles as possible, and that cannot be done by simply adding up the number of principles that represent the pros and cons of Taylor's request, because they do not necessarily carry equal weight in this situation. A strategy of using thought experiments to examine the dilemma in a new way is particularly helpful to advisors in Kai's situation. Specifically, in re-creating the situation, Kai gives it a twist so that it can be seen in a new light.

For example, Kai thinks about a circumstance in which most students avoid this requirement but that in a way Principle 2 (equity) means less injustice in Taylor's escape from the requirement. Comparing the hypothetical situation to the one Taylor presents helps confirm Kai's view that equity is a powerful consideration in this case. In another re-creation strategy, Kai considers a situation in which, notwithstanding Taylor's reluctance to take the math course, Taylor had demonstrated strong quantitative aptitude on standardized tests and had done well in math in high school. With this awareness of Taylor's past performance, perhaps Kai would feel less concern about the application of Principle 1, maximizing learning. Comparing the hypothetical to the actual situation confirms the importance of the learning principle. In another twist, Kai supposes that the dean, who will receive the appeal, is not so accommodating to such appeals. In that case, a meritless appeal from Kai's advisee might hurt the reputation of Kai's advising center; however, because the facts of the hypothetical and actual cases differ, Kai disregards Principle 8 as an important consideration in Taylor's case.

Wisdom, as demonstrated in Kai's situation, as in many other areas of life, lies in appreciating that the more important the problem, the less likely a perfect solution can be identified. Master advisors have learned that they cannot be 100% satisfied with the resolution to every problem, and they do not feel that imperfect resolutions reflect inadequate thinking; rather they accept such outcomes as inherent in their work. Thus the master advisor's approach to ethical advising will include not only guiding principles but also acknowledgment of the limitations of these principles and the strategies for resolving the dilemmas that inevitably arise. However, the more she or he exercises those strategies, the more skilled the master advisor becomes.

Facing Adversity

Being learning-committed, creative, and ethically sophisticated does not make the master advisor immune to adversity. The very practice of taking risks may lead to unsuccessful plans and projects. Moreover, even the advisor who prefers to follow recipes will not completely avoid difficulties because he or she deals with problems created by others. Complications may arise from unanticipated changes in institutions or units, such as from newly hired supervisors or colleagues with poor communication skills, revised organizational models, increased workloads, or altered assigned duties.

Sometimes advisors can use straightforward methods or recipes for addressing their own problems (e.g., a personnel grievance procedure), but more often they need to use improvisation and creativity. In the latter case, master advisors have an advantage because they know how to seek resources and are comfortable with creating unscripted ways of handling unexpected situations.

The Power of Reframing

We have found that intentional reframing of the adverse situation—that is, looking at it through a different lens—changes our perspective and opens up possibilities for resolution. Advisors can choose to perceive an adverse situation as a burden in which they are helpless to improve their circumstances created and controlled by others. However, master advisors actively seek to frame adversity as a blessing that offers opportunities to increase their own self-confidence and agency. Seeing problems as blessings with the potential for agency empowers master advisors.

An insight from existentialist philosophy (Sartre, 1957) reinforces the reframing approach. If people take seriously the implications of free will, they see that they are responsible for their reactions to each situation whether they created it or not. Thus, if advisors work within an environment where the rules are restrictive, they must not hide behind these rules by saying "This is the way it must be" and deny culpability. Rather, those who choose to enforce the rules must own the responsibility for the outcomes.

Moreover, the existentialist philosophy applies to advisors' careers: If advisors settle into roles that they find neither challenging nor empowering and if they are bored and uninspired, then they have freely chosen not to seek other channels through which they can gain stimulation and growth. Sartre (1957) insisted that the responsibility for making one's career and one's life rewarding belongs to oneself.

Nine Questions That Address Adversity

When human beings feel threatened, they go into fight-or-flight mode. To let the adrenaline dissipate and broaden one's thinking about the options for handling the perceived threatening situation, advisors can address the following questions:

- Knowing that everyone faces adversity and learns a great deal from proactively handling challenges, how could I reframe this current painful situation as the best thing that has ever happened to me?
- What lessons am I supposed to learn from handling this issue?
- If I knew I could not fail, how would I handle the situation?
- If I were at my best, how would I handle the situation?
- How can I handle the situation so that all parties can walk away from it with their dignity intact?
- What are three options for dealing with this situation?

o What is one small action I can take right now to make the situation better?

o What resources can I access to help me address the situation?

o What obstacles might I encounter when trying to improve this situation and what strategies could I employ if I encounter one of these obstacles?

Our hope is that by answering these questions, master advisors create a new recipe for addressing the challenge they are facing.

Modeling for Others

In this chapter, we characterize master advisors as lifelong learners who are alert to ethical issues and prepared to create new recipes for handling ethical issues and other problems that arise. True master advisors do not stop at problem solving. Confident in their ability to exemplify traits consistent with their abilities, knowledge, and experience, master advisors seek to model qualities of lifelong learning for both their colleagues and their students.

Modeling for Colleagues

Master advisors lead the way for others in the workplace by inviting colleagues to join a new book club, sharing new ideas, and asking for feedback on drafts of papers and conference proposal abstracts (and offering to reciprocate). When they meet with colleagues either formally or informally, master advisors take the lead in promoting innovative thinking about students' circumstances and continuously look for creative solutions. They also help others think about ways to approach ethical dilemmas that arise in the institution, department, or unit. When groups of advisors meet to commiserate about their helplessness to solve problems in their work and careers, master advisors encourage them to see conflicts as opportunities for creative agency.

Modeling for Students

Master advisors fully realize that students watch them carefully and they recognize the positional power they hold. They bear this responsibility gladly and seek to be good role models for students by sharing with them the latest literature on student success. They freely express that they care about students and share their commitment to helping students succeed.

Master advisors seek to challenge and support students in their endeavors (Sanford, 1966). Some students arrive at college focused on the instrumental value of a degree as a means of getting a job. Unless their career goal requires a graduate degree, these students expect their education to end on graduation day. Master advisors can challenge these advisees to become lifelong learners and demonstrate their proactive efforts to increase their own knowledge.

Students, especially those in their first year, demonstrate a preference for recipes. They may be at a developmental stage in which they believe a single right answer satisfies every question and that good grades are the reward for providing it (Perry, 1970). For example, they may believe that one, and only one, major matches perfectly with every career goal. Students who see the academic world this way may demonstrate risk-aversive behavior when choosing a major and show reluctance in exploring educational choices.

Master advisors look for opportunities to gently and carefully question the assumptions of these students. They recognize that the students must overcome a difficult developmental step. Instead of arguing, they share career-related stories of other graduates (or related to their own careers) to encourage students to consider new educational possibilities.

Opportunities to model ethical reasoning will arise as master advisors resolve issues with students. For example, when Taylor sought to appeal a math class requirement, Kai walked through the steps of the decision, sharing reflections on the values at stake and encouraging Taylor to ask provocative questions that encouraged thoughtful consideration about the comparative weight of each. The personal opinion of the advisor, Kai, was neither shared nor imposed.

In a previous publication, one of us (Lowenstein, 2008) suggested that an advisor (such as Kai) inform an advisee in Taylor's circumstance of the possibility of appeal, because despite the advisor's feelings about it, omission of the fact constitutes a lie. However, the advisor can use the information to encourage the advisee to investigate the implications of the potential choices. In this case, Kai points out the reasons for the math requirement and directs a frank exploration of Taylor's reason for avoiding the course. Kai also asks, "Have you considered that you may need those math skills someday in a way you can't envision now?" Such a conversation may not persuade Taylor to forgo the appeal, a decision that Kai cannot control, but Taylor will have received some educational benefit from the conversation, including some insight into ways to make well-reasoned autonomous decisions, and Kai will have fulfilled the ethical obligations imposed by the situation.

Students often come to visit their advisors for suggestions on handling a problem. These meetings offer excellent opportunities to coach on the reframing process; that is, advisors can show students to find blessing instead of burden and agency instead of helplessness. Advisors may ask students some of the nine questions they use to confront adversity.

Case Study: Modeling Decision Processes

Morgan, a master advisor, greets a distressed undergraduate advisee, Dallas, who wants to switch research labs. "Dr. Jones's lab is more aligned with my research interests than the lab I'm in now, but I don't want my current professor to be mad and maybe give me a bad recommendation later on." Instead of simply telling Dallas the best way to approach the situation, Morgan suggests, "Can you name three options for dealing with this situation?" Dallas pauses for a moment and then replies, "One, I could send my current professor an e-mail explaining my decision to change labs. Two, I could just quit my position and then later join the other lab. Or three, I could sit down with my current professor in person and explain why I want to switch labs." Sensing Dallas already knows the best option, Morgan presses, "If you were handling this as professionally as you could and you were at your absolute best, which of these options would you select?" Dallas looks down and sheepishly says, "I would do option number three and sit down with my professor." Morgan probes further, "Which option do you think would allow both you and your professor to walk away from the situation with both of your dignities intact?" Dallas again answers, with a little more confidence, "Option number three." The advisor replies, "Well, it sounds like you have your answer, and, by the way, I completely agree with it."

Morgan does not stop with encouraging words, but continues to model the behavior and build Dallas's confidence: "Now, let's now role play the conversation so that you can feel prepared and confident going into the conversation. I'll play the role of the professor. The first thing you will want to do is to thank the professor for all the time and effort invested in you. Point out three specific things you have learned while in the lab. Then you can explain the reason you would like to seek this new opportunity." This case study demonstrates the way a master advisor, by asking appropriate questions, can give students the opportunity to reflect and make their own decisions.

Summary

In this chapter, we made a case for comparing master advisors to chefs. Master advisors are lifelong learners who wrestle thoughtfully with ethical problems and seek to devise creative solutions to the challenges that arise. Master advisors display creativity in life and work by approaching both in ways that involve more than simple formulas or recipes. They model for colleagues and students autonomy, success, and ethical professionalism. Master advisors exercise leadership within their advising units and institutions by thinking in creative ways about old and new issues and by showing the courage to suggest new approaches.

Aiming for Excellence

o We used the analogy of short-order cooks and chefs to explain the differences between emerging and master advisors. Create another metaphor that distinguishes emerging advisors from master advisors.

o How do you demonstrate your commitment to lifelong learning? What does being a lifelong learner mean to you? When can you set aside time for reading, thinking, and writing? What obstacles have you encountered, and how have you dealt with them?

o Identify colleagues with whom you might form a reading group.

o What topics are you considering for your next presentation?

o Assume your manuscript will be accepted for publication in a leading journal. What is your topic for the article?

o What have you learned from students in the past six months? Have you shared this information with your supervisors? What does the provost need to know about the experiences students describe?

o Of Lowenstein's (2008) nine principles for dealing with ethical issues, which do you find the most helpful when facing ethical challenges? Can you recall situations in which one or more of these principles may apply? Can you envision circumstances in which you would not want to follow one of these principles?

o Have you experienced a situation—at work or elsewhere—in which your personal beliefs seemed to conflict with each other? How did you handle it?

o Identify a challenge that you are facing and answer the nine questions posited in the chapter for dealing with adversity. Did addressing those questions help you reframe the challenge?

o What single characteristic that you model do you hope your colleagues will most appreciate?

o What characteristic that you model do you hope your students will follow from your lead?

References

Bloom, J. L., & Lowenstein, M. (2013). Embracing lifelong learning for ourselves. *About Campus, 17*(6), 2–10.

Lowenstein, M. (2008). Ethical foundations of academic advising. In V. N. Gordon, W. R. Habley, & T. J. Grites (Eds.), *Academic advising: A comprehensive handbook* (2nd ed.) (pp. 36–49). San Francisco, CA: Jossey-Bass.

McCranie, S. (2015). [*Quote*]. Retrieved from http://www.goodreads.com/author/quotes/4577067.Stephen_McCranie

NACADA: The Global Community for Academic Advising. (2005). *NACADA statement of core values of academic advising.* Retrieved from http://www.nacada.ksu.edu/Resources/Clearinghouse/View-Articles/Core-values-of-academic-advising.aspx

Perry, W., Jr. (1970). *Intellectual and ethical development in the college years.* New York, NY: Holt, Rinehart, and Winston.

Sanford, N. (1966). *Self and society: Social change and individual development.* New York, NY: Atherton.

Sartre, J. P. (1957). *Existentialism and human emotions.* New York, NY: The Philosophical Library.

8

ADVANCED LEGAL ISSUES AND THE MASTER ADVISOR

Matthew M. Rust

Just a few decades ago, colleges and universities were essentially unregulated entities. Their independence, and that of their faculty, was itself a hallmark of the academic enterprise. But in the intervening years, academic institutions have begun to accept millions in federal funds in the form of student financial aid, research grants, Medicare, Medicaid, and direct appropriations. The potential for administrative, faculty, and student negligence, and misconduct in the use of those funds and interactions with students has now become plenary.

—Nathan A. Adams IV (2015, p. 2)

Academic advisors regularly interact with confidential information, maintain trusting relationships with students, and communicate complex academic requirements. Each of these functions has legal implications from various sources of law. Based on short overviews of the law and advanced case studies, this chapter enables the master advisor to understand and apply the complex bodies of jurisprudence that govern academic advising and anticipate the situations and approaches for consulting institutional counsel.

Reader Learning Outcomes

From studying this chapter, advisors will use knowledge gained about legal issues to

- o distinguish between federal law, state law, and institutional policies relevant to academic advising;
- o apply laws and policies to case studies that illustrate the nuanced legal relationships among students, advisors, and the institution of higher education; and
- o anticipate emerging legal issues relevant to academic advising, particularly as they relate to ubiquitous technology and increased legislative scrutiny of higher education.

Master advisors approach the legal issues affecting their advising practice in an informed and sophisticated manner. Marc Lowenstein and Jennifer Bloom's distinctions of advanced advising practice (chapter 7) are paraphrased as follows: The master advisor approaches legal issues in academic advising by (a) recognizing the complexity of legal issues and that legal compliance in academic advising involves more than following simple, static formulas of legal principles; (b) modeling for colleagues the balance of autonomy and consultation with legal counsel to practice advising in a professional, legally compliant manner; and (c) exercising leadership within the unit and institution by proactively monitoring changes in the legal landscape and consulting with legal counsel to update advising policies and procedures as appropriate.

In this chapter, I present advanced-level case studies and discussions in the three broad areas of legal issues in advising as previously discussed in *The New Advisor Guidebook: Mastering the Art of Academic Advising* (Rust, 2015). Specifically, this briefly summarizes and then encourages readers to explore the following areas through case studies: (a) privacy of student information, (b) liabilities created by advisors as agents of the institution, and (c) equal rights and due process for students. This chapter does not provide legal advice for any specific situations; instead it promotes knowledge of general legal principles and applications from which the master advisor continues to build understanding through consultation with institutional administrators or legal counsel.

Confidentiality and Privacy of Student Information

The master advisor recognizes the important role confidentiality plays both in building rapport in the advising relationship and maintaining legal compliance in advising practice. Confidentiality of student information is governed in part by the Family Educational Rights and Privacy Act (FERPA) (1974), an important source of law for academic advising. However, the master advisor does not make the common mistake of assuming that FERPA is the only source—or the most important source—of law governing confidentiality and privacy of student information in advising. FERPA, state privacy laws, and institutional policies all contribute to the landscape that advisors need to negotiate.

Family Educational Rights and Privacy Act

FERPA, a federal funding statute, predicates receipt of federal funding dollars (e.g., for research or student financial aid) on institutional compliance with the privacy protections mandated. FERPA does not require the maintenance of student records, nor does it ever mandate disclosure of student records. Under FERPA, institutions that choose to maintain student records must provide students access to inspect and request to amend their records. Furthermore, no one in the institution may disclose the personally identifiable information contained in those education records except under the circumstances in which FERPA, the legislation, or FERPA regulations, as implemented in institutions per the U.S. Department of Education, permits disclosure.

FERPA and the implemented FERPA regulations have received significant updates in recent years such that a general trend toward greater permissibility of disclosures has emerged. However, the potential permissiveness has been counteracted by the trend toward stricter protection of personal information by evolving state privacy laws.

Education Records. FERPA only applies to the personally identifiable information contained within the student education records maintained by institutions receiving federal funds. The protections of FERPA apply to these education records as soon as the student is considered "in attendance" at the institution, a date that institutions may set to be after the point of admission and no later than the first day the student begins classes at the institution (34 C.F.R. §99.3, 2011; Rooker & Falkner, 2013). As a general rule, FERPA protects the disclosure of personally identifiable information contained in student education records, except for directory information (contact information, dates of attendance, academic major, class standing, etc.), which may be disclosed unless the student has requested that such data be kept confidential (Campbell, Cieplak, & Rodriguez, 2012).

Case Study 1: Protected and Unprotected Data. Tanesha, an academic advisor at a large state university, welcomes a new advisee, Dakota, upon arrival for an appointment. Tanesha opens the meeting with, "How are classes going?" Dakota responds, "I'm doing well, except in English 101," a first-year composition course, and explains, "I received a C and a D on the first two papers." Tanesha realizes that these two grades will account for 50% of Dakota's final grade in the course and logs into the online student information system using her staff user ID and password (which all faculty, staff, and students must use to enter the system) to determine the effect on Dakota's projected GPA. Tanesha needs Dakota's student identification number to find and load her transcript. After noting Dakota's current GPA as listed in her educational record, Tanesha helps Dakota calculate the impact of a low grade in English.

Tanesha now has three pieces of information about Dakota: (a) Dakota is performing poorly in English and has a projected GPA of 2.80; (b) Tanesha has Dakota's student identification number; and (c) Tanesha has Dakota's GPA. At this point in the conversation, Tanesha needs to know which of the three pieces of information are protected from disclosure by FERPA.

Case Study 1: Response. Only the GPA is clearly protected by FERPA. Dakota told Tanesha about the poor English grades; that is, Tanesha did not learn about it from an education record (Family Policy Compliance Office, 2006). Because FERPA only applies to information contained in education records, the undocumented discussion between advisor and advisee is not protected by FERPA. Dakota's student identification number, even if Tanesha had learned of it from education records, may not be protected from disclosure under FERPA. In the 2012 FERPA regulation updates, student identification numbers were listed as directory information such that they could be disclosed under FERPA in situations where the number alone does not lead to protected student information; in this case, records can only be accessed with a user ID and password used in combination. Furthermore, Dakota had not requested to keep her directory information unpublished, so it is not protected under FERPA in this scenario.

This case study illustrates two important points. First, advising involves the exchange of information that—though not necessarily protected by FERPA—should still remain confidential. Tanesha's rapport with Dakota would be compromised if Dakota's poor performance in English had been shared with others. In addition, policies or state privacy laws may prohibit the disclosure of the information Tanesha learns from conversations or directory information.

Second, conversations between advisors and advisees are not legally confidential like the privileged conversations between attorneys and clients or doctors and patients (Tribbensee, 2008). The master advisor recognizes the limits of FERPA, but keeps conversations confidential for ethical reasons and to follow best practices.

However, the standard regarding oral communications differs for academic advisors who hold professional licenses (e.g., in counseling, law, or medicine), which may impose stricter confidentiality requirements than does FERPA. Where conflicting requirements exist, the advisor with a professional license should work with administrators and legal counsel to resolve any conflict. Furthermore, advisors must clarify for students the confidentiality obligations associated with a professional license if the advisor–advisee relationship extends into areas covered by licensure, such as legal advice or mental health counseling.

Disclosures.   Advisors are most likely to disclose FERPA-protected information under four circumstances. Specifically, disclosure is typically granted when a student gives consent, a student's tax dependent status is verified, an education official has a legitimate educational interest in the information, and a health or safety emergency is reported.

Consent-Based Disclosure.   Under typical circumstances, students agree to the release of their information to parents or other trusted friends and family through a consent form, which must be written, signed, and dated. The form should specify the purpose of the disclosure, the records that may be disclosed, and the persons to whom disclosures may be made (Campbell et al., 2012). Advisors contacted for the release of information to a third party must utilize reasonable methods to authenticate the identity of the requester party, a requirement that was clarified in the 2008 regulatory updates.

Disclosures Based on Tax-Dependent Status.   FERPA allows disclosure of a student's protected information to a parent if the student qualifies as a dependent as defined in section 152 of the Internal Revenue Code (26 U.S. § 152). Many employees in institutional registrar's offices receive training on accepting and examining tax documents to determine a student's tax-dependent status. Although disclosure is allowed, it is not mandatory. FERPA clarifies situations in which disclosures are permissible; it never mandates disclosure.

Case Study 2: Tax-Dependent Status. Diego receives a call from Jim, the father of an advisee, John, who asks Diego to confirm John's current GPA as 3.80. Diego does not have a signed consent form on file that allows him to disclose John's protected information. Jim insists that he has a right to the information because John is a minor. Indeed, John's record indicates an age of 17 years, but Diego is not comfortable disclosing on the basis of the age alone. Diego asks if Jim claims John as a tax dependent, and the father answers, "Yes, and I'm scanning and e-mailing the tax forms to you as we speak." Diego receives the scanned tax forms, notes that John is listed as a tax dependent, and then discloses John's GPA to Jim. Has Diego violated FERPA?

Case Study 2: Response. Diego has not violated FERPA in this instance, but he may have violated an institutional policy. Diego was correct in choosing not to disclose simply on the basis of John's status as a minor. The protections afforded by FERPA transfer from the parent to the student once he or she is in attendance at an institution of higher education, regardless of age; therefore, John's status as a minor is irrelevant under FERPA. Diego also correctly chose to disclose the education record information to the parent based on the tax-dependent status; however, FERPA requires that the institution maintain a log of disclosures based on tax-exempt status. Therefore, Diego needs to make a record of this disclosure. (John's educational record would be the most logical place to note this, but institutional policy might designate a separate log.)

Because many institutions train staff members in their registrar's office to receive and review tax documents for these purposes, Diego may have violated institutional policy by receiving and reviewing the documents without consulting the personnel designated to handle requests based on tax status. The master advisor knows and follows institutional procedures regarding proper disclosure of protected information.

Disclosures to School Officials. Advisors may disclose student information when working with school officials who have a legitimate educational interest. Legitimate educational interest is interpreted broadly under FERPA and includes other faculty and primary-role advisors, undergraduate peer advisors, clerical staff who support the work of advisors, and administrators. Even practicum and fieldwork students as well as unpaid interns may qualify as recipients of protected information at the discretion of the institution (73 Fed. Reg. 237, 2008). Because FERPA does not define the persons qualified under the legitimate educational interest exception, institutions should develop policies that specifically define who may have a legitimate educational interest in protected information within a student's education record.

Case Study 3: Legitimate Educational Interest in Protected Information. Kelly knows that Luke, an advisee on academic warning, would benefit from an additional layer of academic support. Kelly's advising office has an academic coaching program that utilizes a highly trained graduate intern, Devyn, who earns academic credit to serve in this capacity. Kelly recommends Luke for coaching and e-mails his academic history to Devyn and copies Luke. Kelly also reaches out to Luke's resident assistant, Paul, to ask for help in to keeping Luke on track. Has Kelly violated FERPA?

Case Study 3: Response. Kelly has not violated FERPA but should double-check institutional policies. Devyn and Paul both qualify under FERPA's broad definition of individuals with a legitimate educational interest. However, the institution may have imposed a stricter definition of individuals with a legitimate educational interest. Kelly also needs to confirm that both Devyn and Paul have been trained on FERPA. The master advisor would take these last two steps prior to e-mailing information to either third party in concurrence with best practices and institutional policies, not FERPA.

What if Kelly required Luke and other students on academic probation to attend a group advising intervention? In such a situation, all of the students present have their low GPAs revealed to the group. Would this be a FERPA violation? Because protected information from a student education record is revealed, Kelly should consult legal counsel to determine whether a consent form should be created for participating students to sign. Advisors should be prepared to discuss with counsel each of the following concerns: the group intervention as a requirement for students on probation or as a private, alternative intervention option; opening up admittance to any student to lessen the inference of probation status; keeping the group large enough to promote some anonymity; and means of maintaining confidentiality of personally identifiable information disclosed at the intervention.

Disclosures Under the Health and Safety Exception.   The 2008 regulatory updates to FERPA, enacted partially in response to the massacre committed at Virginia Tech University in 2007, clarify that when an advisor learns that a student has articulated a threat posing significant danger to self or to any other person, the advisor "may disclose information from education records to any person whose knowledge of the information is necessary to protect the health or safety of the student or other individuals" (34 C.F.R. § 99.36, 2008). Generally, such situations warrant a notification to the campus police. Threat assessment teams on many campuses receive nonemergency information about troubling behaviors and determine whether a risk to safety or security exists (Dunkle, Silverstein, & Warner, 2008).

In addition to encouraging advisors to report troubling behavior to threat assessment teams, most institutional policies identify advisors as mandatory reporters of information pertaining to sexual assault. Due to the 2013 passage of the Campus Sexual Violence Elimination Act (an amendment to the Clery Act of 1990) (U.S. Department of Education, 2014) and recent clarifications to Title IX obligations (U.S. Department of Education, 2015), many institutional administrators are reexamining policies on reporting sexual assault and related crimes and determining the best methods of supporting victims. In response to these new laws and regulations, many institutions have designated faculty members and staff (including student staff) who interact with students as mandatory reporters of sexual misconduct. The policies and procedures for reporting vary among campuses, but likely include academic advisors, who will then be obligated to report sexual misconduct and provide referrals and support resources to victims.

Case Study 4: Confidentiality in Sensitive Situations. Alfonso's advisee, Bella, has disclosed some very troubling information in an e-mail. Bella stated that she cannot focus on classes because of suicidal and homicidal thoughts concerning herself and her classmates. Alfonso realizes that Bella has articulated that she poses a significant danger to her own safety and that of her peers, which is the reason she has been seeking help from the university counseling center. In the e-mail, Bella describes in detail her conversations with the licensed mental health counselor. After reading the e-mail, Alfonso immediately forwards it to the unit supervisor and the local police department. Has Alfonso violated FERPA?

Case Study 4: Response. No, Alfonso has not violated FERPA. Because e-mails qualify as part of a student's education record, FERPA does apply to this case. Bella may pose a significant health and safety emergency, which easily qualifies under FERPA's exception for disclosure. Alfonso made a good decision to share the e-mail with the local police.

Many advisors worry about whether medical and mental health information complicates scenarios for which privacy laws apply; however, in this situation, because the advisor is not the student's mental health care provider, no health-related federal privacy laws apply (e.g., the Health Insurance Portability and Accountability Act of 1996). In general, advisors are given more flexibility to disclose confidential conversations or e-mail messages than licensed medical and mental health providers who must maintain additional legal and professional confidentiality obligations (Tribbensee, 2008).

Should Alfonso respond differently to a student using e-mail to describe distress after experiencing a recent sexual assault? In this difficult situation, Alfonso needs to consider breaking the confidential relationship with the advisee to abide by mandatory reporting expectations likely to be in place on his campus. As a master advisor, Alfonso recognizes that his obligations under law and institutional policy—which serve to protect students—would trump his concerns for maintaining confidentiality. Alfonso should follow the institution's procedures for reporting violence to the designated office and refer the advisee to the campus resources that support survivors of sexual assault.

State Privacy Laws

Advisors at U.S. postsecondary institutions pay attention to FERPA, but state privacy laws often require greater protections of student information than are mandated by FERPA (Nicholson & O'Reardon, 2009). Some states, for example, require encryption for names and identification numbers electronically transmitted; under FERPA, these data are considered directory information that can be disclosed unless the student requests otherwise. Some state laws require institutions to monitor the data security practices of third-party sites that have access to education records, but FERPA does not require this measure. Some states have passed laws that impose strict criminal or tort liability (meaning neither intent nor negligence need be proven) for even single instances where private data are released for unauthorized reasons.

FERPA threatens the loss of federal funding if the institution does not comply after being notified of violation, a threatened punishment that has never been handed down (Daggett, 1997; Zick, 2009). In addition, *Gonzaga v. Doe* (2002) clarified that students do not have an individual right of action under FERPA, which means they cannot sue institutions for violations of FERPA protections.

Case Study 5: Technology.   Ashanti, a student who permanently resides in California, enrolls at a community college in Nevada. Prior to scheduling initial advising appointments, new students receive an e-mail from the advising center requiring them to complete a pre-advising survey on a free webform service not affiliated with the community college. The survey asks students to indicate their major, contact information, full name, and student ID number. The completed survey responses are e-mailed through unencrypted means to the assigned advisors at the college-designated e-mail address so an appointment can be scheduled. Ashanti's advisor, Kiana, loses her smartphone that automatically retrieves all e-mails from her college e-mail account. The phone is not password protected. What potential liabilities exist for Kiana and the community college? Does California law apply to this Nevada institution? Does FERPA apply?

Case Study 5: Response.   Kiana may be liable under Nevada and California state privacy laws, but not under FERPA. California has a long-arm statute, which arguably makes privacy laws applicable to any institution in or out of state that stores a California resident's information (Nicholson & O'Reardon, 2009). Nevada requires encryption every time a business in the state electronically transfers a customer's first name or the combined first initial and last name with an identification card number; Ashanti's information was transferred in this manner. The e-mail creates an education record; however, the information transmitted is consistent with directory information (assuming the identification number alone would not give third parties access to student records), and FERPA imposes no requirements on the means by which private information is stored or transmitted. As a result, FERPA has not been violated.

The master advisor recognizes that FERPA provides a baseline of privacy protection minimums and may be less strict than the privacy laws evolving throughout the various states. The master advisor keeps abreast of policies and procedures developed by the institution's legal counsel to comply with relevant state privacy laws.

Advisors as Agents of the University

Advisors act on behalf of and subject to the control of the universities that employ them. Therefore, they are agents of the university under the common law doctrine of agency (Hynes & Loewenstein, 2008). Agency law varies from state to state, but it continues to be relevant to advising practice. Under agency law, advisors—the agents—are able to create liability for the institutions employing them—their principals—without necessarily creating liability for the advisors themselves. Liability in these cases is most likely created under legal theories of contract or tort (Hynes & Loewenstein, 2008).

Liability in Contract Law

Courts predominantly view the relationship between students and the higher education institutions they attend as contractual in nature (Kaplin & Lee, 2013), but the terms of this academic contract are not always clear. Courts have held that the expressed and implied terms of the academic contract are not neatly contained in a single document but often come from a variety of sources (*Aronson v. University of Mississippi*, 2001). Indeed, court opinions generally hold that "the catalogues, bulletins, circulars, and regulations of a university made available to the matriculant become of part of the contract" (*Amaya v. Brater*, 2013, p. 11). The terms of the academic contract can be changed by agents of the university, particularly academic advisors, who teach students institutional knowledge about degree requirements and academic policies.

Case Study 6: Authority. A very responsible student pursuing a BS in biology, Moraa consults the academic bulletin and meets with her academic advisor every semester. As a senior, Moraa looks to complete her final general education requirement in the humanities. The bulletin lists 10 classes approved for the humanities requirement, but each sounds boring to Moraa, who is relieved to see this statement at the bottom of the humanities entry: "This is not a comprehensive list. Students should consult their academic advisors for further options." Moraa's academic advisor, Lee, agrees that an experimental class, Women in 20th Century Rock 'n' Roll, sounds interesting and aligns with the spirit of the humanities requirement. Lee encourages Moraa to enroll in the course. However, two months before graduation, Moraa receives notice from the registrar's office that she still needs a humanities class to graduate. Thinking this is a mistake, Moraa sends the registrar a copy of the e-mail with her correspondence with Lee, which clearly states that the academic advisor had encouraged Moraa to enroll in the Women in 20th Century Rock 'n' Roll course to meet the humanities requirement.

The registrar responds that advisors do not have the authority to approve courses for general education requirements. According to the registrar, Lee should have simply directed Moraa to the most up-to-date listing of approved humanities courses. The registrar also noted that experimental courses are never approved for general education requirements. The registrar states that Moraa will need to enroll in an approved humanities course in a future semester before she can graduate from the university. Outraged, Moraa hires an attorney to seek possible restitution or resolution. What will the attorney advise?

Case Study 6: Relying on the Advisor.   The attorney might advise Moraa that under a state-specific common law, she could present a case for breach of contract. Although the advisor did not have the actual authority to approve courses for the general education requirements, because of the bulletin statement, Moraa believed him to have apparent authority. The apparent authority concept comes from agency law that states that agents can change the terms of contracts into which their principals (e.g., the university) have entered (Hynes & Loewenstein, 2008). Based on that perceived authority, Moraa enrolled in the course.

The attorney points out that courts have traditionally shown great deference to college and university academic decision making; however, a recent dissenting opinion from the Supreme Court led some commentators to conclude that the judiciary is placing less trust in and therefore giving less deference to the decisions made by university educators (Hutchens, Wilson, & Block, 2013). That is, current courts might be willing to apply ordinary concepts of contract law to disputes arising in the academic context; in which case, the courts could construe ambiguities around contract terms against the interests of the institution (i.e., in favor of the student). The master advisor makes good faith efforts to know the limits of her or his actual authority and not make statements that appear to alter the student's academic contract.

Liability in Tort Law

In addition to the academic contract, violations of state tort laws may create liability for institutions through actions of advisors. Specifically, malpractice in advising might give rise to a negligence claim, which includes four basic elements: duty, breach, causation, and damages. A student bringing an advising negligence claim might argue that advisors have a duty of care in their work with students. This duty involves provision of accurate and timely institutional knowledge of educational opportunities and requirements. If an advisor breaches this duty of care and thereby causes a student to experience damages, such as costs incurred for an extra year of classes due to poor advising, the student can hold the institution liable for those damages, if the state recognizes such claims.

Students have had mixed results in their educational malpractice claims heard in U.S. courts. Successful examples include situations where an advisor repeatedly misrepresented the availability of course sequences to support a 4-year graduation time line (*Byrd v. Lamar*, 2003), where a professional college misrepresented the chiropractic program curriculum as an adequate preparation for students taking the licensure examination in all states (*Enzinna v. D'Youville College*, 2011), and in situations in which advisors did not exercise reasonable care to avoid placing students into dangerous internship situations (*Nova Southeastern Univ. v. Gross*, 2000; *Rinksy v. Trustees of Boston University*, 2010).

Most students unsuccessful in having claims heard were unable to establish the first element of the negligence claim: duty (*Hendricks v. Clemson University*, 2003; Kaplin & Lee, 2013; Tokic, 2014). As states get more involved in the curricular matters of institutions, this trend may change. For example, some states have enacted legislation requiring that degrees be attainable within 4 years, such that effective advising is required and individualized degree maps (i.e., 4-year plans of courses) are mandated for students (see, e.g., Tex. Edu. Code §§ 61.070, 61.077, 2005; Ind. Code § 21-12-14, 2013). The courts in these states now have legislatively set standards of care that must be followed by institutions. Students might rely on these standards as the duty element in any educational malpractice claims they bring. Student plaintiffs who establish a recognized duty of care still need to show that the duty was breached by the advisors, that the breach was the cause of damages, and that real damages (usually financial) were sustained.

Case Study 7: Promises, Promises. Zhang, a new mechanical engineering major at a midwestern state university, hopes to graduate in four years and begin his career. Zhang asks his advisor, Martina, about the feasibility of his plan. Upon hearing Zhang's questions, Martina remembers a new state mandate requiring that advisors provide incoming students with degree maps that show ways to complete a degree program in eight semesters. After orientation, Martina hastily puts together a degree map that she thinks accounts for all of the latest changes to the mechanical engineering curriculum and she e-mails the map to Zhang.

Zhang faithfully follows the degree map received from Martina and checks with her each semester to ensure he is still on track to graduate in four years. In the fall semester of his senior year, Zhang receives a distressing e-mail from Martina who has noticed that Zhang never completed a 200-level engineering course required for his degree. Zhang reminds Martina of his degree map and notes correctly that this 200-level course was not listed. Martina apologizes for the mistake but explains that Zhang will need to take this course when it is offered again the following fall semester, delaying his graduation by a semester. Zhang is furious, not just about the delayed graduation, but because he cannot accept the full-time engineering position he was recently offered. Zhang contacts an attorney to seek legal recourse.

Case Study 7: Possible Outcome. Although Zhang's institution is located in a state that does not recognize the tort of educational malpractice, the legislature has passed a law regarding 4-year degree maps that arguably lays out a standard duty to be followed by advisors. Zhang's attorney might suggest that they pursue a claim of educational malpractice based on a breach of the duty to provide accurate information in the degree map. The attorney may rely on one of the few cases in which the courts recognized a tort of educational malpractice: *Sain v. Cedar Rapids Community School District* (2001). In *Sain,* the Supreme Court of Iowa recognized educational malpractice because a high school guidance counselor had misadvised regarding courses that would help a student maintain NCAA eligibility. The court held that a duty of care existed because the counselor was in the business of providing information and therefore could be expected to provide accurate information. If Zhang's attorney presents a convincing argument that Martina should be held to a duty of providing accurate information—particularly because the state legislature has mandated that advisors do so with regard to graduation requirements—the court may hold that Martina breached that duty and caused Zhang to lose at least a semester's worth of a full-time engineering salary (i.e., damages).

Equal Rights and Due Process

Equal Rights

In the United States, the federal constitution and civil rights legislation afford certain guarantees to college students. The 14th Amendment to the U.S. Constitution contains a clause that guarantees "equal protection of the laws." This clause prohibits racial discrimination at public colleges. At private colleges, federal civil rights legislation, including Title VI of the Civil Rights Act of 1964 and 42 U.S.C. § 1981, prohibit such discrimination (Kaplin & Lee, 2013). Four U.S. Supreme Court cases that have dealt with university admissions practices clarified the equal rights guarantees of these laws: *Fisher v. University of Texas* (2013), *Gratz v. Bollinger* (2003), *Grutter v. Bollinger* (2003), and *Regents of the University of California v. Bakke* (1978). Although these cases dealt with race-conscious affirmative action admission plans, the guidance they provide also applies to retention-related practices in higher education, including academic advising (Coleman, Palmer, & Richards, 2005). These cases had established the constitutional permissibility of race-conscious practices in university programs provided these programs are narrowly tailored to ensure the following conditions are met:

- o Students are not selected for program participation based solely on race; rather, race is one of a number of factors considered for eligibility.

- o Program administrators adequately considered available race-neutral alternatives to achieving the educational goals of a diverse student body.

- o The program does not unduly harm majority students.

- o The program is of limited duration with plans to terminate it as soon as is practicable. (*Grutter v. Bollinger*, 2003) (Rust, 2015, p. 167)

In 2015, the Supreme Court reheard *Fisher v. The University of Texas*. The outcome of that hearing, due in Summer 2016, may change the legal landscape for race-conscious practices. To ensure their practices comply with the law, master advisors must stay abreast of evolving legal issues that affect higher education.

Case Study 8: Discrimination. Advisors at a state university want to encourage students of color to persist through graduation. These advisors developed a first-year seminar in which they, as instructors, explore issues of concern to first-year students of color. At new student orientation, advisors received a list of students who self-identified as ethnic or racial minority on the information they submitted on the admissions application. Advisors recommended the new first-year seminar to students of color, but made no point of mentioning the course to White students. Is this a violation under current 14th Amendment jurisprudence?

Case Study 8: Response. Yes, the actions of the advisors violate the 14th Amendment under current law. Although those in the excluded group (White students) do not necessarily sustain harm and the intention of improving retention rates for students of color meets institutional goals, the advising practice subjects students to different treatment based solely on their race. Although alternate, race-neutral methods may have been explored to reach the retention goal, advisor actions did not reflect such considerations (e.g., they failed to mention the course to all students at orientation). If these advisors consulted with their institution's legal counsel, they would likely be directed to make the support program (the first-year seminar) applicable to all groups of students and then use race as one of numerous factors in targeting potential program participants.

Race cannot be the decisive factor, but could be considered along with other known attrition risk factors such as first-generation status, low family income, or low high school GPA. The master advisor never employs a particular advising strategy based solely on a student's race and challenges his or her colleagues to think twice about race-conscious practices such as creating a race-specific distribution list of advisees.

Due Process

Students enjoy certain due process rights that affect the work of academic advisors. At public institutions, due process rights spring from the 14th Amendment to the U.S. Constitution and prohibit the arbitrary deprivation of property by the government. Students at public institutions have a property interest in their continued enrollment that cannot be taken away without adequate due process (e.g., notice and an opportunity to be heard). Although due process rights apply to both academic and misconduct-related dismissals, courts usually require fewer procedural safeguards in the case of academic dismissals than for those related to behavior.

Case Study 9: Dissimilar Treatment. Midsized State University (MSU) has a progress-toward-degree policy: "Students may be suspended from study at the university if the student's academic dean determines the student is not making adequate, timely progress toward graduation." For the last three years, the College of Arts and Sciences at MSU has been led by Dean Ferris, who has never applied the progress-toward-degree policy to students in his college, despite increasing pressure from the MSU President to hold students to high standards.

When Dean Ferris retired, Dean Mori took the helm of the college and immediately identified all students who had failed to pass at least 24 credit hours per academic year. These students were notified that they would be suspended for the upcoming term and were invited to appeal the decision to Dean Mori directly. Did Dean Mori violate due process right?

Case Study 9: Response. No, Dean Mori did not violate these students' due process rights. The U.S. Supreme Court has held that courts should defer to academic judgments made at the institution unless such a decision reflects a substantial departure from academic norms, the student is not made aware of academic deficiencies, or the academic standards are not applied fairly (*Board of Curators of the University of Missouri v. Horowitz*, 1978; *University of Michigan v. Ewing*, 1985). Dean Mori applied the commonly used standard of credit hours to mark progress, students were notified of their deficiencies and given an opportunity to be heard, and the policy was applied to everyone upon Dean Mori's hire.

The abrupt change in application of the policy between the two deans does not create legal problems, but it certainly would frustrate students and their advisors trying to anticipate the application of academic policies. If Dean Mori had individually reviewed the transcripts of each student and chose to suspend or not each individual for varying and seemingly arbitrary reasons, then Dean Mori's actions would be less defensible.

Private Institutions. At private institutions, students do not have constitutionally protected due-process rights; however, under the academic contract theory discussed previously in this chapter, courts have generally required private institutions to follow the academic dismissal procedures and policies they have established and to which students agreed upon enrollment (Kaplin & Lee, 2013). At both public and private institutions, the master advisor pays attention to whether similarly situated students are treated similarly. A master advisor might be the first to recognize when academic policies need to be applied more consistently or transparently, and the master advisor likely argues for grandfathering in cases where policies change to the detriment of previously matriculated students.

Summary

The legal and regulatory environment within which academic advisors must operate is complex and evolving. The master advisor monitors changes to the most important aspects of law affecting academic advising. The master advisor thinks through the relationships between federal and state laws and the institutional policies designed to promote legal compliance and then encourages discussion in the advising office to keep advising practices up-to-date with new laws and regulations. Through this work in legal compliance, the master advisor maintains not just the trust of students, but also of colleagues and administrators.

Aiming for Excellence

o If you advise in a country outside the United States, the guidance in this chapter may not apply to your situation. Consult with your institution's legal counsel to determine the applicable laws regarding

  o confidentiality and privacy of student information,

  o liabilities created by advisors as agents of the institution, and

  o equal rights and due process for students.

o For Canadian advisors, in particular, consult the Office of the Information Commissioner of Canada (2014), which hosts a helpful web directory of the provincial and territorial offices that enforce the various Candian privacy laws, typically known as Freedom of Information and Protection of Privacy Acts of 1990.

o Which employees in your office (faculty, primary-role, or peer advisors; clerical staff; graduate interns) have access to education records? Encourage them to attend FERPA and related privacy law training available at your institution. Make known web pages maintained by the registrar's office regarding FERPA compliance policies. Refresh your own training in this area every few years as well.

o Research the materials provided by your institution to students regarding FERPA rights and procedures and distinguish between the following three documents or processes:

  o the institution's annual FERPA notification to students (which explains the students' rights and the institutional policies in place to abide by FERPA);

  o the mechanism or form by which students opt out of the disclosure of directory information (and how advisors can see whether a student has opted out of directory information disclosures); and

  o the form(s) for FERPA consent to release information.

o Never purchase vended software (e.g., appointment scheduling, advising notes, predictive analytics, etc.) without following institutional guidelines for procuring products that will store or receive student data. Most institutions require that purchase contracts be vetted by institutional counsel, specifically to ensure compliance with FERPA and state privacy laws.

o Examine the third-party software currently used on your campus. How does it protect student privacy? Do students consent to their information disclosure (and specify to whom it may be given) when they opt into using the campus job-posting system? What consents protect the students included in early alert systems that also notify parties outside the institution (e.g., parents)?

o Research the policies related to the Clery Act of 1990, Sexual Violence Elimination Act of 2013, and Title IX of the Civil Rights Act on your campus. Determine whether you, as an advisor, are expected to report instances of sexual misconduct that students disclose to you. Identify the steps to take in such a situation. Specifically, to which office or which official should you report the alleged misconduct? How should you disclose your reporting obligation to your advisees? Frequently update the list of resources for victims of sexual misconduct. Furthermore, ensure that your office's advisors and peer academic advisors (if applicable under your institution's policy) are regularly trained in the expectations for handling disclosures of any criminal or threatening activity.

o Mentor less-experienced colleagues on the final authority on degree require-ments so that they know the documents to use when conflicts of information arise between the bulletin, online degree requirements listings, paper checklists, electronic degree audits, and any other institutional publications. Anticipate such conflicts might arise and work to resolve them before students and colleagues become confused.

o In addition to complying with any new state-imposed mandates affecting academic advising, seek out opportunities to speak on behalf of the advising profession to lawmakers. Find your representative's contact information online and initiate contact; alternatively, seek out meetings of any state-level agencies that have governing authority over higher education and attend them. Ensure these legislators and policy shapers understand the nature of your work as an educator; help them understand how proposed laws could help or hinder student success. Some institutions have policies regarding whether employees can lobby government officials in their capacities as institutional employees, and those that allow advocacy may impose rules or offer guidelines for con-duct. Consult your employee handbook or human resource publications to find policies on political activity.

o Work with institutional general counsel to determine whether race-conscious advising practices comprise an appropriate strategy; that is, do they elevate the achievement levels of all students on campus?

o Read the policies and procedures for academic dismissals as written in the institutional bulletin or handbook. Then consider carefully the last five students that you know have been dismissed. Did the dismissal process each experienced match the written description? If not, consult with administrators to help ensure that future dismissals more faithfully comply with the process described in the written bulletin or handbook.

o Organize a professional development session for advisors featuring a panel discussion among the on-campus legal counsel, campus police, and the threat assessment team. Clarify the circumstances under which an employee should contact the police or the threat assessment team during interactions with troubled students and produce a web-based guide with the answers.

o Work with a campus advising organization or committee to organize an annual meeting with the institution's general counsel. Use the Legal Audit Checklist from Rust (2015) to determine any recent legal updates that might necessitate the development of new advising policies or procedures.

Audit of Legal Issues in Advising Practice

Privacy and Confidentiality (FERPA and State Privacy Laws)

☐ Does your advising office have a FERPA policy?

☐ Does your advising office annually communicate FERPA policy to students and advisors?

☐ Does your advising office ensure that advisors consistently follow institutional FERPA policy?

☐ Does your institution's general counsel annually review FERPA policy?

☐ Specifically, does your general counsel ensure your office FERPA policies are in line with

  ☐ any new aspect of FERPA law or regulations?

  ☐ institution FERPA policy?

  ☐ state privacy laws applicable to your institution? (State law—common or statutory—may prohibit disclosures that FERPA permits or it may require maintenance of records that FERPA does not.)

☐ Does your FERPA policy

  ☐ define the information to be included in and excluded from advising records? (Once data are included, they are FERPA-protected until the record is destroyed.)

  ☐ give students an option to inspect and request to amend their advising records?

  ☐ provide students a means by which to give informed and voluntary consent to disclose their FERPA-protected education records?

☐ Does this consent form

  ☐ note the specific individuals or class of individuals to whom the education records may be disclosed?

- ☐ state the specific office or individual who may disclose FERPA-protected information?

- ☐ describe how long the consent remains in place? (Consent will be in place until the specified date or until rescinded by the student.)

- ☐ note the specific records that may be disclosed?

- ☐ list the purpose of the disclosure?

- ☐ contain a signature and date line? (This can be a digital form.)

- ☐ require authentication from specified individuals when they call, e-mail, or visit the advising office to gain access to FERPA-protected information (e.g., a password provided by student on consent form)?

- ☐ require advisors to maintain a log of all disclosures of FERPA-protected information? (This is not required when the disclosure is based on consent or when disclosing to school officials with legitimate educational interest.)

Advisors as Agents of the Institution (Contract and Tort Liability)

- ☐ Have you familiarized yourself with all the potential sources of terms that comprise the academic contract to which your students agreed with the institution?

- ☐ Specifically, have you reviewed and kept documentation of
  - ☐ promotional materials by which your advisees were recruited?
  - ☐ institutional bulletins under which your advisees enrolled?
  - ☐ published degree requirements check sheets?
  - ☐ paper- and web-based degree audits you have used to advise individual students?
  - ☐ student handbooks?

- ☐ Have you confirmed with the appropriate academic administrators about the listings of degree requirements deemed authoritative to resolve discrepancies among the various terms of the academic contract?

- ☐ Do you carefully and promptly inform students when changes are made to degree requirements or course offerings?
  - ☐ Do you maintain a record of these notices?

- ☐ Do you avoid making promises regarding future course offerings unless you have obtained reliable, documented commitment from the department teaching the course?

- ☐ Do you regularly consult institutional career- and pre-professional school advisors to avoid overselling the career-related usefulness of a degree or program?

- ☐ When promoting experiential learning opportunities (e.g., internships, service-learning, study abroad), do you refer students to institutionally vetted programs?

- ☐ Do you regularly seek out institutional training on how to comply with any new state-imposed mandates regarding academic advising?

Equal Rights and Due Process

- ☐ Do you ever consider a student's race when deciding which advising approach to use or which educational opportunities to promote?

- ☐ If you make such decisions, do you regularly review this strategy with the institution's legal counsel specifically ensuring that the practice

  - ☐ comports with any new jurisprudence regarding race-conscious practices?

  - ☐ is based on factors other than race alone?

  - ☐ renders greater effectiveness in achieving educational goals than a race-neutral approach?

  - ☐ does not harm majority students?

  - ☐ is of limited duration?

- ☐ Are you familiar with the policies and procedures by which your advisees might be academically dismissed from the institution?

- ☐ Do you make good faith efforts to inform your advisees about dismissal policies and procedures?

- ☐ Do you accurately and promptly inform your students of academic deficiencies in their work?

- ☐ Do you faithfully follow dismissal policies and procedures in whatever roles you play in the process?

Reprinted by Permission. From M. M. Rust, pp. 174–176, in the *New Advisor Guidebook: Mastering the Art of Academic Advising* © 2013 by Jossey-Bass.

References

26 U.S. § 152.

34 C.F.R. §99.3 (2011).

34 C.F.R. § 99.36 (2008).

73 Fed. Reg. 237 (Dec. 9, 2008).

Adams, N. A., IV. (2015). Academic compliance programs: A federal model with separation of powers. *The Journal of College and University Law, 41*(1), 1–24.

Amaya v. Brater, 981 N.E.2d 1235 (Ind. 2013).

Aronson v. University of Mississippi, 2001 WL 1155686 (Miss.App., 10/2/01).

Board of Curators of the University of Missouri v. Horowitz, 435 U.S. 78 (1978).

Byrd v. Lamar, 846 So. 2d 334 (Ala. 2003).

Campbell, E., Cieplak, B., & Rodriguez, B. (2012). *Family Education Rights and Privacy Act (FERPA): FERPA for colleges & universities.* Retrieved from http://www2.ed.gov/policy/gen/guid/fpco/pdf/postsecondary-webinar-presentation.pdf

Civil Rights Act of 1964, Title VI, 42 U.S.C. § 2000D et seq.

Civil Rights Act of 1964, Title IX, 20 U.S.C. §§ 1681–1688.

Clery Act of 1990, 20 U.S.C. § 1092(f).

Coleman, A. L., Palmer, S. R., & Richards, F. S. (2005). *Federal law and recruitment, outreach, and retention: A framework for evaluating diversity-related programs.* New York, NY: College Board.

Daggett, L. M. (1997). Bucking up Buckley II: Using civil rights claims to enforce the federal student records statute. *Seattle University Law Review, 21*(1), 29–67.

Dunkle, J. H., Silverstein, Z. B., & Warner, S. L. (2008). Managing violent and other troubling students: The role of threat assessment teams on campus. *Journal of College and University Law, 34*(3), 585–636.

Enzinna v. D'Youville College, 2011 WL 1733907 (N.Y. App. Div., 4th Jud. Dep't 2011).

Family Educational Rights and Privacy Act of 1974, 20 U.S.C. § 1232g; 34 C.F.R. §99.

Family Policy Compliance Office. (2006, February 15). *Letter to Montgomery County public schools (MD) re: law enforcement unit records.* Retrieved from http://www2.ed.gov/policy/gen/guid/fpco/ferpa/library/montcounty0215.html

Fisher v. University of Texas, 133 S.Ct. 2411 (2013).

Gonzaga v. Doe 536, U.S. 273 (2002).

Gratz v. Bollinger, 539 U.S. 244 (2003).

Grutter v. Bollinger, 539 U.S. 306 (2003).

Health Insurance Portability and Accountability Act of 1996. Pub. L. No. 104–191, 110 Stat. 1936.

Hendricks v. Clemson University, 353 S.C.449, 578 S.E.2d 711 (2003).

Hutchens, N. H., Wilson, K., & Block, J. (2013). CLS v. Martinez and competing legal discourses over the appropriate degree of judicial deference to the co-curricular realm. *The Journal of College and University Law, 39*(3), 541–565.

Hynes, D. J., & Loewenstein, M. J. (2008). *Agency, partnership and the LLC: The law of unincorporated business enterprises: Cases, materials, problems.* Newark, NJ: LexisNexis.

Indiana Code, Ind. Code § 21-12-14 (2013).

Kaplin, W., & Lee, B. (2013). *The law of higher education: A comprehensive guide to legal implications of administrative decision making.* San Francisco, CA: Jossey-Bass.

Nicholson, J. L., & O'Reardon, M. E. (2009). Data protection basics: A primer for college and university counsel. *The Journal of College and University Law, 36*(1), 101–144.

Nova Southeastern Univ. v. Gross, 758 So. 2d 86 (Fla.2000).

Office of the Information Commissioner of Canada. (2014, April 7). *Links.* Retrieved from http://www.oic-ci.gc.ca/eng/links-liens.aspx

Regents of the University of California v. Bakke, 438 U.S. 265 (1978).

Rinksy v. Trustees of Boston University, 2010 U.S. Dist. LEXIS 136876 (D. Mass. December 27, 2010).

Rooker, L. R., & Falkner, T. M. (2013). *2013 FERPA quick guide.* Washington, DC: American Association of Collegiate Registrars and Admissions Officers.

Rust, M. M. (2015). Legal issue in academic advising. In P. Folsom, F. Yoder, & J. E. Joslin (Eds.), *The new advisor guidebook: Mastering the art of academic advising.* San Francisco, CA: Jossey-Bass.

Sain v. Cedar Rapids Community School District, 626 N.W.2d 115 (Iowa 2001).

Sexual Violence Elimination Act of 2013, Pub. L. No. 113–4, 127 Stat. 54.

Texas Education Code, Tex. Edu. Code §§ 61.070, 61.077 (2005).

Tokic, S. (2014). Rethinking educational malpractice: Are educators rock stars? *Brigham Young University Education and Law Journal, 2014*(1), 105–133.

Tribbensee, N. E. (2008). Privacy and confidentiality: Balancing student rights and campus safety, *The Journal of College and University Law, 34*(2), 393–417.

University of Michigan v. Ewing, 474 U.S. 214 (1985).

U.S. Department of Education. (2014, July 14). *Dear colleague letter: Implementation of changes to the Clery Act made by the Violence Against Women Reauthorization Act of 2013* (VAWA). Retrieved from https://www.ifap.ed.gov/dpcletters/GEN1413.html

U.S. Department of Education. (2015, April 24). *Title IX coordinators.* Retrieved from http://www2.ed.gov/policy/rights/guid/ocr/title-ix-coordinators.html

Zick, K. (2009). Issues arising from application of new FERPA regulations. *Proceedings of the 30th Annual National Conference on Law and Higher Education.* Retrieved from http://www.stetson.edu/law/conferences/ highered/archive/media/higher-ed-archives-2009/document/ii-zick-issues-of-new-ferpa-regulations-pdf.pdf

9

A HUMAN CAPITAL APPROACH TO ACADEMIC AND CAREER ADVISING

Leigh S. Shaffer

I know many in academia do not want to frame higher education as preparing people for jobs. But, if higher education does not do that, at least, what is it doing?

—Pamela Shockley-Zalabak (2012, p. 15, emphasis in the original)

The great recession of 2008 dramatized the need for an effective model for integrating academic and career advising. In the new knowledge-driven economy, graduates must develop their human capital and broker portfolio careers. A human capital approach, based on Gordon's (2006) 7-step model of the career advising process, helps students complete their degree program and maximize their employability. In this approach, advisors teach students to develop and maintain human capital, which forms the basis of the college wage premium, and to avoid financially risky behaviors associated with attrition and burdensome debt. With advisor guidance in thoughtful course selection, carefully crafted career paths, and well-documented growth portfolios, students acquire transferable skills and special knowledge applicable to the labor market.

Reader Learning Outcomes

From studying this chapter, advisors will use knowledge gained about human capital and career advising to

- describe maximization of human capital,
- explain the process of calculating the costs of a 2- or 4-year college education,
- identify several different types of academic courses students could select to develop human capital,
- define and illustrate transferable skills,
- explain the behaviors that put students at financial risk,
- list some warning signs that advisees may be financially at risk,
- articulate the rationale for undertaking career interventions with advisees, and
- explain the importance of documenting human capital development.

Many college professors feel ambivalent about the role of colleges and universities as institutions expected to prepare graduates to enter the workforce. However, most students (and many of their parents) realize that job prospects for high school graduates have greatly diminished in the new economy, and they view matriculation into postsecondary education as a necessary step toward employability in the 21st century (Shaffer, 2014). Despite concerns over the large investment in higher education paying off in the future, many students unwittingly prepare for the past industrial economy, which is rapidly being replaced by a new, knowledge-driven economy; in fact, many of today's students will hold jobs in their lifetimes that do not exist today (Shaffer, 1997/2009; Shaffer & Zalewski, 2011b).

Regardless of faculty conscientiousness in preparing college students for the demands of the 21st century workforce, no one knows with certainty the skills and special knowledge needed for success in the future. Economists recognize the risk of investing in higher education: Although most college graduates expect and receive a good return on their investment, many college students face the possibility of little— or even negative—rewards for their postsecondary expenditures (Avery & Turner, 2012). Labor markets now operate in a VUCA (volatile, uncertain, complex, and ambiguous) environment, with both employers and college students forced to take risks with their economic investments. VUCA embodies the difficulties associated with gathering, sharing, evaluating, and interpreting information in dynamic contexts (Bodenhausen & Peery, 2009; Free, 2009).

Difficulties in 21st-century decision making are exacerbated by rapidly changing conditions, uncertain futures, and competing factors that result in developments that may or may not unfold as advantageous for new graduates. Long-range planning in all fields, especially government and politics, health care, and retail sales, must be undertaken with an understanding of the dynamics of a VUCA environment. For example, the impact of new technologies has accelerated the pace of skill and special-knowledge obsolescence among workers. Consequently, some employers have eliminated career ladders and currently avoid investing in on-the-job training; instead they make short-term hires of contingent workers (Shaffer & Zalewski, 2011a, 2011b).

These new hiring practices have radically transformed the labor force. Workers now can expect to change employers and occupations regularly, and they must maintain their own employability through lifelong learning (Shaffer, 1997/2009; Shaffer & Zalewski, 2011a, 2011b). In Latin America, for example, human resources directors reported that workers, whose predecessors remained with one employer for 7 to 10 years, start a new job, learn new skills, develop excellent references for better positions, and leave after 2 or 3 years with one employer (Sanchez-Arias, Calmeyn, Driesen, & Pruis, 2013).

Workers must adjust not only their knowledge base and their skill sets regularly but they must also transform themselves. They now experience protean careers, which require them to reconstruct personal qualities, such as attitudes, to enhance job performance; boundaryless careers, which empower them to develop and use transferable skills in new settings; and portfolio careers, which depend upon development and documentation of new skills and special knowledge related to career growth (Arthur & Rousseau, 1996; Hall, 1996a, 1996b, 1997; Hall & Moss, 1998; Lazarova & Taylor, 2009; Shaffer & Zalewski, 2011a, 2011b). Master advisors help students understand the need to build and document the acquisition of human capital during their college years in anticipation of managing their own personal development after graduating from college.

The transition of the industrial to the new, postindustrial economy began in the second half of the 20th century, but the pace and urgency of it was dramatized during the great recession of 2008 when many established workers lost their jobs and then were not rehired because the skill requirements for performing the job had been upgraded (Shaffer & Zalewski, 2011b). During that same period of dramatic change, newly graduated college students faced one of the most difficult job markets in memory, leaving high proportions of them unemployed—or underemployed—just as they started adult life and their student loan payments came due. These new realities reflect a fundamental change in the new economy (Shaffer & Zalewski, 2011a):

> Businesses and industries no longer expect a positive return on their investment for formal on-the-job-training (OJT) and . . . lifelong career tracks are no longer profitable. [They] have changed the operating economic ground rules for employability . . . and expect workers to develop and maintain their own employability through some combination of postgraduate training, formal training, informal upgrading of skills, or work experience. Workers are increasingly expected to manage and maintain their employable skill set as well as act as brokers for their own employment by finding suitable jobs. . . . (p. 64)

These major developments necessitate important changes in the way students think about their educations and their futures, and they will need academic advisors who can help them negotiate the career implications of the day-to-day decisions they make in preparation to graduate. Advisors will find little value in traditional approaches to career development based on the assumption of relatively stable career ladders; instead, they must help students develop the skills to maintain their employability in a VUCA environment. Specifically, students must understand that formal, academic education serves as a preliminary stage in a process of continuous, lifelong learning, and they need the attitudes and personal qualities that will maintain employability throughout their working lifetimes. The human capital approach to academic and career advising gives advisors a comprehensive vision of the new demands of the global labor market and the skills and special knowledge needed for graduates to be successful.

The human capital approach presented in this chapter is based on the seven-step career advising process developed by Virginia Gordon (2006). In Gordon's model, career advising is introduced at Step 4 (typically at the beginning of the student's second year) and continues throughout students' progress toward graduation. Table 9.1 presents a schematic, sequential plan for using the human capital approach to career advising by describing each of the activities or exercises outlined in this chapter within the seven-step approach and by identifying the master advisor's role at each step.

Table 9.1. Presenting human capital development using Gordon's (2006) model of career advising

Approximate Time of Delivery (Year)	Step	Advisor's Role	Human Capital Activity or Exercise
1st	1	Establish rapport	Explain maximizing human capital
	2	Determine student's knowledge	Costs of college calculation
			Establish plan for financing college education through degree completion
			Identify financially at-risk students
	3	Explain advising process	Select general education courses and begin building human capital
2nd	4	Select career interventions	Initiate portfolio documentation of human capital growth
	5	Set career advising goals	Determine career direction and select appropriate major
3rd and 4th	6	Review goals and develop career plans	Initiate career development
	7	Arrange continuing contacts with student	Continue career interventions as needed
			Continue portfolio development

Human Capital Through Academic and Career Advising

The term *human capital* refers to any characteristic of a worker (including skills, special knowledge, productive behaviors and attitudes, health, and geographic mobility) that helps make him or her productive and successful in the world of work (Schultz, 1961). The pursuit of human capital challenges credentialism, the belief held by many students that graduation embodies the only important outcome of attending college and that a college degree represents a sufficient basis for success in the labor market (Shaffer, 1997/2009). In fact, a student can earn a college degree without developing human capital to the fullest. Therefore, the academic advisor who appreciates the value of human capital integrates the traditional goals and practices of a career advisor with academic advising, a fusion increasingly recognized as both desirable and necessary (Hughey, Burton Nelson, Damminger, & McCalla-Wriggins, 2009; Hughey & Hughey, 2009).

In this chapter, I summarize the human capital approach to academic and career advising and provide suggestions and activities for developing practical skills. Also, a year-by-year framework helps students to grow this valuable asset while completing their college education in a timely and affordable manner. The use of this approach does not justify an anti-intellectual philosophy that higher education is most valuable as a means to make money; rather, this approach reflects the belief that students can pursue the traditional subjects and curricula of a college education (including, and especially, a liberal arts education) and still acquire the skills and special knowledge that lead to positive returns on their postsecondary investment. Human capital development prepares students for a lifetime of successful employment or entrepreneurship.

Human Capital Maximization

The human capital approach to integrating academic and career advising practices involves the conscious consideration of every important academic decision as a potential building block of a student's human capital. With each decision, master advisors encourage students to explicitly ask, "What can this [course or activity] do to my special knowledge base [what do I know?] and to my skill set [what can I do?]?" These inquiries prompted as both academic and career advising ensure that students actively contemplate their futures and connect them to their current educational activities and decisions. This process illustrates human capital development in future-affecting decision making (Shaffer, 1997/2009):

> Students should realize that every choice has consequences for human capital, and be aware of these consequences in making those choices. Choosing a science course with a laboratory over a survey course with no laboratory . . . a course that is writing-intensive over one that uses only objective testing . . . an elective that offers only an interesting topic can increase a student's human capital. . . . Such consideration is at the heart of the developmental model of academic advising. (2009, p. 104)

The human capital approach challenges the check-the-box mentality of course selection. Although each selected course contributes to timely completion of all graduation requirements for a chosen major and degree, students must choose classes that also grow their intellectual capacity, knowledge base, and skill set. The human capital approach challenges the necessary, but limited, perspective of finding a job after graduation. College education prepares a student for a lifetime of success, and the payoff for much of a student's education will only emerge when she or he becomes a leader in a field of expertise (Shaffer, 1997/2009).

Although not applied slavishly in every advising encounter, human capital concepts should be reflected in the typical processes students undertake when making any educational decision. Master advisors remind students, especially at the beginning of their academic careers, to maximize their human capital. They may initiate appointments at the beginning of each academic term by asking students to describe the role of their previous classes in developing their skills, special knowledge, attitudes, or behaviors. They also help students document their human capital development by encouraging them to make additions to a résumé or a portfolio. When students trace the trajectory of their growth and the cumulative quality of their development, they will naturally consider maximizing their human capital development when deciding about course work.

The College Wage Premium

In the new economy, high school graduates face a practical choice: try to find well-paying and satisfying work with their high school diploma or matriculate at a post-secondary institution. Because real earnings for high school graduates have declined significantly in the 21st century, many students believe that the cost of not going to college is higher than the costs of attending (Dewan, 2014; James, 2012; Pew Research Center, 2014). Economists refer to the earnings advantage of college-educated workers over high school graduates as the *college wage premium* (Dewan, 2014; James, 2012).

Evidence supports the belief that the average earnings of college graduates outperform those of high school graduates. The college wage premium is measured by calculating the difference between the median wage for employees holding a bachelor's degree and the median wage for employees holding no postsecondary credential but with a high school diploma (James, 2012). As of 2013, for example, the college wage premium among Millennials (people aged 25 to 32 years) was estimated at approximately $17,500 per year (Pew Research Center, 2014). In other words, the college graduate in the early stages of a career earned, on average, nearly $17,500 more per year than their peers with a high school diploma. If only to motivate students to complete their academic degree, master advisors know and describe the magnitude of the college wage premium.

The economic realities creating the college wage premium mean that students need to persist to graduation; however, the college degree proves most critical for students going into economic debt to finance their education (Shaffer, 2014). The earnings of college dropouts do not exceed those of high school graduates (Dwyer, McCloud, & Hodson, 2012; Gladieux & Perna, 2005; Kadlec, 2014). Therefore, the college wage premium should be called the college *graduate* wage premium, because it only applies to those who earn the degree.

Unfortunately, published research does not elucidate the role of community colleges in human capital development in the postindustrial, information-based economy (Laanan, Hardy, & Katsinas, 2006). The rapid pace of change in the workplace has presented a serious challenge to the development of reliable and valid measures of human capital.

Despite the dearth of research, available evidence suggests that earning an associate's degree holds greater value than a high school degree or incomplete college attendance at either 2- or 4-year institutions; that is, associate's degree holders have benefited from a college wage premium roughly one half the size of that enjoyed by baccalaureate holders (Laanan et al., 2006). Furthermore, some evidence points to community colleges as especially successful in human capital development for local or regional labor markets as well as in placing graduates in well-paying positions when partnered with local businesses and industries to customize training programs (Beach, 2009; Gonos, 2009). Better, systematic data collection can help to clarify the impact of community colleges on students' human capital development.

Student Financial Decision Making

Many college graduates with accrued student loan and credit card debt struggle to repay their debt after they graduate. Studies estimate that college graduates now complete their education carrying a debt load approaching $30,000; on average, students graduate with student loans totaling $25,250 as well as $4,150 in credit card debt (Hogan, Bryant, & Overmyer-Day, 2013; Johannes, 2008). Two 21st century studies (Norvilitis et al., 2006; Norvilitis, Szablicki, & Wilson, 2003) reported that college students owed roughly 24% and 31% of their yearly income in payments toward retiring their credit card debt.

However, the real losers in this debt-to-wage-premium gamble are college dropouts. Depending on their length of stay in college and their spending habits while attending (Shaffer, 2012, 2014), dropouts face the prospect of paying off their debts while making no more in earnings, on average, than a high school graduate (Dwyer et al., 2012; Gladieux & Perna, 2005; Kadlec, 2014). Master advisors encourage students to complete their associate's or bachelor's degree as a way of optimizing their human capital.

In addition to all of the academic challenges associated with completing a college degree, a growing number of students in good academic standing face financial choices that force them to stop out or drop out of college; these financially-at-risk (FAR) students (Shaffer, 2012, 2014) jeopardize their chances of completing a college education and put their economic futures at risk by accruing burdensome debt. Although some use student loans and credit cards to pay for the necessities of a college education, many students also accumulate debt while financing an affluent lifestyle (Shaffer, 2012). This *premature affluence*, a term coined by economists for an expensive lifestyle (Bachman, 1983), cannot be sustained when students leave college and try to live independently.

Although students (and their parents) may be aware of the national problem of student loan debt, many seemingly fail to recognize the insidious effects of students accruing credit card debt to pay for cars, clothes, travel, entertainment, electronics, and the like while attending college. Unlike the deferred payment schedules for student loans, credit card charges become due immediately, and colleges lose more students to credit card debt than academic failure (Goetz, Cude, Nielson, Chatterjee, & Mimura, 2011; Shaffer, 2012, 2014).

College students need a solid plan for financing their education, and they also need the discipline to create and live by a realistic and sustainable budget while working toward their degree (Hitchcock, 2012; Olive-Taylor, 2010; Pellegrin & Zabokrtsky, 2009). Master advisors help students with financial planning and encourage them to take financial responsibility for their lifestyles.

Advising Activities and Techniques

Table 9.1 provides a schematic overview of academic advising integrated with career advising in a human capital approach. The advising activities appear in rough chronological sequence for use in advising students from their first year to graduation. Master advisors adopting the human capital approach provide assistance with course selection, decisions about majors and minors, exploration of future careers, and options for postgraduate education. The table features these familiar responsibilities along with several suggested activities specific to teaching students about human capital development and preparing them for entry into the new, knowledge-driven economy.

Calculating the Costs of a College Education

Table 9.2 provides an example exercise for students to use in calculating the costs of their college education. Useful in a classroom or in an advising setting, the information provided gives an advisor insights into the depth and accuracy of students' understanding of college as an economic investment (Shaffer, 1998). It also brings to light students' knowledge of the earnings associated with careers of interest. In this exercise, students make estimates of their investment in a college education by calculating their total educational costs using projections of their expected expenditures for obvious expenses such as tuition and fees, room and board for students living on campus, and books. Most students fail to recognize the opportunity cost of their college education, defined as the wages they forgo each year while they are enrolled in college. Depending on the tuition of the institution the students attend, the opportunity costs may culminate into the largest single cost of earning a college degree (Li, 2013).

Students experience difficulties calculating their own particular costs for two common reasons. First, many approach the calculation based on the most optimistic assumption time to complete a degree. At this point, advisors can inject some needed perspective by discussing the graduation rates at their institution as well as those at comparable institutions. First-year students pursuing 4-year degrees should choose to make their calculations on the basis of a plan to graduate in 5 years. Calculating 5-year costs for these students makes the resulting total larger, but also more realistic, than calculating the 4-year costs. Advisors at community colleges should make similar adjustments for their students' pursuits if an associate's degree or a certificate typically requires more than 2 years for most students.

Table 9.2. Example of expenditures for 1 and 5 years

Expense Type	Annual Amount per Year	Amount After 5 Years
Tuition and fees costs	$7,562	$42,508
Textbooks	$1,000	$5,000
On-campus room and board	$7,434	$37,170
Opportunity costs	$28,000	$140,000
Total projected costs	$43,960	$224,678

Note. Data from West Chester University, Pennsylvania, 2012

Second, many students do not understand the basis upon which to calculate their individual opportunity costs. Some students can readily supply an approximate annual income based on jobs they held during high school, and other students may supply a number based on information about a close friend or sibling without a college degree who works full-time. Master advisors provide a realistic number for students to use to calculate their opportunity costs. For example, they point to the most recent median annual income for high school graduates (in 2012, it was approximately $28,000) (Dewan, 2014).

Students can complete the exercise through a worksheet on which they enter current annual costs for tuition and fees, textbooks, and on-campus room and board at their institution (Shaffer, 1998), or they can provide an estimate of their annual opportunity costs and then calculate an estimate of the total costs for their education. For example, the costs of an undergraduate education at West Chester University, based on charges for a student matriculating in the fall of 2014 who will graduate in 5 years, is shown in Table 9.2.

Once they determine the final cost of their education, students should also calculate the length of time needed to recoup their investment after graduation and initial employment in their chosen career (Shaffer, 1998). I have asked students to estimate the time to amortize their costs in two steps. First, they find the difference between their anticipated annual earnings in their new career by the annual earnings they would have earned had they worked at the wage used to calculate their opportunity costs. Second, they divide their total costs by the difference in the expected and forgone earnings. As when they estimated the costs of their education, students usually express surprise about the time needed to make the money they have invested in earning a college degree. For example, according to the U.S. Department of Labor, Bureau of Labor Statistics (2014–2015a, 2014–2015b), the 2014 median entry-level salaries for a registered nurse with at least an associate's degree was $66,640, while the median entry-level position for a social worker with at least a bachelor's degree was $45,500. Using the $28,000 estimate of a high school graduate's annual income as a baseline, nursing graduates can expect to earn $38,640 more than a high school graduate, and social workers can expect to earn $17,500 more. Dividing the costs of their educations by these differences yields an estimate that nursing graduates with an associate's degree will require nearly 6 years to amortize their costs, while social work graduates must work for a full 14 years to amortize their investment in a bachelor's degree. As with the opportunity costs of their college education, many students have not fully considered the nature of their future occupations nor do they have any realistic notion of the earnings of any occupation of interest. Master advisors provide a realistic number for students to use in estimating their future annual earnings. For example, they can provide the most recent median annual income for college graduates; in 2012, it was approximately $45,500 (Dewan, 2014).

Master advisors use this exercise to discuss two important issues with students: the college wage premium and the dire economic consequences of dropping out of college. The difference between the earnings of college and high school graduates used to calculate the time needed to recoup the investment in a college education serves as the estimate of the college wage premium for each student. Utilizing the median earnings for college and high school graduates, advisees determine the median value of the college wage premium for the nation as reported by economists. After performing these calculations, they can speak intelligently about the economic payoff for their investment in a college education rather than speak in vague terms about expecting to earn *good money* when they graduate.

Master advisors can also inject the sobering thought that college dropouts earn no more than high school graduates once they enter the labor market, and for that reason, dropouts have no identifiable means to recoup the opportunity cost of lost wages for the time they attended college (Gladieux & Perna, 2005). Furthermore, master advisors offer instruction about the impact of any debt—student loans and credit cards—students have accrued while in college.

The introduction of debt can prompt a discussion of student financial behavior and lifestyle that leads master advisors to identify FAR students. Because of the level of detail involved in completing the wage premium exercise and discussing a student's finances, a master advisor may seek alternative means to present these topics outside the usual advising appointment, such as student success classes, joint workshops with career development or financial services professionals, or online assignments.

Advising Financially-At-Risk Students

Academic advisors are likely to work with students in good academic standing who feel forced to stop out, or drop out completely, because of borrowing practices that make their immediate debt service unsustainable. Even for FAR students who remain in school, financial stress can distort their perspectives on short-term educational choices. For example, they may not appreciate the value of unpaid and volunteer work experiences as means of growing human capital and may forgo these opportunities to work for wages that help offset their accumulating debt (Shaffer, 2012).

In addition, FAR students, in particular, may choose majors based primarily on the belief that such a selection secures a well-paying job. As a result, they may decline the opportunity to study another field with less clear career paths and economic opportunities. Questions such as "What can you do with a sociology degree?" may not be questions at all; they may be criticisms and judgments of student choices couched in figurative language (Roksa & Levey, 2010).

Even master advisors need to acquire the set of skills helpful in advising FAR students. They must detect FAR students and guide them toward responsible financial decisions by helping them plan the financing of upcoming academic terms just as they help them make important academic decisions concerning choice of majors and course work. In a previous publication, I discussed the work and lifestyle decisions that place students at financial risk and outlined steps advisors can take to help students persist and earn a degree while accruing manageable levels of debt (Shaffer, 2014).

Developing Transferable Skills

Transferable skills, which include the so-called soft skills or portable skills, are learned in one context but prove valuable and applicable in others (Parker, 2008). Graduates can advance these skills in any occupation at any level (from entry-level jobs to executive positions) and at any stage of a career (Shaffer & Zalewski, 2011b). Therefore, master advisors confidently encourage students to develop such skills as a complement to the content of any major or degree and as of equal (or more) value than discipline or occupation-specific skills. In fact, 21st-century professionals recognize both the hard skills of formal professional training and soft skills such as the ability to communicate with clients. For example, software engineers learn the hard skill of writing code in formal classes, but they also must use the soft skills of listening to understand their clients' needs, such as solutions to problems with the new software developed for an office system. Despite lack of a definitive listing of transferable skills, the following top any lineup: knowing how to learn (especially self-educating for new skills), reading with comprehension, writing effectively, listening to hear others, creative thinking, problem solving, goal setting, teaching, relationship building, and managing a task or project through to completion. Soft skills also include oral communication and computational skills and the ability to participate in career development, negotiation, conflict resolution, and leadership as well as in teams working toward organizational effectiveness (Shaffer & Zalewski, 2011b).

Formal education offers one of the best opportunities to develop transferable skills. In particular, the general education curriculum encourages students to acquire, or improve upon, transferable skills (Robbins, 2014). Employers hire college graduates hoping that their general education will become valuable human capital when the person is oriented into a new job (Roksa & Levey, 2010). In addition, liberal arts courses provide good sources for transferable skills and special knowledge that increase human capital. Students without an intellectual motivation for personal growth often consider rounding out their education with experiences that also increase their human capital.

McCracken (2010) presented a well-articulated example of identifying transferable skills developed by students of the arts. Noting that many parents assume that the arts hold little value in the job market, McCracken suggested that academic advisors explain that by engaging in the arts students develop valuable soft skills (e.g., critical thinking as well as communicating and understanding ideas). She listed less-recognized skills that transfer readily to the workplace. For example, arts students learn to focus on projects like few other students do: A dancer can stand in front of a mirror for hours working to position his or her feet perfectly while mastering a routine, and a graphic arts student frequently spends 20 or more hours to complete a single project. McCracken also described the ability to synthesize ideas (often in different media) into a new product, visualize the outcome of the creative process, and realize that image. She also explained that artists develop the ability to identify specific, concrete details involved in completing a larger, finished work and the skills to correct any flaws in those details. She emphasized the role that academic advisors play in helping arts students recognize the nature and value of these skills and transferring them to the global marketplace.

Master advisors integrate academic advising and career advising by assisting students with selecting courses—sometimes particular sections of courses—that simultaneously meet students' graduation requirements and develop transferable skills. For example, some general education courses labeled as *public speaking* clearly promise opportunities to develop communication skills. Many colleges and universities also offer writing-across-the-curriculum programs, giving students the chance to improve writing skills in courses outside the general education curriculum with sophisticated subject matter (Shaffer, 1997/2009). Master advisors make clear to students that building human capital does not postpone graduation, nor does it require taking extra course work beyond that needed for graduation. However, to develop human capital, students must develop mindfulness about the relative value of different courses as well as a willingness to take challenging courses in lieu of popular electives with reputations for being easy.

In a previous work, I recommended several strategies for developing human capital through acquiring transferable skills (Shaffer, 1997/2009). The following list offers updated and summarized examples:

o Many jobs demand high levels of numeracy such that students should take either higher level mathematics courses (e.g., calculus) or applied mathematics (e.g., statistics) in addition to those needed to meet general education requirements.

o Many jobs require skill in communicating with non-English speakers. Students who take foreign language courses to read or gain conversational fluency in a second language are valued in the global economy.

o Companies headquartered outside the United States report difficulty finding managers and executives who can work with partners in the States or the United Kingdom (Sanchez-Arias et al., 2013). Students with knowledge of foreign cultures, learned through courses covering the history, geography, or anthropology of a region or particular country—or by studying abroad—will have a head start on the cultural competence needed in the worldwide marketplace. Those who can coordinate courses with foreign language proficiency possess skills that stand out to employers worldwide.

o Many degree programs do not require students to select a formal academic minor; however, students who complete a minor that complements their major choice may increase their human capital. For example, a minor in a technical or applied program (e.g., business or technical writing) added to a traditional liberal arts major (e.g., psychology) may be especially appealing to employers.

Students reluctant to follow suggestions to gain transferable skills may see the ways they help them find an entry-level position after graduation. Master advisors remind them that their college education serves as a platform for success through-out their working lifetimes. Courses in an integrative liberal learning curriculum, taken for human capital development, may change students' attitudes, beliefs, and values, making them better candidates for success in managerial and executive positions later in life (Association of American Colleges & Universities, 2016; Robbins, 2014).

Crafting Career Interventions

In the literature produced and consumed by professionals, *career interventions* refers to a myriad of individually designed initiatives aimed at enhancing an individual's development of skills and special knowledge or helping an individual make better career-related decisions (Hartung, Savickas, & Walsh, 2015). Enabling students to experience career interventions embodies Shockley-Zalabak's (2012) vision of academic advisors as "intentional interaction designers" (p. 13). Examples of career interventions include career counseling sessions, academic career-oriented classes, computer applications (e.g., *Career HOPES*, Herman, 2010), and self-administered career inventories. Master advisors, because of their advanced conceptual under-standing and relational skills, may be particularly qualified to undertake career inter-vention with a foreclosure student, who has made a self-defeating, premature commitment to a career trajectory poorly suited to her or his abilities, values, or long-term interests (Shaffer, 2014; Shaffer & Zalewski, 2011c). They would also benefit from the valuable discussion in *The Handbook of Career Advising* (Hughey et al., 2009) on designing career interventions in the context of career development theories (Niles & Hutchison, 2009).

To offer career interventions, master advisors exercise creativity and design novel exercises and interactions as they play the role of labor market intermediaries (LMIs) (Roksa & Levey, 2010; Smith, 2010). According to Smith (2010),

> LMIs play a major disciplinary role in transmitting expert opinions about the ideal worker of the new economy, the new rules of employment and employability, how to manage impressions of one's self, and how to work in diverse, ever-changing work-sites (p. 285).

U.S. colleges and universities offer academic majors that vary in terms of place-ment in the labor market because the relative level of specific occupational training offered in the course work differs (Roksa & Levey, 2010). Some majors, such as nurs-ing, are clearly linked to specific occupations in the workforce. Other majors, such as sociology, have fewer discernible connections to specific occupations, and graduates must look diligently to identify and land jobs in which they can capitalize on their general, intellective skills. Many graduating in academic liberal arts majors exercise more creativity in entering the labor force than graduates in occupationally specific programs; that is, those in the arts must build bridges between their majors and career opportunities (Roksa & Levey, 2010).

As with FAR students, master advisors arrange career interventions by working cooperatively with other professionals on campus, especially career counselors, career educators, and career development and placement specialists (Niles & Hutchison, 2009). Career interventions can be scheduled in parallel with formal academic course work because they typically involve brief or informal activities. For example, attending a career talk on campus or arranging to take a vocational interest inventory does not require missing any formal course work. Other career interventions, such as service-learning projects, volunteer work, or internships, require advanced planning and coordination because of the extended time commitments they entail (Amundson, 2006). However, the best career interventions are timed to coincide with the period when a student is exploring career options and preparing to make important decisions (e.g., selecting a major) (Shaffer, 2015).

Career interventions provide excellent opportunities for advisors to introduce students to one of the central skills of knowledge workers: the maintenance of an up-to-date portfolio. Master advisors explain the importance and processes of documenting the acquisition and practices of the skills and special knowledge that constitute the student's developing human capital.

Developing Documentation of Students' Human Capital

Because documentation of human capital often supplants formal educational credentials and transcripts in the new economy, master advisors encourage students to begin their portfolio careers even before they graduate (Shaffer & Zalewski, 2011b). They need to identify the skills they intend to present to prospective employers as human capital and accumulate documentation for each element through such means as course syllabi, writing samples, capstone projects, evidence of participation in human capital-building career interventions, letters of recommendation, and so forth. Master advisors realize that most students do not value résumé building or maintaining a portfolio until they approach graduation, when they formally search for employment. Therefore, master advisors explain that in a portfolio career, documentation of experience, learned skills, and special knowledge is a part of the human-capital development process, which is based on the principle: "If you can't document it, you don't have it" (Shaffer & Zalewski, 2011b, p. 82).

Although some students may initiate the process with literal, physical portfolios for retaining hard copies of useful materials, others may prefer to maintain electronic portfolios. Many colleges are making investments in electronic portfolio systems for the purposes of assessment, but these same systems can be used to help students create individual portfolios to track their human capital development (Basken, 2008). Studies of student learning in courses including electronic portfolio components show that maintenance of portfolios encourages students to reflect on their learning as they complete course assignments (Eynon, 2014), especially as they create new skills and special knowledge when completing their assignments. Master advisors encourage this type of reflection so students recognize their human-capital development as well as document it (Shaffer & Zalewski, 2011b).

Summary

Academic advising as a form of teaching helps students get the most value from their college experiences and choices (Drake, Jordan, & Miller, 2013; Robbins, 2012, 2014; Shaffer, 2015). Advising-as-teaching has been increasingly described as an engaging educational enterprise (Campbell & Nutt, 2008) in which advisors design interactive experiences for students to help them reach their objectives through high-impact and scaffolded learning activities (Campbell & Nutt, 2008; Robbins, 2014; Shockley-Zalabak, 2012). Because many students (and some of their parents) go deeply into debt to finance a college education, master advisors integrate long-term financial literacy and responsible decision making into the process of making academic and career decisions (Shaffer, 2015). Master advisors creatively function as LMIs for their students, who will need to seek creative ways to remain employable over a lifetime in the new, knowledge-driven economy.

Many resources can assist advisors and advising administrators with the integration of academic and career advising services. I recently developed a model for career advising training built upon Gordon's (2006) model for a seven-step career advising process (Shaffer, 2015). *The Handbook of Career Advising* (Hughey et al., 2009) covers all facets of career advising services. The American Psychological Association has also published a two-volume reference work on career interventions (Hartung et al., 2015). Articles describing the human capital approach to academic and career advising, including those explaining the nature of the changes in careers and the requirements of employability, have also been published in the *NACADA Journal* (Shaffer, 1997/2009; Shaffer & Zalewski, 2011a, 2011b).

Aiming for Excellence

- In your own words, explain human capital and ways to maximize it.
- Develop a worksheet for calculating the costs of earning a degree at your institution; include the current costs of tuition, room and board, and books and fees.
- Know the published entry-level wages or salaries for jobs related to degree programs offered at your institution.
- Create a plan to talk with advisees about financing their education and develop a set of probes to check for signs of risky financial practices.
- Identify a network of professional contacts for student referrals concerning any financial issues or questions.
- Perform a periodic human capital inventory to help students recognize and document the skills and special knowledge they learn in courses, cocurricular activities, and job experiences.
- Develop an approach to helping students start a human capital portfolio and a plan for reviewing students' progress in maintaining that portfolio.

o Identify career intervention strategies that help students gather information about possible careers and encourage them to explore major and minor curriculum choices.

Assessment Strategy 1: Human Capital Inventory

Perform an initial human capital inventory with students by reviewing their transcripts and written summaries of cocurricular activities, systematically recording students' perceptions of skills and special knowledge acquired with each course on the transcript and each activity reported. Ask students to retain the records of each completed inventory and update the entries at regular intervals until students complete graduation requirements. Document the cumulative growth of human capital throughout the college career for student feedback as well as academic assessment purposes. Collect data including (but not limited to) the following categories: courses taken to improve human capital (e.g., statistics to increase numeracy skills), career exploration activities (e.g., formal career-interest batteries), cocurricular activities (e.g., serving as a staff writer or editor for a school newspaper), and career interventions (e.g., completing a service-learning project in a course required for the student's major).

Assessment Strategy 2: Portfolio

Collect data about student documentation of human capital development. Determine the proportion who have started a portfolio and document the time when they started collecting documents for their portfolio. Analyze the number and types of human capital development activities students have included in their portfolios. Develop a means for collecting these data at intervals both to assess students' progress in human capital development and to provide feedback and suggestions to students so they can improve upon their previous choices of course work and activities.

References

Amundson, N. (2006). Challenges for career interventions in changing contexts. *International Journal for Educational and Vocational Guidance, 6*(1) 3–14.

Arthur, M. B., & Rousseau, D. M. (1996). *The boundaryless career: A new employment principle in the new organizational era.* New York, NY: Oxford University Press.

Association of American Colleges & Universities. (2016, January 4). *Faculty leadership in integrative liberal learning.* Retrieved from http://www.aacu.org/ill

Avery, C., & Turner, S. (2012). Student loans: Do college students borrow too much—or not enough? *Journal of Economic Perspectives, 26*(1), 165–192.

Bachman, J. G. (1983). Premature affluence: Do high school students earn too much? *Economic Outlook USA, 10*(3), 64–71.

Basken, P. (2008, April 18). Electronic portfolios may answer calls for more accountability. *The Chronicle of Higher Education 54*(32), A30–A31.

Beach, J. M. (2009). A critique of human capital formation in the U.S. and the economic returns to sub-baccalaureate credential. *Educational Studies*, *45*(1), 24–38.

Bodenhausen, G., & Peery, D. (2009). Social categorization and stereotyping in vivo: The VUCA challenge. *Social and Personality Psychology Compass*, *3*(2), 133–151.

Campbell, S. M., & Nutt, C. L. (2008). Academic advising in the new global century: Supporting student engagement and learning outcomes. *Peer Review*, *10*(1), 4–7.

Dewan, S. (2014, February 12). Wage premium from college is said to be up. *New York Times* (New York edition), p. B3.

Drake, J. K., Jordan, P., & Miller, M. A. (Eds.). (2013). *Academic advising approaches: Strategies that teach students to make the most out of college*. San Francisco, CA: Jossey-Bass.

Dwyer, R. E., McCloud, L., & Hodson, R. (2012). Debt and graduation from American universities. *Social Forces*, *90*(4), 1133–1155. doi:10.1093/sf/sos072

Eynon, B. (2014). Completion, quality and change: The difference e-portfolios make. *Peer Review*, *16*(1), 1–11.

Free, M. (2009). Managing change, changing management. *Production Machining*, *9*(11), 13–14.

Gladieux, L., & Perna, L. (2005). *Borrowers who drop out: A neglected aspect of the college student loan trend*. The National Center for Public Policy and Higher Education. Retrieved from http://www.highereducation.org/reports/borrowing/borrowers.pdf

Goetz, J., Cude, B. J., Nielson, R. B., Chatterjee, S., & Mimura, Y. (2011). College-based personal finance education: Student interest in three delivery methods. *Journal of Financial Education & Planning*, *22*(1), 27–42.

Gonos, G. (2009). Review of "Staircases or treadmills? Labor market intermediaries and economic opportunity in a changing economy" by C. Benner, L. Leete, & M. Pastor. *Contemporary Sociology*, *38*(1), 85–87.

Gordon, V. N. (2006). *Career advising: An academic advisor's guide*. San Francisco, CA: Jossey-Bass.

Hall, D. T. (Ed.). (1996a). *The career is dead—long live the career*. San Francisco, CA: Jossey-Bass.

Hall, D. T. (1996b). Protean careers of the 21st century. *The Academy of Management Executive (1993–2005)*, *10*(4), 8–16.

Hall, D. T. (1997). Special challenge of careers in the 21st century. *The Academy of Management Executive (1993–2005)*, *11*(1), 60–61.

Hall, D. T., & Moss, J. E. (1998). The new protean career contract: Helping organizations and employees adapt. *Organizational Dynamics*, *26*(3), 22–37.

Hartung, P. J., Savickas, M. L., & Walsh, W. B. (Eds.). (2015). *APA handbook of career intervention* (Vols. 1-2). Washington, DC: American Psychological Association.

Herman, S. (2010). Career HOPES: An Internet-delivered career development intervention. *Computers in Human Behavior*, *26*, 339–344.

Hitchcock, T. (2012). *Mind over money*. Retrieved from http://www.nacada.ksu.edu/Resources/Clearinghouse/View-Articles/Financial-Planning-for-students.aspx

Hogan, E., Bryant, S. K., & Overmyer-Day, L. E. (2013). Relationships between college students' credit card debt, undesirable academic behaviors, and cognitions and academic performance. *College Student Journal, 47*(1), 102–112.

Hughey, K. F., Burton Nelson, D., Damminger, J. K., & McCalla-Wriggins, B. (Eds.). (2009). *The handbook of career advising.* San Francisco, CA: Jossey-Bass.

Hughey, K. F., & Hughey, J. K. (2009). Foundations of career advising. In K. F. Hughey, D. Burton Nelson, J. K. Damminger, B. McCalla-Wriggins (Eds.), *The handbook of career advising* (pp. 1–18). San Francisco, CA: Jossey-Bass.

James, J. (2012, August 8). The college wage premium. *Federal Reserve Bank of Cleveland.* Retrieved from https://www.clevelandfed.org/newsroom-and-events/publications/economic-commentary/2012-economic-commentaries/ec-201210-the-college-wage-premium.aspx

Johannes, A. (2008, August). College bound: Marketers welcome but credit card companies get a warning signal. *Promomagazine,* 22–24. Retrieved from http://www.gpamedia.com/advertisers/national/downloads/2008.08.01_college_bound.pdf

Kadlec, D. (2014, June 9). Here we go again: Is college worth it? *Time.com,* p. 1. Retrieved from http://time.com/2838169/is-college-worth-it/

Laanan, F. S., Hardy, D. E., & Katsinas, S. G. (2006). Documenting and assessing the role of community colleges in developing human capital. *Community College Journal of Research and Practice, 30*(10), 855–869.

Lazarova, M., & Taylor, S. (2009). Boundaryless careers, social capital, and knowledge management: Implications for organizational performance. *Journal of Organizational Behavior, 30,* 119–139. doi:10.1002/job.545

Li, W. (2013, Quarter 3). The economics of student loan borrowing and repayment. *Business Review,* 1-10. Retrieved from http://connection.ebscohost.com/c/articles/90602209/economics-student-loan-borrowing-repayment

McCracken, S. M. (2010). Understanding arts training: Beyond "soft" skills. *Academic Advising Today, 33*(3), 8.

Niles, S. G., & Hutchison, B. (2009). Theories of career development to inform advising. In K. F. Hughey, D. Burton Nelson, J. K. Damminger, & B. McCalla-Wriggins (Eds.), *The handbook of career advising* (pp. 68–96). San Francisco, CA: Jossey-Bass.

Norvilitis, J. M., Merwin, M. M., Osberg, T. M., Roehling, P. V., Young, P., & Kamen, M. M. (2006). Personality factors, money attitudes, financial knowledge, and credit-card debt in college students. *Journal of Applied Social Psychology, 36*(6), 1395–1413.

Norvilitis, J. M., Szablicki, P. B., & Wilson, S. D. (2003). Factors influencing levels of credit card debt in college students. *Journal of Applied Social Psychology, 33*(5), 935–947.

Olive-Taylor, B. (2010, December). We are known by the company we keep. *Academic Advising Today, 33*(4). Retrieved from https://www.nacada.ksu.edu/Resources/Academic-Advising-Today/View-Articles/We-Are-Known-by-the-Company-We-Keep.aspx

Parker, P. (2008). Promoting employability in a "flat" world. *Journal of Employment Counseling, 45*(1), 2–13.

Pellegrin, J. L., & Zabokrtsky, J. L. (2009). *The cash connection: Understanding the role of financial aid in academic advising.* Retrieved from https://www.nacada.ksu.edu/

Resources/Clearinghouse/View-Articles/Understanding-the-role-of-financial-aid-in-academic-advising.aspx

Pew Research Center. (2014, February 11). *The rising cost of not going to college.* Retrieved from http://www.pewsocialtrends.org/2014/02/11/the-rising-cost-of-not-going-to-college/

Robbins, R. (2012). Everything you ever wanted to know about academic advising (well, almost). *Journal of College Student Psychotherapy, 26,* 216–226.

Robbins, R. (2014). AAC&U's integrative liberal learning and the CAS standards: Advising for a 21st century liberal education. *NACADA Journal, 34*(2), 26–31.

Roksa, J., & Levey, T. (2010). What can you do with that degree? College major and occupational status of college graduates over time. *Social Forces, 89*(2), 389–415.

Sanchez-Arias, F., Calmeyn, H., Driesen, G., & Pruis, E. (2013). Human capital realities pose challenges across the globe. *T+D, 67*(2), 32–35.

Schultz, T. W. (1961). Investment in human capital. *The American Economic Review, 51*(1), 1–17.

Shaffer, L. S. (1998). Teaching human capital by calculating the true costs of education. *NACADA Journal, 18*(2), 47–52.

Shaffer, L. S. (2009). A human capital approach to academic advising. *NACADA Journal, 29*(1), 98–105. (Reprinted from *NACADA Journal, 17*[1], 1997, 5–12)

Shaffer, L. S. (2012). Live like the affluent in college, live like a student after graduation. *About Campus, 17*(1), 19–25. doi:10.1002/abc21069

Shaffer, L. S. (2014). Advising financially at-risk students: Detecting and addressing premature affluence. *NACADA Journal, 34*(2), 32–41.

Shaffer, L. S. (2015). Academic advising. In P. J. Hartung, M. L. Savickas, & W. B. Walsh (Eds.), *APA handbook of career intervention (*Vol. 2) (pp. 85–98). Washington, DC: American Psychological Association.

Shaffer, L. S., & Zalewski, J. M. (2011a). Career advising in a VUCA environment. *NACADA Journal, 31*(1), 64–74.

Shaffer, L. S., & Zalewski, J. M. (2011b). A human capital approach to career advising. *NACADA Journal, 31*(1), 75–87.

Shaffer, L. S., & Zalewski, J. M. (2011c). "It's what I have always wanted to do." Advising the foreclosure student. *NACADA Journal, 31*(2), 62–77.

Shockley-Zalabak, P. (2012). Advisors as interaction designers. *NACADA Journal, 32*(1), 12–17.

Smith, V. (2010). Enhancing employability: Human, cultural, and social capital in an era of turbulent unpredictability. *Human Relations, 63*(2), 279–303. doi:10.1177/0018726709353639

U.S. Department of Labor, Bureau of Labor Statistics. (2014–2015a). *Occupational outlook handbook, 2016–17: Registered nurses.* Retrieved from http://www.bls.gov/ooh/healthcare/registered-nurses.htm

U.S. Department of Labor, Bureau of Labor Statistics. (2014–2015b). *Occupational outlook handbook, 2016–17: Social workers.* Retrieved from http://www.bls.gov/ooh/community-and-social-service/social-workers.htm

10

ADVOCATING FOR ACADEMIC ADVISING BY LEADING

Chrissy L. Davis Jones

Leadership is a process by which leaders and followers elevate one another to higher-level morality and motivation.

—James MacGregor Burns (1978)

As the landscape of higher education evolves, so do the definitions of leaders and leadership. Today, master advisors are seen as thought leaders on the front lines of the quest for student success. Master advisors know that self-awareness and acceptance of their leadership potential are the first stepping-stones in their journey to becoming influential campus leaders. When they articulate a leadership vision generated through scholarly inquiry, master advisors identify actionable goals for professional development that becomes the framework for their emerging leadership roles. Master advisors build influence that allows them to speak to be heard, and they remain cognizant of factors that motivate them to engage in effective leadership practices.

Reader Learning Outcomes

From studying this chapter, advisors will use knowledge gained about leading as a master advisor to

- recognize one's place in their leadership journey through self-awareness and Freitag's (2011) academic advising classifications;
- articulate a personal definition of leadership and its importance to leading from their position;
- research and select leadership frameworks that support their personal definition of leadership;
- apply the 3-to-1 professional development plan model that features strategies for engagement; and
- speak to be heard to build their influence.

In 2003, Davis (2003) observed that "leadership has been recognized as an activity that can 'bubble up' in various places in the organization and need not be associated only with formal leadership roles" (p. ix). Master advisors take encouragement that, at their respective institutions, they guide tomorrow's leaders: students. McClellan (2009) referred to academic advisors as *thought leaders* because they understand and navigate the diverse and sometimes conflicting needs of multiple constituencies, including students, of higher education. This kind of leadership embodies the ability to influence and advocate for others through the use of various skills (e.g., effective communication, collaboration, advocacy) (Northouse, 2012). As thought leaders, master advisors must develop the two competencies that Northouse identified—influence and advocacy—while leading from their positions to support the institutional goal of student success.

Several scholars (e.g., Drake, 2011; McClellan, 2013; Pargett, 2011) have researched the influence of advisors on the lives of students; however, few have paid attention to the leadership practices and behaviors of master advisors in relation to colleagues and administrators. In this chapter, I describe the importance of self-awareness in leadership, introduce influential leadership as a framework, and present ways to build influence and advocacy skills. The case of John suggests practical application of the concepts featured.

John has more than 15 years of advising experience at a large, urban community college. Respected across campus because of his willingness to advocate for students and the advising profession, he is considered a master advisor. Based on expertise honed from his practical experience in academic advising, John has contributed to the scholarly literature base. Yet, despite his current scope of influence, John does not view himself as a leader and lacks a thorough understanding of leadership and his potential influence. To become effective leaders from any position within the institution, master advisors must develop self-awareness.

Self-Awareness

Bennis (1989) explained that "leadership is a function of knowing yourself, having a vision that is well communicated, building trust among colleagues, and taking effective action to realize your own leadership potential" (p. 9). McClellan (2009) built upon Bennis's definition by describing thought leaders within academic advising as individuals "whose ideas are so influential [that they] alter the way people think and act in the world" (¶1); however, before they can influence the thinking and actions of others, master advisors must first realize their own leadership potential as it evolves from self-awareness. They also must demonstrate a willingness to embrace the leadership role. Because postsecondary institutions are typically organized hierarchically and positions within the structure determine the acknowledged leaders, a cloud of complexity may prevent a person from recognizing his or her own leadership potential.

The view spawned from institutional structure often forces denizens to look past nontraditional forms of leadership as found in a professional's sphere of influence. Mirsalimi and Hunter (2006) explained that influential leadership relies on leverage as opposed to coercion (¶4). An influential leader, such as a master advisor, may use listening and dialogue to formulate a strategy that includes ideas proposed by others to reach the group's goals.

Master advisors' daily interactions with students, coupled with knowledge of theory, position them to be influential leaders capable of advancing student persistence. For example, John does not view himself as a leader because he does not occupy an administrative position in the traditional hierarchy. However, as a master advisor, his knowledge of student experiences and understanding of their educational journeys make him a valuable resource for those improving systems and processes that currently inhibit student success. As advocates, master advisors look for opportunities to inform and address issues related to student success as well as present possible solutions to problems within and outside of academe (Cohen & Lee, 2012; Nguyen, 2015). To champion student success, however, master advisors must know their place in their own academic advising journey.

Advisor Classifications

Freitag (2011) proposed four classifications that outline an academic advisor's progression toward professionalism and scholarship. Freitag's descriptions apply to both staff whose primary role is academic advising and faculty members. In this chapter, the terms *professional* and *master advisor* reflect Freitag's inclusive definition of both faculty and staff advisors.

Freitag (2011) referred to an *academic advising practitioner* as one who views academic advising as a job rather than a distinct profession. Many experienced advisors fall into this classification because to advance to Freitag's higher classifications, one must intentionally direct efforts to specific well-planned professional development.

Freitag (2011) referred to those seeking learning and engagement opportunities for advancement as *emerging professionals* or *professionals*. Both emerging and fully-fledged professionals view academic advising as more than a job. They earn and value certificates and credentials similar to other professionals (e.g., teachers or physicians), and they advocate for the profession and for students. An emerging advising professional can be differentiated from a recognized professional by the hours spent outside the office on field-related responsibilities. Advising professionals dedicate extra time to self-study and research, including various methods to improve practice that advance students and the institution.

Freitag (2011) called those in the most advanced classification *scholars*; these advisors are recognized for their knowledge of the advising field. The academic advising scholar shows enthusiasm for resolving large issues affecting the field, such as creating new knowledge through scholarly research, a specific activity that sets scholars apart from those in the other Freitag classifications. Academic advising scholars are continually "thinking about ways to improve and promote the field of academic advising" (Freitag, 2011, ¶12). The behaviors of academic advising scholars parallel those of thought leaders in that both express passion for their profession, and they use their knowledge and influence to change the way people think and act (McClellan, 2009, ¶1). Table 10.1 summarizes the classifications for academic advisors and the related characteristics.

Master advisors are classified as either professionals or scholars. The following questions encourage master advisors to reflect upon their current classification before advancing in their academic advising journeys and seeking leadership opportunities:

- o At what point in my journey should I expect to lead effectively from a position of master advisor?

- o What resources (e.g., professional development opportunities) do I need to transition successfully into leadership roles at my institution and within the profession?

- o How can I obtain support for my academic advising journey (e.g., through a mentor or supervisor)?

- o How can I leverage the characteristics of my advisor classification in leading from my position?

The process of determining readiness for leadership is typically initiated through self-assessment. Goleman (1998) described engagement in self-awareness as the first step toward both advocacy and leadership. Before influencing others, a leader strives to distinguish self. Through self-assessment, including research and candid reflection, academic advising professionals actively seek opportunities to evolve as advising scholars.

Self-assessment characterizes an authentic leader and enhances the self-awareness that drives master advisors to successfully embrace a leadership role. Reflecting on their responses to the self-assessment questions, master advisors establish their definitions of leadership and determine their scope of influence. Furthermore, master advisors view shortcomings as opportunities for growth.

Leadership Development

Leadership is not based solely on natural talents (Bennis & Nanus, 2003); leadership is also learned. The process of leadership, whether innate or learned, starts with a vision. Cohen and Bradford (2005) described vision as a graphic that, when well drawn, reveals the ways a realized vision changes the lives of others (p. 234). A leader's vision of outcomes serves as a compass pointing in the right direction, and it proves vital, especially when obstacles—such as discord—obscure the best path. Similar to the individuals who review budget requests and award funding for those projects most closely aligned with the institution's mission, master advisors use their vision as a guide for decision making. Master advisors articulate their visions by recording their responses to leadership questions (see Aiming for Excellence). By establishing this documentation, master advisors

Table 10.1. Characteristics of academic advisors by Freitag's (2011) classification

Classification	Characteristics
Academic advising practitioners	View advising as a job Aware of professional organizations (e.g., NACADA: The Global Community for Academic Advising [NACADA]), but may not be members Disconnected from but cognizant of the larger advising field Comprise the backbone of many advising systems
Academic advising emerging professionals	Express dissatisfaction with the view of advising as a job Seek out professional development Pursue opportunities to become academic advising professionals and improve their own advising practice Rarely take work home with them
Academic advising professionals	View academic advising as a profession and wish to be treated as professionals Demonstrate high qualifications and actively seek further educational opportunities Earn and value certifications and credentials Engage as members of and contributors to the field Advocate for the advancement of the profession
Academic advising scholars	Receive recognition for their advising expertise Remain current on advising literature and participate in their association (e.g., NACADA) Identify with the field of advising; view advising as their passion and calling Contribute new knowledge through scholarship and research Often work beyond the standard 40 hours/week; demonstrate dedication to service or research within the field

analyze their leadership abilities and start to sense the difference between leading and leadership; a truer and more active form of guidance, leadership is undertaken when one recognizes the rationale that affects her or his decision.

Northouse (2012) described leadership as an influential process based on relationship building or relational-based interaction that directs individuals and groups toward goal attainment. Goal creation constitutes part of the self-assessment undertaken in the journey toward self-actualization for a master advisor exploring and defining self under Freitag's (2011) classifications. A master advisor establishes goals as a step toward becoming an actualized self and a leader. More important, because a master advisor's visions must reflect his or her authentic self, professional development must be initiated with self-awareness.

Professional Development Plan

Master advisors are lifelong learners who actively seek engagement opportunities to advance their knowledge and skills through intentionally designed professional development plans. Hones and Sullivan-Vance (2007) outlined four steps to create a personalized professional development plan for new academic advisors:

- o evaluate and update a recent résumé or curriculum vitae,
- o ask a mentor or supervisor to review the résumé and identify possible professional development target areas,
- o establish short objectives that lead to the achievement of long-term goals based on the identified areas, and
- o create a realistic professional action plan (p. 143).

The procedure introduced by Hones and Sullivan-Vance (2007) applies to an initial professional development plan, particularly for new advisors. Master advisors, however, take their professional development plans further than advising newcomers by integrating a section on leadership development. They include research goals for identifying a leadership framework best suited for their work and academic advising classification (chapter 13).

Leadership Framework

A framework offers a complex approach to leadership development in that master advisors draw from a variety of theories, behaviors, and practices to develop frameworks that encourage development as campus leaders (Sandmann & Vandenberg, 1995). For instance, when he contemplates his move into campus leadership, John draws from Kouzes and Posner's (2007) five practices of exemplary leadership. Kouzes and Posner's research indicated that leadership does not emanate from a position within an organization, but embodies behaviors and practices that guide the effort to goal attainment. When he realizes that leadership does not depend upon position title, John gains a new perspective on his potential impact, which had been based on the assumption that change only came from members of the deans' council.

In 1977, Greenleaf described *servant leadership*, which is characterized by management that achieves organizational effectiveness through relationships with people instead of over people (p. 27). In 2010, Spears used Greenleaf's idea to identify 10 key servant leadership skills: listening, empathy, healing, awareness, persuasion, conceptualization, foresight, stewardship, commitment to the growth of people, and building community (pp. 27–29). In interactions with students, master advisors routinely use the skills delineated by Spears and the six pillars of character (trustworthiness, respect, responsibility, fairness, caring, and citizenship) identified by the Josephson Institute of Ethics (2015); therefore, they can readily apply them when collaborating with colleagues.

The full range model of leadership (Avolio & Bass, 1998) suggests that no one style works best for all situations. The model encourages an approach in which leaders move along a continuum of roles (e.g., coach or mentor), behaviors, and practices based on the situation.

The cited descriptions and examples of leadership featured in the literature do not make up an exhaustive list, but offer points of reference that master advisors can use as they explore and define the leadership framework that works best for them. Nevertheless, advisors can apply Mirsalimi and Hunter's (2006) influential leadership definition in many practical situations; that is, to influence others, master advisors first assess their collaboration practices with colleagues and see themselves as leaders. Advisors who use their expertise and ability to influence others possess essential elements of influential leadership. Master advisors employ their well-honed listening and persuasion skills to advocate for student growth and development (Spears, 2010, pp. 27–29) and in this way influence institutional decisions.

Opportunities to Develop a Leadership Framework

According to Hones and Sullivan-Vance (2007), master advisors must establish short-term objectives that support long-term goals aligned with their visions. Then master advisors share their visions, goals, and objectives with their respective advising administrators. The goal must be realistic, and the objectives that support the goal must be actionable. Hones and Sullivan-Vance suggested the use of a 3-to-1 model with each goal divided into objectives that lead to one, two, or three realistic actions. They further recommended that advisors develop a new objective every three months (p. 143).

John applies the 3-to-1 professional development model to build a leadership framework. First, he identifies the goal: identify and build a leadership framework to become an influential campus leader. Then he identifies two action items: research leadership theorists and compare their ideas to his own concepts of self-assessment and vision as well as the institutional culture.

To meet his first objective action item, John conducts a literature review to determine the leadership theorists who espouse ideas that most closely agree with his ideas of leadership. He searches scholarly databases (e.g., ERIC and ProQuest using his institution's online library as well as Google Scholar). As he reads the literature, John identifies influential leadership (Mirsalimi & Hunter, 2006) as an approach that most closely reflects his personal leadership philosophy, as it is rooted in content knowledge, relationship building, and collaboration used to achieve a common goal. John particularly identifies with two practices of influential leadership: use of self and modeling. According to Mirsalimi and Hunter (2006), influential leaders use self to assess themselves and their environment in efforts to respond appropriately to circumstances. They contend that modeling sets an example for others through behaviors and actions.

John has identified a practicable approach to leadership and seeks membership on campus committees, which offer significant opportunities for leadership practice and represent an appropriate and actionable way to meet his goal of developing a leadership framework. He sets a short-term (three-month) objective to identify a committee in which he can use his particular strengths and expertise. John communicates his goals and objectives to ensure that his supervisor considers him for engagement opportunities and will support his activities on the committee.

Master advisors may find one of several committees particularly relevant. For example, although curriculum decisions typically fall to instructional faculty, advisors involved with the curriculum committee can provide vital input because they serve as students' initial point of contact regarding classes. During the advising process, advisors explain to students the material they can expect to learn in their selected courses (i.e., learning outcomes) as well as teach them the ways the learning outcomes and course sequencing are woven together as the fabric for future course work. Through this interaction, master advisors prove crucial contributors to the design, management, and evaluation of effective curriculum: "The excellent advisor plays a role with respect to a student's entire curriculum that is analogous to the role that an excellent teacher plays with respect to the content of a single course" (Lowenstein, 2005, p. 65). When master advisors engage in campus committees (e.g., the curriculum committee), they serve as frontline thought leaders and often as the first to observe how proposed curriculum modifications affect student success.

Whatever framework is established for a professional development plan, master advisors must generate a series of objectives that build upon each other, thereby contextualizing leadership as an ongoing process of goal achievement. In fact, the term *process* implies continuation, which also applies to leadership, which evolves throughout an individual's life cycle (Avolio, 2007). Therefore, master advisors' professional plans must reflect their aspirations for growth as leaders.

Master Advisor: The Influential Leader

Master advisors are coaches, advice givers, teachers, and influential leaders. However, they must garner and continuously develop their skills to effectively lead from their positions. Because leaders and leadership have been historically associated with authority or positional power, the prospect of leaders emerging from nontraditional positions seems improbable. However, some researchers (Hogg, 2001; Yukl, 2010) have revised the definition of *leadership* to focus on relational aspects or personal influence. According to the *Merriam-Webster Online Dictionary*, *influence* is "the act or power of producing an effect without apparent exertion of force or direct exercise of command . . . ; the power or capacity of causing an effect in indirect or intangible ways."

Leadership as described by Webster's definition reinforces Maxwell's (1998) assertion that leadership is not a function of power or position but of influence (p. 16). Within this context, leaders and followers exist because of one another, and the leader's ability to influence is based on relational dynamics that influence outcomes.

Model of Power and Influence

Influential leadership includes the examination of influence as a tactic to generate buy-in to accomplish a common goal. French and Raven's (1959) framework acts as the foundation of their social power model. These two theorists identified five important bases of social power: referent, expert, legitimate, reward, and coercive (Table 10.2).

French and Raven's (1959) five bases of power model has been widely cited in research on social power and influence; for example, it is used to predict a leader's choice of various forms of influence tactics. A leader with positional power may choose to use force as an influence tactic while another chooses consultation to generate buy-in toward a common goal.

Yukl (2010) used French and Raven's (1959) research to identify behavioral outcomes after leaders applied different tactics to influence subordinates, peers, and superiors. Yukl (2010) identified three possible reactions of the target audience based on leaders' behaviors: commitment, compliance, or resistance (see Table 10.3). The ability to affect the behavior of others in a particular way reflects effective influential leadership (Cohen, Fink, Gadon, & Willits, 1992).

To explore the concept of influence and outcomes expressed by Mirsalimi and Hunter (2006), master advisors know the three different outcomes for exertion of influence (Yukl, 2010). The outcomes for influence, derived from the influence tactics model as originally posited by Yukl and Falbe (1990), were later explained by Yukl and Tracey (1992):

> A tactic is more likely to be successful if the target perceives it to be a socially acceptable form of influence behavior, if the agent has sufficient position and personal power to the use of the tactic, if the tactic has the capability to affect the target's attitudes about the desirability request (p. 526).

The direction of the target audience is affected by knowledge that engenders trust and respect by the leader. The content knowledge that inspires trust includes facts, concepts, theories, and principles on a subject; for master advisors, this knowledge could include institutional policies and procedures, job and department functions, and institutional history. Therefore, when coupling content knowledge with leadership skills (e.g., listening, awareness, persuasion, and building community), a person gains the ability to influence outcomes powerfully (Mirsalimi & Hunter, 2006).

Mirsalimi and Hunter (2006) emphasized service, integrity, and authenticity as core values of influential leadership. Master advisors, as influential leaders, know and accept themselves and their importance at the institution. For instance, they comprehend the reasons academic advising helps create student and institutional success. Advisors who do not thoroughly understand their roles lack authenticity and cannot adequately advocate for their profession or their students. The correlation between the importance of advising and service, the second core value, becomes clear to influential leaders. Master advisors seek opportunities to contribute to the greater good because they understand that service to their institution includes committee work, teaching, research, and writing (NACADA: The Global Community for Academic Advising [NACADA], 2005, ¶13). Finally, influential leaders communicate their role with integrity (chapter 7). Through ethical behavior like "walking their talk" (Mirsalimi & Hunter, 2006, p. 77), influential leaders, including master advisors, gain clout and establish trust.

Table 10.2. The French and Raven (1959) five bases of power

Five Bases of Social Power	Description
Legitimate	o Formal authority based on positions, working titles, or formal rights in an authority hierarchy (e.g., president) o The extent of power is usually related to the individual's scope of authority (also referred to as positional power). o Individuals with legitimate power may be perceived as demanding with the expectation that others will comply to accomplish the identified goal(s).
Reward	o The use of rewards, such as a promotion or special project assignments, to achieve the desired goal—partially related to legitimate power
Coercive	o Practice of threats, punishment (coercion), or negative reinforcement to manipulate the behaviors of others to achieve the identified goal—often leading to anger or resentment
Expert	o Information, task-relevant or special knowledge, and skills used to accomplish the identified goals—e.g., subject matter experts
Referent	o The respect of others due to likability, charm, or status of an individual within an organization o It is based on perceived expertise as well as the individual's perceived reliability. o A strong relationship characterizes referent power and the individual's character and integrity. o Individuals with referent power may also be viewed as charismatic or influential.

Table 10.3. Possible outcomes of influence tactics

Possible Outcomes	Characteristics
Commitment	The targeted individual internally agrees with the idea, action, or decision. The person demonstrates behaviors such as expressing enthusiasm, volunteering, or willingly undertaking assignments with full effort, helping others to envision the outcome(s), and inviting others to join the project.
Compliance	The targeted individual reluctantly accepts the idea, action, or decision. The person demonstrates behaviors such as indifference (lack of enthusiasm), partial or minimal effort on tasks, and lack of initiative.
Resistance	The targeted individual internally disagrees with the idea, action, or decision. The person may exhibit outright opposition, avoidance or withdrawal, delayed performance on tasks, or absolute refusal to comply.

Note. Based on Yukl (2010), p. 200

Master advisors know themselves, their roles, and best practices, and they hold themselves accountable. In light of their classification as professionals or scholars (Freitag, 2011), master advisors function as content experts well positioned to act as influential leaders on their respective campuses. They understand and articulate the purpose of their work, seek opportunities to contribute their knowledge, and practice leadership skills, such as advocacy, to promote change (NACADA, 2005, ¶13). Due to their expertise, master advisors wield considerable informational power, and they remain cognizant of the factors that inspire effective leadership behaviors as well as outcomes of various tactics so that they can make the most of each situation.

Advisor John's influence, for example, stems from his expert understanding of the ways students move through their degree programs. With his supervisor's support, John serves on the curriculum committee at his institution. At his third meeting, the committee received a proposal from the Social Sciences Department faculty, who expressed agitation with poorly written student papers. The faculty members had proposed adding completion of first-year composition as a prerequisite for their introductory courses. The majority of the committee members responded favorably to the proposal and supported the department's request to change the curriculum. John, however, expresses some misgivings about the addition of the requirement.

With a unique perspective on the reason some advisees earn low scores on their social science writing assignments, John feels compelled to argue in opposition. Based on his experiences and conversations with students over the years, John explains that many students start working on their assignments far too late into the semester, which may contribute to the poor performance. Also, John points out that a significant number of students who scored poorly on college-level placement exams register for introductory social science courses precisely because these courses have no prerequisite. John concludes that a first-year composition course may not be the appropriate solution for improving student performance on papers. He duly notes that the first-year composition courses do not teach students time management skills. John argues that acceptance of the proposal may create an unnecessary barrier to enrollment for students who are prepared for the introductory courses as well as create a bottleneck for those qualified to enroll in social science courses.

Leading from his position, John uses three leadership skills in this situation: strategic thinking, problem solving, and collaboration to express his reservations to the committee. He suggests that the committee review placement testing data (namely, reading) and grades over the past five years, available from the Office of Institutional Research, to determine whether a relationship exists between reading placement and students' success or failure in various social science courses. He employs his problem-solving skills to propose an alternate solution: John offers to meet with the social science faculty members to brainstorm a tiered approach to the writing assignment and to explore ways to incorporate the writing and tutoring centers as parts of a comprehensive approach while the data are gathered. He demonstrates his collaboration skills by offering to visit the introductory social science courses during the second week of the semester to help students create a calendar of deadlines for their assignments. By using his expertise and vision of the whole curriculum, John contributes to the institutional goal of student success in learning.

Building Influence

Bennis (2007) suggested that leaders identify strategies to build their influence, speak to be heard, and maintain motivation. Leadership is grounded in a relationship comprised of a leader(s), followers, and a common goal (pp. 3–4). Relationships established over time are pivotal to building influence (Covey, 2004) such that master advisors cannot be passive in their commitment to them. Master advisors identify building influence as a goal for their professional development plan on leadership. Specifically, they identify common interests with colleagues, collaborate, and get involved.

Identify a Common Interest. When establishing a relationship, master advisors should look for common ground with others. Most higher education professionals want students to succeed; however, the methods used to accomplish this goal vary (chapter 5). The different approaches to achieve the goal of student success most often create the discord that hinders progress. In situations where strategies conflict, master advisors listen and respond thoughtfully (not react defensively), and they use their problem-solving skills to create consensus.

Collaborate. As leaders, master advisors must include stakeholders when exploring solutions to issues. They view problem solving as an opportunity to collaborate. They rephrase a problem as a question that can be answered through scholarly inquiry (i.e., research and data) on student success. For example, John initiates collaboration with the social science faculty by restating the issue of poor student performance as a question: Does a mandatory time management assignment in Week 2 of introductory social science courses improve students' final grades? Collaboration encourages everyone with a common goal to hear alternative perspectives and demonstrate respect, a rudimentary element of establishing trust that aids in building influence.

Authentic Involvement. Master advisors must demonstrate authenticity by knowing who they are and the importance of their jobs. When master advisors consider involvement on their campuses or external organization (e.g., American College Counseling Association; NACADA; NASPA: Student Affairs Administrators in Higher Education), they volunteer for committees or task forces that will reflect their authentic selves (NACADA, 2005, ¶13). Engaged master advisors not only exert influence but also can be influenced. Being open to the suggestions of others, they contemplate the ways others' talents, skills, and spheres of influence contribute vital support to the proposed endeavor. Once they know their role, master advisors orchestrate their message to ensure that they are heard.

Speaking to Be Heard: The Language of Leaders

Leaders, including master advisors, exhibit effective communication. Master advisors interact with a wide range of individuals, from students to colleagues to administrators, and so they must tailor their communication style to fit the target audience. They need to communicate the problem, propose solutions, and define the future state by creating a vision. In leading from their positions, master advisors must recognize the interrelatedness between their communication style and their capacity to influence others.

Lateral Communication: Colleagues

Cohen and Bradford (2005) explained that "you will have to influence people above or to the side of you in the hierarchy, getting them to provide resources, information, support, or approval" (p. 233). Some of master advisors' best allies are their lateral or horizontally positioned colleagues. The relationship between master advisors and their colleagues, regardless of their levels in the organization, creates the environment for change. Many master advisors develop trusting connections over time and through mutual understanding.

For instance, John openly shares the experiences of advisors with the other members of the curriculum committee. He also involves the staff of the Office of Institutional Effectiveness because of their expertise in research and data collection related to student success. Most important, John uses his long-standing relationships with the social sciences faculty to learn more about their concerns and proposed ideas.

Connections must be nurtured to maintain trust; leadership requires a team of individuals who pursue a common goal. Influential leaders, including master advisors, do not work alone to influence meaningful change (Drucker, 1999) in student success, the act of teaching, or the process of learning.

To develop effective communication skills as an influential leader, master advisors use their listening and observation skills (Spears, 2010). An often overlooked way of understanding the current state of a department, process, or procedure involves exploration of institutional history, which has shaped the identity and culture of the campus and also has exerted influence on academic advising. Programs and individuals have left imprints on the institution, often related by successors, and master advisors recognize how those related experiences (positive or negative) have formed the current institutional environment. Understanding the organizational culture at their institutions, master advisors develop the system thinking necessary for influential leadership (Mirsalimi & Hunter, 2006).

Master advisors take special care to observe language or terminology associated with the institutional culture. Language has the potential to affect master advisors' abilities to establish connections and build influence across campus. For example, terms such as *professional advisor,* which delineate individuals whose primary role is advising students, and *faculty advisor*, which describes those with primary responsibilities in instruction and research, reflect past situations and contribute to current institutional culture. Master advisors use institutional culture, including nomenclature, to connect the different disciplines at their institution to the academic advising field, and they use it to foster their content knowledge and build influence across campus.

John hones his communication skills when his supervisor asks him to lead a task force of 15 advisors (primary role, staff, and faculty) charged with redesigning the college-level academic advising system. John's supervisor outlines the goal, expectations, and time line for accomplishing task force goals. His supervisor also requests an initial report in three weeks. At the first meeting, John shares the charge and expectations with the task force. He then directs that the members brainstorm ideas on ways to promote student success throughout students' advising experiences. He encourages everyone to participate in the activity.

Susan, a tenured instructional faculty member who also serves as an academic advisor, abruptly states, "No one is listening to what I am saying. I do not think any of the ideas we are discussing here will work. We have tried most all of these ideas in the past and none of them have worked. I feel like we are wasting our time on this activity and these ideas." John had noticed that Susan appeared increasingly disengaged from the larger conversation and she had started talking only with a fellow faculty member in an adjacent seat.

Resistance raises a common obstacle during brainstorming because proposed ideas may have been tried and failed in the past. Colleagues with institutional history may feel that their experiences are not heard or valued, which may deter the original purpose of the exercise. In this case, John recognizes that Susan, whose experience and knowledge of institutional history reflect her expertise, offers information that may benefit the group's work.

In leading from his position, John addresses Susan's concerns and reengages her in the larger conversation by asking her to share her knowledge of past advising system redesigns at the institution. As a follow-up, he asks, "Why do you think the previous redesigns failed and how can we avoid those pitfalls?" Using his listening and observation skills, John not only enlists Susan to use her content knowledge but also creates a space for Susan to lead from her position to accomplish the goal.

To build influence, master advisors understand the current institutional agenda. Language such as *student success*, *data-informed decision making*, *retooling* or *reorganization*, *doing more with less*, and *revamping remediation* or *developmental education courses* describes possible institutional agendas. Master advisors engage in the discussions inspired by these phrases and formulate ideas about the way academic advising assists with shaping their institution's future. To direct the future, leaders understand the past. Speaking to be heard, master advisors know the institutional history, culture, and current institutional agenda to influence change laterally and vertically (i.e., administration).

Upward Communication: Administration

Culture determines the leadership style used when addressing specific institutional challenges and opportunities for goal attainment (Blunt & Jones, 1997). Master advisors acquaint themselves with their current administrators (chapter 11). Each administration and administrator, including those of advising units, profess principles that reflect their unique leadership styles, such as autocratic or participatory; administrators will most likely display their leadership style through their communication.

Many administrators communicate using numbers. Wagner and Ice (2012) noted that the use of evidence and learning analytics (predictive data) empowers educators to prepare students for success (¶2). Administrators appreciate anecdotes; nevertheless, they are tasked with making improvements in student success that are measured numerically by federal and state stakeholders as well as accreditation agencies. For example, the numerical measures used to determine student success include the highest level of remedial or developmental math and English courses completed by students, term-to-term and yearly retention rates, and of course, graduation rates.

The data selected for evaluating success reflect the national agenda to increase the percentage of educated workers. In 2009 President Obama stated, "In a global economy where the most valuable skill you can sell is your knowledge, a good education is no longer just a pathway to opportunity—it is a pre-requisite" (The White House, 2009). Furthermore, he noted that the fastest growing jobs require some form of postsecondary education. Responses to this call to action from President Obama and the public fall to postsecondary executive administrators, who must clearly communicate to the academy its roles and responsibilities. As Shaw (1989) asserted, "Communication throughout the college has become a fundamental process not an afterthought" (p. 80). To strengthen their ability to lead and widen their scope of influence, master advisors address both laterally and vertically positioned colleagues and integrate data into their communication toolboxes.

In leading from their positions, master advisors share their knowledge, based on their observations, to build their influence when communicating upward. They pay attention to minutia, such as the proper use of terms, and the behemoth, such as the formation of ideas to support or change the current institutional agenda. For the latter, master advisors use data-based knowledge to construct concepts. Specifically, they employ three steps of the scientific method (Bhattacherjee, 2012): state the question, conduct background research to convey relevancy, and gather the necessary data to answer the question.

Employing the three-step approach, John and the task force identify the problem of the former advising system redesigns: No assessment plans (i.e., evidence) had been used to determine the effectiveness of academic advising practice or the revised advising system(s) in terms of student persistence and completion. The task force members ask themselves the following questions: What are the institutional completion rates over the past five years? Why are students leaving our system before earning their degrees? At what points are students leaving our system? The task force then conducts background research on the assessment of academic advising and student learning outcomes (chapter 14) as informed by Susan's historical knowledge of the previously attempted curricular adjustments.

John informs his supervisor about the data necessary to meet the outlined expectations. In a follow-up meeting with his supervisor, John reports that the task force has agreed to gather term-to-term persistence data and will use early registration for the subsequent term as a leading indicator for persistence. In addition, John explains that the task force used Susan's content knowledge as well as the institution's current agenda to identify questions that focused on effectiveness, assessment, and measures on which the task force members felt they could take action immediately (i.e., early registration) to shape the institution's future (i.e., persistence and completion).

The final step for master advisors in upward communication mirrors the previous step of sharing observations with multiple constituents. They tailor their communication and practice using data for effective upward communication; narratives with data are best for effecting change. Leaders report at all levels, including to those in administration, with data to close the communication loop.

Maintaining Motivation

In addition to effecting change, master advisors build their influence to maintain motivation for themselves and others. Self-motivation includes intrinsically meaningful activities that promote personal growth that an individual undertakes without external prompting and without expectation of rewards from others. According to Malone and Lepper (1987), engagement and completion of the activity constitute the sole reward. Malone and Lepper's definition suggests that leaders are motivated when they work toward meaningful goals that require completion of increasingly difficult, yet attainable, goals; that is, challenging goals motivate leaders because they provide new opportunities for personal growth.

Leaders maintain their motivation within supportive learning environments that offer challenges, pique curiosity, promote cooperation, and provide recognition (Malone & Lepper, 1987). Challenges result in one of three outcomes: commitment, compliance, or resistance (Table 10.3). Influential leaders find that tackling difficult endeavors reinvigorates them, and they also want to learn more about the problem. Influential leaders couple their content knowledge with such curiosity to refuel themselves. For example, an influential leader uses times of little progress to research an idea, develop an alternate influence strategy, or meet with a colleague who is clearly resistant to the proposed change (also a cooperation technique). Malone and Lepper described cooperation as a form of self-motivation because individuals receive satisfaction from helping others achieve a common goal. Finally, recognition for goal attainment makes up the ultimate reward for leaders because it means they advanced their leadership skills by engaging in a challenging goal or situation.

Challenging, yet intellectually stimulating, projects such as redesigning an academic advising protocol (John's situation) can generate change and expand leadership boundaries. Effecting change, such as demonstrating leadership, requires dedication, patience, focus, and appreciation of the importance of timing. To avoid fatigue, master advisors pay particular attention to these factors as they serve in leadership capacities. As influential leaders, master advisors often need to look within themselves to stay motivated during times of conflict and slow (or no) progress. They reflect and focus on the purpose of the change as means of monitoring their own energy and motivation techniques (Mirsalimi & Hunter, 2006).

Recollection of purpose offers another self-motivating strategy for master advisors. Understanding the reason for the effort inspires leadership in general (Cohen & Bradford, 2005; Kouzes & Posner, 2007; Maxwell, 1998; Mirsalimi & Hunter, 2006), especially for influential leaders, including master advisors, who must show assurance to convince others of the value of the project. This is particularly true when influencing a person or situation seems impossible: Leaders recall the purpose of the undertaking and do not allow others to dismiss it. Master advisors, as influential leaders, acknowledge and deal with failed outcomes, not as a stop sign but as a sign of yielding; that is, they may need to consider rerouting, revisiting the purpose, or reassessing the plan. When they yield and thoughts of discarding the plan surface, leaders reexamine the plan and action items before moving forward. Master advisors acknowledge leadership as a process by including regrouping strategies in their leadership development plan. Master advisors' actions connote them as resilient leaders who "analyze the circumstances, ascertain the meaning behind the unexpected, and determine whether there are appropriate adjustments to be made" (Wolinski, 2011, ¶3). Learning and using regrouping strategies are actionable and assessable items.

Summary

Master advisors lead from their positions. Those who succeed demonstrate self-awareness: They know who they are as academic advisors and the reasons their work influences student success. Through self-assessment, master advisors explore their authentic selves to embrace their roles as influential thought leaders on the institutional front lines. Moreover, master advisors generate professional development plans that identify engagement opportunities and develop the communication strategies that ensure they speak to be heard and build influence. Master advisors learn the techniques needed to build influence by maintaining motivation. Finally, to effectively lead from their positions, master advsiors equip themselves with effective leadership practices garnered from scholarly research. These processes and practices support the achievement of student learning outcomes.

Aiming for Excellence

- According to Freitag's (2011) advising classifications, where are you in the academic advising journey? Where would you like to be? Write a vision statement delineating the Freitag classifications that you intend to embody in five years.
- Develop or update your professional development plan to include a section on leadership development with a goal, at least two objectives, and relevant action items.

o Research and identify a leadership framework that best aligns with your self-assessment, vision, and institutional culture. After conducting your research, define *leadership*. Which of the theorists listed in this chapter best describes your leadership style?

o What characteristics do you believe a leader should demonstrate? Of those identified characteristics, which do you currently possess? Which characteristics allow you to effectively advocate for student success and widen your scope of influence? Compare your lists. Which characteristics may be areas for growth? How can you best develop those leadership behaviors?

o What strategies might engage your advising administrator in the development of your leadership skills?

o In leading from your current position, how do you communicate both laterally and upwardly to advocate for student success in learning? How might you use your professional development plan to tailor messages based on the target audiences? How do you want others on campus and in the profession to perceive you?

References

Avolio, B. J. (2007). Leadership is a process, not a role. In G. Brewer & B. Sanford (Eds.), *The best of the* Gallup Management Journal *2001–2007* (pp. 177–182). New York, NY: Gallup.

Avolio, B. J., & Bass, B. M. (1998). You can drag a horse to water but you can't make it drink unless it is thirsty. *The Journal of Leadership Studies, 5*(1), 393–399.

Bennis, W. (2007). The challenges of leadership in the modern world. *American Psychologist, 62*(1), 2–5.

Bennis, W., & Nanus, B. (2003). *Leaders: Strategies for taking charge* (2nd ed.). New York, NY: HarperCollins.

Bennis, W. G. (1989). Managing the dream: Leadership in the 21st century. *Journal of Organizational Change Management, 2,* 7.

Bhattacherjee, A. (2012). *Social science research: Principles, methods, and practices.* Retrieved from http://scholarcommons.usf.edu/oa_textbooks/3

Blunt, P., & Jones, M. (1997). Exploring the limits of Western leadership theory in East Asia and Africa. *Personnel Review, 26*(1/2) 6–23.

Burns, J. M. (1978). *Leadership.* New York, NY: Harper & Row.

Cohen, A. R., & Bradford, D. L. (2005). *Influence without authority* (2nd ed.). San Francisco, CA: Wiley & Sons.

Cohen, A. R., Fink. S. L., Gadon, H., & Willits, R. D. (1992). *Effective behavior in organizations.* Homewood, IL: Irwin.

Cohen, K. R., & Lee, C. M. (2012). The psychology of advocacy and the advocacy of psychology. *Canadian Psychology, 53*(3), 151–158.

Covey, S. R. (2004). *The seven practices of highly effective people: Powerful lessons in personal change.* New York, NY: Free Press.

Davis, J. R. (2003). Preface. In J. R. Davis (Ed.), *Learning to lead: A handbook for postsecondary administrators* (pp. ix–xii). Westport, CT: American Council on Education and Praeger.

Drake, J. K. (2011, July/August). The role of academic advising in student retention and persistence. *About Campus*, 8–12.

Drucker, P. F. (1999). *Management challenges for the 21st century*. New York, NY: HarperCollins.

Freitag, D. (2011, March). Freedom to choose: Advisor classifications and internal identities. *Academic Advising Today*, *34*(1). Retrieved from https://www.nacada.ksu.edu/Resources/Academic-Advising-Tday/View-Articles/Freedom-to-Choose-Advisor-Classifications-and-Internal-Identities.aspx

French, J. R., & Raven, B. H. (1959). The bases of social power. In D. Cartwright (Ed.), *Studies in social power* (pp. 150–167). Ann Arbor, MI: Institute for Social Research. Retrieved from http://web.mit.edu/curhan/www/docs/Articles/15341_Readings/Power/French_&_Raven_Studies_Social_Power_ch9_pp150-167.pdf

Goleman, D. (1998). What makes a leader? *Harvard Business Review*, *76*(6), 93–102.

Greenleaf, R. K. (1977). *Servant leadership: A journey into the nature of legitimate power and greatness*. New York, NY: Paulist.

Hogg, M. A. (2001). A social identity theory of leadership. *Personality and Social Psychology Review*, *5*(3), 184–200.

Hones, S. A., & Sullivan-Vance, K. (2007). Professional development: Looking ahead. In P. Folsom (Ed.), *The new advisor guidebook: Mastering the art of advising through the first year and beyond* (Monograph No. 16) (pp. 141–147). Manhattan, KS: National Academic Advising Association.

Influence [def. 3a & 4]. (n.d.). *Merriam Webster online dictionary*. Retrieved from http://www.merriam-webster.com/dictionary/influence

Josephson Institute of Ethics. (2015). *Making ethical decisions: The six pillars of character*. Retrieved from http://josephsoninstitute.org/MED/MED-2sixpillars.html

Kouzes, J. M., & Posner, B. Z. (2007). *The leadership challenge* (4th ed.). San Francisco, CA: Jossey-Bass.

Lowenstein, M. (2005). If advising is teaching, what do advisors teach? *NACADA Journal*, *25*(2), 65–73.

Malone, T. W., & Lepper, M. R. (1987). Making learning fun: A taxonomy of intrinsic motivations for learning. In R. E. Snow & M. J. Farr (Eds.), *Aptitude, learning, and instruction:* Volume 3. *Conative and affective process analyses* (pp. 223–253). Hillsdale, NJ: Erlbaum. Retrieved from http://ocw.metu.edu.tr/mod/resource/view.php?id=1311

Maxwell, J. (1998). *The 21 irrefutable laws of leadership*. Nashville, TN: Thomas Nelson.

McClellan, J. L. (2009). Thought leaders wanted: What each of us must do to advance the field of academic advising. *Academic Advising Today*, *32*(4). Retrieved from http://www.nacada.ksu.edu/Resources/Academic-Advising-Today/ViewArticles/Thought-Leaders-Wanted-What-Each-of-Us-Must-Do-to-Advance-theField-of-Academic-Advising.aspx

McClellan, J. L. (2013). Contributing to the development of student leadership through academic advising. *Journal of Leadership Education*, *12*(1), 207–233.

Mirsalimi, H., & Hunter, M. (2006). Influential leadership. *Rough Notes, 149*(8), 76–78. Retrieved from http://www.roughnotes.com/rnmagazine/2006/august06/08p076.htm

NACADA: The Global Community for Academic Advising. (2005). *The statement of core values of academic advising: Exposition.* Retrieved from http://www.nacada.ksu.edu/ Resources/Clearinghouse/View-Articles/Core-valuesexposition.aspx

Nguyen, G. (2015, June). Academic advising or advocacy? *Academic Advising Today, 38*(2). Retrieved from https://www.nacada.ksu.edu/Resources/Academic-Advising-Today/ View-Articles/Academic-Advising-or-Advocacy.aspx

Northouse, P. G. (2012). *Introduction to leadership: Concepts and practices* (2nd ed.). Thousand Oaks, CA: Sage.

Pargett, K. K. (2011). *The effects of academic advising on college student development in higher education* (Unpublished master's thesis). University of Nebraska, Lincoln. Retrieved from http://digitalcommons.unl.edu/cehsedaddiss/81

Sandmann, L. R., & Vandenberg, L. (1995). A framework for 21st century leadership. *Journal of Extension, 33*(6). Retrieved from http://www.joe.org/ joe/1995december/a1.php

Shaw, R. (1989). Telling the truth, warming the heart: The future of student development in the community college. In W. Deegan & T. O'Banion (Eds.), *Perspectives on student development* (pp. 73–84). San Francisco, CA: Jossey-Bass.

Spears, L. C. (2010). Character and servant leadership: Ten characteristics of effective, caring leaders. *The Journal of Virtues & Leadership, 1*(1), 25–30.

Wagner, E., & Ice, P. (2012). Data changes everything: Delivering on the promise of learning analytics in Higher Education. *Educause Review, 47*(4). Retrieved from http://er .educause.edu/articles/2012/7/data-changes-everything-delivering-on-the-promise-of-learning-analytics-in-higher-education

The White House. (2009, February 24). *Remarks of President Barack Obama: Address to joint session of Congress.* Retrieved from http://www.whitehouse.gov/the_press_office/ Remarks-of-President-Barack-Obama-Address-to-Joint-Session-of-Congress

Wolinski, S. (2011, January 11). *Adaptability and resilience in leadership* [weblog]. Retrieved from http://managementhelp.org/blogs/leadership/2011/01/12/adaptability-and-resiliency-in-leadership/

Yukl, G. (2010). *Leadership in organization* (7th ed.). Upper Saddle River, NJ: Pearson Prentice Hall.

Yukl, G., & Falbe, C. M. (1990). Influence tactics and objectives in upward, downward, and lateral influence attempts. *Journal of Applied Psychology, 75*(2), 132–140.

Yukl, G. A., & Tracey, B. (1992). Consequences of influence tactics used with subordinates, peers, and the boss. *Journal of Applied Psychology, 77,* 525–535.

11

ADVOCATING FOR ACADEMIC ADVISING

Brett McFarlane and Carolyn Thomas

Never doubt that a small group of thoughtful, committed people can change the world. Indeed, it is the only thing that ever has.

—Margaret Mead (Lutkehaus, 2008, p. 261)

Standing firmly at the intersection of academic and student affairs with networks that span the academy, master advisors are uniquely positioned to advocate for the advising needed to help students persist to completion. Where shackled by structural reporting line constraints, a lack of legitimate power and voice, and competition between positional demands, advisors may grow frustrated with an inability to effect broad political and structural change. In this chapter, we provide master advisors with a tool set to use for effectively advocating for advising, establishing communities of practitioners to develop common definitions of student success, determining best practices in meeting student needs, improving as professionals, and collaborating with administrators at all levels and across all areas of the institution to realize advising excellence.

Reader Learning Outcomes

From studying this chapter, advisors will use knowledge gained about advising advocacy to

- o understand the complex mechanisms, structures, and drivers that influence advising advocacy efforts;
- o utilize four approaches to advocate broadly for academic advising on campus;
- o identify key issues related to advising important to upper level administrators;
- o get involved as a campus thought leader and key member of the broader higher education learning network;

- appreciate advisor training and development as a mechanism for coalition building around academic advising; and

- know the key roles and communication networks necessary to advocate for advising enhancement at the institutional level.

Late on the first Friday of the fall term, Maria, an advising director in the College of Agricultural Science, prepares for her end-of-the week staff meeting. Exhausted, she reflects on the interactions over the past week and realizes that she has advised students in the college and from other colleges exploring fields in agricultural science as well as incoming transfer and international students. She has also met with college faculty members and instructors in partner colleges that offer key feeder courses. In addition, she has consulted with various department chairs and staff from the registrar's office, admissions, and student judicial affairs as well as heads of the academic success, counseling, and career centers. She walked a student contemplating suicide to the crisis center, spent two hours on the phone with an upset parent, and attended three evening welcome events.

In the midst of all the hands-on consultations and appointments, Maria struggles to provide effective professional development to her staff. Her advisors work with approximately 6,000 undergraduates. Some have held their positions for 20 years and others have gained 3 to 5 years of advising experience. In addition, several new professionals joined her unit within the past 2 years. Most of the new hires earned graduate degrees in higher education administration, academic advising, counseling, or adult education. Her advisors with midrange experience hold a combination of bachelor's and master's degrees, and a few of the long-term advisors do not have bachelor's degrees.

The disparity in advisor experience became a source of concern most recently when Maria was called into an emergency meeting with the dean to brainstorm ideas on the best way to respond to the university president who had demanded that the dean "fix" advising. After hearing the request for help and guidance with this charge, Maria immediately wonders what the president means by *fix*. Regardless of the meaning of it, Maria knows that any improvements require the input of master advisors (Miller, 2003) and suggests forming a task force to study the issues and make recommendations. Although she instinctively knows the advising staff members best suited to serve on the task force, Maria acknowledges two confounding facts: The more seasoned staff lack familiarity with the latest theories and research in the field, and the newer staff have not yet developed many of the interpersonal skills that characterize the experienced advisors. Perhaps most important, Maria realizes that the expertise offered in the task force directly reflects on the profession of academic advising and on her ability to advance the profession on her own campus.

Maria works in an environment in which many master advisors and their administrators thrive: They work with a diverse group of students, network with the best people on campus to advocate for students, smooth troubled waters among staff members, enable students to explore and navigate ambiguity, and connect students with tools for success. In this chapter, we focus on how a generalized request, such as a call to fix advising, can serve as a vehicle for change. Specifically, we address the ways uniting advising colleagues across campus raises the visibility and impact of quality academic advising to those less familiar with it.

Through the narrative presented in this chapter, we challenge master advisors to view their career, including duties, abilities, and potentialities, through a new lens. Each week master advisors connect with people of various positions within systems interwoven in the academic advising enterprise. Advisors often struggle with under resourcing, which leads to high workloads and little time to seek improvements. In addition, master advisors may be underrepresented within institutional forums in which decisions about resources and student success initiatives are made. As a result, master advisors face a dual challenge: They must daily seize opportunities to create broader networks, and they must make administrative allies who can partner with them to effect change. Master advisors embrace the opportunity to enhance the positive impact of advising on students and improve the perception of advising on campus.

Master advisors can become more effective advocates for students and for academic advising by

o building an organized community of practice;

o identifying institutional opportunities for coalition building;

o advancing practice through intentional training, development, and assessment activities; and

o working with key administrators to intentionally guide advising decisions.

In addition, master advisors identify and recruit crucial campus leaders outside academic advising to help promote advising, including efforts to address structural barriers and systems that have positioned academic advising in a location from which effecting change can be difficult. In addition to addressing the roles of master advisors in the current postsecondary climate, we discuss approaches to overcome obstacles for advancing practice, career, and the advising field. We also offer tools for constructing potential solutions to vexing issues.

Barriers to Effective Advising Advocacy

Reporting Lines

To advocate for academic advising, the master advisor first recognizes inherent impediments to progress. At many institutions, structural barriers present the most significant challenge. Nonuniform and nonstandardized reporting lines for academic advising pose one such obstacle to advisors seeking to influence important educational processes. According to a recent national survey administered by NACADA: The Global Community for Academic Advising, people conducting advising at three fifths of all surveyed postsecondary institutions report through academic affairs (Carlstrom & Miller, 2013c) while at one fifth of the surveyed institutions, advisors report through student affairs. At other institutions, advisors report jointly through academic and student affairs. Respondents from public doctoral universities indicated that 83% of surveyed campuses had advising reporting through academic affairs. Data also showed that academic affairs served as the primary reporting line for six of eight of the survey's identified institutional types (Carlstrom & Miller, 2013d). This is different from 2-year institutions where the preponderance of survey respondents indicated that advisors report through student affairs (Carlstrom & Miller, 2013d).

The complexity of these reporting lines extends beyond structural divisions between academic and student affairs. Advisors housed in academic affairs may work in one of various academic departments, in a midlevel cluster or divisional-level unit within a college, in a college-centric office, within a clustered or university-wide advising program, or another unique structure (Barron & Powell, 2014; Habley, 1983, 2004; Pardee, 2000, 2004). Advising positions in these various units rarely fall under the same leadership hierarchy. Advisors may report to a faculty undergraduate advisor within a department, an administrator within a department, a department chair, an administrator outside the department, or others. The reporting lines are further confounded by the classification of advisors as faculty members, instructors, staff, graduate students, or undergraduate peers, each with reporting lines unique to the administrative structure.

This complexity also characterizes reporting lines within student affairs. Academic advisors may work out of residential life, tutoring centers, career services, retention programs, international student services, or one-stop enrollment centers, among others (Manning, Kinzie, & Schuh, 2013). Perhaps as equally convoluted as that in academic affairs, the reporting structure in student affairs may consist of one central administrator with a direct hierarchical or a decentralized reporting line.

Lack of Legitimate Power and Voice

Academic advising not carefully threaded with institutional core purpose risks being a marginalized function seen as external to the primary mission (Campbell, 2008, p. 232). In addition, rewards for quality academic advising may be limited or nonexistent for faculty and primary-role advisors who excel at their work (Wallace, 2013). In many cases, "more advisees" comes as the response to "What reward is there for being a good advisor?" Furthermore, the nature of advising responsibilities (e.g., as clerical or student focused) depends on the reporting line, philosophy of administrators, and institutional mission (Self, 2008).

The disincentives for advising excellence extend to faculty advisors. According to the *2011 NACADA National Survey of Academic Advising*, fewer than 30% of all institutions, regardless of type (e.g., 2-year, private bachelor, doctorate, etc.), include any reference to advising in faculty evaluations (Carlstrom & Miller, 2013b), and as pointed out in chapter 12, the extent to which any incentives promote excellence in advising remains unclear.

The distance of primary-role advisors, in particular, from high-level administrative concerns contributes to this lack of attention to advising as a practice and an absence of clear pathways for encouraging advising excellence. The typical president's or chancellor's cabinet is populated by individuals charged with the functions historically considered primary to the institution: research, faculty affairs, graduate and undergraduate studies, international affairs, and resolution of campus-level issues. Advisors, omnipresent but dispersed across student affairs, colleges, departments, and undergraduate studies, are seldom included at that decision-making table. Therefore, with academic advising buried in most high-level administrative reporting structures, advising issues rarely reach upper administration except through elevated complaints from students, parents, politicians, or donors. As a result, senior administrators may think of advising in a negative context that results in the perceived need to fix it, as one sees in the example of Maria and the master advisor task force. This lack of voice, compounded by the vast distribution of advising positions across the campus and the variety of responsibilities and duties that advisors may be assigned outside academic advising, may result in trickle-down funding designed mainly to keep advising afloat while impeding efforts to consider new structures and practices that can develop true advising excellence (Carlstrom & Miller, 2013a; Self, 2008; Wallace, 2013).

Incongruent Paradigms

In addition to the gulf between primary-role advisors and upper administrators, dissonance among various types of advisors on campus contributes to some advisor difficulties in securing a place at the planning table and receiving financial support. The shift in academic advising from a focus on teaching to a focus on learning, since 2000, has pushed the basis of practice from student development theory to close alignment with the learning mission of the institution (Drake, Jordan, & Miller, 2013; Gordon, Habley, & Grites, 2008; Hemwall & Trachte, 2005). This movement follows the broader higher education trend toward the learning paradigm and away from the teaching paradigm as introduced by Barr and Tagg in 1995.

In the midst of this evolving postsecondary shift, several theorists and researchers recognized the significant opportunities for concomitant systemic changes in academic advising (Hemwall & Trachte, 2005; Lowenstein, 2005; Melander, 2005). As a result of the learning paradigm, academic advising is now referenced in a language familiar to the faculty, but primary-role advisors trained under developmental and counseling approaches are challenged to integrate new theories and approaches into practice. Furthermore, advisors must define their positions and roles to facilitate student learning objectives; that is, they need to identify the assessable knowledge and skills that students need to know, do, and value as a result of their interactions with academic advising.

These role conflicts that emerge as advising shifts from a developmental and counseling paradigm to a teaching and learning paradigm may add confusion for advisors trying to collaborate across student affairs and academic affairs. These collaborators may not share the same language or goals. As a result, camps of advising practitioners may unintentionally offer contradictory advice to students and work at cross-purposes, effectively diminishing rather than enhancing student success. Advisors and their administrative advocates, who want to see these structural and political challenges overcome, must seek proactive solutions to ensure that this crucial profession plays an important role in 21st-century strategies for enhancing student success.

Advocating for Advising

The master advisor task force needs to form networks of individuals who advocate with a united voice for advising professionalization, support, and recognized integration into the key campus mission. Advisors, master advisors, advising administrators, and higher education administrators can take one or more of the following approaches to begin forming these networks and using them to push for political and structural change:

o Weave advising into an organized community of practice on campus by building upon existing ecosystems.

o Identify institutional and political opportunities for coalition building in advising through the use of campus networks and committees.

o Enhance and advance practice through intentional training, development, and assessment activities.

o Provide focused administrative-level guidance.

Building an Organized Community of Practice

Wenger (2011) explained, "Communities of practice are groups of people who share a concern or a passion for something they do and learn how to do it better as they interact regularly" (p. 1). Building a community of practice around academic advising requires members to draw on the strength of existing connections, organize across student and academic affairs, develop common language and goals, and formalize campus advising and communication networks.

Utilizing Existing Connections.   Maria knows that master advisors build numerous relationships across campus that include broadly developed connections within their own department or college and other colleges on campus as well as with faculty members and student affairs partners crucial to student success. In chapter 10, Chrissy Davis Jones describes master advisors as influential leaders, and she specifically points to Northouse's (2012) definition of leadership as the ability to influence and advocate for others in an effort to achieve a common goal. A leader influences the behavior of others in a particular way (Marion & Gonzalez, 2013), and Maria enjoys status as a leader because she has gained trust and respect from members of her community.

Master advisors develop this high regard through expert power as defined by Raven and French (1958). The master advisor is a *cultural navigator* of the institution, a campus expert who helps students negotiate a variety of institutional, cultural, and personal barriers (Strayhorn, 2014) (chapter 3). Leaders seek opportunities to contribute to the greater good because they understand their purpose and prove their dedication to students by "walking their talk" (Mirsalimi & Hunter, 2006, p. 77). As a result of these efforts, their power has an impact.

Bridging Academic and Student Affairs. Creating a networked community of practice to support the work of academic advisors starts with strengthening the most crucial partnership—that between academic and student affairs. The research definitively shows that meaningful change in academic advising requires a collaborative partnership between those responsible for academic and student affairs functions (Bourassa & Kruger, 2002; Kezar, 2003; Whitt et al., 2008).

Magolda (2005) noted that ignoring or minimizing differences may seem satisfying in the short term but will undermine efforts in the long term. The values primarily associated with academic affairs center around generating and disseminating knowledge, offering collegiality, and encouraging autonomy (p. 20). Student affairs values tend toward respecting difference, increasing student self-awareness, and meeting students' multiple needs (p. 20). As a result, meaningful progress in creating a community-of-practice network that supports each individual's work with students requires open discussion to avoid misunderstandings or conflict. When the values of academic advisors, regardless of reporting line, can be aired openly and without judgment, then strategies to assess the efficacy of collective efforts can materialize.

The required openness and trust are not always achieved quickly. Yet, out of conflict can come collaboration. With a better understanding of partnership, which Kezar (2003) defined as individuals who work together toward a common purpose with equal voice and responsibility (p. 38), collaboration can emerge.

To undertake this important—but challenging—work of building bridges, the work of Kuh (1996) and his guiding principles for creating seamless learning environments can serve as a road map (pp. 136–143). Kuh proposed a six-step model for altering values through dialogue:

o Generate enthusiasm for renewal.

o Create a common vision of learning.

o Create a common language.

o Foster cross-functional dialogue.

o Examine the influences of student culture on student learning.

o Focus on systemic change.

Research has shown a relationship between institutions that utilized Kuh's strategies and highly successful collaborative programs (Kezar, 2003). Advising administrators and master advisors initiate the open dialogue that facilitates cultural change. The strategies for enhancing student advising outcomes evolve from such an intentionally developed academic culture.

Sharing a Common Language.   Kuh (1996) highlighted the importance of building common language and vision to facilitate cultural change in postsecondary learning environments. Shared terms and desired outcomes benefit from mutual vetting as conducted through advisor training and development as well as advising assessment, technology, and governance. Collaborators in student affairs and academic affairs who aim to create shared responsibility for student success across their domains may find Kuh's strategy particularly helpful.

Construction of a common language in which different approaches to advising success can be expressed and yet subjected to a limited, readily understood vocabulary should be a goal for any group wanting to build an interconnected, cooperative advising effort. If advisors in academic affairs understand student affairs colleagues' goals and desired means for achieving them, then they know when and to whom to refer students (and the same is true in reverse). Questions to address at this point in the collaboration process may include

o How is academic advising defined by campus stakeholders?

o What is the on-campus goal for academic advising?

o What accomplishments currently met through academic advising may be better achieved in other ways?

If people answer these difficult questions honestly, disagreements will necessarily surface. However, discordant perspectives need to be recognized and turned from points of acrimony to bonds of strength within the advising community. A skilled mediator can push through these obstacles to achieve progress. Someone trusted on both sides of the advising community, such as a director of advising who reports jointly to academic and student affairs, may accomplish much in this important role.

In the end, participants should agree to a generalized goal regarding the desired achievements for advising and the terms and language that describe institutional advising practice. A common understanding and language among all advising professionals will strengthen an advising community of practice.

Formalizing Campus Advising Networks.   On some campuses, academic advising networks are informally created and thus lack stability. Irregularly held or untimely meetings (e.g., held over lunch hours) and fleeting, rotating, or nonexistent leadership undermine cohesion. Networks may rely on informal membership unrecognized as a formal body within the organizational structure. Network goals and objectives vary from establishing venues for advisors to vent frustrations, creating informal training opportunities, or resolving key problems. Network activities and achievements may shift year to year as they depend upon informal leadership and sporadic membership. Marginalized status within the organizational hierarchy may prevent the group or member advisors from influencing meaningful policy or structural changes.

Despite the prevalence of informal networks, some institutions formally recognize advising bodies controlled by a faculty senate, student affairs, or executive leadership (NACADA, 2015). Although NACADA has developed partnerships with some of these institutionally recognized organizations (e.g., Purdue Academic Advising Association and the Old Dominion Advising Network, NACADA [2015]), no data indicate their prevalence across institutional types.

Maria knows that to create a formal and recognized advising network she must rely on a variety of master advisors within the task force. Once a starting point for collaboration is identified, the task force must determine the ideal institutional host for a new advising network. The reporting structure for advising within the institution will factor into the decision. At Maria's institution, academic advising is housed in the colleges (at a community college, a one-stop enrollment center may be used). As a result, a home within the broader academic affairs hierarchy offers an ideal position for any professional development network. The master advisor task force may approach upper level administrators (e.g., the provost or vice provost for undergraduate studies) as primary partners and hosts for this new community. If met with resistance, the task force may find success with either human resources or a campus center for teaching and learning, whichever takes charge of developing employee knowledge and assessing performance. Among the possible choices, the institutional home must give the network formal recognition.

Academic advising marginalization within institutions often results from lack of formal authority and reporting structure for practitioners. By establishing a formal home and creating a steering committee for an advising professional development network, Maria and the master advisor task force initiative can make progress toward establishing academic advising as a recognized body on campus. A formalized advising network can influence other important issues on campus such as advising technology and assessment. As understanding broadens, membership in the network increases and advisors see the importance of working with stakeholders within the administration, faculty, and various student affairs units to ensure any proposed formal structures have been vetted appropriately. This appreciation for collaboration both strengthens and broadens the advising community of practice.

Formalizing Campus Advising Communication Networks. Academic advising communication networks may act as powerful forces for change within an institution. Along with advising networks across campus, an active communication channel makes advising visible and pronounced within the institution. The following suggestions may help master advisors create a campus advising communication network:

1. Determine who needs to be included in the network.

2. Determine how key partners align with the work of academic advising.

3. Identify the ideal mode of communication among advising stakeholders.

4. Formalize and institutionalize the defined communication relationship.

The first step in developing a strong advising communication network involves clearly identifying the individuals who can contribute to it. Advisors are an obvious choice, but key partners such as those from admissions, the registrar, career services, information technology (IT), student support services, faculty senate or faculty union, and residential life need to be carefully considered.

The second step is determining ways that these key partners align with the work of academic advising and the ideal connection points for enhanced communication. For example, to prepare recruitment materials and communication plans, the admissions office relies on updates from the advising community. At most institutions, admissions follows a prescriptive plan and time line for developing these materials. The staff identifies every prospective student months in advance and logically sequences each communication to meet important admission deadlines. Advising administrators and master advisors who engage admissions early and actively ensure that accurate information is provided to prospective students.

In contrast, the relationship between advising and IT does not necessarily require regular contact. Much of the communication between the parties concerns noncyclical projects or events; therefore, it may be undertaken more periodically or episodically than communication with admissions.

The third step requires identification of the ideal communication mode among advising stakeholder units. Would reports from a standing committee or a quarterly review meeting offer the best way to keep information flowing? Perhaps regular, informal briefings among key administrators in each respective unit would encourage the most productive communication.

The final step involves formalizing and institutionalizing the defined relationship, which will only survive if each party receives benefits from the established structure. Formalizing and celebrating the relationship ensure that each party understands the terms and schedule for making connections; formalization also encourages regular assessments such that the format and structure of the relationship remain viable and appropriate. Specifically during review periods, participants can ask important questions: Is this partnership helping to achieve both of our goals? Are the right colleagues and partners involved? Are we making positive progress together?

Building advising into an organized community of practice first requires recognition of the many connections that master advisors, such as Maria, already enjoy through the advising profession; these established relationships provide a basis for building a larger community. One of the most important bridges covers the gap between academic and student affairs. A collaborative academic and student affairs community enhances student success as does an agreed-upon common language regarding student success metrics. Therefore, establishment of formal communications may make the greatest contribution to this collaboration goal. However, informal relationships and communication networks on campus may work well when addressing individual student needs but are insufficient to maintain an ongoing community of practice that furthers the profession of advising and the broader needs of the campus advising community. For example, the task force, because of particular expertise held by its members, may identify communication between the College of Agricultural Science and the Career Services Center as an area for improvement. Although useful, such a finding would not indicate all the communication issues involving advising that could be improved. In the next step, each task force member may engage in conversations within their respective colleges and units to determine other key communication networks that need to be enhanced. Informal discussions and the broader structure are ultimately complementary: The task force creates an ongoing formal structure that converts informal findings and local conversations into broad-based learning among all advisors, and ultimately, positive action for change.

Opportunities for Coalition Building in Advising

The community of practice, and advising discussions in general, must align with broad institutional goals and priorities. Although coordination of advising between academic and student affairs generates the first significant step toward this end, another critical step involves senior administrators; they must view advising as an important tool for achieving broad institutional and statewide initiatives.

Data Showing That Advising Matters. An honest appraisal over the past three decades would reveal that the advising community has not done the best job of helping administrators understand the impact and efficacy of academic advising. Too often introductions to potentially convincing data points start with "I had a student once who . . ." or "for many of my students . . ." rather than statements such as "a statistically significant portion of first-year students who participated in . . ." or "student learning on this particular advising outcome indicates that. . . ." Furthermore, when master advisors count the number of advising appointments, focus on student–advisor ratios, or report the number of e-mails that were answered in a given time, they describe volume and activity, which does little to address the challenges facing administrators, who need to show fulfillment of a desired result.

Academic advisors will not occupy a seat at the decision-making table until key administrators see advising as a function—not only as beneficial for students—but also as means to affect the key metrics by which the campus as a whole is evaluated. A positive model of a partnership that achieves this kind of leverage can be seen between chief academic officers and chief business officers who focus on data-driven institutional success (Porter, 2013). Academics now realize the way metrics and data analyses can lead to greater financial resources for the academic enterprise. Master advisors can do the same by delineating their efforts and subjecting them to assessment to determine, and make known, their levels of success (chapters 14 and 15).

Links to Retention, Persistence, and Completion. Master advisors communicate about the power of academic advising to affect key institutional metrics; they also advocate for use of assessment to demonstrate the impact on student learning.

At many public institutions, the completion agenda (Reindl & Reyna, 2011) drives higher level programmatic decisions (chapter 17). As a result, many administrators focus on specific measures that define student-related institutional outcomes, such as time to degree completion (Patel, 2014). Advisors must build a coalition of administrators and faculty members who understand the nature and power of academic advising. While the approach will certainly vary by institutional type and governance, the underlying concepts for coalition building are consistent across academe.

Many academic advisors lack legitimate power and voice in their institutions. Organizational power creates the ability to mobilize resources and to accomplish goals. The ability of that power to effect institutional change depends on one's access to resources and information, support necessary to complete the task, and ability to garner cooperation in undertaking key enterprises (Kanter, 1988). When groups with similar values, interests, and goals coalesce, they become more powerful than if each acted alone (Spangler, 2003).

Maria and the master advisor task force are able to initiate the coalition-building process that increases the power and influence of academic advising throughout the institution by first articulating a collective goal for practitioners, and second, supporting the goal by referencing relevant research and literature in the field. The outcome has an especially strong impact if the goals and research are tied directly or indirectly to the goals and metrics of the institution. These two processes are not easily achieved.

Some on campus will disagree about the goals for advising. When disagreement occurs, Maria directs the task force to revisit Kuh's (1996) steps for building a strong on-campus student-learning success platform. The coalition-building process depends on generalized agreement regarding advising.

In response, master advisors on the task force can help overcome disagreements about defining goals by ensuring that they understand the theories, practices, and scholarly research bases that inform academic advising. NACADA publications feature many important contributions to the literature as do other scholarly sources. However, as reflective of an emerging field, the advising literature offers relatively few resources regarding the efficacy of advising (McFarlane, 2013). Instead, task force members would be well served by looking to emerging research from doctoral dissertations in the field. This scholarly inquiry may provide fodder for discussion among group members, which can help master advisors define their own goals while considering work from the next generation of advising scholar-practitioners.

Secure in a mutual vision on advising goals and armed with a scholarly background gained through a comprehensive literature review, the master advisor task force takes the next step in the coalition-building process: connecting the outcomes of academic advising to administrative concerns. Although task force members recognize that many administrators appreciate the importance of advising, they also know that unless administrators understand the ways advising directly affects institutional outcomes, advising may remain a marginalized function. Maria and the master advisor task force seek to show that academic advising can be a major factor in enhancing students' success.

Research That Supports Priorities. As highlighted in chapter 17, discussions regarding performance-based measures in higher education and the completion agenda have ignited a fire under the topic of student success (Kelly & Schneider, 2012). Two common themes emerge in the literature: student persistence to completion and the timeliness of that completion. Institutional leaders, particularly in public institutions, feel a great deal of pressure to graduate more students in a shorter time period (Patel, 2014; Spellings, 2006). To accomplish this goal, many administrators seek to improve efficiencies in their operations. Although in this chapter we decline to debate the relative merits of these outcomes, we acknowledge that the funding based upon these outcomes serves as an incentive for reflection on institutional practices and consideration of significant structural changes that support student success.

A posited clear relationship between quality academic advising and positive rates of retention and time to graduation can be seen on the ground in U.S. universities. However, a relative dearth of research on direct relationships between academic advising and retention means that little empirical evidence supports the clearly observable (McFarlane, 2013). A few recent studies identify the relationship between frequency of academic advising and student persistence (e.g., Klepfer & Hull, 2012; Yarbrough, 2010; Young-Jones, Burt, Dixon, & Hawthorne, 2013). The majority of the researchers in this area have identified indirect rather than direct links to completion-related metrics associated with academic advising (Allen & Smith, 2008; Campbell & Nutt, 2008; Habley & McClanahan, 2004; Kuh, Kinzie, Schuh, & Whitt, 2005; McFarlane, 2013; Smith & Allen, 2006). Indirect linkages show that a particular action produces a by-product with a direct linkage to a desired outcome. For example, the frequency with which a student meets with an academic advisor correlates with both advising learning and satisfaction with the institution (McFarlane, 2013; Schwebel, Walburn, Klyce, & Jerrolds, 2012). In other words, frequency of academic advising in these studies serves as a proxy for persistence through the variable of student satisfaction.

Research related to the quality and quantity of interactions between student and faculty members or staff connections offers a fertile field for sowing. Several studies have suggested that key interactions with faculty members play a role in either student persistence or degree attainment (Grosset, 1991; Kuh, Kinzie, Buckley, Bridges, & Hayek, 2007; Light, 2004; Pascarella & Terenzini, 2005; Roberts & Styron, 2010). Academic advising provides a place for this one-to-one connection with a faculty or staff member who cares about a student's success (Drake, 2011). Master advisors familiar with these linkages propose programmatic and structural changes grounded in research and tied to key outcomes identified by campus administrators. Also, master advisors willing to ask whether current advising approaches work (and willing to acknowledge if the data suggest otherwise) can alter practice for the better (chapters 14 and 15).

Master advisors on the task force are effective in convincing the greater campus of their positive impact when they present current advising data, respected research, and ongoing assessment results directly relevant to overall campus assessment efforts.

Anecdotal examples or descriptive statistics do not persuade campus leaders because they cannot make a connection between advising and desirable institutional outcomes. Instead, experience must be framed within analyses. Master advisors use language that reflects the highest administrative priorities: *retaining students, ensuring that a diverse community of student learners has the opportunity to succeed, connecting degree pathways to secure postgraduate employment,* and *ensuring that financially sustainable 4-year or 2-year degrees can be achieved at our institutions.* They demonstrate, with direct and indirect data, that academic advising contributes to the success of students and to specific institutional priorities.

Enhancing and Advancing Practice

Early in the process, Maria recognized the diversity in background, training, and advising experience that characterizes her staff; such diversity describes many campus units. Although this chapter is not focused on professional development (chapter 13), we emphasize the need to ensure that faculty members, administrators, and other key stakeholders recognize the scholarship and expert knowledge that distinguishes the field of academic advising. Administrators responsible for advising frequently face the misguided perception that academic advising consists solely of course sequencing, transactional activities, and student resource referral. Of course, advisors regularly undertake these duties, but only as precursors to developmental and learning-focused opportunities for students. The change-of-major form signature does not represent advising; rather, advising is embodied in the discussions about the reasons a chosen major no longer fits a student's changing goals or the discovery of a student's strength that best aligns with an alternate major. Mandatory and proactive advising appointments are not bureaucratic rubber stamps; they offer a chance for students to ensure that they are progressing toward their educational and career goals in the best manner possible. Master advisors find this distinction painfully obvious and unnecessary to state, but such clarity does not necessarily or uniformly pervade the academy.

Infusing a Culture of Learning and Development.   To make sure that campus stakeholders understand the depth and breadth of advising, advocates should clearly articulate the learning necessary for a practitioner to be recognized as an expert, master advisor. The online NACADA Clearinghouse features numerous articles suggesting formats for starting a successful professional development program. It also hosts an article on a framework of five key advisor training components: conceptual, informational, relational, technological, and personal (McClellan, 2007). Master advisors may find this framework useful in developing individualized advisor training programs that encourage advisors and supervisors to finely hone areas for individualized professional growth at all levels of advising. The importance of creating and maintaining a training and development program supersedes the specific format chosen; an institution without a formal training and development program for academic advising does not truly value and recognize academic advising at the level needed to advance practice.

Some master advisors argue that their institution or unit does not offer budgetary resources to create training and development programs. We suggest that funding may not be necessary where a team of dedicated advisors is willing to develop a professional development framework and agree collectively on a format and process to present it to the advising community. For most institutions, grassroots approaches by dedicated on-campus experts have a greater impact than a top-down approach to advisor training and development. Most important, hands-on collective efforts affirm the work done by the people who advise.

Many campus thought partners can help with the training and professional development endeavors, including those from teaching and learning programs, organizational development units, human resource offices, and professional development centers. A campus with visible programs highlighting the scholarship and professional training necessary to advise is likely led by upper administrators who seek the counsel of informed professionals in the field.

Administrators who would not hesitate to contact a psychology faculty member for guidance on a mental health topic may contact persons with no formal training or background in advising to lead initiatives related to advising. This myopic process generally leads to disappointing outcomes and a frustrated advising community. To preempt such misinformed administrative outreach, the advising community must demonstrate academic advising as a scholarly field of inquiry and make clear that master advisors and advising scholars are the content experts for advising. Development of a formal and recognized professional development program for advisors offers a visible step toward the goal of greater appreciation for advising in the institution.

Creating Visibility. Effective master advisors make themselves visible across the institution. They identify key committees, work groups, and task forces where their expert knowledge will benefit the group or charge. Master advisors analyze the entities making and hearing recommendations and determine the scholars producing white papers that address or define student success. They help delineate the faculty committees charged with oversight related to student advising and student success. After completing this evaluation, master advisors identify potential entry points and key people who can help them gain entry to areas of influence.

Establishing a Shared Learning Network. Maria and the master advisor task force identify campus partners who have shared interests in helping students succeed. Because of the deep connections of advising with the student experience and because task force members have established a strong network of allies, they recognize that additional partners include people in both academic and student affairs.

As a teaching and learning enterprise (Campbell & Nutt, 2008), academic advising naturally fits with partners in a variety of curricular programs (e.g., first-year experience, living-learning communities, and supplemental instruction). Banta and Kuh (1998) suggested that integrated learning experiences offer the most effective means of learning, and Maria can identify the programs to explore in her own college and institution.

Becoming a Thought Leader.   Maria, as a recognized thought leader for academic advising on campus, identifies others on campus who also exert influence as thought leaders in advising. Mizell (2010) defined a thought leader as "a person or group of people espousing ideas that influence the thinking and actions of many others" (p. 46). In the context of academic advising, Maria takes the lead and finds other master advisors who visualize and conceptualize a future for academic advising at the institution. A thought leader in academic advising possesses two crucial qualities: a deep knowledge of the theories, research studies, and practices that inform the current state of academic advising, and the ability to imagine an academic world where advisors fully contribute and completely thrive. A thorough literature review by master advisor task force members delineates thought pieces (Frost, 2000; Gordon et al., 2008; Hagen, Kuhn, & Padak, 2010; Lowenstein, 2005, 2013; Schulenberg & Lindhorst, 2008) from the world of academic advising to inspire others to think differently about the future of advising and visualize a new reality for advising at the institution.

Assessing Practice.   A minimal amount of research has focused on the efficacy of advising, particularly in relation to student retention (Smith & Allen, 2014). Although many theories and frameworks inform advising practice, to move institutional leaders, the efficacy of advising must receive more attention, and more master advisors must conduct research to show the ways and areas advising exerts influence on the learning essential to student persistence and graduation. Maria and the master advisor task force bring together key colleagues from across the campus to determine initial advising assessment efforts (chapters 14 and 15).

Administrative-Level Guidance

Administrators at the senior or cabinet level may not have direct experience with academic advising. Therefore, they need access to information about the aims and practices of academic advising. Confounding the effort to make advising visible, lack of broad aims and visions of administrators to back assessment plans may leave advisors within departments and colleges struggling to set assessable goals for their staff. A partnership between informed master advisors and committed upper administrators must be forged to improve the state of advising and to spur the administration into developing the political will to make improvements. With the right approach, the advancement and the determination can be achieved.

The Communication Loop with Administrators.   Maria and the master advisor task force create the needed partnerships. Frustrated by the small number of advisors within the department in the College of Agricultural Sciences and the ever-increasing advisee caseload, Maria pressed to have advising positions added to her department. Furthermore, Maria felt discouraged when the training sessions once available to advisors had been discontinued campuswide. In addition, primary-role advisors, who comprise the majority of her college's advisors, were increasingly asked to do routine work (e.g., make course packets and tend to course scheduling), leaving them less time to meet with more students. Maria shares these concerns with the dean in hopes of creating a partnership that would lead to the allocation of new resources to ameliorate the condition.

The dean hears about acute resource needs within the college on a daily, if not hourly, basis. She encounters department heads asking for faculty positions and development officers asking for staff support. The academic personnel matters pile up as quickly as the advisee load. The dean wonders if she could hire a faculty assistant, but each department has expressed concern that the operating budget could not cover basic services. To complicate matters, the IT professional recently insisted that if smart boxes are not replaced in the college's classrooms, the faculty will completely lose PowerPoint compatibility this fall. In short, Maria's dean, like many upper level administrators, faces competing demands for scarce resources and she will need to hear a compelling argument before agreeing to add resources for advising. If Maria makes funding the only strategy for addressing advising challenges, she risks having her concerns placed in the queue perpetually addressed tomorrow.

Coalition Building With Administrators.   For student success to receive top billing for agendas and resource flow, the administration needs to make advising a key priority. To capitalize on past scholarship, Maria researches recommendations from previous committees charged by upper level administrators. By utilizing the input of her predecessors, she leverages the contributions of many and does not rely on her own, isolated task force to sway others.

Maria turns to this mix of past and present research during the monthly convening of all associate deans and lead college advisors when the agenda item of advising resource shortages is addressed. After a spirited discussion in which everyone agrees that advisor caseloads exceed the U.S. median (Carlstrom & Miller, 2013a), Maria suggests, "Perhaps we can work together to get this message heard beyond our own deans' offices." The new vice provost of undergraduate studies, who has been charged with finding ways to enhance student academic performance across colleges, hears Maria. The group decides to invite the provost to a future meeting and explain the situation.

From her literature review, Maria knows the connection between quality academic advising and measures of student success. She brings that information to the next meeting to inspire a productive discussion. At the second meeting, the group decides to pursue the first cross-campus collective request for advising resource augmentation. The vice provost helps them construct a case, citing research in the field and looking at units with high student–advisor ratios across campus. Most important, he notes that a proposed cost-share initiative will offer the most effective approach:

Deans provide one half of the funding for new advisors for a three-year period, and a matching provost's contribution demonstrates a willingness to ensure these resources are used appropriately. The solution creates a win-win-win: Deans can make scarce resources go further and take meaningful action to improve student performance; advisors and advising supervisors receive relief and new professional thought partners; and the provost can take direct, meaningful action with measurable results for student success efforts. Moreover, through this collaboration, the vice provost has identified a strong advising advocacy group with representation from across campus; this group forms the basis for further efforts to enhance the training, professionalization, and visibility of academic advisors and their impact on campus.

Upper level administrators make headway toward institutional goals when they consolidate advising requests into a single message and communicate it clearly to provosts, chancellors, and presidents committed to undergraduate success. Yet scenarios like the one featuring Maria, by itself, will not change a campus culture that fails to prioritize advising excellence. In addition to work among administrators and advisors, chief administrators for student success must host broad campus dialogues, for example, through working groups or committees charged with student success, in which advising can emerge as a common concern for faculty members, students, administrators, and staff.

A select group created in close partnership with student and staff groups as well as the faculty or academic senate may want to focus on student success rather than advising so that members can engage in a free dialogue about all campus issues that affect student persistence and completion rates. Participants may raise concerns over admissions policies, preparatory courses, cocurricular activities, course sequencing, and advising. When part of an open dialogue among stakeholders in student affairs, academic affairs, and others in areas of undergraduate education leadership, group members explore advising as one of several topics. The group will ultimately arrive at unique conclusions about improvements necessary to advising practice and outcomes.

This secondary coalition approach situates advising in the midst of other concerns that must be simultaneously addressed to meet desired outcomes for students. It also helps administrators well versed in advising issues to learn more about the way others within the larger campus community believe advising can be improved, thereby contributing novel approaches and identifying new challenges. In addition, it allows faculty members, who may not know the responsibilities of primary-role advisors, to hear from students and staff about the situations advisors face without appearing to be working under mandates or sudden new resource allocations to support advising from the administration. In short, such working groups, if managed well and given time to thoroughly examine the issues, can become important sites of advocacy for advising across staff, students, and faculty members. They can prove instrumental to improved awareness of advising performance and opportunity.

Centralized Academic Advising Leadership.   Finally, master advisors and undergraduate administrators work with their provost, deans, associate deans, and advisors to provide centrally coordinated academic advising leadership for ensuring sustainable actions and decisions that support broad efforts to address student needs. An institution without centralized coordination becomes subject to a variety of seemingly positive but innocuous decisions that fail to support the overall needs of students. Examples of ineffective or counterproductive measures include

- technology implemented in only one college or division,
- robust advisor training in one college but none in another,
- advising curricula that vastly differ between colleges and confuse students,
- assessment undertaken based on descriptive data in one division and learning outcomes in another,
- use of completely different student advising communication plans, and
- hiring and compensation that vary dramatically depending on where an advisor is located rather than the specific duties performed.

Central coordination increases the possibility that advising hiring, training, technology, assessment, curricular decisions, communication modes, learning outcomes, and investments are made in economical and efficient ways that align with broad institutional outcomes and initiatives (each institution looks unique because of campus culture).

Although a dean or vice provost for undergraduates will likely serve as an advocate for advising, an administrator with a combined portfolio of experience in student and academic affairs may also prove helpful. An administrative advocate helps coordinate budget requests across colleges, monitors the number of students admitted, ensures advising resources are placed proactively, and helps coordinate internal campus IT resources or vendor-provided solutions for advising tools. In addition, individuals in these positions can ensure that advising training, professionalization, performance, and assessment are offered and systematized across campus. Too frequently, in the absence of deliberately allocated support, advising solutions that work well in one college, department, or unit are not adopted in others, leaving students with unequal levels of service between majors and without an information trail to follow if they switch majors from one college to another.

The momentum gained for hiring advisors can be quickly lost when budgets shrink because staff positions are the easiest to eliminate. When a central administrator takes responsibility for advising excellence, the provost, chancellor, or president can count on a strategist and advocate for academic advisors who takes responsibility and makes decisions that serve as pivot points for positive advising change.

Summary

In this chapter, we introduced the complex structures, institutional relationships, and drivers that influence academic advising advocacy efforts and provided suggestions for advocating for academic advising. We explained the complex nature of the structures, values, and competing demands that affect decision making by upper level administrators as they take the first step on the pathway toward improved stature and practice of advising.

We identified four approaches for advocating for political and structural change:

o Weave advising into an organized community of practice on campus, building upon existing ecosystems.

o Identify institutional and political opportunities for coalition building through the use of campus networks and committees.

o Advance practice through intentional training, development, and assessment activities.

o Provide focused administrative-level guidance.

Master advisors use these four approaches to create productive partnerships. A coalition and community of engaged professionals across academic affairs, student affairs, and throughout the administration bring discussions of advising to the forefront of efforts toward overall student success. Finally, campus advising efforts coordinated centrally help guarantee that all students have access to advising resources and that advisor training, professional development, and assessment remain consistent.

Aiming for Excellence

o Conduct an informal analysis of the educational and experiential backgrounds of your advising staff. Review past positions; work experience outside the department, unit, and institution; formal and informal education; and specific areas of expertise. Utilize Habley's (1987) model or McClellan's (2007) enhanced model to identify gaps that could be addressed through additional professional development or targeted hiring.

o Create a campus advising hierarchical map. Identify structural reporting lines across both academic and student affairs. What existing structures encourage communication? What formalized communication and collaboration lines must be created to improve advising? Do advisors report to advising experts or do they report to administrators who may not fully understand advising?

o How do administrators at your institution hear about challenges and needs related to academic advising? Who are the prime advising advocates in the administration? What mechanisms ensure that advocates have regular communication with master advisors on campus?

o Consider several recent speeches on student success issues given by members of the campus leadership. How does advising relate (or not) to the issues that were discussed? How does the definition of advising communicated through the speech correspond to current practice? What topics would you add to similar addresses? How might in-depth knowledge of the work of advisors have strengthened the leader's remarks?

o On which student success initiatives or programs do student and academic affairs work collaboratively? Identify gaps over which additional bridges can be built using existing relationships and programs.

o Address issues related to developing a common language for advising. How is academic advising defined by campus stakeholders? What do stakeholders try to achieve through academic advising? What achievements made through academic advising may be achieved better by others?

o Map the formal advising-related committees on campus. How were the committees formed? Who serves on the committees and how long is their service period? Are some committees unproductive due to unclear goals and outcomes or a continually transitional membership? What types of decisions do these committees make (or do they primarily offer information to others)? What committee structures associated with advising seem most efficient and what changes could make these committees more effective?

o Identify the most significant initiatives at your institution. What two or three initiatives are most closely associated with academic advising? How are they associated? What connections does the advising community need to make to formalize the potential impact of advising on these initiatives? What programs and professional development opportunities are offered to support the institutional advising community? Does professional development address advisors at all levels? What opportunities for research and scholarly inquiry are related to advising at your institution?

o Who are the formal and informal campus leaders in the advising community? Are specific advisors or master advisors seen as thought leaders? Do leaders in positions interact directly with upper administration? What approaches for more formal connections can be created between advising leaders and upper administration?

References

Allen, J. M., & Smith, C. L. (2008). Importance of, responsibility for, and satisfaction with academic advising: A faculty perspective. *Journal of College Student Development*, 49(5), 397–411.

Banta, T. W. & Kuh, G. D. (1998, March/April). A missing link in assessment: Collaboration between academic and student affairs professionals. *Change, 30*(2), 40–46.

Barr, R., & Tagg, J. (1995). A new paradigm for undergraduate education. *Change, 27*(6), 13–25. doi:10.1080/00091383.1995.10544672

Barron, K. E., & Powell, D. N. (2014). Options on how to organize and structure advising. In R. L. Miller & J. G. Irons (Eds.), *Academic advising: A handbook for advisors and students Volume 1: Models, students, topics, and issues* (pp. 14–23). Retrieved from http://www.teachpsych.org/Resources/Documents/ebooks/advising2014Vol1.pdf

Bourassa, D. M., & Kruger, K. (2002). The national dialogue on academic and student affairs collaboration. *New Directions for Higher Education, 2002*(116), 9–38. doi:10.1002/he.31

Campbell, S. M. (2008). Vision, mission, goals, and program objectives for academic advising programs. In V. N. Gordon, W. R. Habley, & T. J. Grites (Eds.), *Academic advising: A comprehensive handbook* (2nd ed.) (pp. 229–241). San Francisco, CA: Jossey-Bass.

Campbell, S. M., & Nutt, C. L. (2008). Academic advising in the new global century: Supporting student engagement and learning outcomes achievement. *Peer Review, 10*(1), 4–7. Retrieved from https://www.aacu.org/publications-research/periodicals/academic-advising-new-global-century-supporting-student-engagement

Carlstrom, A. H., & Miller, M. A. (Eds.). (2013a). Number of undergraduate advisees that full-time professional advisors are responsible [for] [Table 6.21]. *2011 NACADA national survey of academic advising* (Monograph No. 25). Retrieved from http://www.nacada.ksu.edu/Portals/0/Clearinghouse/documents/Chapter%206%20-%20Professional%20Advisor%20Load%20-%20FINAL.pdf

Carlstrom, A. H., & Miller, M. A. (Eds.). (2013b). How effective faculty advising is rewarded [Table 7.30]. *2011 NACADA national survey of academic advising* (Monograph No. 25). Retrieved from http://www.nacada.ksu.edu/Portals/0/Monographs/nat%-20survey%20upload%20docs/Chapter%207%20-%20Faculty%20Advising%20-%20Final.pdf

Carlstrom, A. H., & Miller, M.A. (Eds.). (2013c). Reporting lines [Table 14.1]. *2011 NACADA national survey of academic advising* (Monograph No. 25). Retrieved from http://www.nacada.ksu.edu/Portals/0/Clearinghouse/M25/rebuilt_chap14final.pdf

Carlstrom, A. H., & Miller, M.A. (Eds.). (2013d). Reporting line by institutional type [Table 14.3]. *2011 NACADA national survey of academic advising* (Monograph No. 25). Retrieved from http://www.nacada.ksu.edu/Portals/0/Clearinghouse/M25/rebuilt_chap14final.pdf

Drake, J. K. (2011). The role of academic advising in student retention and persistence. *About Campus, 16*(3), 8–12.

Drake, J. K., Jordan, P., & Miller, M. A. (Eds.). (2013). *Academic advising approaches: Strategies that teach students to make the most of college.* San Francisco, CA: Jossey-Bass.

Frost, S. H. (2000). Historical and philosophical foundations for academic advising. In V. N. Gordon & W. R. Habley (Eds.), *Academic advising: A comprehensive handbook* (1st ed.) (pp. 3–17). San Francisco, CA: Jossey-Bass.

Gordon, V. N., Habley, W. R., & Grites, T. J. (Eds.). (2008). *Academic advising: A comprehensive handbook* (2nd ed.). San Francisco, CA: Jossey-Bass.

Grosset, J. M. (1991). Patterns of integration, commitment, and student characteristics and retention among younger and older students. *Research in Higher Education, 32*(2), 159–178.

Habley, W. R. (1983). Organizational structures for academic advising: Models and implications. *Journal of College Student Personnel, 24*(6), 535–540.

Habley, W. R. (1987). Academic Advising Conference: Outline and notes. *The ACT National Center for the Advancement of Educational Practices* (pp. 33–34). Iowa City, IA: ACT. Retrieved from www.nacada.ksu.edu/Portals/0/Clearinghouse/advisingissues/documents/AcacemicAdvisingConferenceOutlineandNotes.pdf

Habley, W. R. (2004). *The status of academic advising: Findings from the ACT sixth national survey* (Monograph No. 10). Manhattan, KS: National Academic Advising Association.

Habley, W. R., & McClanahan, R. (2004). *What works in student retention? Four-year public colleges*. Iowa City, IA: ACT. Retrieved from https://www.act.org/research/policymakers/pdf/droptables/FourYearPublic.pdf

Hagen, P. L., Kuhn, T. L., & Padak, G. M. (Eds.). (2010). *Scholarly inquiry in academic advising* (Monograph No. 20). Manhattan, KS: National Academic Advising Association.

Hemwall, M. K., & Trachte, K. C. (2005). Academic advising as learning: 10 organizing principles. *NACADA Journal, 25*(2), 74–83.

Kanter, R. M. (1988). When a thousand flowers bloom: Structural, collective, and social conditions for innovation in organization. *Research in Organizational Behavior, 10*, 169–211.

Kelly, A. P., & Schneider, M. (2012). *Getting to graduation: The completion agenda in higher education*. Baltimore, MD: The Johns Hopkins University Press.

Kezar, A. (2003). Enhancing innovative partnerships: Creating a change model for academic and student affairs collaboration. *Innovative Higher Education, 28*(2), 137–156. doi:10.1023/B:IHIE.0000006289.31227.25

Klepfer, K., & Hull, J. (2012). *High school rigor and good advice: Setting up students to succeed*. The Center for Public Education. Retrieved from www.centerforpubliceducation.org/Main-Menu/Staffingstudents/High-school-rigor-and-good-advice-Setting-up-studentsto-succeed/High-school-rigor-and-good-advice-Setting-up-students-to-succeed-Full-Report.pdf

Kuh, G. D. (1996). Guiding principles for creating seamless learning environments for undergraduates. *Journal of College Student Development, 37*(2), 135–148.

Kuh, G. D., Kinzie, J., Buckley, J. A., Bridges, B. K., & Hayek, J. C. (2007). *Piecing together the student success puzzle: Research, propositions, and recommendations* (ASHE Higher Education Report, Vol. 32, No. 5). San Francisco, CA: Jossey-Bass.

Kuh, G. D., Kinzie, J., Schuh, J. H., & Whitt, E. J. (2005). *Assessing conditions to enhance educational effectiveness*. San Francisco, CA: Jossey-Bass.

Light, R. J. (2004). *Making the most of college: Students speak their minds*. Cambridge, MA: Harvard University Press.

Lowenstein, M. (2005). If advising is teaching, what do advisors teach? *NACADA Journal, 25*(2), 65–73.

Lowenstein, M. (2013). Envisioning the future. In J. K. Drake, P. Jordan, & M. A. Miller (Eds.), *Academic advising approaches: Strategies that teach students to make the most of college* (pp. 243–258). San Francisco, CA: Jossey-Bass.

Lutkehaus, N. C. (2008). *Margaret Mead: The making of an American icon*. Princeton, NJ: Princeton University Press.

Magolda, P. M. (2005). Proceed with caution: Uncommon wisdom about academic and student affairs partnerships. *About Campus, 9*(6), 16–21. doi:10.1002/abc.113

Manning, K., Kinzie, J., & Schuh, J. H. (2013). *One size does not fit all: Traditional and innovative models of student affairs practice.* New York, NY: Routledge.

Marion, R., & Gonzalez, L. D. (2013). *Leadership in education: Organizational theory for the practitioner.* Long Grove, IL: Waveland.

McClellan, J. L. (2007). *Content components for advisor training: Revisited.* Retrieved from http://www.nacada.ksu.edu/Resources/Clearinghouse/View-Articles/Advisor-Training-Components.aspx#sthash.qXX8Xi7V.dpuf

McFarlane, B. L. (2013). *Academic advising structures that support first-year student success and retention* (Unpublished doctoral dissertation). Portland State University, Portland, OR. Retrieved from http://pdxscholar.library.pdx.edu/cgi/viewcontent.cgi?article=2043&context=open_access_etds

Melander, E. R. (2005). Advising as educating: A framework for organizing advising systems. *NACADA Journal, 25*(2), 84–91.

Miller, M. A. (2003). *A guide to restructuring advising services.* Retrieved from http://www.nacada.ksu.edu/Resources/Clearinghouse/View-Articles/A-Guide-to-Restructuring-Advising-Services.aspx

Mirsalimi, H., & Hunter, M. (2006). Influential leadership. *Rough Notes, 149*(8), 76–78. Retrieved from http://www.roughnotes.com/rnmagazine/2006/august06/08p076.htm

Mizell, H. (2010). Thought leaders: Who they are, why they matter, and how to reach them. *Journal of Staff Development, 31*(6), 46–51.

NACADA: The Global Community for Academic Advising. (2015). *Allied members.* Retrieved from https://www.nacada.ksu.edu/Member-Services/Allied-Memberships/Allied-Members.aspx

Northouse, P. G. (2012). *Introduction to leadership: Concepts and practice* (2nd ed.). Thousand Oaks, CA: Sage.

Pardee, C. F. (2000). Organizational models for academic advising. In V. N. Gordon & W. R. Habley (Eds.), *Academic advising: a comprehensive handbook* (1st ed.) (pp. 192–209). San Francisco, CA: Jossey-Bass.

Pardee, C. F. (2004). *Organizational structures for advising.* Retrieved from http://www.nacada.ksu.edu/Resources/Clearinghouse/View-Articles/Organizational-Models-for-Advising.aspx

Pascarella, E. T., & Terenzini, P. T. (2005). *How college affects students* (Vol. 2). San Francisco, CA: Jossey-Bass.

Patel, V. (2014, December 1). To improve graduation rates, advising gets intrusive by design. *The Chronicle of Higher Education, 61*(14), A6-A6.

Porter, M. V. (2013, March). Data point the way. *Business Officer Magazine.* Retrieved from http://www.nacubo.org/Business_Officer_Magazine/Magazine_Archives/March_2013/Data_Point_the_Way.html

Raven, B. H., & French J. R., Jr. (1958). Legitimate power, coercive power, and observability in social influence. *Sociometry, 21*(2), 83–97. doi:10.2307/2785895

Reindl, T., & Reyna, R. (2011). *Complete to compete: From information to action—Revamping higher education accountability systems* (Report for the NGA Center for Best Practices). Retrieved from http://www.nga.org/cms/home/nga-center-for-best-practices/center-publications/page-edu-publications/col2-content/main-content-list/from-information-to-action-revam.html

Roberts, J., & Styron, R. (2010). Student satisfaction and persistence: Factors vital to student retention. *Research in Higher Education Journal*, *6*(3), 1–18.

Schulenberg, J., & Lindhorst, M. (2008). Advising is advising: Toward defining the practice and scholarship of academic advising. *NACADA Journal*, *28*(1), 43–53.

Schwebel, D. C., Walburn, N. C., Klyce, K., & Jerrolds, K. L. (2012). Efficacy of advising outreach on student retention, academic progress and achievement, and frequency of advising contacts: A Longitudinal randomized trial. *NACADA Journal*, *32*(2), 36–43.

Self, C. (2008). Advising delivery: professional advisors, counselors, and other staff. In V. N. Gordon, W. R. Habley, & T. J. Grites (Eds.), *Academic advising: A comprehensive handbook* (pp. 267–278). San Francisco, CA: Jossey-Bass.

Smith, C., & Allen, J. (2006). Essential functions of academic advising: What students want and get. *NACADA Journal*, *26*(1), 56–66.

Smith, C., & Allen, J. (2014). Does contact with advisors predict judgments and attitudes consistent with student success? A multi-institutional study. *NACADA Journal*, *34*(1), 50–63.

Spangler, B. (2003). *Coalition building. Beyond retractability*. Retrieved from http://www.beyondintractability.org/essay/coalition-building

Spellings, M. (2006). *A test of leadership: Chartering the future of U.S. higher education* (Report of the Commission on the Future of Higher Education). Washington, DC: U.S. Department of Education. Retrieved from https://www2.ed.gov/about/bdscomm/list/hiedfuture/reports/final-report.pdf

Strayhorn, T. L. (2014). Academic advisors: Cultural navigators for student success. *NACADA Journal, 35*(1), 56–63.

Wallace, S. (2013). *Implications for faculty advising*. Retrieved from http://www.nacada.ksu.edu/Resources/Clearinghouse/View-Articles/Implications-for-faculty-advising-2011-National-Survey.aspx

Wenger, E. (2011). *Communities of practice: A brief introduction*. Retrieved from http://wenger-trayner.com/wp-content/uploads/2012/01/06-Brief-introduction-to-communities-of-practice.pdf

Whitt, E. J., Elkins Nesheim, B., Guentzel, M. J., Kellogg, A. H., McDonald, W. M. & Wells, C. A. (2008). "Principles of good practice" for academic and student affairs partnership programs. *Journal of College Student Development 49*(3), 235–249.

Yarbrough, E. (2010). *An examination of academic advising style preference in undergraduate students* (Unpublished doctoral dissertation). Auburn University, Auburn, AL.

Young-Jones, A. D., Burt, T. D., Dixon, S., & Hawthorne, M. J. (2013). Academic advising: Does it really impact student success? *Quality Assurance in Education*, *21*(1), 7–19.

12

REWARD SYSTEMS AND CAREER LADDERS FOR ADVISORS

Jeffrey McClellan

Research makes it very clear what [leaders] need to do to motivate individuals to perform well. They need to create agreement on what needs to be done and to clearly tie valued rewards to performance.

—Edward E. Lawler (2008, p. 103)

Master advisors actively promote and contribute to the design of effective reward systems and career ladders, as appropriate, within advising units and academic departments. Research on sources of motivation help them, in collaboration with others, to design and implement appropriate incentives for primary-role and faculty advisors. Master advisors also contribute to conversations and plans for building career ladder structures that encourage retention of primary-role advisors committed to the practices and professional development initiatives that benefit students and institutions as well as the field of advising.

Reader Learning Outcomes

From studying this chapter, advisors will use knowledge gained about rewards and career ladders to

o articulate the distinction between extrinsic and intrinsic rewards;

o contribute to the design of reward systems appropriate for their institutional environment;

o describe how incentives contribute to or diminish motivation as part of a rewards system; and

o describe career ladders and identify appropriate career ladder structures for the institutional environment.

Academic advising, whether undertaken as a career or as part of faculty responsibilities, offers deeply rewarding and intrinsically motivating experiences. The fulfillment that comes from interacting with and assisting students to develop and achieve their academic, career, and professional goals draws many to engage and continue in the field. However, historically the academy has misunderstood and undervalued advising by offering entry-level compensation or treating it as a peripheral add-on to a faculty member's teaching–research–service responsibilities. As a result of these disincentives, many who find fulfillment in advising students do not pursue career advancement in the field (chapter 1).

The appreciation of academic advising has grown because many recognize it as an instructional endeavor that supports the educational mission of the institution (Hemwell & Trachte, 2005; Hurt, 2007; Ryan, 1992). In addition, the increasing emphasis on retention, persistence, and completion (and the role of advising in each) has increased the value and significance of advising as well as the responsibilities of advisors in higher education (Drake, 2011; Nutt, 2003). This increased acknowledgment suggests a need to reinforce the importance of advising as a profession for primary-role advisors and as a professional function for faculty advisors. Efforts to advance the field may ensure that effective primary-role advisors do not seek other career paths more rewarding in terms of career or economic advancement (Shaffer, Zalewski, & Leveille, 2010). Successful promotion of advising may result in faculty advisors who can focus their attention on and receive recognition in a way that validates the importance of the advising function.

To retain and reward top advisors, some institutional administrators have sought or currently seek to establish intentional reward systems or career ladders. The principles and practices associated with the creation of such mechanisms are explored through the lens of the master advisor, an informal leader within the field of advising who is interested in promoting increased recognition for the advising profession.

To the Master Advisor

Master advisors, the target audience for this book, may wonder about the extent to which they can drive the promotion of reward systems and career ladders for all academic advisors. They can have a tremendous impact. Leading change does not require a position of authority. Indeed, sometimes, positions of authority counter a leader's ability to effect change (McClellan, 2010). Specifically, master advisors initiate the process in two ways. First, they advocate for quality academic advising because they understand and articulate the value of advising at every opportunity. They also communicate about the impact of their work on both students and organizational core outcomes.

Second, master advisors get involved. They look for opportunities to interact with others and contribute to the goals of the broader institution through involvement on committees, task forces, and other policy-making bodies. This activism gives them a venue for communicating the value of advising and for raising awareness about the need to incentivize practitioners (chapters 10 and 11).

These two types of engagement increase their credibility and influence so that master advisors can initiate the change of their own choosing (chapter 3), which opens opportunities for them to create or take the lead in task forces charged with designing reward systems or promoting the professionalization of advising through career ladders. Master advisors lead by understanding and accommodating both faculty and primary-role advisors in change processes, reviewing the literature on rewards and motivation within corresponding organizational systems, and implementing the design of reward systems or career ladder structures.

Faculty and Primary-Role Advisors

Great leaders are concerned not only with their own interests but also with the interests of the key stakeholders affected by their leadership. As Gerzon (2003) explained, they "have the clear intention to act on behalf of everyone involved, not just one 'side'" (p. 15). Advising is conducted on most campuses by both faculty members and staff who possess different strengths and limitations in relation to advising. Furthermore, both types of advisors have unique needs and face different challenges in relation to the development of reward systems and career ladders. For example, in a recent webinar, Grites (2014) identified the following differences between primary-role (often referred to as *professional*) and faculty advisors. He stated that primary-role advisors are

- hired via a search process and have specific job descriptions (i.e., they are selected);
- expected to undertake systematic, intentional, and ongoing training (i.e., professional development is expected);
- evaluated through annual performance reviews; and
- rewarded with salary and benefits.

In contrast, faculty advisors are

- expected or required to advise, but also to teach, publish, seek grants, and undertake other significant responsibilities (i.e., they are not selected based on desire or ability to advise);
- provided limited training, typically no more a few days or a few hours;
- subjected to nonsystematic evaluation; and
- rewarded very sparsely (not part of most tenure track evaluations) or with more responsibilities (i.e., increased advising caseload) such that encouragement for advising comes primarily from intrinsic satisfaction.

Such differences between the expectations for and recognition of advisors exert a significant influence on the advising practices of both types of advisors, including the challenges they face in practice as well as the means for assessing, evaluating, recognizing, and rewarding their advising responsibilities.

Reward and Motivation

In preparation for leading an initiative to design or redesign a reward system or career ladder structure, master advisors should review the relevant literature. In general, reward systems comprise essential components of an organization's performance management process. The Council for the Advancement of Standards in Higher Education (CAS) (2015) indicated that effective advising programs should "manage human resource processes including recruitment, selection, professional development, supervision, performance planning, succession planning, evaluation, recognition, and reward" (p. 8). In addition, assessment efforts should be used to "recognize personnel performance" (p. 10) and promote institutional success. Consequently, advising programs should implement reward systems for faculty and primary-role advisors.

These reward systems represent an effective means of complying with an additional recommendation that financial resources are used "to raise awareness of the academic advising program and its value to a range of stakeholders" (CAS, p. 15). As they work with others to advocate for and promote the application of these standards, master advisors should keep in mind the principles of effective motivation and reward.

In general, the research on reward and motivation in organizations has yielded mixed findings. Studies have shown repeatedly that extrinsic rewards do little to promote intrinsic motivation (Deci, Koestner, & Ryan, 2001). Transactional reward systems that offer some tangible incentive in exchange for engagement in a specific behavior do not motivate people to take up a behavior based on the merits of it; in fact, generally speaking, extrinsic rewards diminish intrinsic motivation and only achieve, if anything, temporary compliance (Kohn, 1993). As Lawler (2008) explained, the "carrot and stick approach to motivation can actually demotivate employees" because if "you offer the wrong carrot, . . . employees will feel insulted, misunderstood, or just apathetic" (pp. 103–104).

In contrast, some research suggests that incentive systems motivate individual employee and team performance (Burney & Widener, 2013; Gil, Cuevas-Rodriguez, López-Cabrales, & Sánchez, 2012; Gnyawali, Offstein, & Lau, 2008). For example, Gneezy, Meier, and Rey-Biel (2011) reported significant positive impact on school attendance when financial incentives were used. In another study, customer service–oriented responses (number of calls returned) increased when salespeople were compensated based on customer satisfaction ratings instead of solely for total sales (Sharma & Sarel, 1995).

Perhaps rewards "offered independently of performance, for carrying out a trivial or tedious task, or for meeting a vague performance criteria" (Eisenberger & Shanock, 2003, p. 124)—that is, in a transactional fashion—may be considered manipulative. In addition, when the recipient does not place inherent valuable on the reward, the person may lose motivation, even if she or he finds the task inherently interesting. If the person perceives the task as unimportant, he or she may only perform it to obtain the reward, which may further diminish the individual's innate interest in performing the task and ultimately result in temporary compliance.

Positive feedback and appreciation given to employees appears to positively affect employee motivation and performance (Vansteenkiste & Deci, 2003). Natural enjoyment of an activity may be enhanced with positive reinforcement, which results in employee interest in performing effectively. Therefore, coupling rewards with encouraging gestures can reinforce the motivational impact of the reward. In addition, intrinsically desirable rewards or tasks that require creativity can contribute to motivation (Eisenberger & Shanock, 2003). In situations in which motivation is lacking due to limited self-efficacy, master advisors can suggest that intrinsically motivated individuals be rewarded with encouragement to follow through on performance behaviors. For example, Stockton University (2015) offers a grant-like award for faculty advisors who engage in projects that promote effective advising. Such a simple reinforcement may prove particularly useful in situations marked by lack of resources.

Lawler (2008) explained, "Motivation requires offering rewards that individuals value and that are clearly tied to their performance" (p. 104). Thus, motivation seems related to the extent to which the individual perceives the reward or the task as desirable. Figure 12.1 presents a matrix that illustrates the connection between innate interest in a task and the value placed on a related reward.

Figure 12.1 shows that if a reward is seen as manipulative or undesirable, the actor will remain unmotivated even if she or he has inherent interest in the task. In contrast, if seen as desirable and as supportive of deep-seated interests, a reward will likely positively influence motivation, especially in people with an intrinsic motivation to perform the task. For example, faculty members who tend to publish are intrinsically motivated to write. If they also like to travel, these faculty members will

Figure 12.1. Role of perception of reward on motivation

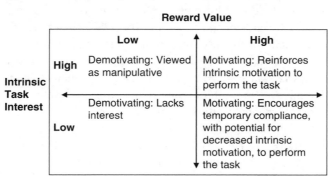

likely feel positively incentivized and appreciate a system that rewards travel funds for their efforts to publish. Faculty members who dislike either writing manuscripts or taking excursions will likely not welcome travel vouchers as incentives to publish.

Reward systems work best when viewed as demonstrations of appreciation and inherently desirable reinforcements for performance-enhancing behaviors, not as a means to manipulate or recompense for an action deemed desirable only by others. In other words, people work harder when leaders appreciate and reward them in meaningful ways for their work. To incentivize others properly, master advisors should work with administrators to design effective reward systems.

Designing Reward Systems

The process for designing an effective reward system begins with understanding the strategy and culture of the organization. Based on this knowledge, master advisors work with others to identify key indicators of performance. In collaboration with other stakeholders, master advisors examine strategic planning processes and advising-related goals for the institution, division or college, and department, unit, or program. For example, if an institutional goal includes assistance with a career plan for every student, then a key performance indicator demonstrates the degree to which advisors assist students in the development of career plans during each advising session. After identifying indicators, the master advisor works with administrators to determine the appropriate and desirable incentives to attach to the achievement of these indicators.

Not all rewards must be linked to performance to confer benefit to the actor. Rewards designed to simply express appreciation can motivate employees when given with sincere gratitude and in a fair way.

Thinking Strategically

To develop an appropriate and motivating reward system, master advisors work with administrators to develop an effective strategy applicable to the organization. The system should address mission and vision statements, values, strategic priorities, and goals (chapter 4). As Drake (2008) explained, rewards must be aligned "with business goals to create a win–win partnership" (p. 398). They must rely on clear and effective strategic planning by advising administrators (Campbell, 2008) as well as advisor understanding of the operational environment of the advising program. Based on this awareness, principals draft guiding documents (mission, vision, and values) (McClellan, 2007) that guide the organization in developing strategic priorities based on environmental analysis. Thus, if an analysis shows, for example, that many commuter students are disproportionately placed on academic probation, then the advising unit may prioritize the development of an outreach program on academic success with particular efforts to include commuter students. To focus attention on such a priority, clear goals for diminishing the numbers of students on probation proportionate to their representation on campus would be articulated and accompanied by action plans to achieve the goals. An appropriate rewards structure recognizes and rewards those who successfully contribute to the achievement of these goals. The development of appropriate, comprehensive learning and organizational outcomes creates the bases for rewards programs (McClellan, 2011).

Development of a reward system will not produce the desired results without effective strategic leaders who implement the plan by encouraging others to enact it. Typically, leaders seek input and feedback from key stakeholders that will help ensure open communication throughout the planning process. Consultations contribute to the likelihood that the plan will be understood and implemented, and they contribute to the creation of a "positive and natural reward experience" (Drake, 2008, p. 397). Furthermore, engaging in effective strategic planning and leadership anchors "the advising program, forming the foundation from which all activities and initiatives are derived and guided" (Campbell, 2008, p. 232).

Identifying Key Performance Indicators

As part of strategic planning processes in advising units and programs, master advisors advocate for and assist in developing comprehensive assessment plans that include both summative and formative outcomes (McClellan, 2011). The summative outcomes represent critical performance indicators that help to measure the success of the advising unit. For example, the Kent Academic Support and Advising Association (2009) identified an outcome for advising that students "understand the purpose and importance of advising" as evidenced by keeping regular appointments and maintaining an advising portfolio. The number of students who keep appointments and maintain the portfolio represents key summative outcomes.

Formative outcomes identify the critical behaviors that contribute to the achievement of summative outcomes. For example, if administrators of an advising unit indicate an essential summative outcome that all students develop a 10-year postgraduation career plan, then a key formative outcome involves advisors discussing postgraduation career plans on a regular basis with students. The more these formative outcomes can be directly tied to summative outcomes, the better they can be used in designing reward systems. For example, a study conducted at Frostburg State University determined that the extent to which students indicated that they trusted their advisors (a student satisfaction outcome) was predicted by the extent to which advisors sought to understand student needs by listening before proffering advice (McClellan, 2013). In this example, effective listening (a formative outcome) drives perceived trust (a summative outcome). Awareness of the relationship between the two types of assessment encourages advisors to extend their "line of sight," especially when these outcomes are tied to broader organizational goals and objectives, by helping them to "understand how what they do has an influence on other members of their organization"(Drake, 2008, p. 398).

Once formative and summative outcomes are developed and the relationships between them identified, master advisors work with advising unit leaders to develop a reward system. That is, they select the behavior- and performance-focused outcomes most essential to achieving the current strategic priorities of the unit. For example, in a recent study of survey respondents, Powers (2012) found that the most frequently used student learning outcome involved the development of long-term educational plans (p. 40). Advisors wanting to assess this or a similar outcome might count the students who articulate a long-term educational plan by a specific point in their educational career. The formative behaviors that contribute to the achievement of this outcome could include advisor direction on ways to develop a plan in the freshman year and help with reviewing and revising it in the student's sophomore year. The formative behaviors should be tied to appropriate incentives to encourage performance.

With Figure 12.1 in mind, master advisors avoid trying to incentivize nonvalued outcomes, which may result in a decline in performance and morale. At one time, I worked for a large for-profit university that used a pay-for-performance program that partially based pay on the number of students individual advisors readmitted to the university. However, advisors felt they had little time to spend on this initiative and disliked doing it. As a result, the pay-for-performance plan had no impact on readmission rates, and advisors frequently spoke disparagingly of this feature of the pay-for-performance system.

Also, the program adopted should allow sufficient flexibility to ensure that advisors can experiment with alternate means of engaging in a desired behavior. Adaptability and encouragement of resourcefulness contributes to increased motivation and creativity (Amabile, 1997; de Treville, Antonakis, & Edelson, 2005). For example, to assess the formative outcome of student satisfaction, leadership may issue a clear but non-enumerated measure that encourages advisors to build rapport with students in meaningful, genuine ways. In contrast, imposed measures for specific dialogue, such as asking students about their hobbies, to create relationship stifles creativity and impedes authenticity, which could result in diminished intrinsic motivation.

Identify Incentives

"It is important for organizations to determine—within the contexts of their missions, values, goals, and cultures—what sorts of rewards, both intrinsic and extrinsic, make sense for their workforces" (Drake, 2008, p. 399). The rewards must be directly related to performance, achievability, desirability, need satisfaction, and motivation (Drake, 2008). Consequently, advising administrators must carefully identify incentives that appeal to the unique interests and desires of the staff. This important undertaking creates challenges because, as multiple research studies have demonstrated, individual preferences for rewards and the factors that contribute to engagement vary among persons, by culture, across job functions, and over time (Fisher & Yuan, 1998; Hofstede, 1972; Kovach, 1995; Silverthorne, 1992; Society for Human Resource Management, 2014). Likewise, the innate interest in their responsibilities likely differs by individual and the task being performed. For example, primary-role advisors who chose the profession likely find advising students intrinsically motivating; however, some faculty members, particularly those who prefer to focus on research, may not perceive advising as intrinsically motivating.

Because of the variation in reward preferences and task perceptions among advisors, administrators must understand the general mind-set that pervades their unit and the specific preferences of each individual. To generate some valid data for the identification of reward preferences among academic advisors, NACADA: The Global Community for Academic Advising conducted a survey of 1,969 NACADA members in 2007 (Drake, 2008). It conducted another survey in 2014 that reached 1,677 academic advisors. The results demonstrate the values of faculty and primary-role advisors.

Survey Results

The results of the 2008 and 2014 NACADA surveys provide insights useful for the development and identification of appropriate reward structures. As a result, master advisors can use the information when advocating for or engaging in the creation of reward systems.

Faculty Advisors

The results of the 2008 and 2014 NACADA surveys suggested that no single practice is used widely by educational institutions to recognize and reward faculty advisors at any type of institution. However, more 4-year public institutions seem to have implemented reward processes. Additionally, the most recent survey revealed that 40% (4-year private), 49% (4-year public), and 56% (2-year public) of respondents reported that no recognition or rewards exist or that they were unaware of the existence of such awards. Among the most frequently used approaches across all three institutional types, minor consideration in tenure review was cited by respondents. However, the percentages of respondents indicating this acknowledgment are decreasing, perhaps because of economic turbulence following the 2008 recession. Rewards for primary-role advisors follow some similar trends as those for faculty members.

Primary-Role Advisors

According to the 2014 NACADA survey, more primary-role advisors receive reward and recognition opportunities than do faculty advisors, but the percentages of respondents had declined between the 2008 and the 2014 NACADA surveys; a difference in institutions represented by respondents may have accounted for some of this discrepancy. Nonetheless, in the economically challenging times between 2008 and 2014, funds were limited for supporting reward and recognition efforts. However, results from the more recent survey suggest that leadership is exerting more effort into development of incentive programs for primary-role than for faculty advisors.

Across all types of surveyed institutions, merit pay and support for professional development are the most cited means of reward. However, according to respondents, specific approaches vary by institutional type (e.g., more respondents from private colleges than from other institutions report hosting banquets and giving cash awards, certificates, and trophies).

The relative value of reward structures is not inherent in their mere existence but in the way rewards are used and how well they align with the deep-seated desires of employees. Consequently, those creating the incentives must examine advisor interest in specific rewards. To this end, the survey explored faculty and primary-role advisor responses regarding the relative importance they give to specific rewards and recognition types.

In an interesting finding, a higher percentage of primary-role respondents indicated that the offered reward and recognition types were not important to them than the percentage who indicated that they were very important to them. Perhaps this result reflects the value that those who chose an advising career place on the innate rewards associated with it. The percentages of primary-role advisors who reportedly appreciate thank you letters, certificates of appreciation, and plaques or trophies remained unchanged or increased between the first and second surveys.

The only 2008 and 2014 NACADA survey item identified as very important to a majority of participants was support for professional development. Merit [pay] was also considered important to a majority of respondents of both surveys. When very important and moderately important rankings were combined, the most important reward and recognition options were recorded as follows: support for professional development (88%), merit [pay] (78%), cash awards (60%), and thank you letters (55%); these acknowledgments may represent the best options for consideration.

When determining the best possible rewards, master advisors realize that extrinsic motivators, while perceived as valuable, tend to diminish motivation unless valued by the recipient and used to reinforce intrinsically motivating activities. Two of the items indicated by survey participants—cash awards and merit [pay]—are characteristic of extrinsic motivators, which Herzberg (1976) identified as "hygiene factors" because increasing them does not significantly increase motivation or satisfaction but removing them creates significant dissatisfaction. The annual report of the Society for Human Resource Management (2014) reinforces Herzberg's contention. The report states that employees rank salary and pay as more important than any other factor. Nonetheless, neither was among the factors that contributed to employee engagement, which included the intrinsic motivators of relationships with coworkers, opportunities to use skills and abilities, relationship with immediate supervisor, the work itself, contribution of work to the organization's business goals, variety of work, and the organization's financial stability. In summary, the use of monetary rewards to improve motivation and engagement will likely not render the desired effect; however, insufficient pay will likely discourage job satisfaction, which could lead to diminished performance and increased attrition (Bedeian & Armenakis, 1981).

The clear advisor interest in financial incentives may reflect concerns regarding the entry-level wages and limited opportunities for pay increases that they face

("Median Salaries of Higher-Education Professionals, 2014–2015," 2015). These concerns may be best addressed by alternative salary and promotion structures as opposed to reward systems.

According to the NACADA (2008, 2014) surveys, respondents serving as primary-role advisors generally view professional development (learning and growth) and certificates of appreciation as appropriate for promoting intrinsic motivation. Herzberg (1976) views these gratuities as motivators because they correlate directly to increased satisfaction and motivation. Consequently, reward planners should emphasize investments in training and demonstrated appreciation; however, a certificate given without genuine gratitude may serve as little more than an extrinsic motivator and have little impact on long-term performance. In contrast, gestures of true appreciation in conjunction with a cash award, an extrinsic motivator, may be valued and encourage motivation, especially for recipients who express concerns over pay.

Faculty Incentives

Survey responses (NACADA, 2008, 2014) from faculty advisors showed some similar trends to those found for primary-role practitioners: Faculty advisors consider professional development and merit [pay] very important, but no more than 50% of respondents indicated that any incentives are very important to them. This finding may suggest a general valuing of the intrinsic rewards associated with advising, but it could also suggest a lack of interest in receiving rewards by faculty members who may suspect that institutional rewards are awarded to compel them to take responsibility for an activity they do not inherently value.

The highest percentages of surveyed faculty advisors (NACADA, 2014) reportedly consider professional development and consideration for promotion and tenure as important and very important (36 and 37%, respectively). Combining moderately and very important scores resulted in the following items identified as most important to surveyed faculty advisors: support for professional development (53%), consideration for promotion and tenure (48%), merit [pay] (46%), and salary supplement for advising (37%). These numbers show that a lower percentage of faculty advisors than primary-role advisors found the listed rewards important, and the responses also suggest that faculty members may be more interested in remuneration than other types of rewards. However, the highest percentage of respondents indicated that the incentives referenced were not relevant to them.

Design a Rewards System

Rewards

The results of the NACADA (2014) survey mirror, in some ways, the results of similar research studies. In general, no universally desirable rewards can be discerned, but some general preferences can be determined. For example, as a motivator or contributor to engagement, gestures of appreciation as well as interesting and meaningful work are valued by more U.S. employees than wages (Kovach, 1995; Silverthorne, 1992; Society for Human Resource Management, 2010, 2014). Furthermore, one individual may value a reward that another individual or group may not appreciate, and this trend may change over time (Kovach, 1995). Thus, a system that one individual perceives as motivational, such as the one that incentivizes publishing with travel money, may demotivate another person, such as one with little interest in publishing or travel.

Based on the 2014 NACADA survey, one may conclude that primary-role advisors appreciate support for professional development, but a supervisor must recognize that some individuals may not feel energized by training opportunities. When the majority of individuals in a department may lack interest in receiving professional development, the department administrator may require professional development for advisors, but he or she must recognize that this opportunity does not qualify as a valid incentive for desired outcomes. Therefore, although data such as those from the NACADA (2008, 2014) surveys offer valuable general sources of information regarding trends, master advisors interested in designing reward systems for academic advising must work with administrators and engage advisors in conversations to identify rewards valued by recipients.

When selecting rewards, program designers must consider institutional resources available and the philosophy of institutional leaders. That is, they must recognize the distinctions between reward systems for faculty and for primary-role advisors.

Faculty Advisors.   In terms of faculty reward systems, O'Connell (2010) outlined three key items that master advisors can promote at their institutions. First, they need to communicate the need for and strive to promote the value of advising. O'Connell provided the following thoughts on the value of academic advising that institutions communicate to the faculty:

> The importance that your university, school/college, or department places on advising is best evidenced by where it is found in your mission, strategic goals, policy, personnel, and procedure documents. What is the place of advising in your position descriptions, position ads, yearly evaluations, and tenure and promotion documents? Do your ads identify advising as a required position activity—or is it hidden under "other duties as assigned"? Do your search committees ask questions appropriate to assessing a candidate's suitability for, skills in, and commitment to student advising? Does your university promote the idea of advising as a teaching activity—or is it always relegated to the "service" category? Does your university convey in its new-faculty orientation the importance of and expectations for advising? (¶5)

Faculty member responses to O'Connell's questions reflect the importance that institutional stakeholders place on the advising function for the faculty. This information reveals the level to which institutional leadership values and rewards effective faculty advising.

Second, O'Connell (2010) suggested that institutions "provide orientation and professional development related to advising" (¶6). Leadership should assign individuals to coordinate or oversee these venues, and all faculty advisors should have access to and participate in them. Furthermore, O'Connell pointed out that professional development, which many advisors view as a valued reward, provides an excellent way to both reward and promote effective advising. However, planners must remember that faculty advisors, who primarily serve as discipline-based experts and teachers, cannot sacrifice their key responsibilities to learn more and develop their skills as advisors.

Third, O'Connell (2010) suggested that specific rewards be given at the department, college, and university levels. A number of universities throughout the country feature an awards event. Table 12.1 summarizes the content of some awards as based on information available on select institutional web sites at the time of this writing.

Although it does not follow the format of acknowledgments listed in Table 12.1, the award offered at Stockton University (2015) is based on recognition of projects related to research and advising improvement projects. Such esteem placed on scholarly endeavors offers an alternative approach that some faculty advisors, in particular, may appreciate.

The examples in Table 12.1 highlight the faculty advising awards offered by a few universities that choose to recognize the value of advising. However, the existence of an award is not enough to promote motivation. To be effective, these recognitions should "have the same stature as similar awards for teaching or research" (O'Connell, 2010, ¶7). For example, at the University of Central Florida (2015), each of the advising, research, teaching, service, and librarian recognitions includes a monetary award of $2,000. Of course, administrators may also bestow nonmonetary awards, such as those outlined in the NACADA (2008, 2014) surveys or articulated by potential recipients.

Primary-Role Advisors. Awards for primary-role advisors fall in many of the same categories as noted for faculty awards and featured in Table 12.1. In some cases, divisional and regional awards are offered. For example, Utah Valley University (2016), which employs mostly primary-role advisors, provides annual awards for different types of specialists, including academic advisors, support advisors, specialty advisors, and advising administrators. Each recipient receives $500, a plaque, and recognition at the annual advising conference. Utah State University models its advising awards on the NACADA awards structure so that an advisor who receives a university award can easily apply for a NACADA award. As a result, many Utah State advisors have won association awards.

The example from Utah Valley University highlights a traditional, highly selective award structure. However, master advisors know the importance of identifying ways to honor all effective advising personnel, and they work with administrators to identify individual and unit standards and rewards that best reflect the individual interests of advisors. I know one administrator who regularly meets with advisors to learn of their interests and career goals. Then she delegates assignments and projects that

Table 12.1. Faculty advisor awards at select U.S. colleges and universities, 2015-2016

Institution	Award Name	Monetary Award	Other Forms of Recognition
CalPoly San Luis Obispo	Outstanding Faculty Advisor Award	$1,200	Recognition at president's fall conference & name on plaque in library
James Madison University	Provost Award for Excellence in Academic Advising	$1,000	Not specified
Nevada Board of Regents	Board of Regents' Academic Advising Award for universities and community colleges	$5,000 (Bylaws indicate that all campuses should also offer a $1,000 award of their own)	Use of the award title in perpetuity
Northern Arizona University	Outstanding Academic Advisor Award: Faculty Advisor	$1,000	Campus recognition
Plattsburgh State University of New York	Outstanding Academic Advisor Award	$500	Certificate, recognition at President's Opening Breakfast, and name on plaque in library
Temple University	Faculty Advisor Award	$1,000	Recognition at annual Advisor Professional Development Workshop and name on plaque
University of Central Florida	University Excellence in Undergraduate Faculty Academic Advising (2 awarded per year)	$2,000	Recognition at Founders' Day Honors Convocation
University of Georgia	Outstanding Academic Advisor Award: Faculty Advisor	Amount unspecified	Recognition at Spring Faculty Awards Banquet
Utah State University	Outstanding Faculty Advisor of the Year Award	$500	Recognition at Robins Awards Banquet
Virginia Tech	Alumni Award for Excellence in Undergraduate/ Graduate Advising	$2,000	Not Specified

align with these interests. She also regularly recognizes advisors for success and nominates her staff for campus awards. In addition, she ensures that department social events and retreats celebrate successes and recognize staff for their hard work. The positive results include a department with low turnover and a high number of internal applicants from other areas of the institution for positions that become available.

An institutional example of the all-encompassing approach to recognition can be found at Missouri State University (2015), where advisor training, evaluation, and promotion fall under the provision of Master Advisor Workshops. Persons who participate in the provisional development earn the designation of master advisor. With this title comes a framed certificate as recognition of achievement and eligibility for the university's Excellence in Advising awards.

Delivery and Implementation of a Reward System

Once valued rewards are identified, master advisors work with administrators to determine the best way to deliver them. They must choose between several systematic approaches. For example, they can attach rewards to the performance management of all employees, develop competitive processes for earning accolades, or create a nomination process for individuals to receive specific recognition.

Once the process for delivering rewards is identified, the planners must see to execution of the program. As with any institutional process, effective implementation depends upon some key factors:

o A steward, either an individual or a committee, must oversee the process.

o A clear delineation of responsibilities and a time line for program progress must be made and clearly communicated to promote accountability.

o Time, money, and supplies must be made available to the steward so the program remains viable.

o The effectiveness of the program needs to be evaluated in terms of employee motivation, productivity, and satisfaction as based on performance-oriented objectives. Furthermore, processes and deadlines for specific assessment tasks must be set under the direction of the steward.

Based on the suggestions outlined, master advisors can work to implement a responsive, motivational, and effective reward system for faculty and primary-role advisors. However, even a well-researched, -planned, and -implemented system will prove insufficient as a motivator if promotion opportunities remain unavailable and advisors leave advising for other fields that offer better pay.

Rewarding Advising Through Promotion

Faculty advisors enjoy a distinct advantage over primary-role advisors in promotion and retention efforts. The faculty structure, complete with tenure and promotion processes, allows for career advancement that generally promotes stability and retention within the field. This does not, of course, mean that faculty advisors are necessarily promoted based on quality advising. As the *2011 NACADA National Survey of Academic Advising* demonstrated, 27.2% of faculty advisors can utilize their advising activities as a part of promotion and tenure (Carlstrom & Miller, 2013). In a related concern, the extent, if any, that advising responsibilities change as a result of promotion and tenure remains difficult to determine. Therefore, although faculty promotion and tenure systems generally promote career stability, doubts about the degree to which they promote excellence in advising linger.

As an entry-level position, academic advising does not provide primary-role advisors with opportunities for advancement or salary increases. Indeed, advancement opportunities have traditionally meant leaving advising to pursue supervisory or administrative responsibilities. Thus, academic advising is often considered a bounded position with an entry-level salary range and no immediate options for advancement. However, the increased attention on the importance of advising and the growing emphasis and need to professionalize the role (Shaffer et al., 2010) support change in the traditional view. As a result, at many institutions, stakeholders seek an alternative approach, and a variety of institutions are implementing career ladders (Taylor, 2011, ¶14).

Career Ladders

Although the concept of long-term employment and career stability continues to change (chapter 9), many practitioners acquire and administrators value specialized advising knowledge and skill. In addition, high costs of retraining and time-consuming learning curves (Folsom, Joslin, & Yoder, 2005) make the retention and development approaches offered through career ladders attractive options for keeping good advisors. In general, by offering opportunities for advancement within a specific role, an effective career ladder system promotes improved retention and recruitment of effective employees. As Taylor (2011) explained,

> A formal career ladder provides the institution with leverage in a search process as job candidates consider the potential for advancement. An infrastructure that offers professional and financial recognition motivates academic advisors by articulating clear expectations for successful promotion and rewarding them for achieving those objectives. Such a model contributes to advisor satisfaction and retention of valued staff members while encouraging innovation and commitment to the institution and the profession. (p. 135)

Taylor (2011) suggested that an effective career ladder is built by first clarifying the role of advising at the institution and understanding the human resources policies and procedures associated with these structures. For example, at the University of Texas Arlington (2012), an Advisor II job description clearly defines the purpose of the position: "understanding and interpreting the needs of specific populations of students to administrators, for interpreting, formulating, and evaluating institutional rules for students, and for facilitating exchange of academic information." The job description for an Advisor II at Temple University states that the position involves "providing comprehensive academic advising to a diverse population of students and assisting with the development and implementation of services geared to achieving, maintaining or enhancing student success and retention" (Higher Ed Jobs, 2015). The former statement emphasizes the role of advising in terms of tasks performed. The latter focuses not only on tasks performed but also on the relevance of these tasks in relation to strategically significant outcomes such as student success and retention. While different in their approaches, both statements provide a description of the role that advising plays in the institution. A well-written job description helps to develop and articulate the role of advising, as well as showcases the importance of advising for use in advocating for financial support.

In addition to developing this kind of clarity, master advisors understand the policies and guidelines associated with the creation of career ladders. Although the rungs of the ladder vary from institution to institution, the gradation between steps must be reflected in the tasks performed at each level as well as the experience and education requirements necessary to perform them. Stakeholders use clearly explained knowledge about job requirements to determine appropriate pay ranges based on benchmarking of the duties performed as determined from data on similar positions nationwide. For example, Texas A&M University (2015) features a career ladder incorporating four levels: Academic Advisor I, Academic Advisor II, Senior Advisor I, and Senior Advisor II. Table 12.2 provides a summary of the key differences in the requirements and pay ranges of these positions as of 2015.

In addition to the differences included in Table 12.2, the number and nature of duties outlined for each position show additional variations. For example, an Advisor I list of duties includes 21 different items, and a Senior Academic Advisor list includes 29 duties. Most of the additional duties provide clarification regarding the supervisory, instructional, and coordination work for the higher level advisor. To justify the creation of a career ladder, the committee writing job descriptions must note, at minimum, the clear differences between the levels in duties, supervisory responsibilities, education levels, and experiences associated with the position.

Financial support for implementation of career ladders is based on advocacy for the importance of academic advising and the need to retain effective advisors. In situations characterized by lack of financial support for pay increases, stakeholders may consider advancement in terms of titles and privileges. The Master Advisor Program at Missouri State University (2015) serves as an example of a successful initiative providing promotion and advancement opportunities that can be adopted in the absence of pay incentives.

After garnering support, planners assemble a team to explore the structure of the career ladder with the objective to "articulate a vision for and the implications of the proposed career-ladder structure" and to determine "the number of rungs in the ladder, the descriptions associated with those rungs, and the distance between them" (Taylor, 2011, p. 136). In addition, they address the procedures for

Table 12.2. Career ladder structure at Texas A&M University (2015)

Position	Description	Supervision Given	Required Education	Required Experience	Salary
Academic Advisor I	Recruits and advises undergraduate students concerning their career goals and academic requirements; provides information on and refers students to University resources that can assist in meeting their needs or solving problems; may supervise projects.	May give detailed instruction and periodic review to support personnel	Bachelor's degree and knowledge of higher education	None	$30,000–$33,000
Academic Advisor II	Recruits and advises undergraduate students concerning their career goals and academic requirements; provides information on and refers students to University resources that can assist in meeting their needs or solving problems; may supervise projects.	May give detailed instruction and periodic review to support personnel	Bachelor's degree	2 years of experience	$33,000–$35,000
Senior Advisor I	Serves as senior level position which may be required to teach courses, manage unit of professional and support personnel, and recruit and advise undergraduate and/or graduate students concerning their educational or career goals, academic requirements, and related personal concerns; provides information on and refers students to University resources that can assist them in meeting their needs or solving their problems; may develop or oversee projects.	May give detailed instruction, training, periodic review, and supervision to academic advisors and other support personnel	Bachelor's or master's degree	4 years of experience or 2 years of experience with master's degree	$35,000–$40,000

(continued)

Table 12.2. (Continued)

Position	Description	Supervision Given	Required Education	Required Experience	Salary
Senior Advisor II	Serves as senior level position which may be required to teach courses, manage unit of professional and support personnel, and recruit and advise undergraduate and/or graduate students concerning their educational or career goals, academic requirements, and related personal concerns; provides information on and refers students to University resources that can assist them in meeting their needs or solving their problems; may develop or oversee projects.	Gives detailed instruction, training, periodic review, and supervision to academic advisors and other support personnel	Bachelor's or master's degree	6 years of experience or 4 years of experience with master's degree	$40,000–$45,000

advancement and promotional reviews. While some universities implement a system based on experience and education, as at Texas A&M University (2015) (Table 12.2), others use a promotion structure based on the faculty model, which typically incorporates portfolio review processes. Iten and Matheny (2008) provide an example of the portfolio-review approach:

> At the College of Liberal Arts and Sciences' Academic Advising Center at the University of Florida [UF], beginning advisors are hired as "Assistant In Advising," which are non-tenure-accruing, 12-month faculty lines. If they remain for five years and excel at advising, service to the campus community, and professional development (generally through involvement in NACADA), then they can be promoted to "Associate In Advising," much like faculty. Another five years of excellence in all three areas leads to promotion to "Senior Associate In Advising." Each promotion comes with a 9% raise in addition to any merit or across-the-board raises. Promotion requires the development of a portfolio demonstrating excellence in all three areas, and the portfolio includes a personal promotion statement, letters from outside UF and inside UF, as well as a Director's letter that ties everything together. The process parallels the teaching faculty's promotion process, and advisors are judged by the Promotion and Tenure Committee of the College, the Dean, and ultimately the UF-wide Academic Personnel Board under the supervision of the Provost. This career ladder has been in place for roughly a dozen years (the third tier was added about five years ago), and has been very successful in rewarding deserving advisors. It has also encouraged many to stay in advising rather than leave for better pay elsewhere. (¶6)

Regardless of the evaluation approach used, implementation and support of the career ladder structure requires master advisors and advising administrators to "position their academic advisors for success, minimize structural barriers to advancement, and avoid disconnects between advisor work and expectations for promotion" (Taylor, 2011, p. 136). To the extent that such structures are incorporated, academic advisors may receive support for remaining in the profession and reaping the rewards associated with their career choice.

Summary

Master advisors work closely with advising administrators to communicate the value of advising and promote the appreciation due to advisors for their work. Communication of efforts ideally leads to the creation of both informal interaction processes and formal structures that offer appropriate appreciation, recognition, and reward for outstanding advising. While developing processes and structures for career ladders, master advisors identify the desired outcomes of their advising programs and the key advising practices and professional development activities associated with these outcomes. They listen carefully to advisors to identify appropriate rewards and develop a reward structure that incentivizes excellence in advising.

To retain effective advisors and promote career satisfaction, master advisors and administrators may explore the option of implementing career ladders for primary-role advisors. A career ladder helps professionalize the role of advising so that effective advisors remain in their roles and continue to support students while advancing in their own careers. The master advisor also supports or stimulates efforts to embed advising into the already existing tenure and promotion structures for the faculty.

Aiming for Excellence

- o Discuss with a group of advisors on your campus intrinsically and extrinsically motivating rewards. Involve both faculty and primary-role advisors in this conversation.

- o Journal daily for two weeks about the most intrinsically rewarding activities and experiences at work. What motivates you to advise?

- o Develop an outline of the reward design process for a department or unit and discuss it with the program director or supervisor.

- o Contact an advising colleague at a similar postsecondary institution with a career ladder and ask about the process used to develop it. Follow up by asking about the impact of the structure on advising.

- o Develop and distribute a survey that explores preferred incentives among advisors. Host a discussion group to review the results.

- o Identify strategic priorities and outcomes within your unit or department and identify the behaviors essential to achieving each. What incentives might encourage these behaviors and increase the intrinsic motivation to pursue them?

- o Offer an on-campus workshop focused on designing reward systems or career ladders in academic advising.

- o Organize a task force to explore the creation of a reward or career ladder system.

- o Ask human resource personnel for examples of career ladders used on campus. Also discuss any policies or procedures related to incentive or reward systems.

- o Acquire a copy of your current job description from the human resource office. Review and update the description based on your current duties. How have your duties and responsibilities changed since you were first hired for advising? Do they match up with the career evolution of other advisors? Does the nature of the changing duties suggest the need for a career ladder?

References

Amabile, T. M. (1997). Motivating creativity in organizations: On doing what you love and loving what you do. *California Management Review, 40*(1), 39–58.

Bedeian, A. G., & Armenakis, A. A. (1981). A path-analytical study of the consequences of role conflict and ambiguity. *Academy of Management Journal, 24*(2), 417–424. doi:10.2307/255852

Burney, L. L., & Widener, S. K. (2013). Behavioral work outcomes of a strategic performance measurement system–based incentive plan. *Behavioral Research in Accounting*, *25*(2), 115–143.

CalPoly San Luis Obispo. (2015). *Outstanding faculty advisor award*. Retrieved from http://advising.calpoly.edu/content/nominate-faculty-advisor

Campbell, S. M. (2008). Vision, mission, goals, and program objectives for academic advising programs. In V. N. Gordon, W. R. Habley, & T. J. Grites (Eds.), *Academic advising: A comprehensive handbook* (2nd ed.) (pp. 229–241). San Francisco, CA: Jossey-Bass.

Carlstrom, A. H., & Miller, M. A. (Eds.). (2013). How effective academic advising is rewarded [Table 7.30]. *2011 NACADA National Survey of Academic Advising* (Monograph No. 25). Retrieved from http://www.nacada.ksu.edu/Portals/0/Monographs/nat%20survey%20upload%20docs/Chapter%207%20-%20Faculty%20Advising%20-%20Final.pdf

Council for the Advancement of Standards in Higher Education. (2015). *Academic advising programs*. Retrieved from http://standards.cas.edu/getpdf.cfm?PDF=E864D2C4-D655-8F74-2E647CDECD29B7D0

Deci, E., Koestner, R., & Ryan, R. (2001). Extrinsic rewards and intrinsic motivation in education: Reconsidered once again. *Review of Educational Research*, *71*(1), 1–26.

de Treville, S., Antonakis, J., & Edelson, N. M. (2005). Can standard operating procedures be motivating? Reconciling process variability issues and behavioural outcomes. *Total Quality Management & Business Excellence*, *16*(2), 231–241. doi:10.1080/14783360500054236

Drake, J. K. (2008). Recognition and reward for academic advising in theory and practice. *Academic advising: A comprehensive handbook* (2nd ed.) (pp. 396–412). San Francisco, CA: Jossey-Bass.

Drake, J. K. (2011). The role of academic advising in student retention and persistence. *About Campus*, *16*(3), 8–12. doi:10.1002/abc.20062

Eisenberger, R., & Shanock, L. (2003). Rewards, intrinsic motivation, and creativity: A case study of conceptual and methodological isolation. *Creativity Research Journal*, *15*(2 & 3), 121–130.

Fisher, C. D., & Yuan, A. X. Y. (1998). What motivates employees? A comparison of US and Chinese responses. *The International Journal of Human Resource Management*, *9*(3), 516–528.

Folsom, P., Joslin, J., & Yoder, F. (2005). *From advisor training to advisor development: Creating a blueprint for first-year advisors*. Retrieved from http://www.nacada.ksu.edu/Clearinghouse/AdvisingIssues/First-Year-Advisors.htm

Gerzon, M. (2003). *Becoming global citizens: Finding common ground in a world of differences*. Retrieved August 13, 2008, from http://www.mediatorsfoundation.org/relatedreading/becoming_global_citizens.pdf

Gil, D., Cuevas-Rodrıguez, G., López-Cabrales, Á., & Sánchez, J. M. (2012). The effects of incentive system and cognitive orientation on teams' performance. *Behavioral Research in Accounting*, *24*(2), 177–191.

Gneezy, U., Meier, S., & Rey-Biel, P. (2011). When and why incentives (don't) work to modify behavior. *Journal of Economic Perspectives, 25*(4), 191–210.

Gnyawali, D. R., Offstein, E., & Lau, R. S. (2008). The impact of CEO pay gap on firm competitive behavior. *Group Organization Management, 33*(4), 453–484.

Grites, T. (2014). *Assessing the effectiveness of your academic advising program* [webinar]. Available from http://www.innovativeeducators.org/Assessing-The-Effectiveness-Of-Your-Academic-p/3421.htm

Hemwell, M. K., & Trachte, K. C. (2005). Academic advising as learning: 10 organizing principles. *NACADA Journal, 25*(2), 74–83.

Herzberg, F. (1976). *The managerial choice: To be efficient and to be human.* Homewood, IL: Dow Jones-Irwin.

Higher Ed Jobs. (2015). *Advisor II* [job description from Temple University]. Retrieved September 28, 2015, from https://www.higheredjobs.com/admin/details.cfm?JobCode=176047805&Title=Advisor%20II

Hofstede, G. H. (1972). The colors of collars. *Columbia Journal of World Business, 7*(5), 72–80.

Hurt, R. L. (2007). Advising as teaching: Establishing outcomes, developing tools, and assessing student learning. *NACADA Journal, 27*(2), 36–40.

Iten, C., & Matheny, A. (2008). Promoting academic advisors: Using a career ladder to foster professional development at your institution. *Academic Advising Today, 31*(3). Retrieved from https://www.nacada.ksu.edu/Resources/Academic-Advising-Today/View-Articles/Promoting-Academic-Advisors-Using-a-Career-Ladder-to-Foster-Professional-Development-at-Your-Institution.aspx

James Madison University. (2015). *Provost award for excellence in academic advising.* Retrieved from https://www.jmu.edu/universitystudies/advising-award.shtml

Kent Academic Support and Advising Association. (2009). *Student survey and academic advising survey: Comparison summary report.* Retrieved from https://view.officeapps.live.com/op/view.aspx?src=http%3A%2F%2Fwww2.kent.edu%2Facademics%2Fresources%2Fkasada%2Fupload%2FSummaryReport_Final.doc.

Kohn, A. (1993). Why incentive plans cannot work. *Harvard Business Review, 71*(5), 54–63.

Kovach, K. (1995). Employee motivation: Addressing a crucial factor in your organizations performance. *Employment Relations Today, 22*(2), 93–107.

Lawler, E. E. (2008). *Talent: Making people your competitive advantage.* San Francisco, CA: Jossey-Bass.

McClellan, J. L. (2007, June 28). Answering the fundamental questions of organizational existence: Developing, implementing, and communicating effective mission statements and goals to guide advising programs or centers. *The Mentor: An Academic Advising Journal.* Retrieved from http://www.psu.edu/dus/mentor/070628jm.htm

McClellan, J. L. (2010). *Bringing about change when you are not in charge. The importance of informal change leadership in academic advising.* Retrieved from http://www.nacada.ksu.edu/Resources/Clearinghouse/View-Articles/Leading-Change.aspx

McClellan, J. L. (2011). Beyond student learning outcomes: Developing comprehensive, strategic assessment plans for advising programs. *Journal of Higher Education Policy and Management, 33*(6), 641–652.

McClellan, J. L. (2013). *The advising process.* Presentation from the CLAS Academic Advisor Training Workshop, Frostburg State University, Frostburg, MD.

Median salaries of higher-education professionals, 2014–2015. (2015, March 30). *Chronicle of Higher Education.* Retrieved from http://chronicle.com/article/Median-Salaries-of/228735/

Missouri State University. (2015). *The Academic Advisement Center: History of the master advisor training program.* Retrieved from http://www.missouristate.edu/advising/10704.htm

NACADA: The Global Community for Academic Advising (NACADA). (2007). *National survey of recognition and rewards for academic advising* [raw data]. Manhattan, KS: Author.

NACADA. (2014). [National survey for academic advising, raw data]. Manhattan, KS: Author. Retrieved from http://www.nacada.ksu.edu/Portals/0/Surveys/Documents/Rec%20and%20reward%20Initial_Report%202014.pdf

Northern Arizona University (2015). *Outstanding academic advisor award: Faculty advisor.* Retrieved from http://nau.edu/University-College/University-Advising/ACADEMIC-ADVISOR-RECOGNITION/

Nutt, C. L. (2003). *Academic advising and student retention and persistence.* Retrieved from https://www.nacada.ksu.edu/Resources/Clearinghouse/View-Articles/Advising-and-Student-Retention-article.aspx

O'Connell, K. L. (2010, October 7). Valuing and rewarding academic advising. *Faculty focus: Higher ed teaching strategies from Magna Publications.* Retrieved from http://www.facultyfocus.com/articles/academic-leadership/valuing-and-rewarding-academic-advising/

Plattsburgh State University of New York. (2016). *Outstanding academic advisor award.* Retrieved from http://www.plattsburgh.edu/academics/advising/outstandingadvisoraward.php

Powers, K. L. (2012). *Academic advising assessment practices: A descriptive study* (Unpublished doctoral dissertation). Kansas State University, Manhattan. Retrieved from http://krex.k-state.edu/dspace/bitstream/handle/2097/14945/KeithPowers2012.pdf?sequence=1

Ryan, C. C. (1992). Advising as teaching. *NACADA Journal, 12*(1), 4–8.

Shaffer, L. S., Zalewski, J. M., & Leveille, J. (2010). The professionalization of academic advising: Where are we in 2010? *NACADA Journal, 30*(1), 66–77.

Sharma, A., & Sarel, D. (1995). The impact of customer satisfaction based incentive systems on sales people's customer service response: An empirical study. *Journal of Personal Selling and Sales Management, 15*(3), 17–29.

Silverthorne, C. P. (1992). Work motivation in the United States, Russia, and the Republic of China. *Journal of Applied Social Psychology, 22*(20), 1631–1639.

Society for Human Resource Management. (2010). *Research quarterly: Motivation in today's workplace: The link to performance* (Second Quarter Report). Alexandria, VA: Author.

Society for Human Resource Management. (2014). *Employee job satisfaction and engagement: The road to economic recovery*. Alexandria, VA: Author.

Stockton University. (2015). *Provost's R & PD award in academic advising*. Retrieved from http://intraweb.stockton.edu/eyos/page.cfm?siteID=245&pageID=12

Taylor, M. (2011). Career ladders and performance evaluations for advising administrators. In J. Joslin & N. Markee (Eds.), *Academic advising administration: Essential knowledge and skills for the 21st century* (Monograph No. 22) (pp. 133–144). Manhattan, KS: National Academic Advising Association.

Temple University. (2015). *Faculty advisor award*. Retrieved from http://www.temple.edu/vpus/resources/AdvisorAwards.htm

Texas A&M University. (2015). *Academic advisor career ladder*. Retrieved from http://employees.tamu.edu/compensation/career-ladders/academic-advisor/

University of Central Florida. (2015). *University excellence in undergraduate faculty academic advising*. Retrieved from https://provost.ucf.edu/files/C__Undergraduate-Faculty-Academic-Advising-16.pdf

University of Georgia. (2015). *Outstanding academic advisor award: Faculty advisor*. Retrieved from https://curriculumsystems.uga.edu/advising/outstanding-academic-advisor-award

University of Nevada Regents. (2016). *Nevada Board of Regents academic advising award for universities and community colleges*. Retrieved from http://www.unr.edu/Documents/provost/provosts-office/forms/2014%20Call%20for%20Nominations%20Regents%20Advising%20Awards.pdf

University of Texas Arlington. (2012). *Office of human resources: Academic advisor II* [job description]. Retrieved from http://www.uta.edu/hr/compensation/job-descriptions/3000/Academic-Advisor-II.php

Utah State University. (2015). *Outstanding faculty advisor of the year award*. Retrieved from http://www.usu.edu/awards/faculty/

Utah Valley University. (2016). *UVU advisement awards and recognition*. Retrieved from http://www.uvu.edu/advising/advisorawards.html

Virginia Tech. (2015). *Virginia Tech alumni award for excellence in undergraduate/graduate advising*. Retrieved December 14, 2015, from http://www.advising.vt.edu/images/pdfs/2016%20VT%20Academic%20Advising%20Award%20Call%20for%20Nominations.pdf

Vansteenkiste, M., & Deci, E. (2003). Competitively contingent rewards and intrinsic motivation: Can losers remain motivated? *Motivation & Emotion, 27*(4), 273–299.

13

PROFESSIONAL DEVELOPMENT

Julie Givans Voller

It's not just learning things that's important. It's learning what to do with what you learn and learning why you learn things at all that matters.

—Norton Juster (1961, p. 233)

Professional development opportunities abound in academic advising. Professional ethics require continuous learning, yet no single path leads to master advisor status. Determining the combination of skills, knowledge, and understanding needed to approach mastery requires reflection on personal strengths, challenges, and goals. Academic advisors must take the initiative to plan, manage, and document their own professional development. To do this, they can create individual professional development plans and portfolios that show advanced achievement in all components of advising: informational, relational, and conceptual. Advisors need to capitalize on formal, nonformal, and informal learning experiences as well as seek opportunities for incremental and major professional growth.

Reader Learning Outcomes

From studying this chapter, advisors will use knowledge gained about professional development to

- articulate the importance of career-long professional development;
- craft an individual professional development plan (IPDP);
- set up and maintain a professional development portfolio;
- balance professional development among informational, relational, and conceptual components; and
- recognize and take advantage of formal, nonformal, and informal learning experiences.

Although lifelong learners, master advisors do not reach this ultimate level of academic advising prowess by following a clear-cut path. Because of the diversity of the profession—with advisors practicing in so many different contexts and with so many different student populations—academic advisors must choose from a multitude of development opportunities to master all they need to know, do, and understand. While the NACADA academic advisor competencies (NACADA: The Global Community for Academic Advising [NACADA], 2003) and New Advisor Development Chart (Folsom, 2015), featured in *The New Advisor Guidebook: Mastering the Art of Academic Advising* (Folsom, Yoder, & Joslin, 2015), provide some guidelines for those who seek to master the distinctive knowledge base of academic advising, very few institutions provide comprehensive professional development programs for primary-role or faculty academic advisors (Givans Voller, 2013). Furthermore, unlike more established professions, such as medicine, law, and counseling, no governmental or professional entity sets licensing, certification, or continuing education requirements for academic advising (Dean, Woodard, & Cooper, 2007). In sum, academic advisors who seek to master their craft and advance the profession have no structure on which to climb.

Academic advisors with two or more years of experience (Folsom, 2015) who have established a solid foundation of informational, relational, and conceptual knowledge in the field seek the next steps toward becoming master advisors. These strides should lead to further engagement with the goals, interests, and contexts of each individual advisor. After a brief review of the importance of continued professional development, I present suggestions on ways an advisor can craft an individual professional development plan (IPDP) and set up a portfolio for documenting learning. I then turn to the knowledge advisors need and ways to acquire it. I conclude the chapter with suggestions for seeking diverse formal, nonformal, and informal learning experiences.

These professional topics harmonize with the larger purpose of this book: to outline the knowledge, skills, and abilities academic advisors must develop as master advisors, who not only stand as experts in their practice but also act as leaders in the field. Thus, this chapter does not present methods to create and deliver professional development programs. Interested readers can find good information on planning and implementing professional development programs through many other sources, including the NACADA Clearinghouse and *Academic Advising Training and Development: Practices that Deliver* (Givans Voller, Miller, & Neste, 2010). In this chapter, academic advisors find encouragement and guidance for taking responsibility to plan, manage, and document their own professional growth over the course of their careers.

Why Bother With Professional Development?

In a world changing faster every day, academic advisors cannot rely on their initial training to remain viable throughout their careers; changes in institutional information, advising approaches, and student populations make ongoing professional development a must for every person who advises students. Professional development, defined as the continuous learning in which experienced advisors engage after their initial year of practice and beyond (Givans Voller et al., 2010), takes an investment of time—arguably any advisor's most precious resource. Yet, the benefits for students and advisors—as well as for the profession as a whole—far outweigh the costs.

Meeting with a knowledgeable academic advisor contributes to student engagement (Kuh, 2008), learning (Light, 2001), and retention (Klepfer & Hull, 2012; Noel-Levitz, 2011; Swecker, Fifolt, & Searby, 2013). Research demonstrates that professional development improves student learning outcomes in K-12 classrooms (Cohen & Hill, 2000; Darling-Hammond, 2010; National Commission on Teaching & America's Future, 1996). With these recent studies in mind, one can conclude that students are likely to learn the most from experienced and well-prepared academic advisors.

Engaging in professional development also benefits individual academic advisors. A national survey of academic advisors (Sofranco, 2004) found that the top incentives for participating in professional development activities included ability to better assist students, professional growth, and personal growth as well as opportunities to engage in lifelong learning and networking. In addition, surveyed advisors indicated that professional development increased their motivation at work and validated the importance of their role (Sofranco, 2004). Indeed, a majority of primary-role and faculty advisors consider support for professional development an important form of recognition and reward (Drake, 2008) (chapter 12).

In addition, professional development may serve as a form of self-care for academic advisors. Engagement in lifelong learning contributes to cognitive wellness for practitioners of counseling, another helping profession (Venart, Vassos, & Pitcher-Heft, 2007). Thus, when determining whether they have time to participate in professional development, advisors should consider the long-term benefits for themselves and their students.

Advisor participation in development activities also results in long-term implications for the profession as a whole. To wit, the definition of a professional includes mastery of a complex and distinctive base of knowledge (Eraut, 1993). Thus, each time academic advisors learn or teach other advisors about the complex informational, relational, and conceptual components of the field, they move the profession forward. Academic advisors' mastery of and contribution to knowledge distinctive to academic advising elevate the status of academic advising as a profession.

A code of ethics characterizes a profession, and competence (Bayles, 1981)—attaining and maintaining the knowledge, skills, and abilities to advise clients accurately—constitutes a core principle of professional ethics. Masters in any field must engage in continued professional development to maintain competence over the course of their careers. NACADA has defined competencies for academic advisors (Gordon, 2003), which are used by a few savvy administrators to establish institutional advisor development pathways (McClellan, Moser, & Waterreus, 2008). The American College Personnel Association and NASPA: Student Affairs Administrators in Higher Education have also published general standards of professional competence for student affairs professionals (Joint Task Force on Professional Competencies and Standards, 2010). In addition, evidence suggests that student affairs practitioners support the idea of a national system of professional development credits administered by a professional organization (Dean et al., 2007). However, to date no entity has yet defined or enforced requirements for certification or continuing education in academic advising. Nonetheless, because quality academic advising constitutes an important component of student learning, professional organizations that support academic advising promote ongoing learning for practitioners.

For example, both NACADA and the Council for the Advancement of Standards in Higher Education (CAS) (2015) provide codes of ethics that include specific calls for continued learning of practitioners. The NACADA Statement of Core Values of Academic Advising maintains that "advisors are responsible for their professional practices and for themselves personally" (NACADA, 2005a). This core value reminds academic advisors of the importance of interacting with and learning about people who differ from themselves, the importance of research, and the need to take care of themselves emotionally. It also speaks directly to the obligation for professional development:

> Advisors seek opportunities to grow professionally. They identify appropriate work-shops, classes, literature, research publications, and groups, both inside and outside the institution, that can keep their interest high, hone professional skills, and advance expertise within specific areas of interest. (NACADA, 2005b, ¶2)

The CAS Standards and Guidelines for Academic Advising Programs (AAP) provide fundamental requirements and expectations for academic advising programs (Miller, 2012). The CAS Standards outline a gamut of expectations—from ethical behavior to organization and leadership. On the subject of continuing education for academic advisors, the CAS Standards state: "AAP personnel must engage in continuing professional development activities to keep abreast of the research, theories, legislation, policies, and developments that affect their programs and services" (2015, p. 10). Clearly, continuous professional learning and growth compose fundamental expectations for academic advisors.

Data from the latest national NACADA survey suggest that institutional professional development structures for academic advising do not meet the needs for the ongoing professional development suggested by the CAS Standards (2015) and NACADA Core Values for Academic Advising (2005a, 2005b) (Givans Voller, 2013; NACADA, 2014c). Thus, academic advisors must seek their own sources for professional learning. While benign neglect, or even discouragement, from supervisors presents a real challenge for many, academic advisors must persevere. With time and commitment, advisors can take advantage of a multitude of low and no cost ways to keep learning. For any academic advisor with the will to identify and take advantage of them, opportunities for professional growth abound. Ascending to the level of master advisor requires individuals to seize the reins and control their own futures.

Charting the Path: Recognizing and Recording Professional Learning

Ongoing professional growth forms an ethical cornerstone of the academic advising profession. Yet, ways to plan and document advisor learning do not follow from the need. Academic advising presents too many complexities for any single practitioner to master every context. The multiple types of postsecondary institutions, the range of academic disciplines, and the diversity of student populations make all-encompassing mastery an unattainable goal. Any advisor who has been overwhelmed by the number of sessions offered at an annual advising conference understands this. Thus, advisors must set priorities for learning.

Without agreed-upon parameters for planning and documenting continued learning, each academic advisor must create a plan for growth specific to his or her goals as well as to the needs of the institution and the advisor's role within it. Many educators find IPDPs and portfolios very effective tools for this type of learning (Janssen, Kreijns, Bastiaens, Stijnen, & Vermeulen, 2013; Jarvinen, 1995; Villegas-Reimers, 2003). In fact, according to a national survey of academic advisors, one half of respondents considered an individual professional growth plan a moderate or major need (Sofranco, 2004). Furthermore, as the most common documentation of student learning, especially as part of teacher preparation programs, portfolios as means for documenting professional learning are garnering favor (Vowell & Wallet-Ortiz, 2003). The IPDP and the portfolio serve as the physical manifestations of the personal learning infrastructure described in chapter 7.

The Individual Professional Development Plan

The IPDP comes from advisor reflection upon personal advising practice, role within the institution, and impact on the profession. When beginning this process, advisors should take time to consider their

- current role(s),
- professional goals and interests,
- personal goals and interests,
- strengths and areas for improvement, and
- personal philosophy of academic advising.

Introspection about a professional destination—and the steps that lead to it—lays the foundation for advancement. Next, an advisor needs to consider the context in which she or he works, or would like to work. Preparing a plan for professional growth cannot be done in a vacuum; instead, the advisor must take into account

- the mission, vision, goals, and metrics of his or her current institution or position and
- the mission, vision, goals, and metrics of the target institution or position.

Weighing these factors prior to embarking on a path of professional learning will help an academic advisor identify areas of harmony and contrast between a personal philosophy and the vision, goals, and realities of the unit.

For example, academic advisor Skylar may be interested in learning about and employing a learning-centered approach to advising; however, Skylar advises at an institution with a high student–advisor ratio. Furthermore, the administration has placed the highest priority on increased student head count. In this particular culture, Skylar's supervisor may not welcome professional growth focused on learning centeredness. To acknowledge this situation, Skylar creates an IPDP that includes a plan for mastering the learning-centered approach. It also includes a plan for learning more about institutional goals and budget practices as well as strategies for managing up the organizational chart.

In the next step, to prepare the IPDP, the advisor writes down these reflections and discusses them with a trusted colleague, mentor, or supportive supervisor—anyone who might serve as a good sounding board. Because of the vastness of the knowledge base and the many opportunities for learning it, advisors make the best use of limited time and resources by setting a learning goal and identifying the knowledge, skills, and abilities needed to reach it. In the process, the advisor looks for and acknowledges gaps in knowledge or opportunity.

The Portfolio

The pieces of the IPDP provide the first artifacts for the academic advisor's portfolio. The plan outlines the advisor's philosophy, states the goals, and charts the intended path; the portfolio documents all that the advisor learns along the way to and through mastery. Portfolios are used for formative purposes: to document learning and also to encourage more reflective practice. In some contexts they may also be summative and used for assessment, promotion, or recognition (Vowell & Wallet-Ortiz, 2003). Although the time required to prepare and maintain a portfolio deter some, the advisor who selects an easy-to-use tool as well as finds or creates a supportive context for maintaining a portfolio will likely keep it updated (Fong et al., 2014). Thus, to support the creation and maintenance of their professional portfolios, advisors should find like-minded individuals with whom to collaborate.

Portfolios may be as individual as the advisors who create them. They may be notebooks or hard-copy file folders. Some advisors choose to keep it simple by storing their learning artifacts in an electronic folder on their hard drive or cloud-based service. Still others choose to use a web-based application, such as Mahara (n.d.), created especially to build, maintain, and share electronic portfolios. Regardless of the methods used to manage the portfolio, advisors benefit from guidelines that ensure the utility of the portfolio. Examples available through the NACADA Clearinghouse (IUPUI University College Advising Center & Buyarski, 2014; Vowell & Wallet-Ortiz, 2003) suggest the following common elements be included:

- o résumé or curriculum vitae,
- o statement of academic advising philosophy,

- advising goals,

- description of current role (e.g., student demographics and job responsibilities),

- feedback from students and colleagues,

- professional development activities attended, and

- reflective writing (e.g., essays on accomplishments and challenges, responses to professional development, and reflections on specific advising interactions).

Of all these elements, perhaps reflective writing offers the best means for learning and growth. Professionals learn the most relevant information informally from colleagues and through experience (Eraut, 1993). Thus, documentation of thoughts, reactions, and outcomes creates a more powerful record of learning than a list of workshops attended. Indeed, reflection on interactions with students, coworkers, and administrators can lead to more useful insights than those gleaned from formal learning experiences. These writings contribute to in-depth learning, especially when personal insights are linked with larger concepts, theories, and trends (Joslin & Yoder, 2015). Whatever form it takes—blog, journal, or a series of essays—the power of the portfolio stems from the deep connections and understandings that arise from the reflective process.

Advisor Knowledge

When they plan, document, and reflect on their learning, academic advisors highlight ways their development integrates with the informational, relational, and conceptual components of the academic advising knowledge base as initially outlined by Habley (1989) and King (2000) (chapter 3). The *New Advisor Guidebook: Mastering the Art of Academic Advising* (Folsom et al., 2015) provides introductory information on these key components of advising and ways new advisors can lay the foundation for their practice. In this chapter, master advisors find information for building upon that foundation.

Informational Component

To get an initial handle on the huge volume of the information in the academic advisor knowledge base, new practitioners focus on grasping curriculum requirements, policies, and procedures that help students navigate the institution. However, informational learning does not end when the advisor can help students negotiate the college experience. Even master advisors will never know everything, and they keep their eyes and ears open to learn details that may someday prove useful to a student. Higginson's (2000) framework organizes this vast array of information that advisors must possess into four categories: internal, external, student needs, and advisor self-knowledge.

Internal Information. Master advisors do more than keep up with the changes in curriculum and policy at their institutions; their knowledge of internal information extends to degree programs and courses outside their assigned area. Master advisors draw upon this knowledge to provide learning-centered academic advising and to help students make connections between courses across the curriculum and understand the purpose of higher education (Lowenstein, 2000, 2013). Advisors seeking to learn also benefit from sitting in classes, talking to faculty members in unfamiliar disciplines, and attending departmental lectures and brown bag discussions.

External Information.   Higginson (2000) categorized information about legal issues as well as the community, the state or province, and higher education as *external*. Aspiring master advisors might inquire about nearby colleges and universities as well as community resources. They also keep abreast of changes in federal and state laws, especially those that affect access to and delivery of higher education: the Family Educational Rights and Privacy Act (FERPA) in the United States and the Freedom of Information and Protection of Privacy Act (FIPPA) in Canada (Beres et al., 2013) (chapter 8).

Student Needs.   Information about student needs exposes ways to be successful in the classroom and includes data on student attitudes, opinions, and demographics. In addition, after mastering basic advising information, advisors should take time to increase their knowledge of local and national student trends. Exploring survey data from the National Survey of Student Engagement, Community College Survey of Student Engagement, Ruffalo Noel Levitz, and other sources increases advisors' knowledge of their students. Moreover, master advisors should understand the concepts and practices these widely used survey resources are measuring, as the results exert influence in shaping legislation and policy.

Advisor Self-Knowledge.   Often overlooked in training programs, advisor self-knowledge appears on well-crafted IPDPs. Self-knowledge includes being aware of one's values, biases, and attitudes toward certain behaviors (Higginson, 2000). For a master advisor, self-knowledge also includes awareness of one's preferred leadership style as well as cognizance of the ways others perceive him or her. To move the profession forward, master advisors must lead from their positions, work across functional areas, and cultivate support for academic advising among stakeholders (chapter 10). Development of self-awareness increases in importance the longer an advisor stays in the field.

Technology.   Although not one of Higginson's four categories, technology has evolved as a ubiquitous, major contributor to higher education and advising practice; therefore, master advisors keep abreast of new technology. Moreover, they seek innovative ways to apply existing technologies to their work (chapter 16). The NACADA Technology in Advising Commission and EDUCAUSE (n.d.), the premier association for information technology professionals in higher education, offer excellent resources. Master advisors should also identify opportunities to participate in technology projects on campus. Volunteering to implement or troubleshoot new software, for example, gives academic advisors a firsthand look at the capabilities of technology and greater appreciation for the hard work required to get such systems in working order.

Relational Component

The interpersonal skills academic advisors must possess to build effective partnerships with students comprise the relational component of advising. Within the first years of practice, advisors focus on basic skills such as active listening and paraphrasing (Jordan, 2015). Once this foundation is laid, aspiring master advisors continue to build their relational skills with students and colleagues.

Although most advisors have a preferred style for interacting with students, master advisors need more than one tool in their supply kit. *Academic Advising Approaches: Strategies That Teach Students to Make the Most of College* (Drake, Jordan, & Miller, 2013) introduces advisors to numerous ways to approach interactions with students. Because of the uniqueness of every student, an advisee who does not respond to a prescriptive approach may blossom when an appreciative style, for example, is used (Bloom, Hutson, & He, 2013). Master academic advisors are familiar with and able to apply different approaches under different circumstances.

Master advisors demonstrate the ability to work well with stakeholders of the field. Relational skills such as collaboration, persuasion, and negotiation advance understanding of the central role academic advising plays in the student experience. Aptitude for working with administrators, business leaders, and legislators broadens awareness about academic advising. To move the profession forward, relational development must include creating networks, identifying political issues, and crafting and sharing compelling narratives about academic advising, student learning, and success (chapters 10 and 11).

Conceptual Component

The knowledge of students and the role of academic advising both within the institution and in higher education more broadly contribute to the conceptual component of advising (King, 2000). Expanding beyond the basics means delving into the theories, philosophies, and studies of academic advising, teaching and learning, social sciences, humanities, and other related fields (chapters 2 and 3). Advanced conceptual knowledge also means understanding the way academic advising fits into the structure of the college, school, or institution as well as the broader conversation about education in each state, province, or country. Master advisors identify and articulate the way laws and initiatives affect individual students to ensure that critical academic advising perspectives are incorporated into administrative decision-making processes.

A comprehensive IPDP includes goals that address each of these three components of academic advising. Readers seeking a more comprehensive curriculum for gaining foundational mastery in their third year of advising and beyond will find it in Folsom's (2015) New Advisor Development Chart. In addition, every chapter in this book provides Aiming for Excellence activities designed to build the skills and knowledge needed to develop as a master advisor. Therefore, advisors should take time to reflect, identify areas for growth, and use the IPDP and portfolio to chart an individualized set of learning goals.

Learning Strategies

Once advisors identify their individual learning goals, they next determine the best way to meet those objectives. For academic advisors determined to master their craft, professional development is not limited to workshops; they see opportunities everywhere. Smith (2002) revived a definition from 1973 by Coombs, Prosser, and Ahmed, who noted the distinctions between formal, nonformal, and informal education; their model provides a useful structure to identify where and how academic advisors learn. The categories in this model are not discrete. For example, a single professional development event or experience may result in the participant learning the information formally presented as well as applications for it as learned informally from colleagues. Nonetheless, the categories not only help advisors distinguish among options for professional growth but also help them see the overlap among opportunities. This method of organizing possibilities encourages advisors to reflect on all the learning acquired from each professional development experience.

Formal Learning

Formal learning is created by a structured system of learning experiences formally measured and graded. Upon successful completion, it culminates in a certification or award recognized by the single, national educational body of the country where the award is earned. Usually housed in schools or classrooms, formal education is characterized by hierarchical grade levels, admission requirements (age or prior educational attainment), and registration criteria (United Nations Educational, Scientific and Cultural Organization [UNESCO], 2006). Formal education is exemplified at K–12 schools and college, university, and technical school classes and degrees.

In terms of professional development, formal education presents some drawbacks. First, it can be expensive. In all but a few countries, formal education beyond high school generally comes with a bill for tuition, and even academic advisors lucky enough to have access to tuition waivers or reimbursement through their workplace must pay for course fees, parking spots, books, and other supplies. Second, while degrees and courses are easy to document, verification of learning is not always easily accomplished.

Although formal education may not offer the most effective way of learning, it confers many benefits. First, advisors may need formal educational credentials, such as advanced degrees, to land specific positions or fill certain roles and offer "significant value for advisors who work in academic departments and in close proximity to faculty" (Taylor, 2013, ¶4). Second, the shared meaning of the credential, both nationally and internationally, makes substantiation fairly easy. Individual degrees and classes have titles that can be listed on a résumé. Practical activities such as internships or clinical positions can be documented by clock and credit hours earned. Syllabi outline specific learning goals students may justifiably claim to have achieved. Moreover, the curriculum is structured by a faculty with expertise in the field. Thus, students may feel confident that they have been exposed to the prominent ideas, theories, and practices of their field of study.

Master's Degrees. Results from the *2011 NACADA National Survey of Academic Advising* reveal that at almost one half (46%) of responding institutions, primary-role academic advisors need not present a credential other than a bachelor's degree (and in some cases a high school diploma or associate's degree suffices) (Carlstrom & Miller, 2013b). Yet, the same survey reveals that at nearly two thirds (65%) of institutions, most primary-role academic advisors have earned a master's degree (Carlstrom & Miller, 2013a). Because of the mobility of today's workforce, rate of change in higher education, and growth of academic advising as a profession, academic advisors should strongly consider getting a master's degree.

The choice of degree should be based upon interests and lifelong goals. Institutions and hiring managers vary widely on preferences. Lowenstein (1999) suggested that well-rounded education in almost any liberal arts discipline benefits advisors, but some administrators in academic units prefer applicants with master's degrees in department-specific disciplines. Those looking to cross disciplinary lines or get a foothold in a competitive market might consider course work or certification specifically in academic advising, such as the graduate certificate in academic advising offered through Kansas State University or the letter of accomplishment in academic advising available through the University of Manitoba. However, some institutions seek applicants with master's degrees in counseling, higher education, college student personnel, or similar areas. Benefits of such a degree include formal learning in psychosocial theories, career development, law and governance in higher education, and basic research methods (McMahan, 2008).

Doctoral Degrees. To move up the academic career ladder, some may consider pursuing and completing a doctorate. The number of advisors pursuing this degree has reached the critical mass and justifies the creation of the doctoral students interest group within NACADA; the group, formed in 2009, provides support and information to prospective and current doctoral students in advising as well a network for research ideas and resources (NACADA, 2014a).

Time-consuming and expensive, earning a doctorate and adding those additional letters after one's name provide both personal and professional benefits. Any institutional online job posting reveals open doors to higher level positions for those with the highest degree. However, because of the limited number of positions for which the degree is compensated, advisors need to know their local job market and consider their own geographical mobility. Also, because return on investment is not guaranteed, the prospective doctorate should enjoy the process. Although one's interests should direct the choice of academic discipline to pursue, a doctoral degree in practice-based fields, such as education, typically bestows the most benefit when paired with some years of experience in the field. Notwithstanding the pros and cons, in many contexts, a doctorate inspires credibility, increased influence, and professional respect. In addition, the research base of academic advising grows stronger through the contributions from the dissertation process and subsequent research projects undertaken by practitioners with doctoral degrees.

Classes.   Those with their terminal degrees or uncommitted, for any reason, to a degree program, may continue formal learning through individual classes. Because they teach students the way courses fit together to form a coherent educational whole (Lowenstein, 2000, 2013), academic advisors benefit from taking courses in almost any area. Certainly, courses in the discipline of the unit where one advises, or hopes to advise, offer useful assets for practice, but classes from any field—similar to or vastly different from those in the discipline—provide material for learning-centered conversations with students.

Teaching.   Although teaching classes is not considered formal learning for the instructor, the expertise acquired contributes to effective advising. After all, teaching is at the heart of academic advising. Although many faculty members undertake classroom teaching as a focus of their on-campus role, many primary-role advisors find that classroom teaching experiences are missing from their toolbox.

Teaching an academic course differs from advising students one-to-one or presenting a series of workshops. Classroom instructors must address issues of classroom management, assess student learning on the fly, select appropriate tests and assignments, and apply grading policies. Over the course of their careers, many master advisors provide instruction in student success classes and freshman seminars. Some choose to seek positions as adjunct instructors. They find classroom teaching an asset that improves academic advising, makes them more marketable, and strengthens their understanding of the challenges faced by advisors who teach as their professional role at the institution.

Nonformal learning

Nonformal learning includes structured learning activities, workshops, and classes that do not lead to a credential recognized by a national educational body. They are organized programs with structured student–teacher relationships and intended for teaching and learning through lectures, seminars, and like venues (UNESCO, 2006). A national association (e.g., National Board of Certified Counselors) may give recognition such as badges or certificates for completion of these programs (Smith, 2002). Most professional development enterprises for academic advisors fit in this category, including handbooks, webinars, lunch-and-learn sessions, conferences, and workshops.

Workshops, Seminars, and Webinars.   Short instructional forums (a day or less), such as workshops, seminars, and webinars, focus on a specific topic. Whether held on- or off-campus, they serve as common sources of professional development for advisors. Although useful, these programs take precious time, so advisors must select those that best match their needs and goals.

Master advisors can maximize the benefits of such programs by writing and reflecting on ways the content relates to larger trends or research in the field. Moreover, master advisors take the initiative to plan and present workshops, seminars, and webinars for their colleagues. They also help others develop such programs. When those experienced in the field provide up-front input, not only on the featured topics but also on the details of presentation, they not only help the presenter but they also learn themselves; the best way to learn something is to teach it to someone else.

Conferences.   Professional organizations sponsor conferences that comprise another nonformal method of expanding professional knowledge. Advisors attend conferences to learn about student needs and new research. Moreover, they can see how different institutions apply theories to address common problems of practice. Because of the many benefits of conferences, advisors should attend them on a regular basis. Although conferences can be pricey, attendance may be offset by scholarships offered by associations.

For maximum return on the investment, advisors should include a mix of opportunities in their conference schedules. Although conferences—and particular sessions offered in them—should match interests and goals, advisors can seek new ideas in these venues. The gain of new perspectives benefits advisors, and the spread of new ideas benefits the field. Advisors can choose from many options, including conferences by the Association of American College & Universities, League of Innovation in Community Colleges, and those offered by constituents within the academic disciplines.

Master advisors also take advantage of the opportunities to practice their relational skills by networking with fellow attendees and presenters between sessions, at mealtimes, and even while waiting at the airport. They document their learning in their portfolios and use the journal or blog to reflect on experiences and encourage new connections among ideas. They also apply to make presentations at conferences. The processes of writing proposals and connecting successful practice with larger theories and trends expand both informational and conceptual knowledge.

Institutes.   Smaller than conferences, institutes offer fewer sessions and fewer people with whom to network. However, all sessions are presented and curated by persons eminent in the field. Thus, attendees are assured of relevant, high-quality offerings. Moreover, at most institutes, attendees spend a significant portion of the time generating an action plan to be launched upon their return to the workplace. Thus, highly interactive institutes not only strengthen foundational knowledge and provide many opportunities to learn from experienced faculty but they also teach the basics of leading change and working across institutional boundaries.

NACADA offers several options for master advisors—NACADA Summer and Winter Institutes, the Assessment Institute, and the Advising Administrators' Institute—as well as programs sponsored by Harvard University, the League for Innovation in the Community College, and others. All NACADA institutes provide hands-on, intensive programs designed to expand advisors' knowledge across the spectrum. Master advisors seeking support to plan and implement an innovation on their campus recognize the value in investing the time and money in an institute.

Microcredentials and Badges.   Microcredentials offer some of the newest options available for nonformal learning and professional development. Learners earn microcredentials, commonly displayed as digital badges, demonstrating mastery of specific, observable skills and competencies. Learners may share their badges via social media or digital backpacks: web links that connect to evidence of the knowledge and skills of the learner (EDUCAUSE, 2015). Learning documentation includes performance-based artifacts such as work samples, self-reflections, endorsements from instructors or classmates, videos, and descriptions of observations. The artifacts are presented for public review, which provides transparency and credibility to the credential (Digital Promise, n.d.).

Use of digital badges to organize, achieve, and display professional skills and competencies gained traction in 2011 when the MacArthur Foundation started the Badges for Lifelong Learning initiative (Grant, 2011) and Mozilla initiated the Open Badges infrastructure (Surman, 2011). Although pursuit of badges for mastering specific skills or meeting certain milestones in academic advising is a new idea, it holds merit. Because of the diversity of the advising profession, the student population, and the contextual environments of where advising is practiced, microcredentialing through badges may make more sense than a single professional development credential.

By embracing microcredentialing, academic advisors would become part of a growing movement. Some institutions, such as the University of California at Davis, have developed badge systems that allow students to demonstrate competency in specific skills learned outside a formal classroom setting (Fain, 2014). The higher education information technology community already accesses professional development badges through EDUCAUSE (n.d.). In addition, Penn State University, the National Aeronautics and Space Administration, and the National Science Teachers Association collaborated to create the Teacher Learning Journey for customized professional development through online microcredentials of primary- and secondary-school science teachers. Assessment of the Teacher Learning Journey revealed that teachers capitalized on the system's flexibility to create and meet personalized professional development goals (Gamrat & Toomey Zimmerman, 2014). Moreover, learners customize the credential by choosing the evidence to share with specific clients or potential employers (EDUCAUSE, 2015). For example, when applying for a position working with exploratory or undecided students, an advisor might choose to high-light microcredentials in guiding student decision making and career counseling, but to apply for a position at a liberal arts college, the same advisor might share micro-credentials demonstrating understanding of the importance of liberal learning.

Open badge systems available through providers such as Google Course Builder (Google Project Hosting, n.d.), Mozilla (Open Badges, n.d.), and some learning man-agement systems put the technology needed to create badges at the fingertips of anyone with Internet access (Presant, 2014). Master advisors can keep abreast of evolving options for nonformal learning through badges offered by academic institu-tions, EDUCAUSE, and, perhaps one day, NACADA.

International Experiences. Master academic advisors seeking new ways to expand their skills and knowledge beyond the ordinary might consider an international edu-cational experience as part of their IPDP. Various options, applicable as depending on the advisor's role and educational background, expand the understanding of advising practices worldwide and increase the advisor's ability to communicate across cul-tures. The Fulbright U.S. Student program offers opportunities for professionals, scholars, and administrators from around the world to apply for opportunities to study and build networks across the globe (Institute of International Education, n.d.). NASPA (n.d.) also offers the International Exchange Program. Targeted at senior-level administrators, the NASPA program arranges one-week exchanges in which three to five delegates learn about student affairs practices at a host institution in another country. International conferences, such as those hosted by NACADA and the National Resource Center for The First-Year Experience, offer another option for gaining cultural awareness. Master advisors can find additional listings of interna-tional opportunities at web sites of professional organizations associated with an academic discipline or the International Association of Student Affairs and Services.

As Schuh (2014) noted, "As one's career matures and develops, international expe-riences can add a great deal of learning to one's understanding of higher education" (p. 23). Advisors who think they have seen it all may gain perspective and a host of new ideas from a trip abroad.

Mentoring. Advice or guidance given to someone less experienced is considered mentoring. Traditionally, mentoring consisted of informally created, serendipitous connections formed between colleagues. To this day, such chance partnerships offer valuable opportunities for relational, internal informational, and personal learning.

As evidence mounts on the powerful learning that transpires through mentoring, more nonformal options are surfacing. Many colleges and universities offer mentor-ing programs for employees who wish to enhance the soft skills and knowledge needed to be successful within the organization. Also, many professional organiza-tions match those new to the profession with volunteer mentors experienced in the field. NACADA, for example, offers mentoring programs at the regional and national levels, most notably the Emerging Leaders Program (NACADA, 2014b).

Mentoring, whether done nonformally or informally, provides a learning experience well suited to documentation through a portfolio. Feedback in the form of e-mails, letters, or formal write-ups demonstrates learning. Also, regular reflective writings done over the course of the relationship provide evidence of enhanced personal growth and matured understanding of conceptual issues.

Informal Learning

In contrast to formal and nonformal education, informal learning is characterized as less structured; it is also voluntary and lifelong (UNESCO, 2006). Informal learning is defined by the method in which

> every individual acquires attitudes, values, skills and knowledge from daily experience and the educative influences and resources in his or her environment—from family and neighbours, from work and play, from the market place, the library and the mass media (Coombs, Prosser, & Ahmed as cited in Smith, 2002, ¶6).

Accounting for the majority of learning in the workplace, informal learning may offer the most effective form of professional growth (Eraut, 2010). Academic advisors should pay attention and reflect upon the informal opportunities in their workplace to maximize their own learning from experiences, colleagues, and students.

Experiential Learning.   To become masters of their craft, academic advisors need more than information. They must skillfully apply their knowledge to new situations as well as build trusting relationships with students. To grow these relational skills and personal knowledge bases, advisors bring their learning close to their practice (Cranton, 1996) by using experiential learning techniques.

Duslak and McGill (2014) suggested several ways advisors can learn through practice. Even experienced advisors benefit from case studies, role plays, and clinical observations in which advisors watch colleagues during student appointments. Role play and case studies offer excellent ways for advisors to learn how to handle complex situations, especially those that might involve emotional situations. Through case studies and role plays advisors expand their repertoire of advising approaches in a low-risk atmosphere.

Although receiving feedback on practice can be disconcerting, advisors learn from the input of others. A colleague who observes, keeps notes, and video records a session provides backup to the observer's assessment as well as artifacts for the advisor's portfolio. Experiential learning can be undertaken by any advisor at any time (with the permission of all participants); a video recording device and a colleague willing to help with documentation and to provide constructive criticism make this type of experiential learning within the reach of most practitioners.

Collaboration.   Conducted within and across academic units or functional areas, collaboration provides a multitude of opportunities for informal learning. Working with others on committees, in work groups, or for planning projects supports master advisors' learning throughout the spectrum of knowledge available. Through collaboration, advisors gain information and relational skills, and they learn about the challenges, trends, pressures, and goals within academic and student affairs programs outside their own units as well as in areas other than advising that affect student learning. Advisors can acquire insights from other perspectives that help them advocate for students and the profession. For example, an academic unit may boast of the 90% retention rate for a learning community cohort, while the budget office is concerned about the extra pay the professors draw and the dean is worried about scalability. Knowledge of these various perspectives makes advisors more effective in their current roles and creates a scaffold for moving up or across the career lattice. Portfolios provide space to document not only achievements made but also the learning gained through collaboration.

Professional Learning Networks.   Like teachers and counselors in the same school or office, advisors—even those in the same unit—often work independent of one another. Master advisors welcome opportunities to ask questions or share knowledge and practices. Members of a professional learning network share time and space, often by getting together regularly for nonformal or informal learning, or they may exist in cyberspace. Social media has removed physical barriers to colleagues. Master advisors who seek access to information outside the institution, insight into student needs, or advice on relational or conceptual topics need look no further than their smartphones. A connection with a single colleague online can spark the creation of an informal professional learning network. In addition, advisors may benefit from joining a nonformal network like an electronic mail service sponsored by a favorite NACADA commission, or the Facebook page managed under the auspices of their NACADA region. Twitter hosts communities such as #sachat or #acadv, where advisors and others share information, ask questions, and support each other's professional development goals.

Reading and Writing.   The least complicated methods for professional development, absorbing and creating the written word, may be the most difficult endeavors to undertake. Attending a workshop is clearly perceived as work; sitting at one's desk reading is perceived as not busy or even goofing off. Besides, who can write when students keep dropping by with questions? Despite these difficulties, advisors need to find ways to incorporate reading and writing into their professional development plans.

Many prominent newspapers have education sections with articles available online. By selecting new or classic journal articles from academic advising or other disciplines, an advisor enjoys a steady stream of information. In addition, the advisor can commit to reading a book chapter every month. Introverts may enjoy reflecting in a blog or journal. Those adept at brevity might share the main take-away ideas on Twitter. Extroverts may enjoy creating a reading group or book club for motivation and support.

Short, written reflections lay the foundation for professional and personal growth. Other writing options include book reviews for the *NACADA Journal* or articles for a campus newsletter or *Academic Advising Today*. Writing supports self-knowledge, conceptual understanding, and informational learning. It also tests one's grasp of the big picture ideas informing academic advising.

Summary

Opportunities for professional development are limited only by the advisor's willingness to invest time in self-awareness and reflection. Master advisors utilize campus funds when available and find creative ways to subsidize professional development when campus resources do not materialize. Although conferences and classes can be expensive, feedback from colleagues is absolutely free. By taking charge of their own professional development, advisors transcend the limits of their current roles and open the door to new ideas that will benefit their students, their institutions, and themselves. They also contribute to the advancement of the profession of academic advising.

The paths to developing advising mastery diverge in as many directions as the number of institutions hosting academic advisors, and they vary as much as the individual interests and goals of advisors. An IPDP pays off as it helps advisors use their time wisely; that is, advisors intentionally participate in activities that support their goals and opt out of those that are worthy but do not advance their professional agenda. Master advisors use the portfolio to document all the formal, nonformal, and informal learning acquired, and they consider and document their own growth. An elusive goal always just beyond the horizon, mastery develops in different forms for different people. While the foundations of academic advising offer a clear and solid base for good practice, master advisors are never done learning.

Aiming for Excellence

○ Draft an IPDP. Start by outlining your goals and anticipating the additional skills, knowledge, and abilities you need to reach them. Share with a mentor, friend, or trusted supervisor. Work together to identify and record the ways you will acquire the learning you need.

○ Create a portfolio club of colleagues. Agree on how each of you will set up your individual advising portfolios. Set a monthly meeting day and time. At the first meeting, share your advising philosophies and give feedback. Each month, share your learning and the artifacts added to your portfolio. Hold each other accountable.

o Keep a personal work journal for a week. Throughout each day, note the activities or interactions that bring you satisfaction or happiness. Note the ones that cause frustration or anger. Consider the ways you manage stress in the moment. Talk about your findings with a mentor, friend, or trusted supervisor.

o Volunteer to be a subject matter expert at your institution's next technology project.

o Research and attend a conference or seminar sponsored by an organization new to you. Check out offerings from the American Association of Colleges and Universities, the League of Innovation in Community Colleges, the European Association for International Education, or the Association of Universities and Colleges of Canada.

o Read the article by Duslak and McGill (2014). Take turns with a colleague observing each other as you advise. Provide constructive feedback on the points of the appointment that went well and ways to improve. Repeat annually.

o Collaborate with others to learn a new aspect of advising, discipline, or institution. Volunteer to serve on a committee with members from across the institution: Examples include, but are not limited to, search committees, the parking citation appeals board, athletics advisory councils, curriculum committee, or strategic planning. After each meeting, write and reflect on relational skills used and the new information and insights you gained about other areas of the institution.

References

Bayles, M. D. (1981). *Professional ethics*. Belmont, CA: Wadsworth.

Beres, K., Drake, J., Givans Voller, J., Jordan, P., King, N., Musser, T., . . . & Yoder, F. (2013). *Foundations of Academic Advising* (Pocket Guide Series No. 14). Manhattan, KS: NACADA: The Global Community for Academic Advising.

Bloom, J. L., Hutson, B. L., & He, Y. (2013). Appreciative advising. In J. K. Drake, P. Jordan, & M. A. Miller (Eds.), *Academic advising approaches: Strategies that teach students to make the most of college* (pp. 83–99). San Francisco, CA: Jossey-Bass.

Carlstrom, A. H., & Miller, M. A. (Eds.). (2013a). Minimum required credentials for academic advising [Table 9.1]. *2011 NACADA National Survey of Academic Advising* (Monograph No. 25). Retrieved from ww.nacada.ksu.edu/Portals/0/Clearinghouse/documents/Chapter%209%20-%20Professional%20Advisor%20Credentials%20and%20Career%20Ladder%20-%20FINAL.pdf

Carlstrom, A. H., & Miller, M. A. (Eds.). (2013b). Most common credential for professional advisors [Table 9.7]. *2011 NACADA National Survey of Academic Advising* (Monograph No. 25) Retrieved from ww.nacada.ksu.edu/Portals/0/Clearinghouse/documents/

Chapter%209%20-%20Professional%20Advisor%20Credentials%20and%
20Career%20Ladder%20-%20FINAL.pdf

Cohen, D. K., & Hill, H. C. (2000). Instructional policy and classroom performance: The
mathematics reform in California. *Teachers College Record, 102*(2), 294–343.

Council for the Advancement of Standards in Higher Education. (2015). *Standards and
guidelines: Academic advising programs.* Retrieved from http://standards.cas.edu/getpdf
.cfm?PDF=E864D2C4-D655-8F74-2E647CDECD29B7D0

Cranton, P. (1996). *Professional development and transformative learning.* San Francisco,
CA: Jossey-Bass.

Darling-Hammond, L. (2010). *The flat world and education: How America's commitment to
equity will determine our future.* New York, NY: Teachers College Press.

Dean, L. A., Woodard, B. R., & Cooper, D. L. (2007). Professional development credits in
student affairs practice: A method to enhance professionalism. *The College Student
Affairs Journal, 27*(1), 45–56.

Digital Promise. (n.d.). *Developing a system of micro-credentials: Supporting deeper
learning in the classroom.* Retrieved from http://www.hewlett.org/sites/default/files/
mc_deeperlearning.pdf

Drake, J. K. (2008). Recognition and reward for academic advising in theory and in practice.
In V. N. Gordon, W. R. Habley, & T. J. Grites (Eds.), *Academic advising: A comprehensive handbook* (2nd ed.) (pp. 396–412). San Francisco, CA: Jossey-Bass.

Drake, J. K., Jordan, P., & Miller, M. A. (Eds.). (2013). *Academic advising approaches:
Strategies that teach students to make the most of college.* San Francisco, CA:
Jossey-Bass.

Duslak, M. P., & McGill, C. M. (2014). *Stepping out of the workshop: The case for experiential learning in advisor training and development.* Retrieved from http://www.nacada
.ksu.edu/Resources/Clearinghouse/View-Articles/Stepping-out-of-the-workshop-The-
case-for-experiential-learning-in-advisor-training-and-development.aspx

EDUCAUSE. (n.d.). *Badges.* Retrieved from http://www.educause.edu/library/badges

EDUCAUSE. (2015, August 3). *Badging in a learner-centered context: How can badges be
most effective in a learner-centered context?* Retrieved from https://youtu.be/
gFn-lpvfk3U

Eraut, M. (1993). The characterization and development of professional expertise in school
management and teaching. *Educational Management, Administration, and Leadership,
21,* 223–232.

Eraut, M. (2010). Informal learning in the workplace. *Studies in Continuing Education,
26*(2), 247–273. Retrieved from http://dx.doi.org/10.1080/158037042000225245

Fain, P. (2014, January 3). *Badging from within.* Retrieved from https://www.insidehighered
.com/news/2014/01/03/uc-daviss-groundbreaking-digital-badge-system-new-sustainable-
agriculture-program

Folsom, P. (2015). New advisor development chart: Building the foundation. In P. Folsom,
F. Yoder, & J. E. Joslin (Eds.), *The new advisor guidebook: Mastering the art of
academic advising* (pp. 19–35). San Francisco, CA: Jossey-Bass.

Folsom, P., F. Yoder, & J. E. Joslin (Eds.). (2015) *The new advisor guidebook: Mastering the art of academic advising*. San Francisco, CA: Jossey-Bass.

Fong, R.W.T., Lee, J.C.K., Chang, C. Y., Zhang, Z., Ngai, A.C.Y., & Lim, C. P. (2014). Digital teaching portfolio in higher education: Examining colleagues' perceptions to inform implementation strategies. *The Internet and Higher Education, 20*, 60–68.

Gamrat, C., & Toomey Zimmerman, H. (2014). Personalized workspace learning: An exploratory study on digital badging within a teacher professional development program. *British Journal of Educational Technology, 45*(6), 1136–1148. doi: 10.1111/bjet.12200

Givans Voller, J. (2013). *Implications of professional development and reward for professional academic advisors*. Retrieved from http://www.nacada.ksu.edu/Resources/Clearinghouse/View-Articles/Implications-for-professional-development-2011-National-Survey.aspx

Givans Voller, J. L., Miller, M. A., & Neste, S. L. (Eds.). (2010). *Comprehensive advisor training and development: Practices that deliver* (Monograph No. 21). Manhattan, KS: National Academic Advising Association.

Google Project Hosting. (n.d.). *Course builder*. Retrieved from https://code.google.com/p/course-builder/

Gordon, V. (2003, September). Advisor certification: A history and update. *Academic Advising Today, 26*(3). Retrieved from http://www.nacada.ksu.edu/Resources/Academic-Advising-Today/View-Articles/Advisor-Certification-A-History-and-Update.aspx#sthash.rm45UI60.dpuf

Grant, S. (2011). *Unpacking badges for lifelong learning*. Retrieved from http://www.hastac.org/blogs/slgrant/2011/09/25/unpacking-badges-lifelong-learning

Habley, W. R. (1989). *Advisor training: Whatever happened to instructional design?* ACT workshop presentation. Iowa City, IA: ACT.

Higginson, L. C. (2000). A framework for training program content revisited. In V. N. Gordon & W. R. Habley (Eds.), *Academic advising: A comprehensive handbook* (1st ed.) (pp. 298–306). San Francisco, CA: Jossey-Bass.

Institute of International Education. (n.d.). *Fulbright Scholars Program*. Retrieved from http://www.cies.org/

IUPUI University College Advising Center, & Buyarski, C. (2014). *Advising portfolio examples*. Retrieved from http://www.nacada.ksu.edu/Resources/Clearinghouse/View-Articles/Advisor-Portfolio-Examples.aspx

Janssen, S., Kreijns, K., Bastiaens, T. J., Stijnen, S., & Vermeulen, M. (2013). Teachers' beliefs about using a professional development plan. *International Journal of Training and Development, 17*(4), 260–278. doi:10.1111/ijtd.12016

Jarvinen, A. (1995). Promoting professional development in higher education through portfolio assessment. *Assessment and evaluation in higher education, 20*(1), 25–36. doi:10.1080/0260293950200104

Joint Task Force on Professional Competencies and Standards. (2010). *ACPA/NASPA professional competency areas for student affairs practitioners*. Washington, DC:

American College Personnel Association, National Association of Student Personnel Administrators. Retrieved from https://www.naspa.org/images/uploads/main/Professional_Competencies.pdf

Jordan, P. (2015). Effective communications skills. In P. Folsom, F. Yoder, & J. E. Joslin (Eds.), *The new advisor guidebook: Mastering the art of academic advising* (pp. 213–229). San Francisco, CA: Jossey-Bass.

Joslin, J. E., & Yoder, F. (2015). Advisor growth and development: Building a foundation for mastery. In P. Folsom, F. Yoder, & J. E. Joslin (Eds.), *The new advisor guidebook: Mastering the art of academic advising* (pp. 301–315). San Francisco, CA: Jossey-Bass.

Juster, N. (1961). *The phantom tollbooth*. New York, NY: Scholastic.

King, M. C. (2000). Designing effective training for academic advisors. In V. N. Gordon & W. R. Habley (Eds.), *Academic advising: A comprehensive handbook* (pp. 289–297). San Francisco, CA: Jossey-Bass.

Klepfer, K., & Hull, J. (2012). *High school rigor and good advice: Setting up students to succeed*. Retrieved from http://www.centerforpubliceducation.org/Main-Menu/Staffingstudents/High-school-rigor-and-good-advice-Setting-up-students-to-succeed

Kuh, G. D. (2008). Advising for student success. In V. N. Gordon, W. R. Habley, & T. J. Grites (Eds.), *Academic advising: A comprehensive handbook* (2nd ed.) (pp. 68–84). San Francisco, CA: Jossey-Bass.

Light, R. J. (2001). *Making the most of college: Students speak their minds*. Cambridge, MA: Harvard University Press.

Lowenstein, M. (1999, November 22). An alternative to the developmental theory of advising. *The Mentor: An Academic Advising Journal, 1*(4). Retrieved from http://www.psu.edu/dus/mentor/991122ml.htm

Lowenstein, M. (2000, April 13). Academic advising and the "logic" of the curriculum. *The Mentor: An Academic Advising Journal, 2*(2). Retrieved from http://www.psu.edu/dus/mentor/000414ml.htm

Lowenstein, M. (2013). Envisioning the future. In J. K. Drake, P. Jordan, & M. A. Miller (Eds.), *Academic advising approaches: Strategies that teach students to make the most of college* (pp. 243–258). San Francisco, CA: Jossey-Bass.

Mahara. (n.d). *Open source eportfolios*. Retrieved from https://mahara.org/

McClellan, J., Moser, C., & Waterreus, J. (2008). *Advisor certification at Utah Valley State College*. Retrieved from http://www.nacada.ksu.edu/Resources/Clearinghouse/View-Articles/Advisor-Certification-.aspx

McMahan, A. B. (2008). *How to become an academic advisor*. Retrieved from http://www.nacada.ksu.edu/Resources/Clearinghouse/View-Articles/Become-an-Advisor.aspx

Miller, M. (2012). *Interpreting the CAS standards for academic advising*. Retrieved from http://www.nacada.ksu.edu/tabid/3318/articleType/ArticleView/articleId/1249/article.aspx

NACADA: The Global Community for Academic Advising (NACADA). (2003). *Academic advisor competencies*. Retrieved from http://www.nacada.ksu.edu/Resources/Clearinghouse/View-Articles/Academic-advisor-competencies.aspx

NACADA. (2005a). *NACADA statement of core values of academic advising: Declaration.* Retrieved from www.nacada.ksu.edu/Resources/Clearinghouse/View-Articles/ Core-values-declaration.aspx

NACADA. (2005b). *NACADA statement of core values of academic advising: Exposition.* http://www.nacada.ksu.edu/Resources/Clearinghouse/View-Articles/Core-values-exposition.aspx

NACADA. (2014a). *Doctoral students interest group.* Retrieved from http://www.nacada. ksu.edu/Community/Commission-Interest-Groups/Advising-in-Academic-Programs-I/ Doctoral-Students-Interest-Group.aspx

NACADA. (2014b). *NACADA emerging leaders program.* Retrieved from http://www. nacada.ksu.edu/Events-Programs/Emerging-Leaders-Program.aspx

NACADA. (2014c). [National survey for academic advising, raw data]. Manhattan, KS: Author. Retrieved from http://www.nacada.ksu.edu/Portals/0/Surveys/Documents/ Rec%20and%20reward%20Initial_Report%202014.pdf

NASPA. (n.d.). *Globalism.* Retrieved from https://www.naspa.org/focus-areas/globalism

National Commission on Teaching & America's Future. (1996). *What matters most: Teaching for America's future.* New York, NY: Author. Retrieved from http://nctaf.org/ wp-content/uploads/WhatMattersMost.pdf

Noel-Levitz. (2011). *Retention practices report: Student retention report for colleges ranks 53 methods for boosting degree completion rates of enrolled students.* Retrieved from https://www.noellevitz.com/about-noel-levitz/press-releases/retention-practices-report

Open Badges. (n.d.). *Mozilla open badges* [Home page]. Retrieved from http:// openbadges.org/

Presant, D. (2014). *Open badges: Making learning visible.* Retrieved from http://www. savvyfolio.net/user/don/overview-open-badges

Schuh, J. H. (2014). International experiences for student affairs educators: There is a world of professional development opportunities out there. *New Directions for Student Services, 2014*(146), 23–31.

Smith, M. K. (2002). Informal, non-formal and formal education: A brief overview of different approaches. *The Encyclopedia of Informal Education.* Retrieved from http://www.infed.org/foundations/informal_nonformal.htm

Sofranco, K. B. (2004). *Factors motivating full-time, non-faculty professional academic advisors to participate in professional development activities* (Unpublished doctoral dissertation). Temple University, Philadelphia, PA.

Surman, M. (2011, September 15). *Mozilla launches open badge project* [web log post]. Retrieved from https://commonspace.wordpress.com/2011/09/15/openbadges-2/

Swecker, H. K., Fifolt, M., & Searby, L. (2013). Academic advising and first generation students: A quantitative study on student retention. *NACADA Journal, 33*(1), 46–53.

Taylor, M. A. (2013). *Professional advisor credentials, career ladders, and salaries.* Retrieved from http://www.nacada.ksu.edu/Resources/Clearinghouse/View-Articles/Professional-Advisor-Credentials--Career-Ladders--and-Salaries.aspx

United Nations Educational, Scientific and Cultural Organization. (2006). *Classification of learning activities—manual.* Luxembourg: Office for Official Publications of the European Communities. Retrieved from http://www.uis.unesco.org/Statistical CapacityBuilding/Workshop%20Documents/Education%20workshop% 20dox/2010%20ISCED%20TAP%20IV%20Montreal/NFE_CLA_Eurostat_EN.pdf

Venart, E., Vassos, S., & Pitcher-Heft, H. (2007). What individual counselors can do to sustain wellness. *Journal of Humanistic Counseling, Education & Development,* 46(1), 50–65.

Villegas-Reimers, E. (2003). *Teacher professional development: An international review of the literature.* Paris, France: UNESCO International Institute for Educational Planning. Retrieved from: http://unesdoc.unesco.org/images/0013/001330/133010e.pdf

Vowell, F. N., & Wallet-Ortiz, J. (2003, February). Using a portfolio to document advising effectiveness. *Academic Advising News,* 26(1). Retrieved from http://www.nacada.ksu.edu/ Resources/Clearinghouse/View-Articles/Advisor-Portfolios-Document-Effectiveness.aspx

14

ASSESSMENT OF ACADEMIC ADVISING

OVERVIEW AND STUDENT LEARNING OUTCOMES

Rich Robbins

The great thing in this world is not so much where you stand, as in what direction you are moving.

—Oliver Wendell Holmes (1809–1894)

All functions of higher education affect student learning and development and must be measured for effectiveness. Academic advising is properly assessed based on the achievement of student development and learning outcomes, which in turn support programmatic goals as well as programmatic and institutional missions. The identified and assessed outcomes culminate in efforts directed toward student engagement, persistence, and completion. Those undertaking assessment, including master advisors, begin the process by crafting student learning outcomes.

Reader Learning Outcomes

From studying this chapter, advisors will use knowledge gained about student learning outcomes and the assessment of academic advising to undertake the following:

o Articulate reasons to perform assessment of academic advising:
  o articulate the importance of assessing an effective advising program using student learning outcomes,
  o understand the difference of assessing a program for effectiveness to identify improvements and secure funding from assessment used for accountability to justify program existence, and
  o know that some assessment data can be used for both improvements and accountability.
o Recognize the differences between evaluation and assessment:
  o know that evaluation is performed for an individual advisor,

o know that evaluation is based on students' perceptions and opinions,

o know that assessment is performed at the programmatic level, and

o identify assessment as appropriate for determining student learning outcomes.

o Identify Maki's four basic components of the assessment cycle:

o identify outcomes,

o gather evidence,

o interpret evidence, and

o implement change.

Assessment of Academic Advising

As evident from other chapters in this book, the mission and goals of an academic advising program influence practice, which may consist of various combinations of responsibilities (e.g., academic mentoring, academic coaching, assistance with course selection, interpersonal mentoring, and career advising). Academic advising is delivered in various ways (e.g., one-to-one and in groups; by telephone, e-mail, or text; through social networking or web sites). Academic advising may be mandatory or voluntary; it may be delivered through a host of approaches, delivered by various parties, and specialized for specific student populations. Whatever the missions, goals, modes of delivery, or other features of a program and practice, academic advising as teaching has been an endorsed practice cited in the literature for decades (e.g., Crookston, 1972/1994/2009; Robbins & Adams, 2013).

Furthermore, as asserted in the NACADA Concept of Academic Advising (NACADA: The Global Community for Academic Advising [NACADA], 2006), academic advising involves both teaching and learning, support of institutional missions and goals through advising curricula, advising pedagogies, and student learning outcomes (SLOs) for advising. By contributing to the teaching and learning mission of the institution, academic advising aligns (or should align) with other aspects of the institutional mission and related goals, including the overall strategic plan and specific enrollment management, retention, persistence, and completion strategies.

The literature further suggests that effective academic advising serves as a robust predictor of student engagement with the college environment (Keup & Kinzie, 2007; Kuh, 2008) as advisors connect students with learning opportunities (Campbell, 2008; Rinck, 2006; Schulenberg & Lindhorst, 2008). Recent research has shown that, in addition to student engagement such as student self-efficacy and development of study skills, effective academic advising influences retention indirectly by affecting desired outcomes (Young-Jones, Burt, Dixon, & Hawthorne, 2013). Once advising practices are implemented, the effectiveness of the academic advising program must be assessed in terms of desired outcomes.

Why Assess Academic Advising?

From an educational perspective, academic advising should be assessed primarily to determine program effectiveness; that is, advisors and administrators need to know whether the goals and desired outcomes for the advising program are being met and whether students are learning through the academic advising process (Maki, 2002, 2004; Robbins, 2009, 2011; Upcraft & Schuh, 1996). Furthermore, assessments help stakeholders determine the effect of improvements to advising practices and programs made in response to prior assessments.

Despite these important reasons, the need for accountability currently inspires most of the assessment directed to academic advising. Many external entities (e.g., boards of regents, state and regional governments, and accreditation agencies) require institutional assessment of nearly all aspects of higher education, including academic advising (Ratcliff, Lubinescu, & Gaffney, 2001; Robbins, 2011; Sims, 1992). In addition, the justification for the existence of institutional offices and units in the face of financial constraints may require assessment data, which may also provide validation for programmatic enhancement to improve effectiveness and to guide future planning, budget, and program decisions. The goals of assessment for academic advising thus include efforts to determine program effectiveness and student learning as well as to initiate program improvement or show accountability (Robbins, 2009, 2011) according to the needs, priorities, and missions of the institution and the advising program.

Assessment or Evaluation?

Some confusion over the terms *evaluation* and *assessment* has emerged in both the academic advising literature and the effort to determine the effectiveness of academic advising (Robbins, 2009, 2011; Robbins & Adams, 2013; Robbins & Zarges, 2011). Advisor evaluation most often involves indirect measurements of the perceived performance of the individual advisor. Indirect measures include parties' recall of past events or reports of opinions, perceptions, or beliefs. Evaluation is typically performed episodically with student satisfaction or student perception ratings and surveys (Habley, 2004; Macaruso, 2007; Robbins, 2011) through which students rate their advising experiences.

In contrast, direct measures are based on empirical or firsthand observation (Robbins, 2011) of student learning, such as derived from a pre- and post-test methodology, items on an instrument or quiz requiring responses that convey student knowledge, or some other demonstration of student learning. Assessment of academic advising is performed at the programmatic, departmental, college, or institutional levels, depending on the specific needs and purposes of the assessment (Robbins & Zarges, 2011) and includes both direct and indirect measures of the effectiveness of the academic advising practices and processes as they affect SLOs (Robbins, 2009, 2011).

Assessment consists of a continuous, systematic process of collecting outcome data through multiple collection points and measures, reflecting upon the information, and utilizing the resulting knowledge to improve student learning and development (Angelo, 1995; Ewell, 2000; Marchese, 1993; Palomba, 1999; Pellegrino, Chudowsky, & Glaser, 2001). This limited definition does not suggest that advisor evaluation lacks importance; in fact, evaluation of individual academic advisor performance may be included in an overall assessment designed to measure outcomes. However, evaluation alone proves insufficient to support claims of program effectiveness (or ineffectiveness) and student learning (Robbins, 2011; Robbins & Zarges, 2011).

Powers, Carlstrom, and Hughey (2014) reported that 57.8% of NACADA national survey participants reported using formal measures to assess SLOs for academic advising. According to this slight majority of respondents, student surveys and questionnaires comprised the primary way in which SLOs are measured. This information illustrates that most of those who reported assessing academic advising were not conducting assessments of student learning.

Overview of the Assessment Cycle

Maki (2002, 2004) illustrated the basic processes of the assessment cycle as seen in Figure 14.1. Maki's model provides the big picture, without the detailed individual steps, of the process.

In the center of the assessment cycle (Maki, 2002), the institutional mission as well as purposes and educational objectives are surrounded by the four basic steps of the assessment process: the identification of desired outcomes, the accumulation of evidence, the interpretation of evidence, and the implementation of change based on the evidence. Following any data-informed changes, stakeholders begin another assessment cycle to determine the effectiveness of those changes. In this chapter, I focus on the first step of Maki's model: identification of desired outcomes. I describe Steps 2 through 4 of this assessment model in greater detail in chapter 15.

Outcomes for Academic Advising

Desired outcomes can be identified or developed for an academic advising program in numerous ways. However, before addressing them, those conducting assessments must distinguish between SLOs and programmatic or process and delivery outcomes (PDOs).

SLOs reflect the knowledge, behaviors, and values students should attain or demonstrate as a result of the academic advising experience (Aiken-Wisniewski et al., 2010; Campbell, Nutt, Robbins, Kirk-Kuwaye, & Higa, 2005; Robbins, 2009, 2011; Robbins & Adams, 2013; Robbins & Zarges, 2011). SLOs are categorized as cognitive, behavioral, or affective. For example, student knowledge of the required general education categories reflects a cognitive SLO, and use of a degree audit to plan a future course schedule demonstrates a behavioral SLO. A student who values the role

Figure 14.1. Maki's (2002) assessment cycle

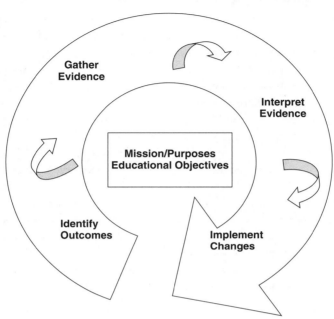

Note. Reprinted with permission.

of academic advising in achieving academic goals engenders an affective SLO. To assert that learning results from academic advising, stakeholders conduct assessment of SLOs.

The three types of SLOs reflect Bloom's (1956) taxonomy of educational objectives. The hierarchy of learning describes a student with the following characteristics:

1. Knows something (knowledge).
2. Comprehends something (comprehension).
3. Applies knowledge (applications).
4. Analyzes information (analysis).
5. Synthesizes information (synthesis).
6. Evaluates information (evaluation).

Knowledge of the required general education categories (a cognitive SLO) represents both the knowledge and comprehension levels of Bloom's taxonomy, but use of a degree audit to plan future course work (a behavioral SLO) relates to the application, analysis, synthesis, and evaluation levels. Valuing the role of academic advising in achieving academic goals (an affective SLO) may fall in Bloom's evaluation level to the extent that the attribution of value culminates in learner affect. Master advisors can use Bloom's taxonomy to identify the sequencing of student competencies (Robbins & Adams, 2013).

PDOs reflect expectations about the delivery and content of academic advising for the achievement of desired SLOs (Aiken-Wisniewski et al., 2010; Campbell et al., 2005; Robbins, 2009, 2011; Robbins & Adams, 2013; Robbins & Zarges, 2011). According to the NACADA Concept of Academic Advising (NACADA, 2006), PDOs represent both the curriculum and the pedagogy of advising. For example, if a student is expected to know the required general education categories (cognitive SLO) as a result of academic advising, then the specific information to learn them must be discussed or presented during the academic advising interaction. To measure student learning as a result of academic advising, the assessment strategy is directed to the desired SLOs that result from the advising process and the PDOs (Robbins, 2011).

The idea of backward design (Wiggins & McTighe, 2006), or starting with the end in mind, is illustrated by the relationship between PDOs and SLOs. Once the desired SLOs (e.g., students know the general education requirements) are defined, the necessary planning and training essential to PDOs (e.g., advisors learn the general education requirements; advisors discuss the general education requirements with students during the advising session) can be implemented.

Steps to Develop Student Learning Outcomes

Mission Statement for Advising.   SLOs are derived from many internal or external sources, each separately or in combination. Important internal sources include institutional values, vision and mission statements, and goals as well as any values, visions, missions, and goals identified for the academic advising program. Campbell (2008) and White (2000), among others, suggested that a clearly delineated mission statement and specified programmatic goals based on that mission contribute to effective assessment of academic advising (Robbins, 2011). Where mission statements have not been created, the team developing SLOs can look at value and vision statements to create a mission statement and related SLOs.

Bill, a master advisor and member of the institutional assessment committee, has been charged with developing an assessment process for academic advising. To start the assessment process, he conducts a review of the institution's mission statement, which includes phrases and terms such as *providing an outstanding learning environment* and for students being *successful in their academic pursuits, technologically adept in a global environment,* and *responsible citizens.* Considering both the institutional mission and the responsibilities of the academic advising program, he developed the following mission statement for academic advising: "The mission of academic advising is to provide a teaching and learning process that engages and assists students in achieving their academic goals and personal successes." This mission statement reflects the aspects of the institutional mission regarding a learning environment and students being successful; it also likely touches upon other aspects of the institutional mission.

Goals for Academic Advising. With an academic advising mission statement in hand, Bill develops goals for academic advising. Goals identify the achievements of the program by describing the way the mission is enacted. More specific than mission statements, goal statements cannot be measured; rather, they guide the identification of specific SLOs (Campbell, 2008; Robbins, 2011; Robbins & Zarges, 2011; White, 2000) (chapter 15).

Based on the mission developed for academic advising, two goals of several that Bill identified for academic advising describe (a) working in partnership to promote student success and (b) advocating for the shared responsibility of academic advising between student and advisor. These goals reflect the advising mission regarding engaging and assisting students to achieve success.

Initial Considerations. When developing SLOs, planners need to account for details that directly affect the practicality of use. First, compound SLOs complicate subsequent assessment measures. For example, a statement such as "students understand and value the purpose of a liberal arts education" or "students understand and utilize their degree progress reports" requires a two-part assessment: understanding and valuing as well as understanding and utilizing. SLOs should articulate single goals and clearly define the objective.

Second, SLO creators must know where and when the students can acquire the opportunities to complete the desired objectives. Effective planners recognize that not all SLOs are achieved at the same time or in the same place, and they specifically identify the time by which students need to demonstrate achievement of a specific SLO. Because student learning and development continues throughout life, advisors and administrators need to take a developmental approach and utilize different SLOs for students at the most appropriate time during the advisee's college career.

Third, when generating SLOs, planners need to think about the appropriate measures to use to determine the achievement (or not) of it. Identifying outcome measures needs to occur simultaneously with the development of outcomes rather than as an afterthought.

Finally, planners must determine the order in which the SLOs will be assessed; therefore, they need to know the priorities of the institution and any other stakeholders who may need specific information to promote student retention and persistence. The SLOs assessed during any cycle will depend on both priorities.

Sources for Development of Student Learning Outcomes. Even in the absence of any formal mission or set of goals for academic advising, practitioners and advising administrators can likely identify specific desired outcomes they want students to achieve as a result of academic advising (Robbins, 2011). Therefore, they may begin the assessment process with identified SLOs based on the goals and missions of the unit and institution as per backward design (Robbins, 2011; Wiggins & McTighe, 2006).

External sources from which to develop SLOs include the Council for the Advancement of Standards in Higher Education (CAS) (2015a) Standards for Academic Advising, the NACADA Core Values for Academic Advising (NACADA, 2005a, 2005b, 2005c), and the NACADA Concept of Academic Advising (NACADA, 2006). Assessment planners do not use external sources simply for the sake of stating measurable outcomes; they utilize them if they reflect the mission and set of goals for the specific academic advising program. However, despite this caveat, the sources noted, which constitute the three pillars of academic advising (NACADA, 2014), will likely include some attributes that reflect desired SLOs for an academic advising program (chapter 4).

CAS consists of a consortium of experts from various areas of higher education engaged in developing standards for functional areas of student support in higher education (Robbins, 2014; White, 2006). The CAS Standards and Guidelines are employed in the development of academic advising programs and services, program-matic goals for advising, and programmatic assessment, among other initiatives (CAS, 2015a; Miller, 2012; White, 2006). The CAS General Standards specifically state that "Academic Advising Programs (AAP) must develop assessment plans and processes" and "Assessment plans must articulate an ongoing cycle of assessment activities" (CAS, 2015a, p. 17). CAS has developed specific standards and guidelines for 44 different functional areas of higher education with six identified learning domains of

- o knowledge acquisition, construction, integration, and application;
- o cognitive complexity;
- o intrapersonal development;
- o interpersonal competence;
- o humanitarianism and civic engagement; and
- o practical competence (CAS, 2015b, p. 2).

Within these domains CAS has identified multiple learning outcome dimensions (Table 4.1). These dimensions of learning within corresponding domains foster a focused approach for the development and assessment of students and student aca-demic support programs and practices (Robbins, 2014).

The CAS Standards for Academic Advising (CAS, 2015a) were developed based on numerous higher education institutional types and academic settings, and they reflect students' experiences as individualistic, developmental, and holistic. SLO developers can utilize CAS Standards (or any other external resource) to develop SLOs for a specific academic advising situation and link them to or classify them within the CAS domains and dimensions. They can also use the specific standards, domains, dimensions, and samples of the general CAS Learning and Development Outcomes (CAS, 2015b) to develop SLOs for a specific academic advising situation.

The NACADA Core Values for Academic Advising (NACADA, 2005b) consist of six important responsibilities of the academic advisor:

o to the individuals they advise;

o for involving others, when appropriate, in the advising process;

o to their institutions;

o to higher education;

o to their educational communities; and

o for their professional practices and for themselves personally.

The exposition of these core values (NACADA, 2005c) provides directions on ways advisors can embrace the six core values and demonstrate them in the advising inter-action, making the values particularly suitable for use in SLOs. For example, advisors may translate the core value that states that advisors maintain responsibility to stu-dents into a goal to "help students establish realistic goals and objectives and encour-age them to be responsible for their own progress and success" (NACADA, 2005c, ¶3). This advisor objective can be transformed into several SLOs, including "as a result of academic advising, students will establish realistic educational goals" or "students know the general education requirements." Developed SLOs may be linked to the relevant NACADA Core Value, or the NACADA Core Values for Academic Advising may serve as the source for developing SLOs for academic advising (NACADA, 2005b, 2005c).

A multidimensional and intentional summary, the NACADA Concept of Academic Advising (2006) is grounded in teaching and learning. It features specific purpose and content statements for practice. It promotes the view that academic advising supports institutional missions and goals through curricula, pedagogies, and SLOs for advis-ing (Robbins & Adams, 2013). The NACADA Concept of Academic Advising includes sample SLOs that, although not universally relevant, may apply to a variety of advising programs. Once identified or developed, appropriate SLOs, such as those suggested by NACADA (2006), are assessable.

In addition to a mission statement and related goals for academic advising, Bill, who is developing academic advising learning outcomes for all first-year students, considers the campuswide focus on increasing students' uses of technology. As a result, Bill identifies one SLO for academic advising as "students use the electronic degree audit to track progress toward degree completion." This SLO reflects the goal of student success and the shared responsibility with the advisee and advisor to achieve that success.

Bill did not begin the SLO development process by consulting the CAS Standards for Academic Advising (CAS, 2015a); rather, this behavioral SLO is based on specific institutional and programmatic missions and needs along with other goals for student learning through advising. However, the SLO is connected to the CAS (2015b) domain of "knowledge acquisition, construction, integration, and application" (p. 5) and more specifically links to the dimension of "connecting knowledge to other knowledge, ideas, and experiences" (p. 5). If he had first consulted the CAS Standards for Academic Advising (CAS, 2015a) while taking into account specific campus factors, then Bill would have developed the same (or a similar) SLO.

Bill's SLO regarding student use of degree audits also relates to the NACADA Core Value (2005b) articulated as "advisors are responsible to the individuals they advise" (¶1–3). His consideration of the institutional emphasis on technology corresponds to the NACADA Core Value that states, "Advisors are responsible to their institutions" (¶5). In summary, SLOs can be developed based on various sources and multiple factors, including those found in the pillars of advising.

Mapping of Student Learning Outcomes

Mapping desired SLOs involves the process of determining when (or by when), where, and through what experiences the outcomes for advising will be accomplished over students' academic careers (Aiken-Wisniewski et al., 2010; Robbins, 2011; Robbins & Zarges, 2011). Mapping specifies the objective, the means, and timing of the identified achievement. For example, to address the way students can achieve the SLO, "students use the electronic degree audit to track progress toward degree completion," Bill must identify the specific opportunities for students to learn the electronic degree audit (e.g., at orientation, first-year seminar or advising appointments, or online module). The timing of these opportunities provides a deadline (e.g., in summer prior to the first semester, by the end of the first-year seminar, before the last advising session of the first year, or by the scheduling period for the fall of the sophomore year, etc.). Bill delineates a point prior to the end of the first year for the SLO he developed.

The opportunities for students to learn a desired outcome will likely emerge at unique instances and in different settings during students' first year, but the points at which the outcome data are collected need to be strategically identified. Therefore, the timing for achieving the SLO as well as the specific opportunities for collecting data remain integral to the SLO-development process.

Summary

The identification of intended SLOs constitutes the crucial first step of the assessment cycle. Departmental and institutional mission statements, as well as the CAS Standards (2015a, 2015b) and NACADA Statement of Core Values of Academic Advising (2005b, 2005c), provide the foundation to outline the SLOs for the institutional or unit context. Once they identify the learning expected of students engaged in academic advising and map the timing and opportunities for students to gain exposure to the information, assessment planners determine the ways to gather evidence and measure student learning. Chapter 15 provides guidance on gathering evidence as well as offers explanations on the remaining steps of the assessment cycle.

A glossary of key terms will be helpful for master advisors communicating with stakeholders about assessment for advising.

Glossary of Terms

Direct measure: Methods of gathering information that require students and advisors to demonstrate their knowledge and skills (e.g., in a portfolio, presentation, or test result); typical direct measures are more observable than indirect measures.

Goals: Specific aims individuals strive to achieve either for or by themselves or with others as part of a program.

Goal statement: Articulation of the specific aims individuals and programs strive to achieve.

Indirect measure: Methods of gathering information based on student or advisor reflection on learning rather than a demonstration of it (e.g., through questionnaires, interviews, or focus groups); typical indirect measures are more inferential than direct measures.

Mission: The statement that reflects the purpose of academic advising in an institution or in an advising unit; it serves as the institutional road map toward vision-inspired goals and affirms value of academic advising.

Student learning outcome (SLO): An articulation of the learning (knowledge, skills, and values) that students are expected to have gained from the advising process.

Aiming for Excellence

o Are any aspects of your academic advising program being measured? Is this measured activity being evaluated or assessed?

o Identify the pragmatic reasons to assess the effectiveness of your academic advising program.

o Identify the accountability reasons to assess your academic advising program.

o Which of the four steps of Peggy Maki's (2002) assessment cycle (Figure 14.1) can your team complete easily? Why?

o Which of the four steps of Maki's (2002) assessment cycle will create difficulties for your team in completing an assessment? Why?

References

Aiken-Wisniewski, S., Campbell, S., Nutt, C., Robbins, R., Kirk-Kuwaye, M., & Higa, L. (2010). *Guide to assessment in academic advising* (2nd ed.). Manhattan, KS: National Academic Advising Association.

Angelo, T. (1995, November). Reassessing (and defining) assessment. *AAHE Bulletin, 48*(3), 7.

Bloom, B. S. (1956). *Taxonomy of educational objectives: The classification of educational goals. Handbook 1: Cognitive domain*. New York, NY: David McKay.

Campbell, S. M. (2008). Vision, mission, goals, and program objectives for academic advising programs. In V. Gordon, W. Habley, & T. Grites (Eds.), *Academic advising: A comprehensive handbook* (2nd ed.) (pp. 229–241). San Francisco, CA: Jossey-Bass.

Campbell, S., Nutt, C., Robbins, R., Kirk-Kuwaye, M., & Higa, L. (2005). *Guide to assessment in academic advising* (1st ed.). Manhattan, KS: National Academic Advising Association.

Council for the Advancement of Standards in Higher Education (CAS). (2015a). *Academic advising programs*. Retrieved from http://standards.cas.edu/getpdf.cfm?PDF=E864D2C4-D655-8F74-2E647CDECD29B7D0

CAS. (2015b). *Learning and development outcomes*. Retrieved from http://standards.cas.edu/getpdf.cfm?PDF=D87A29DC-D1D6-D014-83AA8667902C480B

Crookston, B. B. (2009). 1994 (1972): A developmental view of academic advising as teaching. *NACADA Journal, 29*(1), 78–82. (Reprinted from *Journal of College Student Personnel, 13*, 1972, pp. 12–17; *NACADA Journal, 14*[2], 1994, pp. 5–9)

Ewell, P. (2000). *Assessment of learning*. Denver, CO: AAHE Assessment Forum.

Habley, W. R. (2004). *The status of academic advising: Findings from the ACT sixth national survey* (Monograph No. 10). Manhattan, KS: National Academic Advising Association.

Keup, J. R., & Kinzie, J. (2007). A national portrait of first-year students. In M. S. Hunter, B. McCalla-Wriggins, & E. R. White (Eds.), *Academic advising: New insights for teaching and learning in the first year* (Monograph No. 46 [National Resource Center]; Monograph No. 14 [National Academic Advising Association]) (pp. 19–38). Columbia: University of South Carolina, National Resource Center for the First-Year Experience and Students in Transition.

Kuh, G. D. (2008). Advising for student success. In V. N. Gordon, W. R. Habley, & T. J. Grites (Eds.), *Academic advising: A comprehensive handbook* (2nd ed.)(pp. 68–84). San Francisco, CA: Jossey-Bass.

Macaruso, V. (2007). From the co-editors: Brief report on the NACADA Commission on the Assessment of Advising 2004 survey results. *NACADA Journal, 27*(1), 3–8.

Maki, P. L. (2002). Developing an assessment plan to learn about student learning. *Journal of Academic Librarianship, 28*(1–2), 8–13.

Maki, P. L. (2004). *Assessing for learning: Building a sustainable commitment across the institution*. Sterling, VA: Stylus.

Marchese, T. (1993). *AAHE continuous quality improvement project: Profiles of campuses*. Braintree, MA: The Assessment Institute.

Miller, M. (2012). *Interpreting the CAS standards for academic advising*. Retrieved from http://www.nacada.ksu.edu/tabid/3318/articleType/ArticleView/articleId/1249/article.aspx

NACADA: The Global Community for Academic Advising (NACADA). (2005a). *NACADA statement of core values of academic advising*. Retrieved from http://www.nacada.ksu.edu/Resources/Clearinghouse/View-Articles/Core-values-of-academic-advising.aspx

NACADA. (2005b). *NACADA statement of core values of academic advising: Declaration*. Retrieved from http://www.nacada.ksu.edu/Resources/Clearinghouse/View-Articles/Core-values-declaration.aspx

NACADA. (2005c). *NACADA statement of core values of academic advising: Exposition*. Retrieved from http://www.nacada.ksu.edu/Resources/Clearinghouse/View-Articles/Core-values-exposition.aspx

NACADA. (2006). *NACADA concept of academic advising*. Retrieved from http://www.nacada.ksu.edu/Resources/Clearinghouse/View-Articles/Concept-of-Academic-Advising-a598.aspx

NACADA. (2014). *Three pillars of academic advising*. Retrieved from http://www.nacada.ksu.edu/Resources/Clearinghouse/View-Articles/Pillars-of-Academic-Advising.aspx

Palomba, C. A. (1999). *Assessment essentials: Planning, implementing, and improving assessment in higher education*. San Francisco, CA: Jossey-Bass.

Pellegrino, J. W., Chudowsky, N., & Glaser, R. (2001). *Knowing what students know*. Washington, DC: National Academies Press.

Powers, K. L., Carlstrom, A. H., & Hughey, K. F. (2014). Academic advising assessment practices: Results of a national study. *NACADA Journal, 34*(1), 64–77.

Ratcliff, J. R., Lubinescu, E. S., & Gaffney, M. A. (Eds.). (2001). *How accreditation influences assessment* (New Directions for Higher Education, No. 113). San Francisco, CA: Jossey-Bass.

Rinck, C. (2006, June 28). Student engagement and academic advising. *The Mentor: An Academic Advising Journal, 8*(1). Retrieved from http://dus.psu.edu/mentor/060628cr.htm

Robbins, R. (2009). Assessment of career advising. In K. Hughey, D. Burton Nelson, J. Damminger, & B. McCalla-Wriggins (Eds.), *Handbook of career advising* (pp. 266–292). San Francisco, CA: Jossey-Bass.

Robbins, R. (2011). Assessment and accountability of academic advising. In J. Joslin & N. Markee (Eds.), *Academic advising administration: Essential knowledge and skills for the 21st century* (Monograph No. 22) (pp. 53–64). Manhattan, KS: National Academic Advising Association.

Robbins, R. (2014). AAC&U's integrative liberal learning and the CAS standards: Advising for a 21st century liberal education. *NACADA Journal, 34*(2), 26–31.

Robbins, R., & Adams, T. (2013). Assessment of peer advising. In H. Koring & D. Zahorik (Eds.), *Peer advising and mentoring: A guide for advising practitioners* (Monograph No. B26) (2nd ed.) (pp. 129–140). Manhattan, KS: National Academic Advising Association.

Robbins, R., & Zarges, K. M. (2011). *Assessment of academic advising: A summary of the process*. Retrieved from http://www.nacada.ksu.edu/Resources/Clearinghouse/View-Articles/Assessment-of-academic-advising.aspx

Schulenberg, J., & Lindhorst, M. (2008). Advising is advising: Toward defining the practice and scholarship of academic advising. *NACADA Journal, 28*(1), 43–53.

Sims, S. R. (1992). *Student outcomes assessment: A historical review and guide to program development*. New York, NY: Greenwood.

Upcraft, M. L., & Schuh, J. H. (1996). *Assessment in student affairs*. San Francisco, CA: Jossey-Bass.

White, E. R. (2000). Developing mission, goals, and objectives for the advising program. In V. N. Gordon & W. R. Habley (Eds.), *Academic advising: A comprehensive handbook* (pp. 180–191). San Francisco, CA: Jossey-Bass.

White, E. R. (2006). *Using CAS standards for self-assessment and improvement*. Retrieved from http://www.nacada.ksu.edu/Resources/Clearinghouse/View-Articles/Using-CAS-Standards-for-self-assessment.aspx

Wiggins, G., & McTighe, J. (2006). *Understanding by design*. Upper Saddle River, NJ: Pearson.

Young-Jones, A. D., Burt, T. D., Dixon, S., & Hawthorne, M. J. (2013). Academic advising: Does it really impact student success? *Quality Assurance in Education, 21*(1), 7–19.

15

ASSESSMENT OF ACADEMIC ADVISING

GATHERING OUTCOME EVIDENCE AND MAKING CHANGES

Rich Robbins

Measurements are not to provide numbers but insight.

—Ingrid Bucher (2010, p. 1)

Building upon chapter 14, this chapter features a detailed discussion of measuring student learning outcomes and the ways planners can use the resultant assessment data to validate and support academic advising processes. To gain a full understanding of the assessment process for academic advising, readers are strongly urged to read chapter 14 prior to this chapter.

Reader Learning Outcomes

From studying this chapter, advisors will use knowledge gained about the assessment processes, outcome measures, and reported results to

o identify stakeholders for advising;

o determine the timing for measuring student learning outcomes (SLOs);

o determine the appropriate cycles for measuring SLOs;

o know the purpose of qualitative data;

o know the types of qualitative data;

o understand the meanings of resulting qualitative data;

o know the purpose of quantitative data;

o know the types of quantitative data;

o understand the meanings of quantitative data results;

o distinguish direct from indirect measures;

o recognize sources of benchmarking criteria (threshold values);

o identify criteria for establishing reliability;

o select measures that demonstrate validity;

o understand the importance of using multiple measurements for an SLO;

o determine sources of institutional sources relevant to SLOs;

o determine other established data sources relevant to SLOs; and

o appreciate the various formats for reporting outcomes to different stakeholders.

Maki's (2002, 2004) cycle of assessment consists of four basic steps: identifying desired outcomes, gathering evidence, interpreting the evidence, and implementing change based on that evidence. Chapter 14 provides guidance on the first crucial step: the successful identification of SLOs for academic advising. Once the outcomes have been identified and mapped, master advisors turn their attention to determining empirically if these goals are being met.

Identifying Stakeholders

A complete assessment process includes the appropriate identification of stakeholders. Messia (2010) provided an excellent classification framework for different types of stakeholders for academic advising; they include others involved with, affected by, and providing influence over the academic advising program (Robbins, 2011). The choice of stakeholders for any specific academic advising program depends on the programmatic mission as well as the goals and desired outcomes for the program. For example, Bill, the master advisor introduced in chapter 14, member of his institution's assessment committee, and developer of academic advising SLOs for all first-year students, must determine the stakeholders for his initiative.

Students are the primary stakeholders in all assessment processes because they coparticipate in advising. In Bill's case, all first-year students comprise the stakeholders. In addition, Bill recognizes the instructors of the first-year seminar as stakeholders. He also understands the roles of advisors, faculty instructors, and parents of first-year students in the assessment process. Other stakeholders include those in and associated with the institution, such as individuals in the enrollment management and registrar's offices, alumni, and people with potential influence in the program (Robbins, 2011). As Messia (2010) noted, some stakeholders are considered "core" (¶3), others "internal but indirect" (¶4), and some qualify as "external and indirect" stakeholders (¶5). All stakeholder categories will likely include protagonists, who support assessment efforts, and antagonists, or naysayers, who challenge assessment initiatives. Some may be influenced to support or challenge the advising assessment. All stakeholders, regardless of position as supporter, naysayer, or uncommitted, must be included in the assessment efforts. Considering and including perceptions, opinions, and suggestions from all parties will promote a shared language and an understanding of academic advising. Engagement of stakeholders may also facilitate buy-in for assessment.

Stakeholders should be included at each step of the assessment process, from preplanning through the reporting of results and implementing data-informed changes. While not all stakeholders participate in the detailed assessment process, facilitators and planners must collaborate and communicate with them to promote a shared terminology, agreement of programmatic goals and desired SLOs, and support for the program and the assessment process (Campbell, Nutt, Robbins, Kirk-Kuwaye, & Higa, 2005; Robbins, 2011).

Members of the assessment team, which implements and conducts the processes, are the heart of the stakeholder group. The team, by definition, includes core stakeholders and identifies the outcome measures, the timing of data collection, and the implementation of the measurements. It also orchestrates the collection and analysis of data and the report of the results. Team members work with other stakeholders to determine specific actions to take based upon the resulting data (Robbins, 2011).

Outcome Measures and Data

Once the desired SLOs have been developed and mapped, the assessment team must identify the type of evidence that determines whether the desired SLOs have been achieved. They then need to refine those choices so that the achievement is attributed to academic advising. As a result of these considerations, the typical evidence is composed of multiple outcome measures for any SLO.

Because of the complex nature of the evidence, planners must take care in determining the gathering mechanisms for the outcome data. To establish validity, multiple and mixed measures are needed for each individual SLO. One measure (e.g., student perception or satisfaction) without a source of comparison data provides no validity for the results. Although frequently used, student surveys typically do not measure learning; rather, they record students' expressed experiences with the advising processes. Even surveys that include questions about student learning tend to reflect indirect measures based on perceptions. Multiple outcome measures must include some combination of qualitative, quantitative, direct, and indirect measurements (Aiken-Wisniewski et al., 2010; Campbell et al., 2005; Robbins, 2009, 2011; Robbins & Adams, 2013; Robbins & Zarges, 2011).

Qualitative measurement provides data described in the form of rich, in-depth responses to open-ended questions (Creswell, 2009; Neuman, 2006; Robbins, 2009, 2011; Robbins & Adams, 2013; Robbins & Zarges, 2011). Interpretation of the data is emergent and subjective, typically coded into themes. Examples of means that yield exploratory information through qualitative measures include focus groups, case studies, and naturalistic observations; they contribute useful baseline data to better understand a topic or when closed-ended items that yield quantitative data cannot be determined. For example, to explore the best way to measure "students use the electronic degree audit to track progress toward degree completion," Bill creates a focus group of students who explain the ways they determine their own academic progress. Bill listens for all comments related to the electronic degree audit.

Quantitative measurements result in descriptive numbers or statistical measures that are interpreted more objectively than the themes revealed through qualitative data (Creswell, 2009; Neuman, 2006; Robbins, 2009, 2011; Robbins & Adams, 2013; Robbins & Zarges, 2011). Measures taken from participants (e.g., students) include surveys and questionnaires with items that force choices; that is, they are not open ended and include multiple choice items, rating scales, and true-false statements. Other quantitative measures of academic advising may include retention rates, grade-point averages, percentages, advisor–advisee ratios, and counts of student advising appointments.

Quantitative measures are typically utilized when target cohorts are unavailable for extensive observations or interactions, when time and funds are limited, or when the stakeholders require numerical information (Robbins, 2011; Robbins & Adams, 2013). Bill uses a quantitative measure to assess whether students utilize the electronic degree audit to track their progress toward degree completion. To establish a direct outcome measure, Bill seeks to document the number or percentage of students who use the electronic degree audit system during an advising session to accurately complete a 4-year course plan. He also uses an indirect measure by asking students to rate the frequency with which they utilize their degree audit to track their progress toward graduation. The respondents must choose on a 5-point scale that ranges from *never* to *always* on an instrument provided to them. This measure is considered indirect because the data are based on students' perceptions.

Optimally, qualitative and quantitative methodologies are used to complement each other and provide a broader understanding of the phenomena under study (Smith & Ortloff, 2010). Furthermore, despite the long-standing perceived dichotomy between qualitative and quantitative measures, similarities between the two measures exist. For example, whether assessment involves a qualitative or quantitative measure, the process is conducted in a controlled environment (either purposely or as a natural consequence of the process) with results extrapolated to a more complex environment or real-world situation. In addition, direct and indirect measures may be qualitative or quantitative, depending on how the data are collected (Robbins, 2009, 2011; Robbins & Adams, 2013; Robbins & Zarges, 2011). Both methods also involve a combination of inductive and deductive reasoning; that is, judgments are made about the outcome data to provide meaning to the topic of investigation (Creswell, 2009). For more detailed comparisons of these two methodologies, see Luyt (2012), Terrell (2012), and Yoshikawa, Weisner, Kalil, and Way (2008). In any case, all methodologies present strengths and weaknesses such that multiple and mixed outcome measures need to be used for any single SLO.

For each individual measure of an SLO, the planners must determine the threshold, or minimum criterion, that demonstrates that the desired SLO has been achieved. In the case of Bill's SLO, the assessment team needs to decide the level of electronic degree audit use to track progress toward degree completion that indicates confirmation that students use the degree audit for planning purposes. Identification of a minimum performance criterion for defining success (threshold) requires informed decision making of various types. For example, existing institutional data may be used to determine the minimum criterion (Robbins, 2009, 2011), or national benchmarking or peer institutional data may be useful as a substitute for or a supplement to institutional data. The first assessment cycle is considered a pilot, a baseline, or a benchmarking endeavor that can be examined to set minimum criteria (Robbins, 2009, 2011).

Assessment teams can take heart that not every student must be assessed on every outcome measure for an SLO. Basic sampling techniques can be used to ensure generalizability to the student population of focus (Creswell, 2009; Troxel & Campbell, 2010), making data gathering a relatively less daunting task.

Assessment Matrix Example

In individual efforts and with others, I have developed a template including 10 detailed stages of an assessment cycle for academic advising (Robbins, 2009, 2011; Robbins & Adams, 2013; Robbins & Zarges, 2011). The matrix builds on Maki's (2002, 2004) assessment cycle (Figure 14.1) featured in the previous chapter, with added specific steps within the four major phases involved in assessment.

Figure 15.1 shows a completed matrix based on Bill's first-year SLO: Students use the electronic degree audit to track progress toward degree completion. This SLO incorporates the Council for the Advancement of Standards in Higher Education (CAS) (2015) domain of "knowledge acquisition, construction, integration, and application" (p. 5) as well as dimensions of "connecting knowledge to other knowledge, ideas, and experiences " (p. 5) and "managing career development" (p. 6) specific to academic advising.

The matrix in Figure 15.1 provides an example, but in some cases, fewer columns may fully account for the necessary assessment (e.g., users can combine *outcome measure*, *minimum performance criteria for success*, and *data instruments* into a single column). Other cases may inspire addition of columns (e.g., *stakeholders, relevant CAS Standards,* or *points of outcome measurement*).

Interpreting Results

The first-year population at master advisor Bill's institution consists of 1,000 students. The assessment team used Bill's suggestion to assess the specific SLO of "students use the electronic degree audit to track progress toward degree completion." As shown in Figure 15.1, three separate outcome measures yielded valuable information.

A qualitative, indirect measure involved samples of 15 students in 1 of 10 focus groups ($N = 150$; 15% of the total first-year population). The focus groups were conducted during the final exam week of the spring semester, and students self-selected (i.e., could choose to attend or not) into specific focus groups. All participating students knew that their names had been entered into a drawing for a

Figure 15.1. Assessment of student learning outcomes in academic advising example matrix

Institutional Mission Statement	Local Mission Statement	Goal or Objective	Student Learning Outcome	Where Learning Occurs (Opportunities for Student Learning)	When or by When Learning Should Occur	Outcome Measure	Data Instruments	Minimum Performance Criteria for Success/ Threshold	Action(s) Based on Data
Specific to institution	Specific to academic advising program	Specific to academic advising program	"Students use the electronic degree audit to track progress toward degree completion."	Orientation First-year seminar course First-year advising meetings Online training module	By the end of the first year	1. Number or percentage of students reporting they use the electronic degree audit system to track their progress toward degree completion (qualitative, indirect)	1. Focus group	Baseline for first assessment cycle for SLO	Advisor development programming
	e.g., "The mission of academic advising is to offer a collaborative process between the student and advisor to promote student academic success."	e.g., "To provide accurate and timely information to students to assist with their curricular choices."	CAS Domains of Knowledge acquisition, construction, integration, and application Connecting knowledge to other knowledge, ideas, and experiences			2. Number or percentage of students responding that they always use the electronic degree audit system to track progress toward degree completion (quantitative, indirect)	2. Likert-scale survey item asking students how often they use their degree audit to track progress toward degree, ranging from *never* to *always*		Additional student learning opportunities Request for resources
						3. Number or percentage of students who use the electronic degree audit system during an advising session to accurately complete 4-year course plan (quantitative, direct)	3. Advisor completed rubric during the advising session		Revision of assessment methodology Other?

← Mapping of Outcomes →

Note. Matrix compiled based on previous works (Robbins, 2009, 2011; Robbins & Adams, 2013; Robbins & Zarges, 2011).

$100 bookstore gift certificate. During the focus group meeting, students were asked the open-ended question, "How do you track your academic progress?" In response, 68 students (45%) reported using the electronic degree audit.

Another outcome measure for Bill's SLO involved a quantitative, direct measure of advisors observing students during an advising session. The facilitating advisor asked the assessed student to demonstrate how he or she tracks academic progress. The advisor then noted the number of students who accessed the electronic degree audit system to complete the request. Of 300 randomly selected students advised by 15 advisors, 180 (60%) utilized the electronic degree audit system. This result demonstrates the value of using randomly chosen samples and distributing the process among various facilitators, which alleviates the burden on a single advisor.

The third outcome measure was based on student self-reports of using the electronic degree audit system to track their academic progress. This indirect, quantitative measure was captured by responses to an e-mail survey administered at the end of the spring semester of the first year. The students self-selected, and all participants were informed that their names were entered into a drawing for a $100 bookstore gift certificate. Three hundred students (30% of the total first-year population) responded to the e-mail invitation to participate, with 285 (95%) reporting that they use the electronic degree audit system to track their academic progress.

In determining the meaning behind the three assessment measures, Bill and the assessment team need to consider the nature of the outcome measures as direct or indirect, any baseline assessments conducted for comparison, the ways the participating students were selected, any possible confounding factors in any of the measures, and the minimum extent to which the three separate measures triangulate to guide the conclusions. For example, the first outcome measure was based on focus group data, so specific questions, if not part of the initial design or when conducted by external evaluators, must be addressed: How were students selected to participate? What incentives did they receive? Who facilitated the discussion in these focus groups? Were the facilitators trained? Were the questions clear to the students in the group? Were the questions truly open ended and not leading? What kind of probing did the facilitators employ to engage students? Also, the committee needs to ensure that the focus group transcripts and coding of responses were conducted according to a prescribed, accepted plan.

Although outcome data from direct measures typically provide the best evidence of student learning, some of the data from the second outcome measure may prove problematic. Because the assessment was conducted during a meeting in the presence of the facilitating academic advisor, the student may have experienced pressure to answer in a specific way. Also, who could determine whether the instructions for the task were communicated clearly, correctly, and consistently to every student? Could any of the advisors have unintentionally led the students to access the electronic degree audit system?

The third outcome measure, as an indirect measure with responses based on students' beliefs, may generate the most problems. Perhaps the question posed to students on the survey was neither valid nor reliable; for example, in the survey authors may have used a compound verb or leading language. The students could have misinterpreted the statement. Developing a sound, valid, and reliable survey takes skill and time, including that necessary to offer a pilot phase and testing. Moreover, the students self-selected to participate in the survey thus creating issues that a random sample does not.

With so many pitfalls with each measure, can the assessment team make any conclusions from the resulting data? Even if the students demonstrate achievement of the desired SLO by meeting the thresholds for each measure, how will an advisor know that learning adds value to academic advising? That is, how does the assessor know where the students learned the information? For example, the outcome depends on whether the focus group consisted only of students who had demonstrated ability to use the degree audit system to track academic progress and the nature of their answers to a specific question about the acquisition of this ability: "Where did you learn how to use the degree audit system to track your degree progress?" In an alternative tool, the question about learning could be included on an assessment questionnaire that directly measures students' knowledge levels regarding the SLO. In this way, the stakeholders can match those demonstrating knowledge of the SLO with their self-reported learning sources.

Interpretation of outcome data based only on students' self-reports of their learning proves difficult. An assessment team may use the best, most precise assessment processes, but the multiple outcome data for a single SLO can yield unclear and contradictory results that confound any conclusion. Because the interpretation of assessment results is more of an art than a science, key team members should ruminate over data for a while rather than jump to immediate conclusions. They need to take the time to review the results carefully and discuss them thoroughly because all the science of the assessment process will not counteract interpretations hastily conducted without intentional and thoughtful consideration.

Reporting Results

After the assessment team interprets the outcome data, the results of the assessment cycle are reported to the various stakeholder cohorts. Depending on the specific audience, results may be communicated in an executive summary, as part of a self-study, as a contribution to an accreditation report, in a strategic plan, or other format (Robbins, 2011). Considerations for the reporting platform include the reason the assessment was performed, the story the data tell, the amount of information shared, the people with the need for the information, the best form to communicate the information, and the necessary timing of the reports to different audiences (Aiken-Wisniewski et al., 2010; Campbell et al., 2005; Robbins & Zarges, 2011).

For example, the team members responsible for sharing results may need to determine if a detailed report should be available on a protected web site for a select group or provided to all identified stakeholders. Should a report include both written text and graphics, such as charts? Should students and administrators receive the same information? The team must take into account the institutional culture and political climate. They also should understand the way communication of assessment results will benefit academic advising.

Acting Upon Outcome Data

Data-informed changes have emerged as a hallmark of higher education in this age of accountability, transparency, and limited resources. The results of the advising assessment may inform revisions in the pedagogy or curriculum of the academic advising program, or they can be used to develop or revise academic advisor development and training, justify the need for additional resources, or help shape institutional decisions (Robbins, 2011; Robbins & Zarges, 2011). In any case, the goals of the academic advising program and the needs of students remain the primary consideration in any initiative that rests on the results.

Based on the interpretation of the outcome data in Figure 15.1, the assessment team may conclude from the results procured from investigation of Bill's SLO that advisors must emphasize instructions for use of the electronic degree audit system with first-year students. Based on the goal of increasing student understanding and use of the system, instructions on degree audits will be included in advisor development for one-to-one advising, web site information, first-year experience courses, and the like. However, those concerned with implementation may realize that to teach the degree audit, advisors may need to change the advising curriculum or delivery method to allow the time needed to instruct students effectively. They may need to add advisors so that each can spend enough time with students to demonstrate and discuss the system. Full use of the assessment often extends beyond those associated with accountability.

Outcome data may indicate needed changes in the assessment process. Figure 15.1 shows the possible options for data collection: a focus group, a self-report survey, and advisor-completed rubrics; however, unique data-collection points or even different assessment processes may be best in a specific situation. Assessment teams may investigate additional opportunities for students to learn the desired information such that data can be collected. When baseline data are absent, how must the process be designed to assess an SLO for the first time? Was the question or instrument used valid (accurate and generalizable) and reliable (meaningful and repeatable)? What improvements to the process would yield better data on self-reports? A review of and improvements in the assessment process should be part of all assessment cycles.

The results of assessment can also add to the body of research on academic advising through a professional presentation or publication. According to Suskie (2009), assessment is a form of action research conducted to inform and improve one's own practice. In fact, the assessment cycle of establishing learning outcomes, providing opportunities for students to learn, assessing student learning, and using the results for improvement mirrors the steps of action research: plan, act, observe, and reflect.

Assessed SLOs provide information on the student population measured, the institutional type involved, and the academic advising delivery system utilized such that features can be compared among similar institutions. In these cases, the results of assessment can be generalized, to some extent, to other academic advising programs, and assessment serves as a form of scholarly inquiry (The National Academic Advising Association [NACADA: The Global Community for Academic Advising], 2008).

The assessment team develops a timetable for making changes informed by the outcome data. It must determine whether all changes will be implemented at once or on a task-specific schedule, and it also needs to identify personnel engaged at each implementation step. The time frame depends upon specific programmatic goals, the results of the assessment, and the campus culture of the institution. A tentative time line should be established and reported along with specific suggestions regarding ways to implement the results. However, the timetable may change as identified resources are needed to respond to the suggestions stemming from the results.

Next Steps

The assessment process does not end with the delineation of a timetable to implement data-informed changes. Any actions designed to improve student learning also need to be assessed for effectiveness in a process many call *closing the assessment loop*. At this point in the process, the SLOs for assessment need to be revisited, and the outcome measures, points of assessment, and all other aspects of the process reviewed. In addition, SLOs not previously assessed should be placed in the assessment cycle as well as the initial SLOs assessed. As a result of these many factors included in the time line, stakeholders account for the manageability and sustainability of the assessment process for academic advising.

Sustainability of Assessment

Ideally, assessment becomes part of the everyday culture of the academic advising program with the various aspects of the process included in daily routines. This commitment fosters sustainability of assessment over time. To this end, administrators should capitalize on current efforts to gauge student learning. For example, academic advisors who routinely assign homework to students, such as bringing a hard copy of their degree audit report to an advising meeting, can use compliance as one of the multiple outcome measures for a behavioral SLO such as "students utilize their degree audit reports" or "students access the necessary technology to develop their schedules." Tracking of student follow-through on referrals to a campus resource, such as tutoring, serves as a direct measure of the behavioral SLO that "students utilize campus resources" or "students follow up on advisors' suggestions." Tracking can also act as an indirect measure of a cognitive SLO such as "students know the available resources on campus." In addition, planners should recognize that using sampling techniques and avoiding attempts to assess every individual student on every SLO make the efforts more feasible.

Assessment teams should gain familiarity with the data collected by institutional research offices, such as the registrar, and know the data maintained in centralized data warehouses. Available data may contribute to indirect measures for a desired SLO. In addition, institutions that participate in commercially administered inventories, such as the Beginning College Survey of Student Engagement (BCSSE), the National Survey for Student Engagement (NSSE), and the Cooperative Institutional Research Program (CIRP) Freshman Survey, among others, likely keep relevant data for assessment initiatives. Management platforms, such as Blackboard, Moodle, Haiku, or others, offer ways to manage information, organize longitudinal data, assign advising homework, review e-portfolios, and perform other activities that help sustain assessment efforts. Survey programs such as Qualtrics and SurveyMonkey can be used to develop indirect measures through survey instruments. Planners need to use technologies that best demonstrate student learning as a result of academic advising while contributing to the analytics already used at the institution (Campbell, Joslin, Lechtenberg, & Robbins, 2015). Assessment teams seek to produce meaningful data that promote understanding and management of institutional efforts, such as retention and completion, so that the importance of academic advising to an institution's mission can be communicated to stakeholders (chapter 11).

To expand the database, assessment planners may identify courses requiring projects and students looking for research topics. An upper level or graduate marketing or social science class may embrace the opportunity to conduct surveys or focus groups. An undergraduate or graduate student interested in student development or higher education issues may be looking for a research topic, and the resulting data can be included in the assessment plan.

Perhaps the most important sustainability strategy requires individual SLOs to be assessed in varying cycles. A few significant SLOs must be assessed every year or cycle, but most can be placed on 2-, 3-, or even 4-year (or longer) cycles so assessment does not become overwhelming.

Summary

Assessment of academic advising involves developing consensus around the collective expectations about student learning that should result from academic advising, gathering evidence to better understand this student learning, and using this evidence to support improvements in student learning through academic advising (Campbell et al., 2014). Assessment is also a change-management process such that successes must be communicated and celebrated after every assessment cycle. Perhaps the most critical aspect of any initiative is the identification of one or two desired SLOs (Robbins, 2011), as attempting to do too much in a given cycle will likely result in lack of support and in perceptions of the assessment process as onerous.

The assessment team needs to demonstrate the utility for assessment and the ways it can be incorporated into everyday activities of the academic advising program. Assessment in higher education is here to stay; the information needed to demystify it is presented to make the assessment journey successful. Master advisors can use the glossary of key terms when discussing the process and outcomes with other stakeholders also striving to help students succeed.

Glossary of Terms

Action research: Research conducted to inform and improve one's own practice rather than to make broad generalizations.

Direct measures: Methods of gathering information that require students or advisors to demonstrate their knowledge and skills (e.g., portfolio, presentation, and test result); direct measures are more observable than indirect measures.

Indirect measures: Methods of gathering information that ask students or advisors to reflect on learning (e.g., questionnaires, interviews, and focus groups) rather than demonstrate it; indirect measures are more inferential than direct measures.

Qualitative methods: Assessment methods that provide a narration or description of learning (e.g., logs, journals, participant observations, and open-ended questions on interviews and surveys).

Quantitative methods: Assessment methods that rely on numerical scores or ratings (e.g., standardized tests, and surveys).

Reliability: Items are related in meaningful ways (internal reliability); individuals would respond similarly to the same test or experience on a different day, location, or time (test–retest reliability); two similar and reasonable people would record similar scores based on viewing, reading, or interpreting the same event (interrater reliability).

Validity: Accurate measurement and description of construct to be measured (internal validity); results generalizable to a similar group, setting, or population (external validity).

Aiming for Excellence

o Identify the stakeholders for your advising program. For a detailed discussion of stakeholders, including comprehensive classifications, see Messia (2010).

o Identify three things that students should know as a result of the advising program. This knowledge can be based on an advising mission statement (if available), specific advising program goals (if identified), institutional mission, or the various areas of advising provided. They could also be based on external sources such as the Council for the Advance of Standards in Higher Education

(CAS) (2015) or the NACADA Statement of Core Values of Academic Advising (NACADA, 2005) (hereafter, NACADA Core Values). This knowledge will comprise the desired cognitive SLOs for the advising program.

o Identify three skills or activities students should be able to do as a result of the advising program. These descriptions of capabilities can be based on an advising mission statement (if available), specific advising program goals (if identified), institutional mission, or the various areas of advising provided. They could also be based on external sources such as the CAS Standards or the NACADA Core Values. These skills or activities will comprise the behavioral SLOs for the advising program.

o Identify three experiences or benefits students should appreciate or value as a result of the advising program. These values can be based on an advising mission statement (if available), specific advising program goals (if identified), institutional mission, or the various areas of advising provided. They could also be based on external sources such as the CAS Standards or the NACADA Core Values. These articulated values will comprise the affective SLOs for your advising program.

o Relate each of the nine SLOs to the appropriate CAS domains and dimensions.

o Select one of the nine identified SLOs and delineate the opportunities for students to achieve this specific outcome. See the mapping outcomes featured in Figure 15.1.

o Determine the time by which students should achieve each SLO (Figure 15.1). Identify one direct and one indirect outcome measure for the SLO.

o Collaborate with other campus constituents and stakeholders to determine if any institutional data are available to inform or serve as an outcome measure for the specific SLO.

References

Aiken-Wisniewski, S., Campbell, S., Nutt, C., Robbins, R., Kirk-Kuwaye, M., & Higa, L. (2010). *Guide to assessment in academic advising* (Monograph No. 23) (2nd ed.). Manhattan, KS: National Academic Advising Association.

Bucher, I. (2010). [Quote]. In V. J. Shute & B. J. Becker (Eds.), *Innovative assessment for the 21st century: Supporting educational needs*. New York, NY: Springer Science and Business Media.

Campbell, S., Joslin, J., Lechtenberg, S., & Robbins, R. (2015, February). *Identifying and using multiple measures*. Plenary session presented at the 2015 NACADA Assessment Institute, Orlando, FL.

Campbell, S., Lechtenberg, S., & Robbins, R. (2014, February). *Sharing and acting upon the outcome data*. Plenary Presentation 5, NACADA Assessment Institute, Albuquerque, NM.

Campbell, S., Nutt, C., Robbins, R., Kirk-Kuwaye, M., & Higa, L. (2005). *Guide to assessment in academic advising* (Monograph No. 23). Manhattan, KS: National Academic Advising Association.

Council for the Advancement of Standards in Higher Education. (2015). *Academic advising programs*. Retrieved from http://standards.cas.edu/getpdf.cfm?PDF=E864D2C4-D655-8F74-2E647CDECD29B7D0

Creswell, J. W. (2009). *Research design: Qualitative, quantitative, and mixed methods approaches*. Thousand Oaks, CA: Sage.

Luyt, R. (2012). A framework for mixing methods in quantitative measurement development, validation, and revision: A case study. *Journal of Mixed Methods Research*, 6(4), 294–316.

Maki, P. L. (2002). Developing an assessment plan to learn about student learning. *Journal of Academic Librarianship, 28*(1–2), 8–13.

Maki, P. L. (2004). *Assessing for learning: Building a sustainable commitment across the institution*. Sterling, VA: Stylus.

Messia, J. (2010). *Defining advising stakeholder groups*. Retrieved from http://www.nacada.ksu.edu/Resources/Clearinghouse/View-Articles/Defining-Advising-Stakeholder-Groups.aspx

NACADA: The Global Community for Academic Advising (NACADA). (2005). *NACADA statement of core values of academic advising*. Retrieved from https://www.nacada.ksu.edu/Resources/Clearinghouse/View-Articles/Core-values-of-academic-advising.aspx

NACADA. (2008). *Final report from the Taskforce on Infusing Research throughout NACADA*. Unpublished report.

Neuman, W. L. (2006). *Social research methods: Qualitative and quantitative approaches*. Boston, MA: Pearson.

Robbins, R. (2009). Assessment of career advising. In K. Hughey, D. Burton Nelson, J. Damminger, & E. McCalla-Wriggins (Eds.), *Handbook of career advising* (pp. 266–292). San Francisco, CA: Jossey-Bass.

Robbins, R. (2011). Assessment and accountability of academic advising. In J. Joslin & N. Markee (Eds.), *Academic advising administration: Essential knowledge and skills for the 21st century*. (Monograph No. 22) (pp. 53–67). Manhattan, KS: National Academic Advising Association.

Robbins, R., & Adams, T. (2013). Assessment of peer advising. In H. Koring & D. Zahorik (Eds.), *Peer advising and mentoring: A guide for advising practitioners* (2nd ed.) (Monograph B26) (pp. 129–140). Manhattan, KS: National Academic Advising Association.

Robbins, R., & Zarges, K. M. (2011). *Assessment of academic advising: A summary of the process*. Retrieved from http://www.nacada.ksu.edu/Resources/Clearinghouse/View-Articles/Assessment-of-academic-advising.aspx

Smith, J. S., & Ortloff, D. H. (2010). Connecting the quantitative and qualitative continuum. In P. L. Hagen, T. L. Kuhn, & G. M. Padak (Eds.), *Scholarly inquiry in academic advising* (Monograph No. 20) (pp. 65–72). Manhattan, KS: National Academic Advising Association.

Suskie, L. (2009). *Assessing student learning: A common sense guide* (2nd ed.). Bolton, MA: Anker.

Terrell, S. R. (2012). Mixed-methods research methodologies. *Qualitative Report*, *17*(1), 254–280.

Troxel, W. G., & Campbell, S. (2010). Quantitative methodologies for the academic advising practitioner-researcher. In P. L. Hagen, T. L. Kuhn, & G. M. Padak (Eds.), *Scholarly inquiry in academic advising* (Monograph No. 20) (pp. 73–84). Manhattan, KS: National Academic Advising Association.

Yoshikawa, H., Weisner, T., Kalil, A., & Way, N. (2008). Mixing qualitative and quantitative research in developmental science: Uses and methodological choices. *Developmental Psychology*, *44*(2), 344–354.

16

TECHNOLOGY AND ACADEMIC ADVISING

George E. Steele

*Technology is just a tool. In terms of getting the kids working
together and motivating them, the teacher is the most important.*

—Bill Gates (n.d.)

Forces internal and external to higher education will challenge the limited ways
in which technology has been used to date in academic advising. To harness technologies that promote advising as teaching will require creative efforts and new
ways of thinking. To assist with this endeavor, the intentional use of technology
model can be used to categorize types of technologies used in advising. The cat-
egorizations explain the ways the designs, functions, and limitations of different
types of technologies align with advising goals of learning, service, and engagement. The model incorporates consideration of security and legal issues. By con-
ceptualizing technology in a framework, those who support an advising-as-teaching
approach can better achieve their goals and document their successes. Implications
for training and professional development are also addressed in this chapter.

Reader Learning Outcomes

From studying this chapter, advisors will use knowledge gained about the use of
technology to

- o identify, compare, and contrast the internal and external pressures that encourage the adoption of more technologies in academic advising;
- o employ the intentional use of technology model to identify technologies
currently used and categorize them by the learning outcome classifications of
teaching, service, and engagement;
- o evaluate the distribution of technologies in light of advising program goals and
planned technology adoption plans;
- o identify new skills and knowledge that effectively promote and defend advising
as teaching in a technology rich environment; and
- o articulate the way technological skills and knowledge relate to appropriate
advisor training and professional development plans.

No one needs a crystal ball to predict that the use of technology in academic advising will expand and evolve. As chapter 17 highlights, groups internal and external to higher education are promoting technology integration into academic advising to address challenges such as retention and completion as well as a means to control costs and improve administrative efficiencies (Schneider, 2010; U.S Department of Education, 2012). For example, advocacy groups, such as the Lumina Foundation (2014), are interested in reforming postsecondary education from outside the academy by advocating for specific policies to effect change in higher education. Use of technology is seen as critical to bring about effective change, and if a portion of the predicted implementation of technology is undertaken, academic advising will be conducted differently than in the past.

Academic advisors can employ technology in many ways, and the uses that advisors collectively choose will exert a long-lasting impact on practice. Because instruction on campus is increasingly offered in blended and distance formats, the academic advising community needs to focus on informing about and arguing for the adoption and deployment of technologies that advance a model of advising as teaching. If advisors do not select the best technologies to face future challenges, then other on-campus groups that may or may not support the vision and mission of an advising-as-teaching approach will impose their technology choices on practitioners. Advisors must select and champion technology because, more than merely providing information, they help students develop deeper meaning and understanding about their personal, academic, and career plans and passions.

The intentional use of technology model (Steele, 2014) shows the relationship between types of technologies and different types of advising outcomes. Academic advisors can use these distinctions to explain the ways practice and technological solutions can help address the challenges advisors face and improve the educational outcomes for students.

Using Technology to Support Advising as Teaching

Many practitioner-scholars advocate the advising-as-teaching model as the best approach to align the mission of academic advising with the larger objective of higher education (e.g., Hemwall & Trachte, 2003; Lowenstein, 2005). Those who support this model point to similarities between teaching and advising. For example, Lowenstein (2005) identified four key endeavors that teachers with a learning-centered philosophy of advising undertake: They help students (a) find and create the rationale behind their education, (b) comprehend the seemingly disconnected pieces of their curriculum, (c) base educational choices on a developing sense of self-efficacy, and (d) continually enhance learning experiences by relating them to knowledge that has been previously gained at appropriate places (such as cocurricular activities) (p. 72).

Also, Martin (2007) argued for application of intentional teaching through use of learning objectives with defined elements of the curriculum that guide student learning and assessment of advising. She stated, "Learning objectives answer the question: What should students learn through academic advising?" (¶3). Consistent with the works of Lowenstein and Martin, NACADA: The Global Community for Academic Advising (NACADA, 2006) endorsed a curricular outline and a focus on the learning objectives as stated in the NACADA Concept of Academic Advising.

Although institutions are increasingly adopting technology applications for academic advising, the selections do not necessarily support the advising-as-teaching paradigm. This conclusion was discerned from the results of the *NACADA 2013 National Technology Survey* (Pasquini, 2013), which was sent to all NACADA members and achieved an approximate 10% return rate. Question 5 stated, "Please identify how often you use these technologies." Respondents indicated that e-mails, personal face-to-face interactions, locally installed software for office and administrative use (e.g., Microsoft Office), and telephones were used in practice between 76 and 100% of the time spent advising. Fifty percent or fewer respondents indicated using other technologies listed on the survey, such as a learning management system (LMS), cloud storage, and social media, 50% of the time in their practice. Furthermore, respondents indicated that they used 18 of the 30 listed technologies (e.g., web cameras, customer relationship management systems, mobile technologies, etc.) less than 25% of the time.

The technology needed to advance an advising-as-teaching approach should not be confused with that required for distance-learning advising. In the 11th annual survey of tracking online education in the United States, Allen and Seaman (2014) reported that 33.5% of all students in higher education take at least one online course, and the rate of distance-learning enrollment exceeds that of overall higher education (p. 4). Of course, academic advisors of distance learners use technology to communicate with advisees (Varney, 2009); however, technology to advance the advising-as-teaching model must also ensure continuous learning. Technology used to establish a call center–based service in which each contact with a student is treated as an episodic event rather than a continuous learning experience does little to advance teaching or learning. Furthermore, technology use does not guarantee desired outcomes, and it must be intentionally chosen and applied to both traditional and distance advising. Therefore, advisors must wisely choose teaching and learning values to inform the practice that drives the choice of technology.

Case Study: Creating an Intentional Use of Technology Plan

The dean informs Blair, a master advisor, that the unit has received a grant to reach out and engage students who enroll in blended and distance learning courses. Recent survey results confirm the impressions that these students, as well as students taking traditional courses, spend less time on campus than their predecessors. This trend has called into question the delivery of all aspects of student services and support.

The original plan was based on a survey of a cross-section of campus students, and technology was grounded in a student-as-customer approach to advising. The dean has challenged Blair to rework the plan so that an advising-as-teaching approach is used to enhance engagement of the targeted students. Within a week of receiving this assignment, Blair needs to submit a short summary statement addressing the following questions:

o What are the academic advising goals for the unit?

o What types of technologies should the unit adopt to help achieve these goals?

o What advising goals may need to be revised to implement the advising-as-teaching plan?

o How can adoption of selected technologies help produce data needed to show student learning and assist with program assessment?

o How will the adoption of this plan affect training and professional development for advisors in the unit?

Intentional Use of Technology Model

NACADA recently posted the intentional use of technology model (Steele, 2014) to help practitioners recognize the inherent capabilities of different technologies. This technology selection model can help advisors choose the most appropriate technologies to achieve desired advising goals.

The model is based on an analysis of technology presentations at NACADA Annual Conferences from 1988 to 2012 (Steele, 2013). From the analysis of 485 regular conference sessions and the 52 preconference technology sessions, three types of technology emerged:

o Enterprise-level tools, such as student information systems (SIS) and degree audits, serve the entire institution. They are often used to provide institutional services through personalized student accounts.

o Communications technologies, including e-mail, social media, mobile technologies, and web conferencing, may or may not serve the entire institution. They facilitate advisor-to-student, student-to-student, and institution-to-student interactions among others.

o Web pages provide information in a variety of media formats.

Figure 16.1 shows overlap among these three technology groups in both function and structure. Although they maintain characteristics of their original fundamental design and capability, technologies have increasingly shared one or more characteristics of other types. For example, an SIS in the 1990s often relied on manually entered data to process course registrations. Now students use their phone (communication tool) and the Internet (web based) to register.

Figure 16.1. Regrouping of technologies

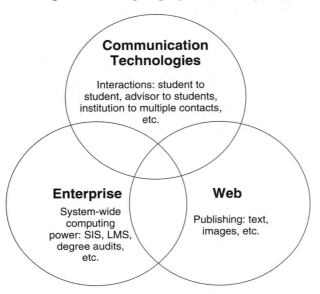

Technologies That Support Learning

The three technology groups intersect at the student portal, defined as "the online gateway where students can log into a school web site to access important program information" (Windsor, n.d., ¶1) (Figure 16.2). Within the portal, a number of campus-based tools, such as LMSs, e-portfolios, and early alert systems, inform the discussion of technology use for advising. Because they can be personalized to individual students, these program information tools in combination offer a robust learning platform for advisors to use in advancing an advising-as-teaching approach. The tools share the enterprise characteristics of institutional-wide data management, feature some form of web interface, and incorporate a number of communication tools.

Despite the obvious convenience and personalization, not all learning-platform tools are tied to the student portal, but they may expand access to learning, reporting, and communicating for students, teachers, and administrators. For example, advisors use e-mail and social media in contexts outside the portal to reach students and support their learning. However, institutional stakeholders must give special consideration to the safety and privacy of tools used outside a secure portal.

Although vendors declare security policies for their products, learning-platform tools available outside the student portal typically do not meet security measures that prevent unauthorized disclosure per institutional policies or legal requirements (e.g., Family Educational Rights and Privacy Act [U.S. Department of Education, n.d.]; Freedom of Information and Protection of Privacy Act [Office of the Privacy Commissioner of Canada, n.d.]) (chapter 8). For example, institution-sponsored

Figure 16.2. Technology grouping showing student portal and privacy and security line

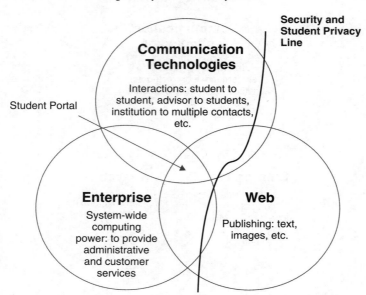

social media pages that do not require a login to access and many forms of e-mail do not offer protection from third-party access. The curved line drawn through the grouping of technologies in Figure 16.1, as shown in Figure 16.2, separates technologies compliant with student security and privacy measures and those that could pose threats to the privacy of student educational records or personal communications.

The security and student privacy line illustrated in Figure 16.2 shows the level of personal interaction that an advisor can pursue with a student and ensure basic privacy. If academic advising is teaching and students engage in self-assessment and development of their own academic and career plans as the goals of advising, limits on personal interactions between an advisor and advisee largely prohibit the type and quality of interactions that benefit students.

Technologies That Support Learning Outcomes

The intentional use of technology model (Steele, 2014) delineates three intended outcomes: service, engagement, and learning. In general, service outcomes are related to enterprise technologies, engagement outcomes are associated with web pages and some communication technologies, and learning outcomes are linked to learning platforms (Figure 16.3).

Service.   Service outcomes are reached through the use of technologies that provide access to campus resources through personalized student accounts such as SIS as well

Figure 16.3. Intentional use of technology model

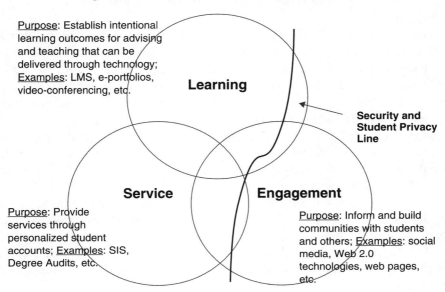

Purpose: Establish intentional learning outcomes for advising and teaching that can be delivered through technology; Examples: LMS, e-portfolios, video-conferencing, etc.

Learning

Security and Student Privacy Line

Service

Engagement

Purpose: Provide services through personalized student accounts; Examples: SIS, Degree Audits, etc.

Purpose: Inform and build communities with students and others; Examples: social media, Web 2.0 technologies, web pages, etc.

as degree audits and appointment schedulers. These technologies typically feature secure enterprise-level systems built on massive amounts of personal and institutional data; however, some are being transitioned from enterprise-level to cloud-based models (Kepes, 2012). These systems provide the foundation for institutional portals, which offer access to pertinent personal information and permit individuals to transact critical business within institutions (McCracken, 2005).

Service systems used in higher education feature characteristics similar to enterprise systems found in other industries, such as banks and airlines, in which persons enter secure sites and perform several tasks with communication tools as necessary. These systems allow users to perform numerous transactions and produce personalized results almost instantly. For scheduling courses, viewing available class sections, or comparing the requirements of different majors, students use these technologies to perform rudimentary cognitive functions that offer a reliable level of accuracy. These systems were introduced as labor-saving devices so that advisors could spend more quality time with their advisees.

Sophisticated service technologies using predictive analytics are coming to market. Predictive analytics are based on examination of extracted information from data sets to discover patterns and predict trends in student behaviors. For example, the Austin Peay State University (n.d.) program, Degree Compass, "pairs current students with the courses that best fit their talents and program of study for upcoming semesters" by using a "model [that] combines hundreds of thousands of past students' grades with each particular student's transcript to make individualized recommendations for each student" (¶1). The emergence of algorithms that purportedly dispense such wisdom lead some to conclude that academic advisors will become as necessary to higher education as blacksmiths have become to the transportation industry.

However, advisors not only teach students how to access and use these systems but they also teach them to evaluate critically the personalized results. The results that these systems produce for scheduling, appointments, degree audits, or course recommendations and the like simply provide information for students (Steele & Thurmond, 2009). As information gathering falls to the lowest level of cognitive functioning, as described by Bloom (1956), advisors must engage students to operate at higher cognitive levels through critiquing and understanding the personalized information produced by these systems. Students must consider results of analytics through an affective perspective to place appropriate value on them (Krathwohl, Bloom, & Masia, 1973).

A degree audit might show a student the most efficient way to graduate on time along with recommended courses to take, but this recommendation may not comport with the student's desired path. The question must be asked: Is the institution led by people interested in students' thoughts and values or by those who define *best* and *desired* solely in terms that advance a business-like efficiency to retention and completion efforts?

Engagement.   Through the intentional use of technology model, engagement goals relate to endeavors that inform and build virtual communities for increasing social networks with students and others in an institution. Strong communities have proven effective in supporting student retention and success (Habley, Valiga, McClanahan, & Burkum, 2010).

Types of technologies related to engagement fall on either side of the security and student privacy line identified in the model (Figure 16.3). For example, a secure version of a vendor's social media tools, which typically are used outside the institution portal, may be operationalized for security within the institutional portal. Tools such as wikis, instant messaging, and chat demonstrate this flexibility.

Advising practice is affected in cases when communication tools fall outside the security line depicted in Figure 16.3: for example, text-based static web pages that link to interactive communication tools, such as vendor-based social networking sites (e.g., Facebook, LinkedIn, and Pinterest), and Web 2.0 applications, such as wikis and photo-sharing platforms. These means of communication facilitate interactivity and expanded connectivity with students in a bound system. Furthermore, social media offer utility in addition to means to distribute top-down information. For example, Joosten, Pasquini, and Harness (2013) suggested that a platform should encourage all participants to contribute. Through these channels, public information can be shared through a series of social networks in which individuals can discuss, comment, share, and promote timely messages, concerns, and issues.

In addition, through these virtual communities, students may experience increased motivation (Cerdà & Planas, 2010). To instigate learning through interactions within communities of students, advisors can facilitate discussions, share important information, guard against the exchange of inaccurate information, and help maintain civil discourse. Use of social media can foster a type of learning that Eisner (1979) described as an *expressive outcome*: "the consequence of curriculum activities . . . intentionally planned to provide fertile fields for personal purpose and experience" (p. 103).

However, other considerations must balance the use of social media. First, more students use social networks for interacting with friends than for engaging in academic communications (Dahlstrom, 2012). Second, communication tools outside the institution's secure portal can only be used for sharing public information. Thus, critical advisor-advisee interactions, as defined by Gordon (1992), are minimized through such impersonal means (p. 53).

Learning. Outcomes compose a part of formal learning (Johnson, Pasquini, & Rodems, 2013). Through formal learning, students are expected to show, through both summative and formative evaluations, that they have mastered some content, developed a skill, produced a project, created a plan, or reflected on a topic or issue. A number of enterprise technologies within secure institutional portals can assist in this type of formal learning. Combined, many technologies can create robust learning platforms.

The most familiar technology used for learning, the LMS, combines space for publishing content, tools for evaluating learning, and venues for interaction within and construction of communities. However, advisors typically limit the use of LMSs for orientation and first-year experience courses (Steele, 2013).

The e-portfolio enables individuals to share examples of projects, ideas, and their best work by providing a platform for collecting and organizing artifacts. Most e-portfolio tools include evaluation and communication tools for instruction as well as means for students to demonstrate their learning through written reflection pieces and artifacts they have created (Chen & Black, 2010). Programs such as the State of Minnesota Goals + Planning = Success (GPS LifePlan) (Minnesota State Colleges and Universities, 2015) and the University of Notre Dame (2015) e-portfolio programs provide examples of self-assessments integrated with academic and career planning. LMSs and e-portfolios help structure the advising content in a manner that supports the pace of individual learners, thus partially fulfilling the goal of adaptive learning (Waters, 2014).

Mobile technologies, such as smartphones, tablets, and videoconferencing systems (with laptops and wireless networks) can extend advising sessions beyond a brick-and-mortar location. Whereas the LMS and e-portfolio rely on student products to demonstrate learning, advising through videoconferencing or smartphones depends on quality interactions with students as judged by an advisor. By integrating these systems, advisors can boost the institutional learning platform and provide a venue for multiple types of learning. Institutionally secure tools such as Web 2.0 applications, wikis, chat, and social media can be included in this configuration.

Like all paradigms, the intentional use of technology model (Steele, 2014) provides a generalized perspective to help users make sense of complex situations. The model proposes the ways the designs, functions, and limitations of different types of technologies align with the general advising outcomes of learning, service, and engagement. For realism, the model addresses the security and legal responsibilities of those working in higher education. It also helps advisors focus on student service, engagement, and learning. With regard to adopting and using technologies, advisors should be able to answer the following questions (among others):

o Do students know the reasons to use enterprise-level service technologies such as degree audits?

o When students use engagement technologies, such as social media, can they relate their experiences to other advising learning outcomes?

o Are students engaged in learning technologies, such as the LMS, challenged to integrate and reflect upon their experiences?

At its core, the intentional use of technology model promotes the view that using the best technology to achieve desired academic advising outcomes improves practice. It also provides a means of interpreting the way new technologies might best be associated with desired advising outcomes of service, learning, and engagement. The model puts forth ways in which technologies help advisors and students achieve objectives; it does not emphasize a sizzle factor. Through creative approaches, practitioners can integrate old and new technologies to achieve multiple academic advising outcomes. By embracing technologies in this thoughtful manner, those who support advising as teaching will better achieve, demonstrate, and promote their efforts and successes.

Learning Outcomes and Student Learning

The importance of learning outcomes to intentional, direct instruction for academic advising has been noted often over the past decade (e.g., Martin, 2007; Trabant, 2006) (chapter 14). McTighe and Wiggins (2012) provided a unique perspective, understanding by design (UbD), which has been implemented primarily by K–12 curriculum and instructional planners. Under UbD, educators establish goals for learning that achieve a level of enduring understanding rather than for mastery in knowledge or breadth of material. To arrive at an enduring understanding in advising practice at the postsecondary level, practitioners must consider institutional, national, and professional standards and they must honor the views of those in the advising community made up of primary-role advisors, faculty members, and administrators.

In brief, to determine learning objectives, planners establish a value-ranking approach. McTighe and Wiggins described a process of unifying learning outcomes with learning activities as *backward design* (chapter 14). First, planners identify long-term desired learning outcomes. Second, they must select the evidence that demonstrates student learning. The third and final step involves choosing instruction and activity that align with the first two steps. This approach contrasts with one in which individual activities are undertaken without consideration about their fit with learning goals in the advising syllabus or curriculum or in which a post hoc evaluation of learning is completed (Steele, 2015).

Content Creation and Technologies for Academic Advising

By applying UbD as described by McTighe and Wiggins (2012) to educational and career planning processes, advisors can integrate many established practices with technology. For example, Gordon (1992) created a four-part conceptual guide used for developing learning outcomes and curricular modules in academic and career exploration; it features self-assessment, educational information, career information, and decision making (p. 75). Through the intentional use of technology model, one can easily create content units and modules in an LMS that address each of Gordon's components for exploration. The content modules could be titled *exploration* and the submodules called *self-assessment*, *educational information*, *career information*, and *decision making*. The three key advantages of using technology to advance Gordon's career decision-making model include:

o The content remains in the protected area of the student portal.

o The material can be arranged in a coherent and focused fashion for convenient access (students need not surf all over the Internet for the information).

o Tools to evaluate student learning can be tied to the intended learning outcome for each module; for example, students can demonstrate their learning of the exploration process with other technologies, such as an e-portfolio system.

Creating curricular modules by utilizing the engagement and service technologies based on the intentional use of technology model, an advisor can generate opportunities that encourage student in-depth understanding of the planning process. For example, through social media tools, students can conduct informational interviews with alumni willing to share their career experiences or seniors about the reasons they selected their majors.

Technology offers a new twist to an old practice. In the 1980s, Gordon (1992) assembled groups of alumni and seniors every year to act as informational resources. In the mid-1990s, this student–alumni networking was conducted through the University College at The Ohio State University by e-mail. Now, people can connect more easily through social media tools than through e-mail. Evaluation exercises for such a social-media networking activity might be directed at helping students develop deeper understanding and clearer meaning of the effective planning processes. For example, students submit a reflection paper on the informational interviews through the LMS such that a digital copy of their efforts and the evaluation of it can be added to and maintained in a portfolio. These data maintain the history of a student's learning, and collectively, these records form the foundation for a program assessment.

The degree audit system offers another service technology related to the exploration process. Students can submit several different degree audit reports to show how their proposed educational planning routes might vary in terms of programs and time to completion. They upload the created planning documents to an LMS to demonstrate their ability in using degree audit technology and submit an accompanying reflection paper describing interpretations of the audit to show their understanding of it.

The networking and degree audit examples illustrate that the integration of technologies across the service, engagement, and learning experience provides for a robust way to organize the self-assessment, educational and career information, and decision-making components that Gordon (1992) identified for student exploration. Each technology offers specialized and intentional features that help advisors develop a rich learning environment. By coordinating the tools in creative ways, advisors can better assist students in achieving levels of deeper learning and understanding.

Of course, the usefulness of content units and modules extends beyond the exploration process. A content unit created for student success might include modules addressing study skills, campus resources, use of technology, students' rights and responsibilities, and time management. Another appropriate content unit relates to campus engagement with modules on campus extracurricular activities, student groups, and learning circles. Community college students may benefit from a module on transfer, and graduate students would likely appreciate a unit on writing the thesis or dissertation.

Most institutions use a cross-section of technologies from the service and engagement categories to promote and provide services and resources (Steele, 2013). Through content units and modules in various technologies, advisors integrate services and resources that can be evaluated to show an individual's understanding of and meaning applied to learning. At a metacognitive level, programs such as the Goals + Planning = Success (GPS LifePlan) (Minnesota Colleges and Universities, 2015) and the University of Notre Dame e-portfolio programs (2015) address both student success and campus engagement because students document reflections on their experiences in a tool other than an LMS.

The creation of content units and modules need not fall to a single advising unit or an individual campus effort. The nonprofit organization Creative Commons (CC) (n.d.) offers advisors a means to collaborate safely by addressing important legal issues. CC offers free copyright licenses to provide standardized permissions for the public to share and use creative works. By collaborating, advisors can adopt and disseminate content regarding a multitude of topics typical of an advising curriculum. Beyond academic and career planning, they can use units or modules to present information on studying, learning, developing critical-thinking skills, managing time, using the library, or understanding student rights and responsibilities. Although adapting content to local practice is required, the general framework for content collaboration through CC helps everyone.

New methods of delivery and content will continue to emerge, and some approaches will give advisors less control over creation of content. For example, some vendor-based solutions, such as e-textbooks, offer a top-down implementation strategy. Many electronic versions of traditionally printed books incorporate multimedia and can be read in various ways, such as with a computer, tablet, LMS, e-reader, or mobile device.

The future of another potential advising mechanism, MOOCs (massive open online courses), remains unclear because the definition of them is evolving. MOOCs were originally described as web-based distance learning courses designed for access by many students distributed over wide geographic areas. As originally proposed, a star faculty member designs the content with the understanding that student learning is predominantly self-paced because of the high student–teacher ratio. Vendors most associated with MOOCs are Coursera, Udacity, and edX.

Those supporting an advising-as-teaching approach rightfully express concerns with the MOOCs model, as it now stands, applied to academic advising. The concept of providing high-quality content to many students at a dramatically reduced cost is appealing to those advocating a short-term cost-savings model; however, the cost of adopting MOOCs must be assessed through the long term of student retention, success, and satisfaction.

A cautionary position seems prudent in light of the mixed results of the research on MOOC effectiveness reported by Straumsheim (2014). However, the use of CC and MOOCs allows on-campus professionals to adapt informational content created by others and apply it to their own programing missions and goals.

Advising-as-Teaching Approach

Creating a digital learning environment can facilitate a flipped classroom approach for advising in which "the core idea is to flip the common instructional approach: With teacher-created videos and interactive lessons, instruction that used to occur in class is now accessed at home, in advance of class" (Tucker, 2012, p. 82). When they use institutional learning platform technologies to create curricular units and modules, advisors demonstrate the flipped classroom approach; that is, students prepare their educational plans before the advising session through rich multimedia resources. Time in the advising session, whether conducted face-to-face or virtually, is dedicated to higher order cognitive and affective domain questions addressed through the advisor–advisee interaction (Bloom, 1956; Krathwohl et al., 1973).

According to the intentional use of technology model, service-oriented technologies, such as degree audits, provide students with personalized information about educational planning. Degree audits offer a high-tech approach to the work a good advisor performs when helping students with planning. With degree audit reports included in the advising session, the advisor directs the advisee to explore the higher order cognitive and affective elements of the information. From an affective focus, in particular, they can concentrate on examining the underlying values inherent in courses or programs suggested by the audit report to help students determine if they reflect personal values, life goals, and passions. This personalized process comports with students' development of their own human capital (chapter 9) and encourages the integration of academic and career advising; specifically, students learn to identify their skills, knowledge, and values to direct their own careers.

Examples of student planning enhanced, in a holistic way, with the assistance of modules in an LMS include the following:

o Content modules can be created with local institutional considerations primarily addressed, such as educational programs and campus resources and services.

o With the ability to create relatively inexpensive vodcasts and podcasts, advisors can generate content guides in the LMS to help students identify critical information and learn the planning process. Students also can use multimedia for creating plans and demonstrating their learning. Examples of multimedia tools include, but are not limited to, surveys and Web 2.0 features such as wikis and blogs (Pasquini, 2010; Steele, 2006).

o Because the LMS e-mail or video tools offer secure communications, advisors can respond easily to student requests for help; that is, students need not make an appointment to ask questions or seek assistance.

o Evaluation tools within the LMS help students organize their learning. In 2014, Smith Jaggars, Fletcher, and Little proposed the use of combined learning technologies to facilitate integration of the student experience. They argued that such an approach can help identify areas of student struggle caused by excessive complexities in the academic decision-making process. This evaluation-as-learning method leads to two important consequences: It can help advisors determine whether students have actively engaged or experienced difficulties in the learning process.

o Students can share their information and explorations through a constructivist process with other students through social media (Mbati, 2013). In this manner, social media can be used to help support informal learning by showcasing students' successful efforts for other students to see (Johnson et al., 2013).

o Students can complete assignments in nontraditional ways. Although modules can be easily aligned to any course or workshop (with appropriate academic credit), students can work on them when most appropriate—at the advisable moment.

Before considering new technologies, master advisors need to determine whether implementation will force traditional-aged, community college, or graduate students to rely on fewer one-to-one, in-person advising sessions for serious interactions. One could argue that within the secure learning platform, the opportunity for virtual and group advising approaches may create opportunities to assign peer advisors as overseers of some tasks or ask students to work in a peer-to-peer environment. In short, by digitizing content, practitioners can flexibly modify the approach, time, and delivery of advising while monitoring students' progress and successes in achieving advising program outcomes.

Technology and Program Assessment

The use of big data and predictive analytics to address student retention and completion issues will likely appeal to many higher education institutions. As an explanation, Eduventures (2013) suggested that "colleges and universities can deploy predictive analytics to determine which students are most at risk for attrition and—armed with deep, historical data—craft segment-specific retention strategies designed to compel them to persist toward degree completion" (p. 3).

The interest in related methodologies is illustrated in the growth of organizations such as the Predictive Analytics Reporting (PAR) Framework (n.d.) and in enterprise-level designs, often called *early alert systems*. A 501(c)(3) entity and representative of this type of group, PAR promotes learner analytics as a service to its membership. PAR is composed of a cross-section of institutional types that address retention and completion issues by identifying effective practices that support students' progress toward their academic goals. PAR claims to focus on practices such as comparative benchmarking and localized predictive modeling as well as linking predictions of risks to interventions used at each point in the college-completion life cycle.

Early alert technologies perform predictive analytics to support student retention and completion efforts. These tools integrate big data from throughout the institution's systems to define and target student populations. For example, the SIS may be used to consider demographic and educational history information; scheduling systems can be used to review data about use of campus services and access to specific events; the LMS could provide information on class attendance behaviors. Results guide development of specific student interventions and align them with staff support agents, including those in advising roles. A formal feedback system helps to deliver positive and often personal messages to audience members for action and a means of keeping continuous communication with selected students receiving services.

The integration of an early alert system with student evaluation data from advising modules enables data gathering for process delivery outcomes (PDOs) and student learning outcomes (SLOs) (Aiken-Wisniewski et al., 2010; Campbell, Nutt, Robbins, Kirk-Kuwaye, & Higa, 2005; Robbins, 2009, 2011) (chapters 14 and 15). Robbins and Zarges (2011) described the importance of differentiating PDOs and SLOs for program assessments in advising. PDOs "are anchored in the academic advising interaction, are concerned with what occurs and what information is exchanged during that interaction" (¶9). "SLOs are the statements which articulate what students are expected to know (cognitive learning), do (behavioral learning), and value (affective learning) as a result of their involvement in the academic advising experience" (¶9). Data for SLOs are generally not utilized in early alert systems.

Aggregated student evaluations for SLOs in program assessment advance advising as teaching. In the past, when relying on only face-to-face advising sessions, advisors experienced difficulty acquiring data for SLOs. They witnessed learning, but the interaction yielded few data. The lack of uniformity makes advising notes, which offer much information, difficult data resources for use in program assessments. By contrast, early alert systems, deeply integrated in the institutional learning platforms that support advising modules, yield rich dividends. For example, many researchers have compared the retention and completion rates of students who attended advising sessions, individually or in a group, to those of students who received no advising (Center for Public Education, 2012).

By using the learning platform with modules related to retention and completion, advisors can focus on individual experiences and those of student groups. The technology provides a natural feedback loop to drive modifications to modules to make them more effective. More important, by embracing the use of the learning platform, advisors can more fully assess the positive claims that advising is teaching and continuously improve the approach and delivery.

Using SLO data in program assessment may help determine whether students learned from advisors' teaching as well as the impact of the learned information on retention and completion. Also, SLO data may provide insight into whether students who had learned specific SLOs would consequently require interventions for these same issues later in their academic careers. Such data would also provide information on ways that a curriculum or module should be adjusted in scope and sequence.

Implications for Advisor Training and Professional Development

The future direction of technology and academic advising relates to training and professional development (chapter 13). Bryant, Chagani, Endres, and Galvin (2006) distinguished training from professional development: Training allows advisors to execute their job functions more effectively; professional development confers a range of skills that promote advisor maturation throughout their careers. Using this distinction, training—which advisors generally receive during the first year of their employment—should focus on effective use of the technologies offered by an institution, such as those within and outside the student portal. This technology training should be undertaken within the broader conceptual framework of advising as teaching. As McClellan (2007) argued, technology training for advisors should not occur in isolation from the informational, conceptual, and relational components of training. Professional development activities for technology and advising, by contrast, are enhanced when recipients consider topics such as instructional design, student evaluation, program assessment, and learning theory.

Advisors and those interested in improving technological applications to advance the advising-as-teaching model would benefit from working with personnel in a local instructional design program or by gaining familiarity with Internet programs such as Quality Matters (n.d.). Finally, with greater reliance on the use of predictive analytical tools, advisors will need preparation in interpreting reports of advising research in light of their institutional vision, mission, retention, and completion goals.

The suggested topics for professional development should help master advisors evaluate emerging technologies with the perspective of an advising-as-teaching model. Not all technologies are designed to assist in this effort, but by remaining true to the NACADA Statement of Core Values of Academic Advising (NACADA, 2005), master advisors can build (and assist in building) technology-rich environments designed to improve student success. Those interested in directing change through advising and technology adopt learning platforms that advance advising as teaching. Rather than focusing on the next set of shiny technology objects that might catch one's eye for a short period, advisors can embrace existing technologies on campus, as well as those on the horizon, for supporting student learning. Although novel technologies should be explored and shared for application in advising, the intentional use of technology for promoting student learning should be emphasized and valued.

Aiming for Excellence

- In a widely quoted statement, Schneier (2013) posted, "Surveillance is the business model of the Internet." How does Schneier's view that privacy on the Internet is a pipe dream raise challenges to those who want to use technology to support an advising-as-teaching model?

- The increasing cost of higher education, along with hikes in student debt, will create the following situation, as described by Clayton Christensen (2014) of the Harvard Business School: "Fifteen years from now more than half of the universities in America will be in bankruptcy" (p. 21). If Professor Christensen's projections are accurate, how would more stringent economic conditions affect adoption of technology to advance an advising-as-teaching model?

- What new or evolving technologies have been recently introduced on your campus? How can these technologies be integrated into an intentional use of technology model (engagement, services, and learning) to promote advising as teaching?

- How would you respond to an advisor who, with great enthusiasm, wants to use a new social media tool with students?

- Technology, along with other factors, will likely lead to the evolution of five work profiles for full-time academic advisors (Steele, 2006):

  - as call-center personnel,

  - as part of financial aid and admissions,

  - as professional with a career path,

  - partly unchanged with portions of advising outsourced, or

  - unchanged.

o What changes do you expect to affect advising practice? How is technology influencing this change?

o In chapter 6, Karen Archambault addresses many different types of advisees. Describe ways that technology could enhance your ability to engage two or three of the student cohorts you advise. How should technology be adjusted for the different populations in a teaching-as-learning approach?

o In chapter 13, Julie Givans Voller outlines use of individual professional development plans (IPDPs) and the portfolio to organize, direct, and provide a platform for reflection of professional development activities by advisors. What technology goals will you consider adding to an IPDP?

References

Aiken-Wisniewski, S., Campbell, S., Nutt, C., Robbins, R., Kirk-Kuwaye, M., & Higa, L. (2010). *Guide to assessment in academic advising* (2nd ed.) (Monograph No. 23). Manhattan, KS: The National Academic Advising Association.

Allen, I. E., & Seaman, J. (2014). *Grade change: Tracking online education in the United States*. Retrieved from http://www.onlinelearningsurvey.com/reports/gradechange.pdf

Austin Peay State University. (n.d.). *Degree compass and my future*. Retrieved from http://www.apsu.edu/academic-affairs/degree-compass-and-my-future

Bloom B. S. (1956). *Taxonomy of educational objectives, handbook I: The cognitive domain*. New York, NY: David McKay.

Bryant, R., Chagani, A., Endres, J., & Galvin. J. (2006). *Professional growth for advisors: Strategies for building professional advising networks*. Retrieved from http://www. nacada.ksu.edu/Resources/Clearinghouse/View-Articles/Building-professional-advising-networks.aspx

Campbell, S., Nutt, C., Robbins, R., Kirk-Kuwaye, M., & Higa, L. (2005). *NACADA guide to assessment in academic advising*. Manhattan, KS: National Academic Advising Association.

Center for Public Education. (2012). *High school rigor and good advice: Setting up students to succeed (at a glance)*. Retrieved from http://www.centerforpubliceducation.org/ Main-Menu/Staffingstudents/High-school-rigor-and-good-advice-Setting-up-students-to-succeed

Cerdà, F. L., & Planas, N. C. (2010). Facebook's potential for collaborative e-learning. *Revista de Univerisidad y Sociedad del Conocimiento, 8*(2), 197–210.

Chen, H., & Black, T. C. (2010, December). Using e-portfolios to support an undergraduate learning career: An experiment with academic advising. *Educause Review*. Retrieved from http://www.educause.edu/ero/article/using-e-portfolios-support-undergraduate-learning-career-experiment-academic-advising

Christensen, C. (2014, June 28). Creative destruction. *The Economist*. Retrieved from http://www.economist.com/news/leaders/21605906-cost-crisis-changing-labour-markets-and-new-technology-will-turn-old-institution-its

Creative Commons. (n.d.). [Home page]. Retrieved from http://creativecommons.org

Dahlstrom, E. (2012, September). *ECAR study of undergraduate students and information technology, 2012*. Louisville, CO: EDUCAUSE Center for Applied Research. Retrieved from http://www.educause.edu/library/resources/ecar-study-undergraduate-students-and-information-technology-2012

Eduventures. (2013). *Predictive analytics in higher education: Data-driven decision-making for the student life cycle*. Retrieved from http://www.eduventures.com/wp-content/uploads/2013/02/Eduventures_Predictive_Analytics_White_Paper1.pdf

Eisner, E. W. (1979). *The educational imagination: On the design and evaluation of school programs*. New York, NY: Macmillan.

Gates, B. (n.d.). [Quote]. Retrieved from http://www.brainyquote.com/quotes/quotes/b/billgates390682.html

Gordon, V. N. (1992). *Handbook of academic advising*. Westport, CT: Greenwood.

Habley, W., Valiga, R., McClanahan, K., & Burkum, K. (2010). *What works in student retention?* (Research report). Iowa City, IA: ACT.

Hemwall, M. K., & Trachte, K. C. (2003). Academic advising and a learning paradigm. In M. K. Hemwall & K. C. Trachte (Eds.), *Advising and learning: Academic advising from the perspective of small colleges and universities* (Monograph No. 8) (pp. 13–20). Manhattan, KS: National Academic Advising Association.

Johnson, M. L., Pasquini, L. A., & Rodems, M. R. (2013). Connecting first year students to formal and informal learning. In H. H. Yang & S. Wang (Eds.), *Cases on formal and informal e-learning environments: Opportunities and practices*. Hershey, PA: IGI Global.

Joosten, T., Pasquini, L., & Harness, L. (2013). Guiding social media at our institutions. *Society for College and University Planning—Integrated Planning for Higher Education, 41*(2), 1–11. Retrieved from http://www.slideshare.net/LauraPasquini/guiding-social-media-at-our-institutions

Kepes, B. (2012, October 30). *On cloud and disruption* [web log post]. Retrieved from http://www.rackspace.com/blog/on-cloud-and-disruption/

Krathwohl, D. R., Bloom, B. S., & Masia, B. B. (1973). *Taxonomy of educational objectives, the classification of educational goals. Handbook II: Affective domain*. New York, NY: David McKay.

Lowenstein, M. (2005). If advising is teaching, what do advisors teach? *NACADA Journal, 25*(2), 65–73.

Lumina Foundation. (2014). *Equity imperative*. Retrieved from http://www.lumina foundation.org/publications/Equity_Imperative.pdf

Martin, H. (2007). *Constructing learning objectives for academic advising*. Retrieved from http://www.nacada.ksu.edu/Resources/Clearinghouse/View-Articles/Constructing-student-learning-outcomes.aspx

Mbati, L. (2013). Online social media applications for constructivism and observational learning. *The International Review of Research in Open and Distributed Learning, 14*(5). Retrieved from http://www.irrodl.org/index.php/irrodl/article/view/1579/2709

McClellan, J. L. (2007). *Content components for advisor training: Revisited*. Retrieved from http://www.nacada.ksu.edu/Resources/Clearinghouse/View-Articles/Advisor-Training-Components.aspx

McCracken, H. (2005). Web-based academic support services: Guidelines for extensibility. *Online Journal of Distance Learning Administration, 8*(3). Retrieved from http://www.westga.edu/~distance/ojdla/fall83/mccracken83.pdf

McTighe, J., & Wiggins, G. (2012). *Understanding by design framework*. Retrieved from http://jaymctighe.com/wordpress/wp-content/uploads/2011/04/UbD_WhitePaper_revised_0612-FINAL.pdf

Minnesota State Colleges and Universities. (2015). [Home page]. Retrieved from http://www.gpslifeplan.org/

NACADA: The Global Community for Academic Advising (NACADA). (2005). *NACADA statement of core values of academic advising*. Retrieved from https://www.nacada.ksu.edu/Resources/Clearinghouse/View-Articles/Core-values-of-academic-advising.aspx

NACADA. (2006). *NACADA concept of academic advising*. Retrieved from http://www.nacada.ksu.edu/Resources/Clearinghouse/View-Articles/Concept-of-Academic-Advising-a598.aspx

Office of the Privacy Commissioner of Canada. (n.d.). *Freedom of information and protection of privacy act* (FIPPA). Retrieved from https://www.priv.gc.ca/resource/fs-fi/02_05_d_15_e.asp

Pasquini, L. A. (2010). Emerging digital resources: Easy and accessible online tools. In J. Voller, M. A. Miller, & S. L. Nest. (Eds.), *Comprehensive advisor training and development: Practices that deliver* (Monograph No. 21) (pp. 123–129). Manhattan, KS: National Academic Advising Association.

Pasquini, L. A. (2013). *NACADA 2013 national technology survey*. Unpublished manuscript, University of Northern Texas, Dalton, TX.

Predictive Analytics Reporting (PAR) Framework. (n.d.). *About*. Retrieved from http://www.parframework.org/about-par/

Quality Matters. (n.d.). [Home page]. Retrieved from https://www.qualitymatters.org/

Robbins, R. (2009). Evaluation and assessment of career advising. In K. Hughey, D. Burton Nelson, J. Damminger, & B. McCalla-Wriggins (Eds.), *Handbook of career advising* (pp. 266–292). San Francisco, CA: Jossey-Bass.

Robbins, R. (2011). Assessment and accountability. In J. Joslin & N. Markee (Eds.), *Academic advising administration: Essential knowledge and skills for the 21st century* (Monograph No. 20) (pp. 53–64). Manhattan, KS: National Academic Advising Association.

Robbins, R., & Zarges, K. M. (2011). *Assessment of academic advising: A summary of the process*. Retrieved from http://www.nacada.ksu.edu/Resources/Clearinghouse/View-Articles/Assessment-of-academic-advising.aspx

Schneider, M. (2010). *Finishing the first lap: The cost of first-year student attrition in America's four-year colleges and universities*. Retrieved from http://www.air.org/sites/default/files/AIR_Schneider_Finishing_the_First_Lap_Oct101.pdf

Schneier, B. (2013, November 25). *Schneier on security: Surveillance as a business model* [web log post]. Retrieved from https://www.schneier.com/blog/archives/2013/11/surveillance_as_1.html

Smith Jaggars, S., Fletcher, J., & Little, J. (2014). Simplifying complexity in student experience. *Community College Research Center*. Retrieved from http://ccrc.tc.columbia.edu/publications/simplifying-complexity-student-experience.html

Steele, G. (2006). Five possible future work profiles for full-time academic advisors. *NACADA Journal, 26*(2), 48–64.

Steele, G. (2013, October). *Technology and academic advising: Where have we been these past 25 years?* Session presented at the annual meeting of the NACADA, Salt Lake City, UT.

Steele, G. E. (2014). *Intentional use of technology for academic advising*. Retrieved from http://www.nacada.ksu.edu/Resources/Clearinghouse/View-Articles/Intentional-use-of-technology-for-academic-advising.aspx

Steele, G. E. (2015). *Using technology for intentional student evaluation and program assessment*. Retrieved from http://www.nacada.ksu.edu/Resources/Clearinghouse/View-Articles/Using-Technology-for-Evaluation-and-Assessment.aspx

Steele, G. E., & Thurmond, K. (2009). Academic advising in a virtual university. *New Directions for Higher Education, 2009*(146), 85–95. doi:10.1002/he.349

Straumsheim, C. (2014). *Data, data everywhere*. Retrieved from http://www.insidehighered.com/news/2014/06/10/after-grappling-data-mooc-research-initiative-participants-release-results#sthash.xYev6iBl.dpbs

Trabant, T. D. (2006). *Advising Syllabus 101*. Retrieved from http://www.nacada.ksu.edu/Resources/Clearinghouse/View-Articles/Creating-an-Advising-Syllabus.aspx

Tucker, B. (2012, winter). *The flipped classroom: Online instruction at home frees class time for learning. Education Next*, 82–83. Retrieved from http://educationnext.org/files/ednext_20121_BTucker.pdf

University of Notre Dame. (2015). *ePortfolio@ND*. Retrieved from http://eportfolio.nd.edu/

U.S. Department of Education. (n.d.). *Family educational rights and privacy act (FERPA)*. Retrieved from http://www2.ed.gov/policy/gen/guid/fpco/ferpa/index.html

U.S. Department of Education. (2012). *Promising and practical strategies to increase postsecondary success*. Retrieved from http://www.ed.gov/college-completion/promising-strategies

Varney, J. (2009). *Strategies for success in distance advising*. Retrieved https://www.nacada.ksu.edu/Resources/Clearinghouse/View-Articles/Distance-advising-strategies.aspx

Waters, J. K. (2014). *Adaptive learning: Are we there yet?* Retrieved from http://thejournal.com/articles/2014/05/14/adaptive-learning-are-we-there-yet.aspx

Windsor, S. (n.d.). *What is a student portal?* Retrieved from http://www.ehow.com/facts_7331470_student-portal_.html

17

EXTERNAL CONDITIONS THAT INFLUENCE THE PRACTICE OF MASTER ACADEMIC ADVISORS

Thomas J. Grites

The future isn't what it used to be.

—Anonymous

Higher education has probably changed more rapidly in the past decade than in the entire previous century. These changes have not always been stimulated by introspective analyses but by pressures and demands from sources outside the academy. Master advisors remain abreast of these external conditions and sources and bring them to the attention of all who directly engage students. Several significant conditions could change the fundamental nature of the academic advising process; therefore, master advisors must stay current with social, economic, and political forces. The chapter provides strategies, resources, and examples of the conditions resulting from the completion agenda, legislative and political activity, and the debate about the worth of college.

Reader Learning Outcomes

From studying this chapter, advisors will use knowledge gained about the influences on higher education and academic advising to

o identify at least one unfamiliar external condition that could influence day-to-day advising;

o identify at least three new sources of information or data affecting internal or external conditions in higher education and on academic advising;

o identify at least one new source for reviewing research or commentary on external conditions;

o develop a plan or strategy for communicating the potential impact of evolving agendas, regulations, and policies to academic advisors, advising administrators, and other campus constituencies;

o design professional development activities to introduce and discuss the impact of conditions inside and outside the academy;

o suggest action plans to address changes to higher education and academic advising; and

o review policies, procedures, and programs for their current applicability and effectiveness vis-à-vis the potential effects created by the external conditions.

In his essay, "The Miseducation of America," William Deresiewicz (2014), summarized the movie *Ivory Tower* by describing how the American public and the higher education community are influenced by media sound bites that continually offer reminders of a wavering, eroding, or failing system of higher education. He observed that the system is squeezed between two monetary conditions: rising tuition costs on the front end and increasing student loan debt at the back end when students' educational pursuits are completed, interrupted, or delayed. These conditions make the work of academic advisors critical to students between these end points.

In another report on the future of higher education, Henry, Pagano, Puckett, and Wilson (2014) identified five trends—all based on monetary considerations—that higher educators must address:

o diminishing revenues from the primary sources (tuition and public funding);

o demands for a greater return on investment in the higher education enterprise;

o demand for demonstration of student outcomes;

o development of new delivery models (online education, 3-year degrees, industry accreditations); and

o accelerated globalization in the recruitment of international students and in the establishment of campuses abroad.

These developments are evolving as stakeholders address the rising costs and funding shortfalls as well as ensure that the quality of the "product" is expediently realized.

Academic advisors are often charged with helping ensure student completion in a timely manner; however, advisors rarely create the conditions under which they must function, which typically originate outside the academic advising process. Advisors must anticipate and adjust to the conditions that arise, advocate for students, and perform with the highest standards in the situation encountered. Master advisors demonstrate their awareness of current conditions and engage in professional development to ensure that they meet these responsibilities.

Academic advisors must know available new technologies, understand alternative financing strategies, and identify the new sources of academic credit being created (e.g., MOOCs [massive open online courses], badges, and other competency-based recognitions). Master advisors enter the debate about the value of higher education that often arises during weak economic conditions and includes topics on employer demands, accreditor expectations, and the rapidly growing debts student accrue.

The conditions and the data reported in this book frequently change. Therefore, to be better informed and to see additional examples and updates, readers are directed to the Clearinghouse of Academic Advising Resources from NACADA: The Global Community for Academic Advising, *The Chronicle of Higher Education* (CHE), *Inside Higher Education* (IHE), and *Academic Impressions* (AI).

The Completion Agenda

In an address to a joint session of Congress on February 24, 2009, President Barack Obama announced his goal for postsecondary education: "By 2020, America will once again have the highest proportion of college graduates in the world" (The White House, 2009, ¶66). This goal is called *the completion agenda*. In the same year as President Obama set the bar for 2020, the Lumina Foundation (2009) established Goal 2025: "to increase the proportion of Americans with high-quality college degrees, certificates or other credentials to 60% by 2025" (¶1). Together these objectives set the target for the United States to return to its once-held status as the most-educated society in the world as measured through awards of new degrees and certificates. These agendas have driven much of the recent and rapid change in higher education.

Completion goals have shaped various efforts in higher education and as a result some institutions have called for enhanced academic advising efforts (McPhail, 2011). Recently, academic advising has emerged as a key factor in the student retention necessary for completion (Klepfer & Hull, 2012), which stands as the most important higher education outcome sought in the United States.

Meeting the completion agenda means that students persist to completion. If students are not retained, they cannot persist to graduation. However, aggregated 2- and 4-year retention and graduation rates have not changed much over the years (ACT, 2015b). In fact, Tinto (1982) reported that 4-year completion rates have hovered below 60% since 1880! These data do not indicate that higher education will meet the completion agenda goal without expanding the measurement of completion (Shapiro et al., 2013; Shapiro, Dundar, Yuan, Harrell, & Wakhungu, 2014). The total completion rate recognizes students who graduated from any institution; that is, they completed a degree somewhere. The Student Achievement Measure (2013) was introduced as a tool for viewing institutional progress as a total completion rate, which includes the previously unrecognized student populations of part-time, transfer, and continuing students.

To meet the completion agenda, academic advisors help students negotiate new degree plans when circumstances change. Academic advisors promote the quality of the student's complete education, as described by Lowenstein (2007), even when the advisee's only goal is earning the degree. Master advisors stay abreast of changing academic policies and know of learning opportunities created on campus. They also recognize the importance of the expected outcomes of their work, even if these outcomes are imposed and defined by others' agendas. Master advisors frequently consult the aforementioned sources. Additionally, master advisors review the Lumina Foundation annual reports of the progress made on Goal 2025.

Enrollment Patterns

A significant factor that affects the completion agenda, but not always acknowledged, is the number of students attending postsecondary institutions during the time lines established for these goals. This number remains unknown and unpredictable. Students initiate the matriculation process as they decide to attend college and subsequently determine the timing and preferred institution for application. Most 4-year institutions measure both the quantity and the quality of the students they invite to enroll; however, most 2-year institutions follow open enrollment policies so the numbers enrolled is neither controlled nor restricted. Parameters may vary (domestically and internationally) according to a series of marketplace conditions, including the number of potential students likely to matriculate, the costs of attending college, institutional capacities, and funding expectations. The uncertain student numbers and demographics make the academic advisor's job more complex.

Although nearly 3 million more U.S. college students are expected to enroll in 2022 than attended in 2014, this figure represents a 30% smaller growth rate than the one describing the previous decade (Hussar & Bailey, 2013; National Student Clearinghouse Research Center, 2014; Noel-Levitz, 2014). Even more significant, the racial and ethnic makeup of these students will continue to increase diversity on campus. Hussar and Bailey (2013) projected increases of 7% for White and Asian/ Pacific Islander students and increases of 26 to 27% for Black and Hispanic students, respectively.

Furthermore, the U.S. Department of Education (2011) reported that 66% of college students transfer institutions before earning a baccalaureate degree, and the National Student Clearinghouse Research Center (2014) reported that 9% of all students attended more than one institution in the same year. These alternative pathways have enabled students to move as desired or necessary to complete a degree. A nonlinear pathway to a college degree has emerged with some certainty from these recent developments.

Although most academic advisors are not held responsible for the recruitment of new students, they play a significant role in their ultimate success (Klepfer & Hull, 2012; Ross & Kena, 2012). In fact, the enrollment management function at many institutions relies on the work of academic advisors as they help students navigate the curriculum, course offerings, supportive resources, opportunities, and expectations of the institution, which Lowenstein (2007) described as helping "students understand the structure or logic of their entire education" (¶5).

With every change in enrollment patterns, the academic advisors' role becomes more complicated and more easily influenced by factors beyond their control. Lower enrollments may result in lost positions or added responsibilities and expectations;

higher enrollments may mean larger workloads but no new resources. Master advisors remain aware of projected enrollment patterns for their institutions so that they can assist all students in crafting their educational plans for success. Master academic advisors should also regularly access the National Student Clearinghouse Research Center and the National Center for Educational Statistics for periodic reports on current and projected enrollment patterns.

Legislative and Political Agendas

"Societal expectations and public resources for higher education are undergoing fundamental shifts" (Zusman, 2005, ¶1) in the 21st century, and these changes often stimulate legislators to propose and adopt a wide variety of actions modifying higher education. Thus, master advisors must remain aware of legislation being considered on the local, state, province, and national levels. Some may react to legislative actions with "It's about time!" and hope that governing entities will pay attention to the efforts expended in higher education. Others may feel that legislative actions are proposed and approved without sufficient consultation with the institutional administrators charged with their implementation and shout, "Wait a minute!"

Although far removed from politically motivated propositions, master advisors need to stay abreast of policy considerations in legislatures to be informed and prepared to take necessary specific actions for compliance. Perhaps even more important, master advisors need to inform their national and state (province) legislators of the potential good or bad consequences of specific actions being considered.

The National Level

The most significant federal legislation affecting U.S. colleges and universities is the 50-year-old umbrella Higher Education Act of 1965 (HEA) that governs federal student and institutional aid. Like similar laws in other countries (e.g., The Swedish Higher Education Act of 1992), the HEA is periodically renewed and was last proposed for reauthorization in 2014. Regulations pertaining to a number of conditions within the U.S. higher education framework—Pell grants, student loan debt, accountability measures, accreditation regulations, a unit-record data and tracking system, and teacher preparation—are embedded in the law. One example of U.S. federal legislative actions that could affect academic advisors in any reauthorization, the gainful employment rule, has already been applied in many technical programs in community colleges.

The gainful employment rule was introduced into the U.S. legislative agenda in 2009, but several legal challenges were issued and two revisions made. One revision (Gainful Employment, 2014) added subtle language that could be significant for academic advisors: "whether certain educational programs prepare students for gainful employment in a recognized occupation" (¶1). A similar movement is under way at both the federal and province levels in Canada (Chiose, 2015).

The subtle message found in the U.S. legislation implies that all academic programs could be measured based on postgraduation performance. The metrics are based on projections of specific majors to confer opportunities for employment such that the graduate can repay federal loans and on determinations of the major program as worthy of federal grants. In the face of these measures, how should advisors respond to a student who wants to follow a passion for a particular major for which "gainful employment" is not predicted by available data? What if the law leads to decisions that only STEM (science, technology, engineering, and mathematics) majors meet the gainful employment criteria and thus will receive all the commensurate support? How will advisors respond to students not interested in or not adequately prepared to pursue only those majors deemed worthy by the gainful employment regulations?

If the most inclusive interpretation of the gainful employment rule is enacted, academic advisors may need to tailor their guidance by the job market salary projected, particularly for students needing to use the federal student loan program to attend college. Advisors of major changers or transfers will need to know who takes responsibility to check the loan eligibility at the receiving institution. Advisor training will need to address the interpretation of the gainful employment rule, especially if it is narrowly applied. Many academic advisors will face situations created by the gainful employment regulations, and master advisors need to be prepared to address these potential challenges.

The State or Province Level

Whatever the outcomes of national or state (province) legislative actions, legislatures often create expectations, policies, and mechanisms for meeting public demands of access, affordability, and accountability without input from experts operating in the field. Finney, Perna, and Callan (2014) astutely observed: "Helping more people get a postsecondary education is a national challenge that will be won or lost primarily at the state level" (p. 2). Academic advisors can expect to respond to legislative actions to which they did not have a voice during the discussion, creation, or regulation of them. To provide the best set of alternatives available for students and colleagues during times of change, master advisors know the ways legislatures affect earned transfer credit, remediation, and funding.

Transfer of Credits. Although some advocates of competency-based education have challenged the use of it, the credit hour as a standard unit of measurement remains the primary determinant of completion, and various efforts to increase production of academic credits, especially in transfer, are already in place. For example, academic advisors typically use the credit hour to review the potential transfer status for students wishing to apply to specific institutional programs or pursuing alternatives to meet specific educational goals.

Articulation efforts are commonly used to ensure transferability of credits within state systems. Smith (2010) found that 36 states had passed legislation to facilitate the transfer of credits from 2- to 4-year institutions within the state. Some elements of articulation include guaranteed admissions, course articulation guides, common core (general education) requirements, or common course numbering systems. These elements serve to inform and ensure community college transfer students that their credits will be accepted and applied to certain degree programs at designated 4-year institutions.

Five states have extended this principle of articulation to reach beyond their own boundaries in a pilot project to support "friction-free transfer" within the region. The Interstate Passport Initiative (2014) uses mutually developed learning outcomes as the common element for transfer and articulation in the institutional, lower division, general education core requirements. These courses are transferred as a block rather than evaluated individually.

Perhaps the most promising strategy for increasing the number of degrees awarded is embodied in reverse transfer: Students who move from a 2-year institution to a 4-year institution without earning an associate's degree or certificate are permitted to transfer certain courses (credits) back to the 2-year institution to earn the credential. The student gains an official recognition of the previous work completed, the graduation profile of the 2-year institution is improved, and the 4-year institution has made contact with a transfer student who is more likely to complete a 4-year degree than others without the associate's degree (Shapiro et al., 2013).

The Credit When It's Due project initially identified over 27,000 community college students eligible for reverse transfer programs in the 12 states that participated in the grant-funded baseline study. Three other states have subsequently joined the effort (Taylor, Bishop, Makela, Bragg, & Ruud, 2013; Taylor & Bragg, 2015).

The completion agenda has generated a heightened interest in alternative methods and approaches to validating college credits and degrees. Competency-based (new) learning and prior learning assessments are the most advocated means to achieve this end. The U.S. Department of Education gave support to competency-based education (CBE) when it attempted to redefine the credit hour in a way that allowed for an equivalency to the historical definition (Laitinen, 2012) and when it approved eligibility for financial aid based on mastery of competencies (Field, 2013). Kelchen (2015) provided a comprehensive description of the enrollments, demographics, and affordabilities of nine U.S. institutions with stand-alone CBE programs. In Ontario, CBE programs cost about the same as traditional programs (Abner, Bartosh, Ungerleider, & Tiffin, 2014).

For decades, The American Council on Education (2014, 2015) has provided the assessment of and credit recommendation for prior learning experiences, and it recently announced the development of online general education courses that enable nontraditional learners to earn degrees more readily. Also, badges are gaining popularity as a way to acknowledge learned and acquired competencies (chapter 13).

Remediation. Between 19 and 64% of all college freshmen (70% of those entering community colleges) need some form of remediation (ACT, 2015a; Gianneschi

& Fulton, 2014; Mangan, 2015; Sparks & Malkus, 2013) and an estimated $7 billion has been spent on this effort (Sparks, 2013). The students do not earn credit toward graduation for completing remedial courses. Furthermore, the data on these students suggest dismal rates of graduation and completion of gateway and remedial courses; many do not show up for the first class (Complete College America, 2012).

Legislatures in Florida, Ohio, Texas, Indiana, Connecticut, and Colorado (among more than 20 other states) introduced or passed legislation to address the remediation issue. The actions ranged from a one-semester limitation of remedial courses at 4-year institutions to allowing most students to opt out of remedial courses (Complete College America, 2012; Mangan, 2015). Early results in Florida indicate that students who opted out "were more likely to fail college-level or gateway courses" (Smith, 2015, ¶2).

All such actions, especially those limiting remedial courses, affect the many academic advisors who determine appropriate levels of courses for students, especially in math and writing. Master advisors need to monitor potential legislative actions in their own state (province) and regularly review the trends emerging elsewhere.

Funding.   The terms *cost, price, value,* and *worth* drive much of the discussion about higher education. As the weakened economic conditions of many states (provinces) fluctuate, more legislators, skeptics, pundits, and researchers focus on the growing imbalance of the payment burden of students and the accountability required of degree-granting institutions (Hiltonsmith & Draut, 2014). These fluctuations and resultant budget changes mean that academic advisors might encounter challenges that could include diminished resources. Funding reductions may result in less effective and efficient academic advising programs as well as less-motivated and less-committed academic advisors.

Master advisors remain alert to the potential (or real) funding changes and plan accordingly. This means asking tough questions: Can some services or programs be reduced or eliminated? Can we shift any responsibilities to other offices or units? Do we need to examine our operational protocols? Answers to these questions should help advising programs continue to meet student needs.

Historically, U.S. public institutions received their primary funding through public governing bodies. This trend declined over the recent 25-year span (Hurley, Harnisch, & Nassirian, 2014); in some locales, funding is projected to improve, although at a slightly lower pace than in the past (American Association of State Colleges and Universities, 2014; Grapevine, 2015; State Higher Education Executives Officers Association, 2015). Baum, Ma, and Payea (2013) reported that only four countries provided public funding for higher education at a lower percentage than the United States.

As a result, many public institutions have increased their efforts to obtain supplemental funding from external sources. This strategy has historically been used much more frequently and ardently by private institutions, but public institutions have entered the competition. Grants, contracts, and voluntary contributions are sought vigorously.

The latter grew substantially through targeted campaigns from sources such as alumni, parents, foundations, and corporations (Council for Aid to Education, 2015).

Absent public funding, private institutions experienced fiscal challenges when revenues decreased due to low enrollments. Private institutions compensated for the enrollment declines with higher tuition discounts that approach the sticker price (Carlson, 2014). Similarly, proprietary institutions, which receive only indirect public funding through student loans and grants, contended that they have saved states between $8.5 and $11.0 billion in five years (Klor de Alva & Schneider, 2014). Arguably, if students at private institutions enrolled in public institutions, the net state appropriations would diminish considerably.

The job of the academic advisor gets no easier as funding sources change. Uncertain and fluctuating funding levels can seriously affect the work of academic advisors. Fewer positions can result in larger caseloads and only enough time to handle routine course scheduling. With less available time, master advisors must choose between many competing enterprises, and their campus involvement, professional development, research, writing, and presentation efforts could suffer. However, these conditions also provide many new opportunities for master advisors to develop new skills, offer new programs, and assume new leadership roles on their campuses. Master advisors find or create alternative strategies to maintain their successful efforts.

The most significant impact of public funding declines is summed up in performance-based funding; that is, monies are based on specific institutional outcomes. No longer does enrolling more students automatically result in more funding. In many locales funding is based upon "greater institutional productivity, accountability, and educational attainment" (Harnisch, 2011, p. 10). Thirty states have established or are transitioning to performance-based funding strategies (National Conference of State Legislatures [NCSL], 2015). Claeys-Kulik and Esterman (2015) found that the majority of 28 European university systems also engaged in some form of performance-based funding, but they pointed out that the approaches employed vary due to differences in the regulatory frameworks, institutional profiles, current funding structures, and internal governance—not unlike the differences in the United States.

Some criteria used to calculate (performance) funding levels include the number of degrees awarded; number of graduated at-risk students; 6-year graduation rates; persistence or transfer rates; postgraduate status (continued education or employed); standard retention rates; reduced costs; increased research and development grants and awards; quality assessments in general education, majors, or licensure tests; and credit completion benchmarks (NCSL, 2015). Many of these are considered, but inconsistently, among the states (Jones, 2013).

Implications for Master Advisors

The implications for academic advisors abound as each performance criterion is related to the advising process. Academic advisors on the front lines can affect positive outcomes in many ways, but if they must take the responsibility such that their funding depends on meeting institutional—rather than student—goals, then the entire dynamic of the advising process could be challenged. To meet their responsibilities to students, master advisors know the funding process and can develop ways to enhance it without sacrificing the relational and conceptual components of a quality advising experience. Master advisors adhere to the NACADA Core Values of Academic Advising (NACADA, 2005), but could easily find themselves in a dilemma as they may struggle with maintaining a balance between their responsibilities to their students and to their institutions.

Faculty advisors might also find themselves in similar dilemmas as primary-role advisors. An example of this possibility was when a funding approach linked to performance was established at New College, The Honors College of Florida (Mulhere, 2015; Rivard, 2014), which had lost approximately $1 million and subsequently created the Performance Improvement Plan (New College of Florida, 2014) to recoup the losses. The plan includes "small group and individual faculty–student advising sessions . . . [and] follow-up actions by administrators, such as sending checklists to faculty and students three times each semester as deadlines approach" (p. 4), asserting that "stronger advising will increase student retention and six-year graduation rates" (p. 5). New College uses a faculty-based advising model. Florida has also introduced this funding strategy for state colleges (née community colleges) (Larrabee, 2015).

The performance-based criteria can influence both individuals and departments. The imposed mandated criteria may have little to do with the advising of individual students, and the resulting unpredictable funding situation could trigger a review of the entire institutional academic advising process. Questions about delivery and results may lead to changes in advising models, advisor responsibilities, space allocations, and technology choices, especially if funding is withdrawn or the levels are flattened or reduced.

Assessment strategies, important for all master advisors, become critical under these tenuous circumstances. To advance their influence, master advisors review (and share with other advisors) chapters 14 and 15 on assessment, and they also may review another process for determining the economic value of an advising unit that I previously described (Grites, 2011).

The role of academic advising evolves as changes in expectations and mandates emerge. As state, province, and national legislatures continue to learn about issues in higher education, they often propose and enact laws that affect each campus, advising unit, advising administrator, master advisor, individual advisor, and student. Master advisors, as advocates for academic advising on the campus, must maintain awareness of various legislative initiatives to prepare for new rules, policies, practices, or processes while maintaining the primary goals of assisting students. Master advisors remain up-to-date about the actions that potentially affect their work with students, their advising colleagues, and other campus constituencies.

Daily scans of the readily available publications (e.g., CHE, IHE, and AI) provide ongoing sources, plans, issues, and outcomes of numerous events in higher education across many institutions, states, and the nations. These summary articles almost always provide links to the original documents that contain the complete research report, legislative action, program proposal, or attempted activity. Reviewing one's own state legislative agenda (via local newspapers and other media, legislators' newsletters, and governmental relations personnel on campus) keeps master advisors apprised of proposed political action for which a plan must be devised to assist students.

The Value—or Worth—of College

Amid the influences and conditions afoot, the deliberations on the cost-benefits of higher education and discussions on responses to students and parents questioning the value of college remain overarching topics of concern. The debate has mainly focused on the monetary return on investment in higher education (Carnevale & Rose, 2015; Carnevale, Cheah, & Stohl, 2012; Kearns, 2015; Zaback, Carlson, & Crellin, 2012). Most studies compare lifetime wage and salary gains among degree holders (2- and 4-year), college attendees with no degree, and those with high school diplomas but no college experience (chapter 9). Both the Federal Reserve Banks of New York (Abel & Deitz, 2014) and of San Francisco (Daly & Bengali, 2014) agree that college graduates receive more long-term economic benefits than those without a degree.

Others reviewed indirect or noneconomic benefits of a college degree (e.g., more active citizenry and healthier personal choices and lifestyles), which include lower unemployment, less obesity, more volunteer work, and higher voting rates (Baum et al., 2013; Economic Modeling Specialists International, 2014; Grusky, Red Bird, Rodriguez, & Wimer, 2013; Taylor, Fry, & Oates, 2014). Such positive noneconomic outcomes clearly project an overall improved human condition, stronger communities, and a reduced achievement gap, especially for first-generation college students. However, in many ways, adding these issues into the milieu muddies the water— much like the many notions of student success described in chapter 5 make less clear the path to student success—because the many variables make the correlations less clear. Is *college completion* only defined as an earned degree? Does one's academic major affect the value of the degree? Are employment earnings the best metric to determine the outcomes of college? What population(s) of students should be included in the assessment? What are the personal and societal benefits (or losses) of having attended or graduated from college?

The debate surrounding the worth of college has generated research that has stimulated those in the higher education community to rethink the fundamental assumption (worthiness) upon which institutions were developed. As the economy calls for an increasing number of workers with technology skills and managers with problem-solving and critical-thinking skills, employers have decried the lack of available skilled workers within the job market (Hart Research Associates, 2015).

Despite the results pointing to benefits of higher education, the projections of the future of higher education are not without critics and not all predictions are positive.

Vedder, Denhart, and Hartge (2014) asserted that a college graduate's earning potential is deteriorating while college costs are rising and underemployment (degree holders working in jobs that do not require a degree) of college graduates is more prevalent than ever. They also argued that these graduates experienced reduced academic standards and grade inflation, both of which devalued their human capital (chapter 9) as employees to prospective employers. The authors further criticized the massive loan indebtedness, especially when the lending is not apportioned by academic majors (gainful employment), and they advocated for significantly altering the conditions for awarding student financial aid. These are considerations that should not be taken lightly.

A resolution of the college value debate seems unlikely; therefore, the worth of a degree may become one of the most significant, perhaps even the most frequent, conversations between academic advisors and students (and their families). Mainstream media outlets seem to thrive on reports that support the extremes regarding the value of college, and social media outlets provide instant opportunities to publicize such results. Two topics seem to surface most frequently in these reports and commentaries: student debt and student performance in the workplace.

Student Debt

Tuition (and other) cost increases have resulted in a massive student debt that has created a spectacle for the public. Although the conclusion of the reports on student debt remains the same—students accumulate too much of it—the figures to back up the contention are reported in different ways and in different contexts. As a result, each report must be evaluated carefully.

Although not expected to become financial aid experts, academic advisors frequently hear concerns about finances in many student inquiries related to academic decisions: "Should I change majors?" "Should I transfer?" "When?" "Should I live on campus?" "Can I work full-time and carry a full schedule?" "Can I do this all online or at night?" "Should I go to graduate school?" "What if don't get a good job?" These concerns about finances affect a student's comprehensive academic planning and require thoughtful and well-informed responses.

Academic advisors must maintain an up-to-date awareness of their own institution's costs because ability to finance the experience affects students' abilities to succeed. The cumulative cost of earning a degree in a reasonable time places a burden on many students with limited financial resources. Thus, legislators seek new ways to diminish student costs without increasing government support. Often they advocate for cost-cutting measures by the institutions. Academic advisors will surely be asked to assist students not only in their academic pursuits, but also in finding the most cost-effective means of doing so. Two such efforts have already received support.

Texas was the first state that challenged each public institution in the state to create 4-year degrees that cost the student no more than $10,000 to earn (Perry, 2011).

A similar $10,000 challenge was issued to Florida's state colleges, formerly community colleges (Kelderman, 2013; Wang, Bousquet, & Solochek, 2012). Each plan carries specific conditions for offering this low-cost education or degree, and academic advisors must know them all. For example, a limited choice of major programs of study is offered and remediation is not required. In addition, students must attend full-time, maintain a 3.0 grade-point average, demonstrate past pursuit of dual credit in high school, and meet with an academic advisor. Questions related to these conditions will certainly become part of the academic advising process.

For students, the most appealing of the cost strategies remains the free community college degree. Tennessee first passed such a measure, the Tennessee Promise (Drive to 55 Alliance, 2014), which was implemented in Fall 2015. To cover their tuition and fees, all Tennessee high school graduates receive the opportunity to combine and apply financial aid awards as well as a portion of the state lottery proceeds. On January 9, 2015, President Obama introduced a similar federal proposal, America's College Promise (The White House, 2015), for a free community college degree in states that agree to fund the balance of costs not covered by federal funding, which amounts to 75 percent of the average cost of a community college degree (or certificate) in each state. Oregon enacted a similar bill in 2015 (KATU, 2015).

Master advisors need to know if or when their state (province) will consider or adopt such a plan. How will community colleges plan for an extraordinary influx of students? How will 4-year institutions address the predictable shortfall of first- and second-year students? How will students adjust to new course demands of upper level classes without the benefit of university-level general education classes? Master advisors must engage in conversations on responding to such changing circumstances. When they can support ideas with data that reflect their institution and students, master advisors contribute to the discussions. Therefore, master advisors should seek such data through institutional career centers or the offices of admissions, alumni, and institutional research.

All academic advisors need to demonstrate familiarity with the general findings about the value (worth) of college as reported in published studies because students and parents will likely ask them questions about it at some point. In fact, academic advisors might raise questions themselves when confronted with students planning an impossible dream; the advisor may need to break the news about the potential pitfalls generated by changing funding conditions in higher education.

The student's goals, passions, abilities, and other characteristics will drive the discussion about the value of college, but advisors need knowledge of current available evidence from current external reports, data, and proposals to engage in difficult conversations more confidently. In these conversations, master advisors include strategies for keeping abreast of issues about the costs and benefits of higher education in their professional development plans. They also understand the ways the ultimate external influence—the workplace—will influence higher education and academic advising.

Jobs, Careers, and Employers

Irrespective of the value that a college education (degree) adds to life, advisees must examine career options, prepare to enter the workforce, and secure (gainful) employment. Although some might argue that the career center addresses these student interests, all student concerns, including those related to employment, fall under the purview of academic advising process (chapters 2 and 9). A well-informed academic advisor gives relevant and helpful advice about the world of work.

Studies on the workforce can be viewed as either good news or bad news, depending on one's perspective. For example, the U.S. Bureau of Labor Statistics (2014) projected the 20 fastest growing occupations through 2022. Although most are in the health care industry or may not require a bachelor's degree, others may surprise an advisee (or uninformed advisor): industrial-organizational psychologists, interpreters and translators, and genetic counselors.

Additionally, Staklis and Soldner (2014) found that for college graduates the rate of unemployment and the number of those holding multiple jobs have both increased over the past 15 years, but the numbers of those holding one full-time job have decreased. These results likely reflect the relatively stagnant global economy and the significant increases in student debt, and they will enter the academic advising conversation in the future. Even if students do not question the status of the workforce, the master advisor remains alert to relevant employment data to anticipate an opportunity (or a specific need) for students.

Although the value (worth) of a college education or degree seems obvious to those invested in the processes and outcomes, perhaps the most significant and relevant data are used for examining the relationship between a student's major and future employment. Although always a part of academic advising, the research and opinion on the major-to-career discussion abound throughout the academy. How advisors approach the discussion can vary, but they must confront the topic with available evidence routinely reported through vetted sources, including those published in higher education and through professional journals (chapter 13).

Students with degrees in the STEM fields fare financially better than those in the arts, humanities, social sciences, and business. Higher unemployment rates and lower earnings distinguish the data of these basic groupings. Anthony Carnevale and his colleagues at Georgetown University have frequently reported data related to earnings (Carnevale et al., 2012; Carnevale, Strohl, & Melton, 2011), and most recent studies have confirmed their findings (Abel & Deitz, 2014; Cataldi, Siegel, Shepherd, & Cooney, 2014; Staklis & Soldner, 2014). However, one study pointed out a potential dilemma. Sjoquist and Winters (2015) reported that students may avoid high-demand STEM fields in favor of receiving and retaining merit-based scholarships to reduce their debt. Master academic advisors should maintain a certain diligence about seeking updates on these and future studies that indicate shifting trends in specific fields of study.

One of the biggest controversies associated with this research, the efficacy of a liberal arts degree or major for approaching employment in the marketplace, remains unresolved. Liberal arts majors do not compete well with STEM majors in the arena of earnings. However, a composite of 2008 graduates showed that they had earned more credits in the humanities than in STEM fields (American Academy of Arts & Sciences [AAAS], 2014). Academic advisors discussing the value of liberal arts, not necessarily as a major but as an opportunity to invest in one's human capital (chapter 9), need to keep in mind information like that presented by the AAAS.

According to Hart Research Associates (2013), employers continue to report the need for employees with a blend of intellectual and interpersonal skills, including the capacities to think critically, communicate clearly, and solve complex problems, the importance of which surpasses the specifics of the undergraduate major. The 2013 report indicated that employers want employees with both broad knowledge and specific skills, especially those typically gained through internships, research projects, and community engagement; that is, they value the employee's ability to apply skills rather than know discrete bodies of information. In a subsequent report, Hart Research Associates (2015) found that students express far more confidence than their employers (2:1) of being prepared across 17 learning outcomes and skills categories, including written and oral communication, ability to work in teams, and awareness of diverse cultures as well as staying current on global developments. In a similar finding, Stein and Irvine (2015) showed results from 14 countries in which discrepancies emerged between students and employer reports on the extent that the college experience prepared students for careers and the workplace.

The significant discrepancy between the workplace expectations of students and employers may be material for exploration in academic advising sessions, especially in the context of Shaffer's human capital approach (chapter 9). Specifically, students should note how skills are developed and changed as they move toward completion of their educational plans. Master advisors query students about the ways their colleges experiences and courses enhance the characteristics that employers desire. They help students assess and document ways they meet, or intend to meet, these workplace expectations.

In an inaugural report by the U.S. Census Bureau, Ewert and Kominski (2014) showed that nearly 12 million bachelor's degree recipients held some additional professional license or certification. Documentation of such postgraduate or other credential could be created through comprehensive (electronic) portfolios, badges, or professional development activities (chapter 13). The report does not indicate the college majors of these recipients, but one can envision the application to students in a wide variety of majors (STEM, liberal arts, business, education, etc.).

Many of the indicators cited in this chapter point toward an overall positive value of a college education (degree). Most academic advisors know the worth of the college experience and as a result choose to advocate, reinforce, and enable the fundamental purposes of higher education; that is, they promote the education that creates an informed and engaged citizenry ready for the workplace.

Students face many questions and dilemmas as they encounter the higher education landscape. Academic advisors are challenged to stay cognizant of all the conditions that affect that landscape as they assist students to negotiate it. From the initial enrollment—whether as a first-time, full-time, transfer, or older returning adult, a military veteran, a student-athlete, or the member of some specific ethnic, cultural, or interest-based cohort—students turn to academic advisors, who need to be well-informed and well-trained, to help them navigate the campus environment. Advisors recognize the circumstances of the students and those under which the campus operates. The master advisor serves as the leader who is aware of these conditions—whether internally created or imposed by external sources—that affect the campus academic advising milieu. The master advisor engages others in discussions about the trends in higher education and initiates action when response to change is required.

What Is a Master Academic Advisor to Do?

Although all academic advisors must consider the issues raised in this chapter and choose strategies that best fit their approach to advising specific students, they also need to stay connected to the external world. The resources mentioned throughout this chapter (e.g., CHE, IHE, and AI), along with those directed to specific institutions (e.g., by the Community College Research Center and Association of American Colleges & Universities), as well as EDUCAUSE and NACADA publications (e.g., the *NACADA Journal, Academic Advising Today*, and the Clearinghouse) help advisors link with the entire academy. NACADA-sponsored social media outlets (e.g., LinkedIn, Facebook, and Twitter) provide ample opportunities to stay connected.

The issues precipitated by external conditions often affect internal advising practices, assessment strategies, and even personnel decisions. The completion agenda may drive the metrics used to assess advising programs; legislation may require shifts in advising conversations; researchers, pundits, and employers will continue to judge the higher education community and inform the public of their findings and opinions. However, the overall expectation and opportunity to facilitate individual student success will remain with academic advisors.

How advisors respond to these externally imposed conditions may change, sometimes quite dramatically, but the fundamental responsibilities, motives, and ethics should not. For example, advisors may examine the level to which each general education course enhances students' intellectual and personal skill, human capital, or the application of desired job competencies. Advisors might suggest an extra course or promote electives to complete an additional license, certification, or minor. Or they might help students build an internship, service learning, or international study experience into their academic plans. Likewise, master advisors may explore the reasons for students' choice of major more deeply. Is the reason for this major financial gain, perceived limits in job availability, the shortest route to completion, parental pressure, or does it reflect a passion?

Master advisors use every opportunity to assist students in achieving their desired goals. Because students likely know little about the many conditions affecting higher education and the related career fields, the academic advising experience is crucial to their success. Despite the various external conditions that may seem remotely relevant, effective advisors must recognize that they cannot achieve success alone or in a vacuum. They engage in collaborative efforts across campus, institutions, and the profession. They take advantage of resources and professional development opportunities mentioned throughout this chapter and in chapter 13. They remain current on the issues that affect the higher education community as a whole and advising in particular.

Each master advisor acknowledges the often-stated observation that academic advisors are perhaps the only persons on the campus who have regular, sustained, and sometimes required contact with students and can provide "the only opportunity for all students to develop a personal, consistent relationship with someone in the institution who cares about them" (Drake, 2011, p. 10). Each advisor must, therefore, identify and use a variety of resources to gain the knowledge and practice the skills that help students succeed while maintaining the overall quality of the institutional mission and the value of the degrees awarded.

Aiming for Excellence

- o What are the three most significant external conditions that influence academic advising practice at your institution?
- o What external conditions had you not realized as such prior to reading this chapter?
- o Which of the conditions new to you may influence your role as an academic advisor (administrator) the most?
- o Describe the anticipated results of external conditions to your practice (administration).
- o What types of professional development plans might help academic advisors, higher level administrators, other professionals on campus, or students recognize the potential of external conditions that might influence academic advising practice on your campus?
- o What existing communication vehicles and strategies can you use to raise the awareness of current, pending, proposed, or potential issues?
- o How do you answer the question "Is college worth it?" Explain your rationale for this response.

References

Abel, J. R., & Deitz, R. (2014). Do the benefits of college still outweigh the costs? *Current Issues in Economic and Finance, 20*(3). Retrieved from http://www.ny.frb.org/research/current_issues/ci20-3.html

Abner, B., Bartosh, O., Ungerleider, C., & Tiffin, R. (2014). *Productivity implications of a shift to competency-based education: An environmental scan and review of the relevant literature*. Retrieved from http://www.heqco.ca/en-ca/Research/Research%20 Publications/Pages/Summary.aspx?link=139

American Academy of Arts & Sciences. (2014). *Enclosed in a college major? Variations in course-taking among the fields*. Retrieved from https://www.amacad.org/content/ research/dataForumEssay.aspx?i=1571

American Association of State Colleges and Universities. (2014). *U.S. economic forecast*. Retrieved from http://www.aascu.org/SearchResult.aspx?searchtext=policy&folderid= 0&searchfor=all&orderby=id&orderdirection=ascending

American Council on Education (ACE). (2014). *ACE alternative credit project to increase attainment levels for nontraditional learners with some college, no degree*. Retrieved from http://www.acenet.edu/news-room/Pages/ACE-Alternative-Credit-Project-to-Increase-Attainment-Levels-for-Nontraditional-Learners-With-Some-College-No-Degree.aspx

ACE. (2015). *Alternative credit project institutions*. Retrieved from http://www.acenet.edu/ news-room/Pages/Alternative-Credit-Project-Institutions.aspx

ACT. (2015a). *The condition of college & career readiness: First-generation students*. Retrieved from http://www.act.org/newsroom/data/2014/states/firstgeneration.html

ACT. (2015b). *Trends and tracking charts: 2000–2015*. Retrieved from http://www.act.org/ research/policymakers/pdf/14retain_trends.pdf

Baum, S., Ma, J., & Payea, K. (2013). *Education pays 2013: The benefits of higher education for individuals and society* (Trends in Higher Education Series). New York, NY: The College Board.

Carlson, S. (2014, July 2). Rising tuition discounts and flat tuition revenues squeeze even harder. *The Chronicle of Higher Education*. Retrieved from http://chronicle.com/article/ Rising-Tuition-Discounts-and/147465/

Carnevale, A. P., Cheah, B., & Strohl, J. (2012). *Hard times: College majors, unemployment and earnings: Not all college majors are created equal*. Washington, DC: Center on Education and the Workforce.

Carnevale, A. P., & Rose, S. J. (2015). *The economy goes to college: The hidden promise of higher education in the post-industrial service economy*. Retrieved from http://www. sheeo.org/resources/publications/economic-benefit-postsecondary-degrees

Carnevale, A. P., Strohl, J., & Melton, M. (2011). *What's it worth? The economic value of college majors*. Retrieved from http://cew.georgetown.edu/whatsitworth

Cataldi, E. F., Siegel, P., Shepherd, B., & Cooney, J. (2014). *Baccalaureate and beyond: A first look at the employment experiences and lives of college graduates, 4 years on (B&B:08/12)*. Retrieved from http://nces.ed.gov/pubsearch/pubsinfo. asp?pubid=2014141

Chiose, S. (2015, April 22). Conservatives seek to align postsecondary and labour market with budget measures. *The Globe and Mail*. Retrieved from http://www.theglobeandmail.com/news/politics/conservatives-seek-to-align-postsecondary-and-labour-market-with-budget-measures/article24060886/

Claeys-Kulik, A-L., & Estermann, T. (2015). *Define thematic report: Performance-based funding of universities in Europe*. Brussels, Belgium: European University Association.

Complete College America. (2012). *Remediation higher education's bridge to nowhere*. Retrieved from http://completecollege.org/docs/CCA-Remediation-final.pdf/

Council for Aid to Education. (2015). *Voluntary support of education 2014*. New York, NY: Author.

Daly, M. C., & Bengali, L. (2014, May 5). *Is it still worth going to college? FRBSF Economic Letter*. Retrieved from http://www.frbsf.org/economic-research/publications/economic-letter/2014/may/is-college-worth-it-education-tuition-wages/

Deresiewicz, W. (2014, July 4). The miseducation of America. *The Chronicle Review*, B6-B9.

Drake, J. K. (2011). The role of academic advising in student retention and persistence. *About Campus*, 16(3), 8-12. 10.1002/abc.20060

Drive to 55 Alliance. (2014). *Tennessee promise*. Retrieved from http://www.driveto55.org/tennessee-promise/

Economic Modeling Specialists International. (2014). *Where value meets values: The economic impact of community colleges*. Retrieved from http://www.aacc.nche.edu/AboutCC/Pages/economicimpactstudy.aspx

Ewert, S., & Kominski, R. (2014). *Measuring alternative educational credentials: 2012*. Retrieved from http://www.census.gov/hhes/socdemo/education/data/files/p70-138.pdf

Field, K. (2013, March 19). Student aid can be awarded for '*competencies,*' not just credit hours, U.S. says. *The Chronicle of Higher Education*. Retrieved from http://chronicle.com/article/Student-Aid-Can-Be-Awarded-for/137991/

Finney, J. E., Perna, L. W., & Callan, P. M. (2014). *Renewing the promise: State policies to improve higher education performance*. Philadelphia, PA: Higher Education Policy Institute, University of Pennsylvania Graduate School of Education.

Gainful employment, 79 Fed. Reg. 64890 (2014) (34 CFR 668).

Gianneschi, M., & Fulton, M. (2014). *A cure for remedial reporting chaos: Why the U.S. needs a standard method for measuring preparedness for the first year of college*. Denver, CO: Education Commission of the States. Retrieved from http://www.ecs.org/search/ecssearch.html?q=cure

Grapevine. (2015). *An annual compilation of data on fiscal support for higher education*. Retrieved from http://education.illinoisstate.edu/grapevine/

Grites, T. J. (2011). The economic value of an advising unit. In J. E. Joslin & N. L. Markee (Eds.), *Academic advising administration: Essential knowledge and skills for the 21st century* (Monograph No. 22) (pp. 199–203). Manhattan, KS: National Academic Advising Association.

Grusky, D. B., Red Bird, B., Rodriguez, N., & Wimer, C. (2013). *How much protection does a college degree afford? The impact of the recession on recent college graduates*. Retrieved from http://www.pewtrusts.org/en/research-and-analysis/reports/0001/01/01/how-much-protection-does-a-college-degree-afford

Harnisch, T. L. (2011). *Performance-based funding: A re-emerging strategy in public higher education financing*. Retrieved from http://www.aascu.org/uploadedFiles/AASCU/Content/Root/PolicyAndAdvocacy/PolicyPublications/Performance_Funding_AASCU_June2011.pdf

Hart Research Associates. (2013). *It takes more than a major: Employer priorities for college learning and student success*. Retrieved from http://www.aacu.org/liberaleducation/le-sp13/hartresearchassociates.cfm

Hart Research Associates. (2015). *Falling short? College learning and career success*. Retrieved from https://www.aacu.org/leap/public-opinion-research/2015-survey-results

Henry, T., Pagano, E., Puckett, J., & Wilson, J. (2014). *Five trends to watch in higher education*. Retrieved from https://www.bcgperspectives.com/content/articles/education_public_sector_five_trends_watch_higher_education/?chapter=2

Higher Education Act of 1965. 20 U.S.C. (1965).

Hiltonsmith, R., & Draut, T. (2014). *The great cost shift continues: State higher education funding after the recession*. Retrieved from http://www.demos.org/publication/great-cost-shift-continues-state-higher-education-funding-after-recession

Hurley, D. J., Harnisch, T. L., & Nassirian, B. (2014). *A proposed federal matching program to stop the privatization of public higher education*. Washington, DC: American Association of State Colleges and Universities.

Hussar, W. J., & Bailey, T. M. (2013). *Projections of education statistics to 2022* (NCES 2014-051). Retrieved from http://www.insidehighered.com/news/2014/02/28/us-projects-college-enrollment-grow-14-through-2022#sthash.K5bvEGZh.dpbs

Interstate Passport Initiative. (2014). *A policy brief on Phase I*. Retrieved from http://www.wiche.edu/passport/research

Jones, D. P. (2013). *Outcomes-based funding: The wave of implementation*. Washington, DC: Complete College America and National Center for Higher Education Management Systems.

KATU. (2015). [Newscast]. Retrieved July 27, 2015 from http://www.katu.com/politics/local/Gov-to-sign-bill-allowing-2-years-of-free-community-college-316144411.html

Kearns, J. (2015). *Why college is worth the money for almost everybody*. Retrieved from http://www.bloomberg.com/news/articles/2015-04-02/does-college-pay-almost-always-yes-san-francisco-fed-says

Kelchen, R. (2015). *The landscape of competency-based education: Enrollments, demographics, and affordability*. Retrieved from http://www.aei.org/publication/landscape-competency-based-education-enrollments-demographics-affordability/

Kelderman, E. (2013, March 4). *Getting to the bottom of the $10,000 bachelor's degree*. Retrieved from http://chronicle.com/article/Getting-Down-to-the-Reality-of/137637/

Klepfer, K., & Hull, J. (2012). *High school rigor and good advice. Setting up students to succeed*. Retrieved from http://www.centerforpubliceducation.org/Main-Menu/Staffingstudents/High-school-rigor-and-good-advice-Setting-up-students-to-succeed/High-school-rigor-and-good-advice-Setting-up-students-to-succeed-Full-Report.pdf

Klor de Alva, J., & Schneider, M. (2014). *Do proprietary institutions of higher education generate savings for states?* San Francisco, CA: NEXUS Research and Policy Center.

Laitinen, A. (2012). *Cracking the credit hour*. Retrieved from http://newamerica.net/publications/policy/cracking_the_credit_hour

Larrabee, B. (2015). *Board of Ed approves college performance funding*. Retrieved from http://www.tallahassee.com/story/news/local/state/2015/07/23/board-ed-approves-college-performance-funding/30604969/

Lowenstein, M. (2007, February 12). The curriculum of academic advising: What we teach, how we teach, and what students learn. *The Mentor*. Retrieved from http://dus.psu.edu/mentor/old/articles/proc01ml.htm

Lumina Foundation. (2009). *Goal 2025*. Retrieved from http://www.luminafoundation.org/goal_2025.html#sthash.62odlW2S.dpuf

Mangan, K. (2015, July 28). Remedial educators warn of misconceptions fueling a reform movement. *The Chronicle of Higher Education*. Retrieved from http://chronicle.com/article/Remedial-Educators-Warn-of/231937/?cid=cc&utm_source=cc&utm_medium=en

McPhail, C. J. (2011, April). *The completion agenda: A call to action*. Summary report from the meeting of the American Association of Community College Commissions and Board of Directors, November 10-11, Washington DC. Retrieved from http://www.aacc.nche.edu/Publications/Reports/Documents/CompletionAgenda_report.pdf

Mulhere, K. (2015, April 10). When a formula doesn't add up. *Inside Higher Ed*. Retrieved from https://www.insidehighered.com/news/2015/04/10/some-gain-others-fall-floridas-performance-based-funding-system

NACADA: The Global Community for Academic Advising. (2005). *NACADA core values of academic advising: Declaration*. Retrieved from http://www.nacada.ksu.edu/Resources/Clearinghouse/View-Articles/Core-values-declaration.aspx

National Conference of State Legislatures. (2015). *Performance-based funding for higher education*. Retrieved from http://www.ncsl.org/research/education/performance-funding.aspx

National Student Clearinghouse Research Center. (2014). *Current term enrollment—Spring 2014*. Retrieved from http://nscresearchcenter.org/currenttermenrollmentestimate-spring2014/

New College of Florida. (n.d.). *The New College of Florida College performance improvement plan* 2014–15. Retrieved from http://www.flbog.edu/about/budget/docs/performance_funding/NCF_PerfImprovPlan_6-13-14.pdf

Noel-Levitz. (2014). *Fall 2014 new student enrollment and retention outcomes at four-year institutions*. Coralville, IA: Noel-Levitz.

Perry, R. (2011). *State of the state address*. Retrieved from http://governor.state.tx.us/news/speech/15673/

Rivard, R. (2014, August 7). Punished for its mission? *Inside Higher Ed*. Retrieved from https://www.insidehighered.com/news/2014/08/07/one-liberal-arts-college-loses-money-after-its-state-adopts-performance-funding

Ross, T., & Kena, G. (2012). *Higher education: Gaps in access and persistence study*. Retrieved from https://nces.ed.gov/pubs2012/2012046.pdf

Shapiro, D., Dundar, A., Yuan, X., Harrell, A., & Wakhungu, P. K. (2014, November). *Completing college: A national view of student attainment rates—Fall 2008 cohort*

(Signature Report No. 8). Herndon, VA: National Student Clearinghouse Research Center.

Shapiro, D., Dundar, A., Ziskin, M., Chiang, Y. Chen, J., Torres, V., & Harrell, A. (2013, August). *Baccalaureate attainment: A National view of the postsecondary outcomes of students who transfer from two-year to four-year institutions* (Signature Report No. 5). Herndon, VA: National Student Clearinghouse Research Center.

Sjoquist, D. L., & Winters, J. V. (2015, August 10). The effect of Georgia's HOPE scholarship on college major: A focus on STEM. *IZA Journal of Labor Economics*. doi:10.1186/s40172-015-0032-6

Smith, A. A. (2015, June 25). When you're not ready. *Inside Higher Ed*. Retrieved from https://www.insidehighered.com/news/2015/06/25/floridas-remedial-law-leads-decreasing-pass-rates-math-and-english

Smith, M. (2010). *Transfer and articulation policies*. Retrieved from http://www.ecs.org/transfer-and-articulation-policies/

Sparks, D., & Malkus, N. (2013). *First-year undergraduate remedial course taking: 1999-2000, 2003-04, 2007-08*. Retrieved from http://nces.ed.gov/search/?q=remedial coursetaking&spell=1&site=nces&showall=&entsp=a&sort=date%3AD%3AL%3Ad1&client=nces&entqr=3&access=p&sitesearch=&ip=192.168.132.61&output=xml:no_dtd&filter=

Sparks, S. D. (2013). Many students don't need remediation, studies say. *Education Week, 32*(21), 1, 21. Retrieved from http://www.edweek.org/ew/articles/2013/02/20/21remediation_ep.h32.html?qs=many+students+don't+need+remediation

Staklis, S., & Soldner, M. (2014). *New college graduates at work: Employment among 1992-93, 1999-2000, and 2007-08 bachelor's degree recipients 1 year after graduation*. Retrieved from http://nces.ed.gov/pubsearch/pubsinfo.asp?pubid=2014003

State Higher Education Executive Officers. (2015). *SHEF–State higher education finance FY14*. Retrieved from http://www.sheeo.org/projects/shef-%E2%80%94-state-higher-education-finance

Stein, J., & Irvine, A. K. (2015). *Career preparedness and lifelong learning: A global perspective*. Retrieved October 25, 2015, from http://www.canvaslms.com/higher-education/stories

Student Achievement Measure. (2013). [Home page]. Retrieved from http://www.studentachievementmeasure.org/about

The Swedish Higher Education Act of 1992. [Description]. Retrieved from https://www.uhr.se/en/start/laws-and-regulations/Laws-and-regulations/The-Swedish-Higher-Education-Act/

Taylor, J. L., Bishop, C., Makela, J. P., Bragg, D. D., & Ruud, C. M. (2013). *Credit when it's due: Results from the baseline study*. Champaign: University of Illinois at Champaign-Urbana, Office of Community College Research and Leadership.

Taylor, J. L., & Bragg, D. D. (2015). *Optimizing reverse transfer policies and processes: Lessons from CWID states*. Champaign: University of Illinois at Champaign-Urbana, Office of Community College Research and Leadership.

Taylor, P., Fry, R., & Oates, R. (2014). *The rising cost of not going to college*. Retrieved from http://www.pewsocialtrends.org/2014/02/11/the-rising-cost-of-not-going-to-college/

Tinto, V. (1982). Limits of theory and practice in student attrition. *Journal of Higher Education, 53*(6), 687–700.

U.S. Bureau of Labor Statistics. (2014). *Fastest growing occupations*. Retrieved from http://capseecenter.org/medium-term-labor-market-return-to-community-college-awards/

U.S. Department of Education. (2011). *College completion tool kit*. Washington, DC: Author.

Vedder, R., Denhart, C., & Hartge, J. (2014). *Dollars, cents, and nonsense: The harmful effects of federal student aid*. Retrieved from http://centerforcollegeaffordability.org/research/studies/harmful-effects-of-federal-student-aid/

Wang, S., Bousquet, S., & Solochek, J. (2012, November 26). Gov. Rick Scott's challenge to state colleges: $10,000 bachelor's degrees. *Tampa Bay Times*. Retrieved from http://www.tampabay.com/news/education/gov-rick-scotts-challenge-to-state-colleges-10000-bachelors-degrees/1263272

The White House. (2009). *Remarks of President Barack Obama—As prepared of delivery address to Joint Session of Congress*. Retrieved from http://www.whitehouse.gov/the_press_office/Remarks-of-President-Barack-Obama-Address-to-Joint-Session-of-Congress/

The White House. (2015). *Fact sheet—White House unveils America's College Promise: Tuition-free community college for responsible students*. Retrieved from http://www.whitehouse.gov/the-press-office/2015/01/09/fact-sheet-white-house-unveils-america-s-college-promise-proposal-tuitio

Zaback, K., Carlson, A., & Crellin, M. (2012). *The economic benefit of postsecondary degrees: A state and national level analysis*. Retrieved from http://www.sheeo.org/resources/publications/economic-benefit-postsecondary-degrees

Zusman, A. (2005). Challenges facing higher education in the twenty-first century. In P. G. Altbach, R. O. Berdahl, & P. J. Gumport (Eds.), *American higher education in the twenty-first century: Social, political, and economic challenges* (2nd ed.) (pp. 109–148). Baltimore, MD: The Johns Hopkins University Press. Retrieved from http://www.educationanddemocracy.org/Resources/Zusman.pdf

18

CHALLENGES FOR THE FUTURE

DEVELOPING AS A PROFESSION, FIELD, AND DISCIPLINE

Craig M. McGill and Charlie L. Nutt

The purpose of life is not to be happy. It is to be useful, to be honorable, to be compassionate, to have it make some difference that you have lived and lived well.

—Ralph Waldo Emerson (1803–1882)

A variety of external influences on higher education and academic advising are creating—even demanding—significant changes. Students today present diversity in every aspect imaginable, and members of the higher education community struggle to deal with colleges and universities that differ significantly from those they attended as students. Change creates instability, challenges competence, and adds confusion. It causes conflict with others and creates uncertainty within as advisors grapple with their evolving roles. We explain the forces likely to influence academic advising, describe two principal areas of necessary expansion to meet the upcoming challenges, and direct advisors to stand at the fore of change for the professionalization of the field.

Reader Learning Outcomes

From studying this chapter, advisors will use knowledge gained about changes in higher education and academic advising to

o recognize issues in higher education today that will influence the future of academic advising,

o identify potential changes in academic advising and the higher education culture by 2025,

o describe the kind of research needed to promote academic advising, and

o reflect on ways the predicted changes will affect institutions and academic advisors.

In his study *Continuing Learning in the Professions*, Cyrile Houle (1980) distilled 17 classic professions down to the elements that form them. Although a select few (e.g., law, medicine, and theology) have existed for ages, many others have taken shape during the past century. Houle argued that these professions and their practitioners exhibited many, if not all, of the following learning-related characteristics: clarified defining function(s); mastery of theoretical knowledge; capacity to solve problems; use of practical knowledge; expectations for self-enhancement; participation in formal training; appreciation and establishment of credentialing; evolution of a subculture; evidence of legal reinforcement, public acceptance, and ethical practice; creation of penalties; and maintenance of relationships with those in other vocations and users of service. In studying the classic professions that have emerged throughout the centuries, those in evolving professions can learn to direct their fields in a similar manner (Shaffer, Zalewski, & Leveille, 2010). Academic advising, as one such emerging profession, has grown tremendously since the professional flagship association—NACADA—was created in 1979 (chapter 1).

In 1992, when I (Nutt) joined NACADA, academic advising was viewed much differently than it is today. As a faculty member who advised, I was charged by a new president with restructuring the academic advising program on campus. The president was most concerned with the faculty understanding items related to the informational component of academic advising (Habley, 1986): how to deal with long lines, students who waited until the last minute to be advised (i.e., "register for classes"), and issues presented by undecided students. In other words, instead of viewing academic advising as an important responsibility that could affect a student's life, the leadership, invoking the historical strategy of the campus, basically expected new faculty members to advise as a rite of passage. Neither I nor the former president of my institution had any idea that a whole set of professionals, whose primary role was advising, was defining key concepts in quality academic advising experiences as conceptual or relational. The previous chapters have provided a variety of ways that academic advising today is viewed differently than it was in 1992.

However, the future of academic advising will diverge even more from the status ascribed to it in 2008 (at the beginning of the recession) when the second edition of *Academic Advising: A Comprehensive Handbook* (Gordon, Habley, & Grites) was published. Not only are more diverse students enrolling, the members of the higher education community struggle to navigate within colleges and universities that significantly differ from those they had attended as students. As the 1988 television commercial touted "This is not your father's Oldsmobile" (Rutland, 2014), higher education is not the stable, traditional academy of yesterday; instead, colleges and universities are exciting and vibrant, but often frustrating, places to work and learn.

Changes in Higher Education That Transform Academic Advising

Although change within the academy may seem slow, an event that alters the course of the academy can happen in an instant (e.g., 9/11 or the 2008 stock market crash). A multitude of issues and agendas has and will instigate transformations in academic advising. In 2015, for example, forces in and out of U.S. higher education focused greater attention on student retention, completion, and persistence than had been directed to these goals at any point in history, and more than 30 states have since implemented some form of performance funding based on levels of student retention, persistence, and completion (National Conference of State Legislatures, 2015).

As higher education across the globe acclimates to the disequilibrium caused by change, the stature and legitimacy of academic advising will rise, which will further inspire and require practitioner engagement on campus. During this time, all academic advisors, whether primary-role or faculty, will be increasingly judged on their expertise and knowledge as well as their abilities and the results of their work. As a result, they will be seated at the decision-making tables at colleges and universities across the globe. That is, instead of advisors being the last to know about key decisions affecting students, they will be involved in driving higher education agendas. We predict that by 2025, academic advisors will garner respect from all institutional leaders and faculty members.

However, to gain positions for influencing the future, academic advisors must now get involved in data mining and analysis. Today, institutions turn to for-profit companies for predictive analytics to inform decisions about programs, initiatives, interventions, or campaigns targeted to specific students or student populations, which are often presented to and absorbed by campuses without the input of the academic advising community. Yet, academic advisors will typically be held responsible for the implementation of programs based upon these analytics-based models. As they increase their empirical and action research efforts, expand the depth of their professional development, and earn increased respect for their expertise, academic advisors will become more actively involved in their institutions' efforts to gather and utilize data to predict risk factors and to create the interventions that ensure student success.

The evolving higher education landscape and the active involvement of state and local communities in holding higher education accountable for increased student success and completion demand more advising collaborations with stakeholders across institutions (chapter 11) as well as with state, community, and civic leaders. A November 2015 gathering of institutional and community leaders in San Antonio, Texas—one of the fastest growing metropolitan areas in the United States—clearly demonstrated how academic advising, as a profession and a field of study, has recently received attention as a key to student success. The Alamo Area Consortium—400 constituents from all higher education institution types (community colleges, state universities, and private colleges), 10 area school districts, city and county governments, area community agencies, area municipalities governments, and major local industries—held the Alamo Area College Access and Completion Summit (2015) to work together across all institutions and the community to build essential pathways for student success. The full-day event focused primarily on the role that academic advising plays in the success of students across all levels of education to ensure student access and successful completion of some form of higher education. The consortium gathered input in a variety of workshops offered throughout the day and concluded the event with a two-hour think tank exercise in which all participants discussed both the strengths and the challenges of the academic advising experienced by students. The ideas generated included

- o formulating a consistent definition and purpose of academic advising among all institutions,
- o clearly defining learning outcomes for academic advising,
- o increasing professional development opportunities for primary-role academic advisors at all levels of the education system,
- o recognizing problems with institutional competiveness rather than collaboration across the area,
- o increasing funding in all areas of education, and
- o incorporating consistent technology support for academic advising.

The consortium participants considered the ideas generated and developed a set of goals, outcomes, expectations, and needs to present to Alamo-area citizens. Consortium members hope to develop action plans to deal with the issues uncovered during the summit, including identifying additional funding sources to fill the identified gaps. Based on this one meeting in one U.S. city, we predict that other large urban conglomerates across the globe will approach problem solving in this collaborative way, and by 2025 academic advising will lead the community in making changes that enhance student success. To meet the calls for accountability, which will continue to increase as governmental funding continues to decline, leaders of higher education must work more closely with all stakeholders, including those in local government agencies, industries, and community agencies. Those in the advising profession must step forward as leaders of future, exciting endeavors (chapters 10 and 11).

Principal Areas of Necessary Expansion

The anticipated changes in the focus and direction of higher education will affect the scope and trajectory of academic advising. Two areas of necessary expansion in the next decade and beyond include (a) research and publication by and for members of the field and (b) professional development for advisors at all levels of expertise.

Expansion of Research and Publication Within the Field

Scholars in the field must produce more literature illustrating the impact of academic advising on student learning, persistence, and completion. Currently, the primary research cited regarding the importance of academic advising has been conducted by those outside the field (e.g., Gardner, 1995; Kuh, 2006; Tinto, 1999). Although recognized experts in areas of student success and the undergraduate experiences of students, these oft-cited authors are not on the front lines of academic advising. Of course, future research must include data acquired through a variety of methodologies and types—empirical, action based, quantitative, and qualitative—but most important, it must come from those active in the field of academic advising: primary-role advisors, faculty advisors, academic advising administrators, and graduate students. Without research by practitioners in academic advising, others will continue to define it such that practitioners may be seen as lacking the interest in or the ability to address the preeminent issues affecting practice (Shaffer et al., 2010) (chapter 4). To create a culture of success that permeates all aspects of the academy, primary-role and faculty advisors must collaborate on the research highly desired and valued in higher education globally.

Publications within the field necessarily follow from the expansion of advising research. NACADA: The Global Community for Academic Advising features print and electronic publications (e.g., the *NACADA Journal,* the quarterly *Academic Advising Today*, the Clearinghouse for Academic Advising Resources) that will continue as the primary venues for research within the field during the next decade. However, publications addressing the role of academic advising in higher education will continue to influence forums in other fields and disciplines as well. In fact, we expect that the primary expansion in research will be seen in discipline-based journals and publications as the fields of student success and academic advising grab the attention of and acceptance by faculty advisors in the academic community.

This envisioned upswing in scholarship hinges on a major culture shift in the acceptance, value, and recognition of student success research by faculty advisors in the tenure and promotion process. For example, in July 2015, Purdue University highlighted the mentoring and advising role that the faculty plays in the lives of undergraduates, putting significant emphasis on student success in the tenure process (Jaschik, 2015). This shift points to a possible trend in which the research and publication required for faculty tenure and promotion may expand from investigations primarily focused on an academic discipline to also encompass scholarship on influences affecting the institution, higher education, and student success. As faculty members expand their research to include inquiries on teaching and learning, academic advising, and undergraduate student success, the culture of higher education will shift dramatically toward student learning and success (chapter 5). Despite these positive indicators, this changing scenario of higher education may be placing the current environment of the institution in flux. Specifically, tenure and academic freedom are being questioned in North American higher education (Flaherty, 2015a, 2015b; Nel, 2013; "Should Tenure for College Professors Be Abolished?" 2012).

Although not a focus in the NACADA international conferences—first sponsored in 2013 in Maastricht, Netherlands—faculty tenure connected to research in student learning and success may be forthcoming in countries where research on student success is emerging as a valued outcome of higher education. For example, the Higher Education Academy in the United Kingdom conducts and sponsors research on all areas of student success and access (Action on Access, 2015). Although a focused area of scholarship materializing in the past decade, student success as a field of study is growing widely across the country in all postsecondary institutions.

The role academic advisors play in student success, retention, and persistence to graduation has been recognized in recent studies and research (Klepfer & Hull, 2012; Ross et al., 2012). To continue the promotion of student success and advising, primary-role advisors must get actively involved in both empirical and action-based research, and they must acquire new skills for this endeavor. In previous decades, the research and writing skills needed for academic publication were not required, expected, or encouraged for primary-role academic advisors; however, with the shift of higher education toward student success (chapter 5), institutions must set criteria for research and publication when hiring primary advisors.

No growth in research and publication within a discipline can occur without the development of a scholarly community that values and expects scholarship. The research and publication skills needed by advisors will expand as the number and quality of graduate programs for academic advising increase. Likewise, emphasis on academic advising research in traditional college student personnel and higher education graduate programs promotes scholarship in the field. As a consequence of deliberate efforts to develop the skills, experiences, talents, and interests in research and publications, primary-role advisors, particularly those entering the field, can contribute to the scholarship that demonstrates the impact of advising on students and higher education.

With an eye toward the future, advising leadership must set an expectation for research and publication for practitioners. However, this expectation cannot be realized without commensurate instruction and support for primary-role advisors who have not yet acquired the necessary skills and knowledge for researching, writing, and publishing. In addition to the ways individual institutions support such professional development, NACADA will take a significant lead in providing support for all levels of research and publication. Since 2002, NACADA has made significant strides in scholarship by

- o adding advising content experts to the NACADA Executive Office staff to support member understanding of advising issues and expansion of the professional literature;
- o significantly increasing the quality and quantity of publication venues and opportunities for the membership as well as the professional development resources in the field;
- o making research and dissemination of results a primary strategic goal of the association;
- o increasing funding for research grants in the field;
- o shifting the culture of the *NACADA Journal* to value and appreciate studies using quantitative, qualitative, and mixed methods as well as conceptual, theory-based, and other nonempirical articles;
- o empowering the NACADA Research Committee to
  - o develop a culture of scholarly inquiry in the field of academic advising for the association,

o develop a research agenda for the association and the field, and

o produce publications and conduct specific training and professional development to support the skills and experiences of primary advisors in research; and

o supporting the Center for Excellence and Research in Academic Advising and Student Success, to open in 2017, in collaboration with the College of Education at Kansas State University (NACADA, 2015).

As the future becomes the present, NACADA is expanding partnerships with other associations and institutions, as well as with for-profit entities, to increase the financial support for research in the field. The association continues to procure outside funding because it cannot realistically support the research critical to the growth of the field from member dues alone. For example, in 2015, as a means of conducting research in a cost-effective way for the association, NACADA worked with Tyton Partners to administer a survey of NACADA members on the status of academic advising and the use of technology in practice. Furthermore, to remain the primary resource for research, professional development, and resources in the field, NACADA has connected with entities across the globe that procure and advise on analytical data collection and utilization.

The Role of Professional Development

Closely tied to the issue of research, changes in the nature, scope, and delivery of professional development mean that leadership needs to ensure that primary-role advisors are equipped to embrace new opportunities and related challenges. Although small areas of change are emerging in specific programs, such as those at the University of California Berkeley, Florida State University, and Alamo Community College Districts, professional development continues to be information based, with few or random experiences focused on the conceptual or relational components of academic advising (Givans Voller, 2012). The current status of academic advising (chapters 7 and 12) and of professional development for academic advisors perpetuates the myth of academic advising as a clerical, routine activity of course selection or information sharing rather than an educative enterprise. In the next decade, professional development must be revolutionized to impart a holistic and comprehensive understanding of the field. Efforts must clearly delineate critical learning experiences of students and the varying strategies and approaches available to academic advisors as part of their foundational skill base. Planners and facilitators of professional development address the foundational competencies that all academic advisors should possess (Folsom, 2015; NACADA, 2003) and the essential teaching and learning strategies that ensure quality academic advising experiences for students. They also must promote an understanding of student learning styles so that academic advisors can develop curricula that take into account the growth of students from their first semester through completion of their educational goals.

Furthermore, planners for professional development must advance processes for measuring the attainment of competencies and skills (Folsom, 2015) (chapter 13) as well as for measuring effective teaching and learning strategies utilized with advisees. The results from assessment offer feedback on the continual, hands-on experiences that best provide opportunities in the conceptual, relational, and informational domains (chapter 3); that is, they help advisors identify and implement the best strategies for building strong, effective, and appropriate relationships with students. Toward this end, academic advisors need to take part in role-playing experiences and case study discussions that demonstrate knowledge of and ability to utilize a variety of communication and teaching styles (Duslak & McGill, 2014). After taking part in professional development, advisors should be able to forge the authentic relationships with students that foster the trust and respect that have far-reaching impacts on the students' undergraduate experiences.

As a consequence of the foundational competencies gained from strong professional development programs in place by the next decade, primary-role advisors will specialize in working with a specific type of student or student group and adopt specific advising strategies or approaches. Consequently, they not only need to demonstrate knowledge of basic competencies and skills but they also need to develop a special area of focus that will increase their employability in institutions across the globe. Whether evidence of knowledge and skills is established through microcredentials, certificates, or badges is irrelevant; academic advisors will advance past general baseline knowledge and skills to exhibit deep learning and understanding of the field as a discipline with specializations in key areas.

By reaching these standards for professional development, those in and out of the field will gain a clear understanding of the competencies, skills, and talents that all academic advisors need to provide effective and impactful academic experiences to students. Although issues of certification or licensure will likely continue to plague the field, by 2025 the knowledge and skills of academic advisors will be trackable and verifiable. Furthermore, postsecondary institutions will use these established competencies to build a framework for primary-role advisors similar to that for the tenure and promotion of faculty members. The resulting career ladders will create appropriate incentives for the professionalization of primary-role advisors (chapter 12). At the same time, leadership will adopt professional development programs for faculty advisors such that advising competencies will be recognized and rewarded in tenure and promotion decisions (e.g., Missouri State University [2010] Master Advisor Training Program and Old Dominion University [2015] Master Advising Certificate Program).

To create relevant professional development for the next decade and beyond, master advisors must conduct action-based research that will influence assessment, decision making, and planning. They need the tools to conduct research at a variety of levels and develop the skills needed for the effective written and oral communication expected of professionals for publication and presentation (chapters 13, 14, and 15).

Summary: Preparing to Meet the Challenge

Having considered the changes to higher education that will influence academic advising, as well as two principal areas of necessary expansion for the field, we ask: How do master advisors, and the profession as a whole, prepare for the predicted changes in the field? We leave academic advisors with several key challenges in developing their practice and for professionalizing the field:

- Academic advisors must intentionally define the role of academic advising on campus to drive institutional policy directives and decision making. In action plans developed at the NACADA Academic Advising Summer Institutes, Academic Advising Administrators' Institutes, and Academic Advising Assessment Institutes over the past decade, representatives from many institutions of all types across the globe have developed academic advising definitions or mission statements and have established goals and student learning outcomes. In the recent past, regardless of how well constructed, many of these plans remained underutilized as forces for effective changes in the academic advising experiences of students or in policy or procedural decisions affecting academic experiences. Members of academic advising communities must rekindle conversations surrounding the key elements of advising and set goals and outcomes for practice. Furthermore, the outcomes must form the basis of key priorities for educating students as well as inform practices and policies. Without purposeful planning and follow-up with completion of actionable and assessable goals, academic advising will be viewed as peripheral rather than as integral to the institutional mission and purpose.

- Academic advisors must step up, welcome change, and embrace the opportunity to demonstrate the impact of their work on student success by conducting research and assessment of outcomes. They must take responsibility and remain accountable for showing that advising changes students' lives, and they must provide evidence to validate the role of academic advising in student learning.

- Clear and definitive roles must be delineated for primary-role advisors, faculty advisors, peer advisors, and academic advising administrators across higher education. Although implementation differs by institution based on type, mission, and purpose, leaders in the field must identify the roles of those advising students. This clarity is important in forging necessary collaborative relationships and in providing professional development.

- Collaborative research across institutions and the globe must become the norm by 2025. Members of the academic advising community must acquire the research skills needed to conduct such scholarship. Academic advisors must sharpen their writing skills so they can publish the research results, theories, and practices that provide a basis for changes in higher education. In addition, administrators and other advising stakeholders must commit the necessary resources to designing and implementing appropriate assessment tools to measure the important work of advising, student learning (regardless of institutional type or location), and the influence of academic advising on student success and persistence.

o Finally, the present and future leadership of NACADA needs to work harder and more definitively for recognition of NACADA within higher education as the leader in supporting academic advising and student success initiatives. When they step into association leadership roles, master advisors become beacons for others facing predicted and inevitable changes.

Each decade alters higher education in unpredictable ways due, at least in part, to the vast changes in technology (chapter 16) and the rapid increase in student diversity (chapter 6). However, the more intimately connected to student success, completion, and graduation goals, the more influence academic advising exerts on higher education. Goals set not only by those in higher education at large but also by state legislatures and private foundations (e.g., Gates or Lumina) increasingly drive change within the academy. As we have aimed to show, higher education will affect academic advising, but academic advising matters to students (Klepfer & Hull, 2012; Ross et al., 2012). Therefore, academic advising will continue to stand as among the most important aspects of higher education. We contend that this is an exciting and rewarding time for the field, and academic advisors must be at the helm and steering that change.

Aiming for Excellence

o Reflect on the changes in advising experienced on your campus.

o Has the value of advising risen, diminished, or remained the same at your institution?

o How has the role of the teaching faculty changed with respect to the academic advising experiences of students?

o What research would affect the impact of academic advising on student success and completion?

o How has professional development changed for academic advisors on your campus?

o How will you meet the future challenges to advising?

o Describe the factors you see driving change within higher education that affect academic advising as a whole and your advising practice in particular.

o Describe the changes that will influence academic advising roles in the next decade and beyond.

o Based upon the challenges outlined in the chapter, what do you see as the biggest challenge to your advising practice?

References

Action on Access. (2015). *The national co-ordination team for widening participation and access to higher education*. Retrieved from http://actiononaccess.org

Alamo Area College Access and Completion Summit. (2015, November 5). *Seamless pathways . . . Endless possibilities* [program agenda]. Retrieved from http://alamo.edu/uploadedFiles/District/Employees/Departments/Student_Success/Summit/fileAssets/Event-webpage-agenda.pdf

Burr, G. S., Scott, H. D., & Shaw, V. L. (2011). *I was here. On lessons learned.* n.p.: Sony Masterworks.

Duslak, M., & McGill, C. M. (2014). *Stepping out of the workshop: The case for experiential and observational learning in advisor training and development*. Retrieved http://www.nacada.ksu.edu/Resources/Clearinghouse/View-Articles/Stepping-out-of-the-workshop-The-case-for-experiential-learning-in-advisor-training-and-development.aspx

Flaherty, C. (2015a, June 15). *AAUP censures 4 institutions*. Retrieved from https://www.insidehighered.com/news/2015/06/15/aaup-censures-four-institutions-calls-out-others

Flaherty, C. (2015b, March 3). "*De-tenure*" *do-over*. Retrieved from https://www.insidehighered.com/news/2015/03/03/u-tennessee-system-backtracks-de-tenure-language

Folsom, P. (2015). Mastering the art of advising: Getting started. In P. Folsom, F. Yoder, & J. E. Joslin (Eds.), *The new advisor guidebook: Mastering the art of academic advising* (2nd ed.) (pp. 3–35). San Francisco, CA: Jossey-Bass.

Gardner, J. (1995). Perspectives on academic advising for first year students: Present and future. In M. L. Upcraft & G. L. Kramer (Eds.), *First-year academic advising: Patterns in the present pathways to the future* (Monograph Series, No. 18) (pp. 163–172). Columbia: University of South Carolina, National Resource Center for the Freshman Experience and Students in Transition.

Givans Voller, J. (2012). *Advisor training and development: Why it matters and how to get started*. Retrieved from http://www.nacada.ksu.edu/Resources/Clearinghouse/View-Articles/Advisor-training-and-development-Why-it-matters-and-how-to-get-started.aspx

Gordon, V. N., Habley, W. R., & Grites, T. J. (Eds.). (2008). *Academic advising: A comprehensive handbook* (2nd ed.). San Francisco, CA: Jossey-Bass.

Habley, W. R. (1986). *Advisor training: Whatever happened to instructional design?* ACT workshop presentation. Iowa City, IA: ACT.

Houle, C. O. (1980). *Continuing learning in the professions*. San Francisco, CA: Jossey-Bass.

Jaschik, S. (2015, July 20). Mentoring as a tenure criterion. *Inside Higher Ed*. Retrieved from https://www.insidehighered.com/newss/2015/07/20/purdue-moves-make-mentoring-undergraduates-criterion-tenure

Klepfer, K., & Hull, J. (2012). *High school rigor and good advice: Setting up students to succeed (at a glance)*. Retrieved from http://www.centerforpubliceducation.org/Main-Menu/Staffingstudents/High-school-rigor-and-good-advice-Settingup-students-to-succeed#sthash.yizFgEcO.dpuf

Kuh, G. (2006, June). Thinking DEEPly about academic advising and student engagement. *Academic Advising Today, 36*(2). Retrieved from http://www.nacada.ksu.edu/Resources/Academic-Advising-Today/View-Articles/Thinking-DEEPly-about-Academic-Advising-and-Student-Engagement.aspx

Missouri State University. (2010). *History of the master advisor training program.* Retrieved from http://www.missouristate.edu/advising/10704.htm

NACADA: The Global Community for Academic Advising (NACADA). (2003). *Academic advisor competencies.* Retrieved from https://www.nacada.ksu.edu/Resources/Clearinghouse/View-Articles/Academic-advisor-competencies.aspx

NACADA. (2015, October 3). Board of Directors annual meeting [notes]. Las Vegas, NV.

National Conference of State Legislatures. (2015, July 31). *Performance-based funding for higher education.* Retrieved from http://www.ncsl.org/research/education/performance-funding.aspx

Nel, P. (2013). Kansas Board of Regents revokes right to freedom of speech [web log post]. Retrieved from http://www.philnel.com/2013/12/18/kansasregents/

Old Dominion University. (2015). *Master advising certificate program.* Retrieved from https://www.odu.edu/facultystaff/advising/resources/master-advising-certificate-program

Ross, T., Kena, G., Rathbun, A., KewalRamani, A., Zhang, J., Kristapovich, P., & Manning, E. (2012, August). *Higher education: Gaps in access and persistence study.* Retrieved from https://nces.ed.gov/pubs2012/2012046.pdf

Rutland, M. (2014, May 21). "Not your father's Oldsmobile"—A cautionary tale [web log post]. Retrieved from http://globalservants.org/connect/blog/165-not-your-fathers-oldsmobile

Shaffer, L. S., Zalewski, J. M., & Leveille, J. (2010). The professionalization of academic advising: Where are we in 2010? *NACADA Journal, 30*(1), 66–77.

Should tenure for college professors be abolished? (2012, June 12). *Wall Street Journal.* Retrieved from http://www.wsj.com/articles/SB10001424052702303610504577418293114042070

Tinto, V. (1999). Taking retention seriously: Rethinking the First Year of College. *NACADA Journal, 19*(2), 5–9.

AUTHOR INDEX

A

Abel, J. R., 337, 340
Abner, B., 333
Adams, N. A., 137
Adams, T., 276–278, 280, 283, 291–294
Aiken-Wisniewski, S. A., 13–14, 275, 278, 280, 284, 291, 296, 319
Alberts, B., 55
Allen, I. E., 307
Allen, J. M., 66, 211, 214
Amabile, T. M., 232
Amundson, N., 171
Angelo, T., 278
Annan, K. A., 83
Applegate, J. L., 66
Archambault, K. L., xxvi, 47, 57, 107–109, 121, 322
Armenakes, A. A., 234
Aronson, J., 112
Arthur, M. B., 160–161
Atkinson, D. R., 109
Aud, S., 12
Avery, C., 160

B

Bachman, J. G., 165
Bailey, T. M., 330
Banta, T. W., 52, 53, 214
Barr, R, 203
Barron, K. E., 50, 58, 202
Bartosh, O., 333
Basken, P., 172
Bass, B. M., 184
Bastiaens, T. J., 255
Baum, S., 334, 337
Baxter Magolda, M. B., 70
Bayles, M. D., 253
Beach, J. M., 164
Bean, J. P., 66
Bedeian, A. G., 234
Bengali, L., 337
Bennis, W., 180, 183, 190
Beres, K., 258
Berra, Y., 65
Bhattacherjee, A., 193

Bishop, C., 333
Black, T. C, 313
Block, J., 146
Bloom, B. S., 279, 280, 312, 317
Bloom, J. L., xxix, 47, 123, 126, 137–138, 259, 312
Blunt, P., 192
Bodenhausen, G., 160
Bourassa, D. M., 52, 205
Bousquet, S., 339
Bradford, D. L., 183, 191, 195
Bragg, D. D., 333
Bridgen, S. T., 13
Bridges, B. K., 86, 211
Brown, M., 55
Bryant, R., 46, 320
Bryant, S. K., 165–166
Bucher, I., 289
Buckley, J. A., 86, 211
Burkum, K., 312
Burney, L. L., 228
Burns, J. M., 179
Burt, T. D., 211, 276
Burton Nelson, D., 162
Buyarski, C., 256

C

Callan, P. M., 332
Calmeyn, H., 160
Campbell, E., 140, 281, 296
Campbell, S. M., xxvii, 54, 65, 66, 72–75, 172, 202, 211, 213, 230, 231, 276, 278, 280, 281, 291, 293, 299, 319
Carlson, A., 335
Carlson, S., 337
Carlstrom, A. H., 50, 52, 202, 203, 215, 240, 261, 278
Carnevale, A. P., 337, 340
Carstensen, D. J., 11
Cataldi, E. F., 340
Cate, P., 2, 11–13
Cerdà, F. L., 312
Chagani, A., 46, 320
Champlin-Scharff, S., 13
Chang, C. Y., 256
Chatterjee, S., 165
Cheah, B., 340
Chen, H., 313

Chen, J., 333
Chiang, Y., 333
Chickering, A. W., 21–23, 30
Childs, M. W., 12
Chiose, S., 331
Christensen, C., 321
Chudowsky, N., 278
Cieplak, B., 140
Claeys-Kulik, A.-L., 335
Cohen, A. R., 181, 183, 187, 191, 195
Cohen, D. K., 253
Coleman, A. L., 148
Confucius, 1
Cook, S., 3, 12–13
Cooney, J., 340
Cooper, D. L., 109, 252, 254
Covey, S. R., 190
Cranton, P., 266
Cregan, C., 55
Crellin, M., 337
Creswell, J. W., 291–293
Crookston, B. B., xxvi, 10, 77, 276
Cross, W. E., Jr., 110, 111
Cude, B. J., 165
Cuevas-Rodriguez, G., 228
Cuseo, J., 51, 58, 91

D

da Vinci, Leonardo, 21
Daggett, L. M., 144
Dahlstrom, E., 313
Daly, M. C., 337
Damminger, J. K., 162
Danielson, C., 45
Darling-Hammond, L, 253
D'Augelli, A. R., 109
Davis, J. R., 180
Davis Jones, C. L., xxix, 59, 179, 204
de Pree, M., 107
de Treville, S., 232
Dean, L. A., 252, 254
Deci, E., 228, 229
Deitz, R., 337, 340
Denhart, C., 338
Deresiewicz, W., 328
Dewan, S., 163–164, 166, 167

SUBJECT INDEX

Page references followed by *fig* indicate an illustrated figure; followed by *tab* indicate a table.